RESILIENT AMERICA

American Presidential Elections

MICHAEL NELSON

JOHN M. MCCARDELL, JR.

RESILIENT AMERICA

ELECTING NIXON IN 1968, CHANNELING DISSENT, AND DIVIDING GOVERNMENT

Revised and Expanded

MICHAEL NELSON

FOREWORD BY MARC J. HETHERINGTON

UNIVERSITY PRESS OF KANSAS

Published
by the
University
Press of Kansas
(Lawrence,
Kansas 66045),
which was
organized by the
Kansas Board of
Regents and is
operated and
funded by
Emporia State
University,
Fort Hays State
University,
Kansas State
University,
Pittsburg State
University,
the University
of Kansas, and
Wichita State
University

© 2014 by the University Press of Kansas

Library of Congress Cataloging-in-Publication Data

Nelson, Michael, 1949–

Resilient America : electing Nixon in 1968, channeling dissent, and
dividing government / Michael Nelson ; Foreword by Marc J.
Hetherington.

    p. cm. — (American presidential elections)

Includes bibliographical references and index.

ISBN 978-0-7006-1963-4 (cloth)

ISBN 978-0-7006-2442-3 (paperback)

1. Presidents—United States—Election—1968. 2. Nixon, Richard M.
(Richard Milhous), 1913–1994. 3. Divided government—United
States—History—20th century. I. Title.

E851.N45 2014

324.973090'46—dc23

2013047051

British Library Cataloguing-in-Publication Data is available.

Printed in the United States of America

10 9 8 7 6 5 4 3 2 1

The paper used in this publication is recycled and contains 30
percent postconsumer waste. It is acid free and meets the minimum
requirements of the American National Standard for Permanence of
Paper for Printed Library Materials Z39.48-1992.

To the lady chosen by God, and to her children,

whom I love in the truth

   2 John 1:1

Linda

Michael

Sam

McClain

CONTENTS

What didn't happen in 1968? The Tet offensive occurred in January, turning Walter Cronkite and ultimately the American people against the war in Vietnam. In April, Martin Luther King was felled by an assassin's bullet in Memphis, robbing the civil rights movement of its most effective leader. Two months later, Robert F. Kennedy was murdered after having won the California primary, eliminating the best chance that either party would nominate an antiwar presidential candidate. In September, the Democratic National Convention went off the rails in Chicago, ensuring the party's eventual nominee, Hubert H. Humphrey, an uphill climb in his quest for the presidency. Throughout the year, urban race riots in several cities rocked the country, causing scores of deaths and millions of dollars in damage. Among the few bright spots, I was born in June, making 1968 a subject of particular interest to me.

What makes understanding the election of 1968 so important is the political aftershocks that continued to rock the nation for decades. Most notably, the Republicans, often the losing party since 1932, became regular winners in presidential elections. Of the six elections starting in 1968, the Democrats won only one, and that was mostly the result of the fallout from Richard Nixon's Watergate scandal. Moreover, three of these victories were landslides, two of historic proportions. In 1972 and 1984, Richard Nixon and Ronald Reagan, respectively, won 49 of 50 states. And, in 1980, Reagan won 45 of 50 states from an incumbent, Jimmy Carter, an unprecedented feat. These victories owe, in part, to the new issue agenda set in motion by the politics of 1968.

Throughout the 1960s, and climaxing in 1968, race became the central issue dividing both the parties and ordinary Americans. When the "race issue" meant integrating public facilities, especially in the South, it benefited Democrats. Witness Lyndon B. Johnson's landslide victory in 1964 over Barry M. Goldwater. The events of the mid- to late 1960s, combined with the skill of Richard Nixon's political operatives, transformed race into a Republican issue that would last decades. No longer was the "race issue" about odious things such as turning fire hoses on peaceful protesters and standing in the schoolhouse door to bar African American students from attending all-white schools. As Edward Carmines and James Stimson skillfully argue in their 1989 book *Issue Evolution: Race and the Transformation of American Politics* (Princeton University Press), it came to be about the degree to which the federal government should be involved in the struggle for civil rights. Later the issue evolved again to be about violence in inner cities. Racial conservatism, then, no longer required one to be a racist as was the case in preintegration days. The evolution of the race issue turned out to be bad news for liberals.

The politics spawned by 1968 reordered party coalitions. Conservative southern whites, once the Democratic Party's most stalwart supporters, have only cast a majority of their presidential votes for a Democrat once since 1968, and that was for native son Jimmy Carter of Georgia in 1976. Working-class whites, another bulwark of Franklin D. Roosevelt's New Deal coalition and a socially and racially conservative group, began to vote for Republicans on a regular basis as well. Less dramatically, but no less importantly, racially liberal northern and western cities began to pull these regions toward the Democratic Party over time.

This reordering of groups and regions is the basis for the partisan polarization that grips the country in the 2000s. Ideological diversity within the parties became a thing of the past. Before 1968, the Republican Party did well in some liberal parts of the country, such as the Northeast and Pacific West, and the Democratic Party did well in conservative parts of the country, such as the South. As a result, both parties had to balance liberal and conservative wings within them. The 1968 election set in motion a process in which that would no longer be the case. The GOP, the conservative party, came to dominate the conservative parts of the country where Democrats once thrived while its liberal wing shriveled. Democrats, the liberal party, came to dominate liberal parts of the country where the GOP once thrived while its conservative wing all but disappeared. The absence of intraparty differences allowed the parties to pursue much more ideological politics, creating the situation that weighs on the nation today. The election of 1968 is the root of all this change.

For all the divisiveness that ultimately followed and the lasting imprint it has left, 1968 goes down in history as a watershed election. Michael Nelson's book is extraordinary in capturing the relevant twists and turns. More than that, it also provides a fresh perspective on this tumultuous time. Given all that happened that year and in the decades that followed, most scholars tend to frame their focus on the period's coming apart. But, as Nelson demonstrates, that story is too simple and ultimately incorrect. The country did not, in fact, come apart as it might have given all the political stress that foreign and domestic events produced. In fact, leaders through this fraught time produced unity as well. The executive and legislative branches worked together to solve problems, despite the presence of divided government. Whereas divided government has caused a governing crisis in the present era, political leaders regularly came together to overcome it in the late 1960s and early 1970s. Nelson's concluding argument is compelling and well made, which is not surprising given his status as one of the political science profession's most esteemed scholars of the American presidency.

Marc J. Hetherington

America coming apart has been the theme, both at the time and in the half century since, of most commentary on politics in 1968. Three of the leading books about the period in which that year's election occurred convey this theme in their titles: *America Divided: The Civil War of the 1960s,* by Maurice Isserman and Michael Kazin; *The Unraveling of America,* by Allen J. Matusow; and Todd Gitlin's *The Sixties: Years of Hope, Days of Rage,* with "hope" morphing into "rage" as the decade unfolded. A blizzard of new commentaries on 1968, timed for its fiftieth anniversary, echoes this theme. Hence the need for an expanded edition of *Resilient America,* the first edition of which received the American Political Science Association's Richard E. Neustadt Award for best book on the presidency published in 2014. I have thoroughly revised that edition to take account of both the literature and, in the concluding chapter, the events of the past few years.

Certainly there was no shortage of unusual, even alarming events in 1968: in January, the Tet offensive in Vietnam, which severely undermined public confidence in President Lyndon B. Johnson's conduct of the war; in March, the challenges to Johnson's renomination by antiwar senators Eugene McCarthy of Minnesota and Robert F. Kennedy of New York, which triggered the president's withdrawal from the election; in April, the assassination of civil rights leader Martin Luther King and the scores of race riots that erupted in its wake; in June, the assassination of Senator Kennedy on the night of his victory in the California primary; in August, the violence surrounding the Democratic National Convention in Chicago; and, all year long, the simmering anger that attended the third-party candidacy of former Alabama governor George C. Wallace. Nineteen sixty-eight was, by any reckoning, a turbulent year.

Yet the year culminated in a peaceful election between the candidate most favored by Republican voters, former vice president Richard Nixon, and the candidate most favored by Democratic voters, incumbent vice president Hubert H. Humphrey. Both nominees worked hard to placate the loudest dissident elements of their parties. Humphrey moved far enough left to win back many antiwar Democrats. Nixon moved far enough right to keep on board conservatives whose loyalties lay with the GOP's 1964 nominee, Senator Barry M. Goldwater of Arizona, and the recently elected governor of California, Ronald Reagan. The largest dissident element in the electorate was even further to the right, at least on racial and cultural issues, and neither Nixon nor Humphrey was willing during the campaign to move sufficiently in that direction to capture the 14 percent who constituted the core of Wallace's support.

Just as significant as the events of 1968 was the aftermath of the election. President Nixon, the Democratic Congress, and both major parties worked actively and, for the most part, successfully to woo still-alienated sectors of the electorate into the normal channels of constitutional politics and government. Nixon was rightly driven from office partway through his second term for the crimes and other abuses of power he committed as president. But during his first years in the White House he surprised the left with his diplomatic openings to the country's leading enemies, China and the Soviet Union, as well as with his acquiescence to a wide range of environmental, feminist, civil rights, and other domestic reforms. By reducing draft calls and then eliminating the draft, he took much of the wind out of the sails of the campus-based antiwar movement. At the same time Nixon courted Wallace's supporters by alternately honoring and pandering to their cultural fears and concerns.

On Capitol Hill, congressional Democrats pushed Nixon leftward on domestic policy and became a vehicle through which opponents of the war in Vietnam could advance their cause. The Democratic and later the Republican parties opened up the presidential nominating process so that most of those who felt shut out in 1968 were emboldened to pursue their goals through the two-party system.

America holding together, not America coming apart, is my theme in this book—the resilience of a political system that, after enduring great strains, largely recovered from them. Conventional political processes—peaceful demonstrations, congressional legislation, executive initiatives, Supreme Court decisions, party reforms, and presidential politics—were flexible enough to absorb most of the dissent that tore America deeply in 1968 and may otherwise have torn it asunder. The system also proved able to endure—and at least in the short term benefit from—a lasting problem of governance to which the 1968 election gave birth: a federal government chronically divided between a president of one party and a Congress wholly or partially controlled by the other party—with serious long-term consequences for, among other things, the third branch of government, the judiciary.

Although the resilience of the political system is my theme, the 1968 election was too rich in event and character to be shoehorned into a single argument. Among the other claims I make in this book are these:

- Like Nixon in 1952 and 1956, Johnson was in serious danger of being dropped from the Democratic ticket in 1964 if President John F. Kennedy had lived.
- As president, Johnson faithfully pursued his predecessor's policy in Vietnam and had reason to worry that he would be attacked as a weak leader by Robert Kennedy if South Vietnam fell to the communists.
- Among the dissident candidates in 1968, Wallace and McCarthy regarded getting their widely diverging points of view taken seriously as reason enough to enter the race. Kennedy had no interest in running unless he thought he could win.
- McCarthy's surprise showing in the New Hampshire Democratic primary was facilitated by Republican contender George Romney's withdrawal from the GOP contest, which freed up considerable media time and attention for the McCarthy campaign.
- Although Reagan posed the greatest risk to Nixon's nomination, Nixon worried more about Gov. Nelson A. Rockefeller of New York. In many ways, Nixon's insecurities and resentments toward Rockefeller resembled Johnson's toward Robert Kennedy.
- Nixon, a risk-taker throughout his political career, ran a superb campaign for the 1968 Republican nomination. His main appeals to the voters—foreign policy statesmanship and cultural populism—reflected authentic aspects of who he was. But Nixon nearly lost the general election by running a cautious campaign for which he was temperamentally unsuited.
- In choosing a running mate, Nixon sought someone in his own vice presidential image: loyal, hardworking, and willing to attack the opposition relentlessly so that he could take the high road. He decidedly did not want someone like the languid, independent-minded running mate he chose in 1960, the Massachusetts patrician Henry Cabot Lodge.
- Of all the candidates who ran in 1968, only Nixon had a campaign organization that was talented and integrated from top to bottom. In the fall campaign, his was the only organization that had been battle-tested in the primaries.

- Humphrey would have been nominated for president by his party even if Robert Kennedy had lived, and the contest came down to him, Kennedy, and McCarthy.
- RFK's death, the stalled peace talks with North Vietnam, and the president's belief that he had a better chance to defeat Nixon in November than Humphrey did led Johnson to seriously reconsider reentering the race on the eve of the Democratic convention.
- Humphrey severely underestimated how much the power balance between him and Johnson shifted away from the lame-duck president when Humphrey became the nominee of the Democratic Party. As a result, he refused to make even a modest break with Johnson until just five weeks before the election.
- The Wallace campaign was crippled by his offhand selection of former air force general Curtis LeMay as his vice presidential running mate. Wallace was too easily dissuaded by influential right-wing backers of his campaign from picking his first choice, former Kentucky governor A. B. "Happy" Chandler, an experienced campaigner.
- Wallace's supporters, so different in most ways from those attracted to the extreme left wing of the antiwar movement, resembled them in their certainty that the political system was controlled by a small elite that scorned their values and neglected their concerns.
- The judiciary's recent transformation into a political football kicked back and forth by the political parties was foreshadowed by the Senate's reaction to Johnson's nomination of Justice Abraham Fortas to be chief justice in June 1968.
- As a way of channeling dissent into mainstream politics, the much-criticized reforms of the presidential nominating process that followed the 1968 election were of tremendous value.
- McGovern's landslide defeat in 1972, like Goldwater's in 1964, helped lay the foundation for the future success of their parties.

These arguments emerge from rather than organize *Resilient America*. The book is built on a triad of character, narrative, and analysis from which my arguments emerge. I take my cue from Robert A. Caro, who once wrote that because Johnson's narrow election to the Senate in 1948 "was thrilling," then "if your account of that campaign isn't thrilling, it's false, even if it's factually accurate." At the risk of inviting invidious comparison with a superb practitioner of the art of political journalism, I can only say that

1968 also was a thrilling election, and I have tried to write about it in a way that at least doesn't drain it of its dramatic power.

In terms of how the book is organized, to appreciate the stresses that the American political system endured in 1968 and how it bounced back from them means seeing events as they unfolded in time. It also means understanding the individuals who dealt with those events as candidates for the presidency. The 1968 election was not *sui generis*; it arose from circumstances previously in the making and played out through the nominating process, the general election campaign, the voting, and the events that followed. Narrative and character therefore govern the organization of this book.

Chapter 1 takes the view from 1964, an election that seemed to place the continued existence of the Republican Party in jeopardy; it also introduces the nine political leaders who later played the leading roles in 1968: Johnson, Humphrey, McCarthy, Kennedy, Wallace, Nixon, Rockefeller, Reagan, and Romney. Chapter 2 describes the events of 1965 and 1966: Johnson's simultaneous pursuit of the Great Society and a satisfactory outcome in Vietnam, as well as the GOP's steady recovery from recent defeat, culminating in a major rebound for the party in the 1966 midterm elections.

Chapters 3 (the Democrats) and 4 (the Republicans and Wallace) chronicle the parties' parallel presidential nomination campaigns from 1967 until the end of the primaries in early June 1968. Chapter 5 is about the lead-up to the conventions and the conventions themselves.

The general election campaign between Nixon, Humphrey, and Wallace is the subject of chapters 6 (September) and 7 (October and early November, including an analysis of the congressional, gubernatorial, and, especially, presidential results). Chapter 8 returns to the theme of resilience by describing the efforts of both the parties and the government to bring back dissenting elements of the electorate on both the left and right into the institutions and processes of the American political system.

In the course of researching and writing this book, I incurred debts too great to pay with words of thanks—but here goes anyway. Bruce Miroff read the manuscript carefully and provided exactly the sort of pointed but helpful criticism that an author needs. Bruce's entire motivation was to help me construct the best version of my argument that I could. Marc J. Hetherington's comments on draft chapters were very helpful, as were those of Andrew E. Busch, Richard J. Ellis, and my fellow series editor, John M. McCardell. In addition, Marc wrote a foreword that is not only gracious but also deeply insightful in its own right.

Rhodes students Mathew Jehl, Kyle Ference, and especially Alex McGriff provided able and timely research assistance. Jackie Baker, departmental assistant for the Rhodes political science department, did so many small favors for me as to equal at least a half dozen big ones. I am also grateful to Greg Paraham of Rhodes's Paul Barret Jr. Library and to Rhodes College for sabbatical support. John Lynch, director of the Vanderbilt Television News Archive, and Larry Romans, head of government information and media services for the Vanderbilt University Libraries, were enormously helpful to me in gaining access to the archive's coverage of the 1968 election. I was able to spend the spring 2008 semester as a visiting professor of political science and make use of these resources at Vanderbilt thanks to the late department chair C. Neal Tate and colleagues Bruce I. Oppenheimer and John G. Geer.

Thanks as well to Charisse Kiino, publisher of CQ Press, who granted me access and permission to use the data in the appendices.

In addition to the University Press of Kansas's former director Fred M. Woodward, who patiently supported this book at every stage, I thank these others at the press: Kelly Chrisman Jacques and Jane Raese, project managers for the book, who oversaw its production; Lori Rider, who copyedited the original manuscript and Linda Lotz, who copyedited this one; art director Karl Janssen, who designed the jacket; Rebecca Murray Schuler, publicist; proofreader Aimee Anderson; Mike Kehoe, marketing and sales manager; Joyce Harrison, editor-in-chief; and Larisa Martin, production editor.

This book is dedicated to my family with love and gratitude: my sons Michael and Sam, my grandson McClain, and above all the woman who completes me, my wife Linda.

1

THE VIEW FROM 1964

On election night in 1964 it was clear that the times were changing, but it was less clear how.

The results presented one of the strangest maps in the history of presidential elections. As in 1932, the election that ushered in the generation-old New Deal Democratic majority, the Democratic nominee lost only six states to his Republican opponent. In 1932 the six states that Republican president Herbert Hoover carried against Gov. Franklin D. Roosevelt of New York were all in the Northeast: Connecticut, Delaware, Pennsylvania, New Hampshire, Maine, and Vermont. Thirty-two years later, the Northeast was Republican presidential nominee Barry Goldwater's worst region. Aside from his home state of Arizona, Senator Goldwater carried only the five states that constituted the Deep South, the region with the nation's largest African American population but also, because blacks were still substantially disenfranchised, an almost monochromatically white electorate. Alabama, Mississippi, Louisiana, Georgia, and South Carolina, states in which Hoover had averaged 7 percent of the vote in 1932, voted overwhelmingly for Goldwater. As recently as 1960, except for South Carolina, all of the Deep South states that Goldwater carried were among Republican nominee Richard Nixon's least successful states, and the vice president lost all five of them to his Democratic rival, Sen. John F. Kennedy of Massachusetts, or to independent conservative Democratic electors.

The Republicans' success in 1964 was regional, but that of the Democrats was national. The ticket of incumbent Lyndon B. Johnson for president and Sen. Hubert H. Humphrey of Minnesota for vice president prevailed in forty-five states with 486 electoral votes, including nine states that no Democrat since FDR had carried and one, Vermont, that no Democrat had ever carried. Johnson won 61.1 percent of the national popular vote, exceeding Roosevelt's previous record of 60.8 percent in 1936. His party's national sweep extended to a thirty-seven-seat gain in the House of Representatives, increasing the Democrats' 82-seat majority to 155. Even their one-seat increase in the Senate was a triumph. Because the party had done so well in the 1958 Senate elections, twenty-six Democratic seats were on the 1964 ballot compared with only nine seats occupied by Republicans. With much more to lose, the Democrats actually won, leaving the Senate, like the House, more than two-thirds Democratic. Nearly all of the new Democrats in both chambers were northern and western liberals, tilting leftward a congressional party that had long been dominated by conservative southerners. Meanwhile, the loss of dozens of moderate-to-liberal Republican members and the gain of seven new conservatives in the Deep South—the Republicans' first representatives from that region since Reconstruction—tilted the congressional GOP rightward.

In an equal and opposite reaction to their gains among Deep South whites in 1964, the Republicans lost the African American vote almost entirely. Just four years before, Nixon had earned the support of 32 percent of black voters. Dwight D. Eisenhower had done even better, earning 39 percent in 1956.[1] Although Kennedy introduced what became the Civil Rights Act of 1964 and Johnson shepherded it to passage after succeeding to the presidency when Kennedy was assassinated on November 22, 1963, only about three-fifths of House and Senate Democrats voted for the bill, compared with more than four-fifths of congressional Republicans.[2] Among the GOP senators opposed to the act, however, was the party's candidate for president, whose share of the black vote on Election Day dropped to 6 percent. In fact, while doing well in the Deep South, Goldwater lost the four Outer South states carried by Eisenhower in 1952 and 1956, Nixon in 1960, or by both Republican nominees: Florida, Texas, Virginia, and Tennessee. As for Hoover's six northeastern states in 1932, they were among Johnson's best in 1964, auguring the Northeast's eventual transformation from the GOP's strongest region to the Democrats' main stronghold.

Goldwater ran an ardently ideological campaign, arguably the most conservative of any major party nominee in history. Long a big-tent Republican who, as chair of the National Republican Senatorial Committee in the mid-1950s and early 1960s, had worked as hard to elect liberal Republicans as conservatives, Goldwater nevertheless made no serious effort to unite all the wings of the party behind him in his presidential campaign. At the GOP nominating convention he insisted on a strongly conservative platform and chose a conservative vice presidential running mate, Rep. William Miller of New York. Defending "extremism" and attacking "moderation" in his acceptance speech, Goldwater told convention and country: "Those who do not care for our cause, we don't expect to join our ranks in any case."[3] Apart from his strong ideological views, Goldwater also frightened many voters with off-the-cuff comments about wanting to "lob" a nuclear weapon "into the men's room of the Kremlin" and "drop a low-yield atomic bomb on Chinese supply lines into North Vietnam."[4] Along with William Jennings Bryan in 1896, Tom Wicker observed, Goldwater "was only the second presidential challenger in history who became *the* issue."[5]

In contrast, Johnson ran a serenely nonideological campaign whose main theme was that he was the safe alternative to a dangerous extremist. "Vote to save your Social Security from going down the drain," Johnson told voters. "Vote to keep a prudent hand which will not mash the nuclear button."[6] He used this theme to good effect in uniting labor with management, blacks with whites, women with men, Protestants with Catholics and Jews, young with old, and moderates with liberals. Except for self-identified Republicans, Johnson carried every demographic and political group polled by Gallup.[7] Members of the Business Council, who had donated to Republicans over Democrats by 73 to 7 in 1960, broke only 36 to 33 for the GOP in 1964.[8] "We're in favor of a lot of things and we're against mighty few," Johnson said in campaign speeches.[9] The *New York Herald Tribune* was one of many old and staunchly Republican newspapers to endorse a Democratic presidential candidate for the first time. Yet neither Johnson nor the Democratic platform had much to say about what he intended to do if he was elected to a full term. By David Broder's count, "The Democratic Platform devoted three times as much space to reciting the accomplishments of the previous four years as to listing the promises of the next four."[10] As a rule, the recitations were specific and the promises general. The result of "failing to make explicit where he intended to take the country in the next four years," Robert Dallek has argued, was that "Johnson won less than a solid consensus for bold change in either domestic or foreign affairs."[11]

The Democratic sweep was massive: in addition to winning the White House and 363 of 535 seats in Congress, the party gained 540 new state legislative seats and an additional governorship, reducing the number of Republican state chief executives to sixteen. Postelection handwringing immediately ensued among established Republican leaders and political pundits about what the GOP needed to do to survive. "He has wrecked his party for a long time to come," wrote *New York Times* columnist James Reston about Goldwater.[12] Another leading political journalist, Robert J. Donovan, foresaw a quarter century of Democratic control of the White House, with Johnson reelected in 1968, Vice President Humphrey succeeding him in 1972 and 1976, and either Sen. Robert F. Kennedy of New York or Sen. Edward M. Kennedy of Massachusetts winning the elections of 1980 and 1984.[13] Prominent liberal Republicans, including Gov. Nelson A. Rockefeller of New York and Gov. George Romney of Michigan, felt vindicated by their decision not to endorse Goldwater against Johnson. Rep. John V. Lindsay of New York, speaking for the small group of surviving liberal House Republicans, said they would "have to rebuild the Republican party out of the ashes . . . to return the party to the tradition of Lincoln."[14]

Leading scholars of American politics buttressed the establishment consensus. James MacGregor Burns predicted that, having ceded the nomination once to its rural, retrograde "congressional party," the more "urban, liberally oriented presidential Republicans" would "not display the fumbling grasp of convention politics in 1968 or 1972 that they had in 1964," thereby regaining control of the GOP.[15] Gerald Pomper suggested that 1964 was a critical election on the scale of 1896, "the classical critical contest" in all of American history and one in which the majority party secured its supremacy for another generation.[16] Lending weight to this interpretation was that Goldwater's defeat was the GOP's seventh in the last nine presidential elections. The party's only successful nominee, former World War II Supreme Allied Commander Dwight D. Eisenhower, could just as easily have been elected as a Democrat. And despite Ike's personal popularity, his party's congressional ranks were considerably smaller when his two terms ended than when they began.

Nevertheless, conservative Republicans were cheered by Goldwater's success at energizing a broad network of grassroots supporters. Nearly four million people worked to elect him in some capacity, and more than a million donated money to his campaign (compared with just 22,000 who donated to Kennedy in 1960). They also were heartened by Goldwater's sweep of the Deep South. Except for Louisiana, which voted for Eisenhower in 1956, no Deep South state had gone Republican since Reconstruction—indeed, to the extent that Goldwater's electoral map resembled anyone's, it was that of the States' Rights Party nominee, Gov. J. Strom Thurmond of South Carolina, in 1948. Goldwater carried all four of Thurmond's states by margins ranging from 13.6 to 74.2 percentage points, meaning that except for Arkansas and North Carolina, every state in the heretofore solidly Democratic South had gone Republican in at least one recent presidential election. The GOP could now compete in every region, conservative Republicans claimed, which meant they no longer would have to win about 70 percent of the North and West to elect a president or control the House. And, devoted though they were to Goldwater, conservatives also argued that their political philosophy did not receive a fair test in 1964 because most voters perceived their candidate not as a conservative but as an unstable extremist who was "trigger-happy," "radical," and "impulsive—shoots from the hip."[17] The messenger may have been flawed, they conceded, but not the message. Goldwater, who had been a reluctant candidate, happily abandoned presidential politics after the election.

Other political figures emerged from the 1964 election with their gaze fixed on 1968 and beyond. Among Democrats these included Johnson and Humphrey, who looked forward to being reelected as a ticket in four years; Robert Kennedy, the slain president's oldest living brother, who was elected to the Senate from New York in 1964; Sen. Eugene McCarthy, Humphrey's fellow Minnesotan and finalist for the vice presidential nomination; and Gov. George C. Wallace of Alabama, who had run a socially conservative protest campaign against Johnson in three northern primaries and won surprisingly strong support from white working-class Democrats.

Four Republicans rose from the wreckage of their party's 1964 defeat in varying states of ambition. Nixon, defeated narrowly for president in 1960 and handily for governor of California in 1962, campaigned ardently for Goldwater against Johnson with an eye toward a possible political comeback. Ronald Reagan, best known as a screen actor, gave a brilliantly effective nationally televised speech for Goldwater a week before the election that raised conservatives' hopes that he might become the appealing advocate of conservatism that the candidate himself was not. In contrast, Governors Rockefeller and Romney were determined to take back the GOP from the conservatives who had—temporarily, they hoped—seized it.

THE DEMOCRATS

In the view from 1964, no Democrat foresaw anything other than a reelection campaign for Johnson and Humphrey in 1968. Kennedy, like Humphrey, had his eye on 1972, when Johnson would be barred by the Twenty-second Amendment from seeking another term. McCarthy, who believed that he, not John Kennedy, should have been the nation's first Roman Catholic president, reluctantly returned to the Senate, where he was bored and restless. Meanwhile, Wallace resolved to find a way to translate his vote-getting ability as a critic of Democratic liberalism into something bigger.

JOHNSON

Lyndon B. Johnson was a product of the Texas Hill Country west of Austin, where he grew up and spent his first twenty-three years. But he was a creature of Washington and, in particular, of Congress. Johnson had more congressional experience than any other president before or since. Starting in 1931, he spent three years as a House staffer, two years as the Texas director of the New Deal's jobs-giving National Youth Administration, eleven years as a House member, and twelve years as a senator. In 1955, after two years as Senate minority leader, he became the youngest and, soon, the most influential majority leader in history when the Democrats regained control of that chamber.

Being from Texas was a burden when Johnson sought the Democratic presidential nomination in 1960. No southerner had been elected president since before the Civil War, largely because most southern voters expected their elected officials to oppose legislation advancing national causes such as civil rights, labor unions, and business regulation. Johnson did so during his nearly thirty years in and around Congress, especially after making the move from the moderately liberal Tenth District to a Senate seat representing a conservative state. In hopes of rebranding himself as a westerner, Johnson bought a 418-acre ranch where he raised cattle, wore a cowboy hat, and hosted numerous political leaders and reporters to impress on them his ties to a region most Americans admired rather than distrusted.

Being from Washington, on the other hand, offered certain advantages. The federal government enjoyed the trust of the American people during the 1950s, and the Cold War rivalry with Soviet communism placed a political premium on service in the Senate because of that body's distinctive constitutional responsibilities in foreign affairs. From 1952 to 1972 seventeen of twenty major party nominees for president and vice president were experienced federal office holders, most of them senators.[18] As one of the two or three most powerful leaders in Washington, Johnson was a *prima facie* serious presidential contender.

But Johnson's experience in the capital blinded him to some inconvenient political realities. It convinced him that support from his fellow Democratic senators could secure the votes of their state delegations at the 1960 convention. In truth, governors and other state and local party leaders, who were on the scene in their communities and had jobs and contracts to dispense, typically led their delegations. "It was not easy to find men and women who knew Johnson outside the District of Columbia and Texas," said LBJ supporter India Edwards.[19] The Senate lens through which Johnson looked at presidential politics also veiled the public appeal and political shrewdness of John Kennedy, who as a Senate colleague Johnson had found to be "a weak and indecisive politician, a nice man, a gentle man, but not a man's man."[20] As a Catholic, Kennedy saw clearly that he needed to enter and win primaries to convince state party leaders that his religion would be no barrier to election in November. (No Catholic had ever been elected president, and the only one whom the Democrats nominated, Gov. Al Smith of New York, lost by a landslide in 1928.) As a southerner, Johnson faced similar skepticism about his electability from party professionals. But he refused to enter primaries even in politically congenial states such as conservative Indiana and Protestant West Virginia. Kennedy competed for votes successfully, Johnson did not compete at all, and Kennedy won the nomination on the first ballot.

Kennedy's decision to invite Johnson to join the ticket as his vice presidential running mate was an easy one, despite the opposition of his brother and campaign manager Robert Kennedy, who was channeling liberals' and labor leaders' concern that Johnson was too conservative, as well as his own personal animus toward the Texan. For a generation, nearly every Democratic vice presidential nominee had been from a southern or border state, in recognition that the Democrats needed the South in order to win competitive elections even if they were unwilling to choose a southerner for the top of the ticket.[21] "He's the natural," Kennedy told Rep. Tip O'Neill of Massachusetts, speaking of Johnson. "If I can ever get him on the ticket, no way we can lose."[22] Kennedy also dreaded the prospect of having to deal with an independently powerful Johnson as Senate majority leader if he won the election. "Did it occur to you that if Lyndon becomes the vice president, I'll have Mike Mansfield [of Montana] as the leader, . . . somebody I can trust and depend on?" he asked political aide Kenneth O'Donnell.[23]

Johnson no more wanted to be Senate leader under a Democratic president than Kennedy wanted him in that role. But Johnson did want to be president, and as Vice President Nixon had demonstrated in the 1960 Republican contest, the vice presidency had become a solid stepping-stone to securing a future presidential nomination.[24] Winning and holding a national office would enable Johnson to emerge as a national leader, liberated to some extent from the Texas brand. And, perhaps influenced by Kennedy's troubled medical history—one source of the evolving hatred between Johnson and Robert Kennedy was the accurate charge made by Johnson surrogates that JFK had Addison's disease—Johnson told Republican writer Clare Booth Luce: "I looked it up: one out of every four presidents has died in office. I'm a gambling man, darling, and this is the only chance I got."[25]

Johnson also thought he could turn the vice presidency into a powerful office—after all, the position of Senate party leader had been weak until he transformed it. Specifically, Johnson thought that after the election he could persuade Senate Democrats to let him continue functioning as their leader and get Kennedy to sign an executive order granting him a large staff, a West Wing office, and authority as a de facto national security adviser. The election results, he believed, strengthened his hand. More than any other vice presidential candidate in history, Johnson had been instrumental in securing the president's victory. Without his effective campaigning in the South, North Carolina, South Carolina, Texas (where the mayor of Blanco had declared Kennedy-Johnson a "kangaroo ticket, one with all its strength in the hind legs"), and perhaps Georgia would have gone Republican, handing Nixon the election.[26] But even before inauguration day, both Johnson's Senate colleagues and the president-elect rebuffed his power grabs. "Power is where power goes," Johnson had boasted when accepting the vice presidential nomination.[27] Not this time. "Being vice president is like being a cut dog," he reflected after being consigned to the sidelines in the White House and on Capitol Hill.[28] After the Cuban missile crisis of October 1962, in which Johnson's advice was consistently—and, in the president's view, unhelpfully—bellicose, Kennedy "was prodding Johnson less now, sending him fewer memos and giving him fewer assignments and, as a result, Johnson was fading into the background," wrote Kennedy's secretary, Evelyn Lincoln. She calculated from her appointments calendar that in 1963 the president spent only about ten minutes per month with Johnson, about one-sixth as much as in 1961.[29]

Unwilling to blame the president for his diminished status, Johnson focused his resentment on Robert Kennedy, who was both attorney general and his brother's closest adviser. "Jack Kennedy's as thoughtful and considerate of me . . . as he can be," Johnson told an associate. "But I know his snot-nosed brother's after my ass."[30] The lowest point of Johnson's vice presidency came when he was chairing a 1963 meeting of the President's Committee on Equal Employment Opportunity, a toothless entity whose purpose was to increase minority hiring in the federal government. Partway into the meeting Robert Kennedy charged in flanked by aides, interrupted the discussion by firing brutally disdainful questions at Johnson protégés Hobart Taylor and James Webb, and then stormed out. RFK loyalists spread word of the incident around Washington. It was the latest example, they suggested, of how hopelessly inadequate the vice president was. As for Johnson, "I was humiliated."[31] Seeing him in late summer, a close former aide observed, "It was a time of deprivation. He grew very fat and drank a lot."[32]

Johnson was convinced that Robert Kennedy wanted him off the ticket in 1964 and feared that this time the president would take his brother's advice. He may have been right. The cool rationality about politics and governance that led JFK to choose Johnson in 1960 pointed to a different choice in 1964. Politically, Kennedy calculated, his administration's first-term support for a strong civil rights bill meant that winning the South again would be impossible. The eighty-one southern electoral votes Kennedy received in 1960 would have to be replaced by carrying the large northern and western states he had lost to Nixon: Ohio (twenty-six electoral votes), Wisconsin (twelve), and California (forty). Johnson could not help him there; indeed, as a weak vice president in a liberal administration, he had even lost popularity and influence in Texas. Nor was there any need for Kennedy to worry, as in 1960, about the problems that Johnson could cause if he was not in the administration. As a possible obstacle to governing, Johnson had been neutered, a condition that would not change if he became a former vice president. Compounding Johnson's political woes, in November 1963 *Life* magazine was deep into its reporting of an investigative story about his dramatic increase in wealth from various Texas properties during his Senate years, when his annual salary never exceeded $22,500.

The president's trip to Texas on November 21–22 underscored Johnson's status as a declining political asset. Kennedy was mad that he had to make the trip at all—why hadn't Johnson been able to unite the Texas Democratic Party by muting the hatred between the conservative faction led by Gov. John Connally and the liberal faction led by Sen. Ralph Yarborough? The trip itself, marked by petty spats over protocol among Connally, Yarborough, and Johnson, underscored the vice president's diminished standing even in his own state.

"I am nothing," said John Adams, the first vice president, "but I may be everything."[33] Johnson went from nothing to everything at 1:00 p.m. CST on November 22, when Kennedy was officially pronounced dead after being shot in the head by Lee Harvey Oswald, an erratic supporter of various communist causes, during his motorcade through Dallas. But Johnson's succession to the presidency was complicated in ways that were wholly without precedent. Not only had Kennedy been killed in Johnson's home state, but he now succeeded to the presidency closer to the end of the term than any vice president in history. The election was less than twelve months away, and the Democratic convention just nine months. Beyond that, Robert A. Caro has written: "The President, the King, was dead, murdered, but the King had a brother, a brother who hated the new King. The dead King's men—the Kennedy men, the Camelot men—made up in Shakespearean terms, a faction."[34] The day after the assassination White House aide Arthur M. Schlesinger gathered a group of fellow Kennedy loyalists to discuss replacing Johnson with Robert Kennedy at the head of the Democratic ticket in 1964.

With flattery and feigned humility ("I need you more than President Kennedy needed you . . . the knowledge, the skills, the understanding"), Johnson persuaded most members of the Kennedy administration to stay on, especially those in the national security arena and the cabinet.[35] He was so solicitous of the slain president's widow, Jacqueline Kennedy, remarked Johnson aide Harry McPherson, that he probably would have renamed the country the United States of Kennedy if she had asked.[36] (He did rename Cape Canaveral as Cape Kennedy at her request.) No longer the cut dog of his miserable thousand days as vice president, Johnson took to the presidency "like Popeye after a can of spinach," in David Greenberg's apt phrase.[37] Striking exactly the right chords of resolve and reassurance in a televised speech to Congress and the nation five days after the assassination, Johnson declared that his mission was to continue what Kennedy had begun—specifically, to enact into law his major civil rights and tax cut bills, which had been mired for months in the legislative process. "I had to take the dead man's program and turn it into a martyr's cause," he said years later.[38]

Johnson persuaded a Senate that was ill disposed to approve anything more than a diluted version of the civil rights bill to pass the full-strength version: the Civil Rights Act of 1964. "As a southerner," Johnson knew, "I had to produce a civil rights bill that was even stronger than the one they'd have gotten if Kennedy had lived."[39] The bill was resisted by southern Democratic senators led by Richard B. Russell of Georgia, but it was accepted once it became law. As Clay Risen has pointed out, for some time, numerous southern merchants had wanted to serve black customers, but individual store owners were afraid to go first and risk the wrath of the racist Ku Klux Klan and White Citizens' Council. The region's commercial and industrial leaders had come to regard racial discrimination as a huge impediment to attracting investment from northern and foreign firms. Now they and their political leaders—including Russell, who proclaimed "our duty as citizens" to obey the new law—could say their hands were tied.[40] Robert Kennedy's warning to Johnson not to sign the bill until after July 4, for fear that troublemaking blacks would use "the day off . . . to go into every hotel and motel and every restaurant," proved groundless. Most business owners were grateful for the surge of new customers.[41]

Johnson also persuaded the fiscally conservative southern Democrats who controlled tax policy in the House and Senate to mute their resistance to Kennedy's proposed income tax cut in return for keeping the fiscal year 1964 federal budget under $100 billion. And then, with RFK convinced that his brother had been on the verge of trying to end poverty at the moment of his death, Johnson took on that issue as well. He used his January 8, 1964, state of the union address to "declare unconditional war on poverty in America, . . . not only to relieve the symptoms of poverty, but to cure it and above all, prevent it."[42] Urged on by Johnson, Congress passed the Economic Opportunity Act in August.

Johnson's domestic policy triumphs removed any effective grounds for resistance by Kennedy loyalists to his nomination for a full term as president. But these triumphs also entailed political costs. Johnson was aware that by championing civil rights he was alienating southern whites. "I think we just delivered the South to the Republican Party for a long time to come," he told press secretary Bill Moyers the night the bill passed.[43] In contrast, he was unaware of the problems latent in the War on Poverty. Johnson took for granted that ending poverty meant giving government jobs to poor people, preferably by hiring unemployed young men to build big things in the fresh air, as he had when serving FDR as National Youth Administration director in Texas. "He had this sort of concrete idea," recalled Council of Economic Advisers chair Walter Heller. "Bulldozers. Tractors. People operating heavy machinery."[44] But in order to attract Robert Kennedy's support for his program, Johnson accepted without fully understanding "community action," a nascent idea percolating in the Kennedy Justice Department's juvenile delinquency commission. Community action was grounded in the assumption that the poor themselves, not local government and party officials, were the best judges of what they needed and that they would become more self-sufficient if they were allowed to decide how antipoverty programs were run in their neighborhoods. In the jargon of the day, the Kennedyites' theory was that "maximum feasible participation" would overcome the "culture of poverty." In practice, the only clear consequence of community action was heightened political discord between local activists and local elected officials—most of them Democrats.

In a speech delivered on May 7, 1964, four months after declaring his War on Poverty, Johnson embedded that effort in a larger vision of the Great Society. FDR's New Deal, Harry S. Truman's Fair Deal, and Kennedy's New Frontier had already made the United States "the rich society and the powerful society," Johnson said. The new challenge was to stretch the helping hand of government both downward (by bringing "an end to poverty and racial injustice") and upward (to "advance the quality of our American civilization"). The Great Society, he pledged, "is a place where the city of man serves not only the needs of the body and the demands of commerce, but the desire for beauty and the hunger for community."[45]

Johnson inherited more on taking office than Kennedy's domestic agenda, which the new president readily embraced and was able to pass through a legislative process that he understood completely. His inheritance also included the 16,300 military advisers whom Kennedy had dispatched to South Vietnam—seventeen times more than the 900 Eisenhower had sent there—to prevent that nation's pro-American regime from being toppled by the combined communist forces of North Vietnam and the National Liberation Front, or Vietcong, the insurgent group waging civil war within South Vietnam. Kennedy, whose "main issue [in 1960] was the Cold War and how to stop losing it," had begun escalating American involvement in 1961, shortly after the failed Bay of Pigs invasion of communist Cuba in April.[46] In May, Kennedy approved National Security Action Memorandum 52, which stated that the "U.S. objective" was "to prevent Communist domination of South Vietnam" and that his administration would "initiate, on an accelerated basis, a series of mutually supporting actions of a military, political, economic, psychological, and covert character designed to achieve this objective."[47] In June, following the verbal drubbing Kennedy took from Soviet leader Nikita Khrushchev when they met in Vienna, he told the *Times*'s James Reston that "we have a problem in making our power credible," and "Vietnam is the place."[48] At the January 18, 1962, meeting of the National Security Council, the president observed, "The record of the Romans made clear that their success was dependent on their will and ability to fight successfully at the edges of their empire."[49]

The State and Defense Departments and the CIA buttressed the president's judgment that the Chinese and Soviets, despite their differences, were united in their commitment to foment revolutions in the developing world. The pro-American regime in Saigon could not be allowed to fall to

Whether as vice president or, in this photograph, as president, Lyndon B. Johnson's meetings with Attorney General Robert F. Kennedy always were tense. (Credit: Yoichi Okamoto, provided by the Lyndon B. Johnson Presidential Library)

the communists. If it did, Kennedy and nearly everyone in the government agreed that the neighboring nations of Southeast Asia also would fall. Kennedy not only adopted Eisenhower's concept of cascading dominos but also resolved to intervene muscularly to prevent the first one from falling. "In my opinion, for us to withdraw would mean a collapse not only of South Vietnam, but of Southeast Asia," he said. "So we are going to stay there."[50]

Weeks before he died, Kennedy doubled down on the American commitment by authorizing South Vietnamese generals to launch a coup against the country's strong but unpopular leader Ngo Dinh Diem, a coup that Vice President Johnson "was against—strongly against."[51] To the president's dismay, the coup resulted not just in Diem's overthrow but also his assassination. "Without the United States," Kennedy told a gathering of Dallas business leaders on the morning of November 22, 1963, "South Vietnam would collapse overnight."[52] To the president, said his brother Robert Kennedy, "the strong, overwhelming reason for being in Vietnam was that we should win the war in Vietnam or face the loss of all of Southeast Asia."[53]

As president, Johnson felt bound to continue Kennedy's course in Vietnam, just as he had continued his domestic policies. (In his memoirs,

Johnson titled the first chapter on Vietnam "Steady on Course."[54]) Less confident about Vietnam than he was about domestic matters, however, Johnson regularly asked the foreign policy advisers he inherited from Kennedy—chiefly Secretary of State Dean Rusk, Secretary of Defense Robert S. McNamara, and National Security Adviser McGeorge Bundy—what Kennedy would have done, and then he did it. Their judgment, based on claims of expertise, was that the American commitment must be maintained, which was consistent with Johnson's own judgment. Vietnam was a "little piss-ant country," in Johnson's view, and had become "just the biggest damn mess."[55] But he "knew that Harry Truman and [Secretary of State] Dean Acheson had lost their effectiveness from the day that the Communists took over in China" and that a communist victory in Vietnam would be even worse for him. "This time there would be Robert Kennedy out there in front leading the fight against me, telling everyone that I had betrayed John Kennedy's commitment to South Vietnam. That I had let a democracy fall into the hands of the Communists. That I was a coward, an unmanly man. A man without a spine."[56]

Politically, Johnson walked the tightrope of Vietnam in 1964 with perfect balance. In early August, when North Vietnamese gun boats reportedly fired on American naval destroyers in the Gulf of Tonkin, he harnessed the public's traditional "rally round the flag" response to military action and secured the sweeping Gulf of Tonkin Resolution from a nearly unanimous Congress.[57] The open-ended resolution authorized the president "to take all necessary measures to repel any armed attack against the forces of the United States and to prevent further aggression." In the short term, Johnson ordered a small retaliatory air strike on North Vietnam but sent no additional troops. Having established his firmness, he went back to portraying himself as the peace candidate in the election against the supposedly trigger-happy Goldwater. "We are not about to send American boys nine or ten thousand miles to do what Asian boys ought to be doing for themselves," he told a cheering audience at the University of Akron on October 21.[58] More than anything else, however, Johnson did everything he could to tamp down public interest in the war—and succeeded. In five press conferences held between mid-August and mid-October, the president was not asked once about Vietnam.

Johnson was nominated by acclamation at the Democratic convention in Atlantic City, as was his popular choice for vice president, Hubert Humphrey. Polls throughout the year attested that his election was never in doubt.

President Kennedy's assassination meant that Robert Kennedy, the second youngest of the four Kennedy brothers, was now, after his two elder brothers' deaths, the oldest and, by implication, the legatee of his family and its retinue's ambitions for national leadership.[59] Nothing about this role was temperamentally appealing to Kennedy, who was much more comfortable behind the scenes than in the political limelight. He spent much of the 1950s assisting Senate committee chairs of both parties—initially Republican senator Joseph McCarthy of Wisconsin and later Democratic senator John McClellan of Arkansas—in investigating alleged communist infiltration of the federal government (McCarthy) and the nexus between organized crime and organized labor (McClellan). Kennedy was a fierce (critics said ruthless) investigator with what two supporters called "a Puritan's sense of right and wrong, good and evil"—a quality that in later years would be redirected into crusades against poverty, racism, and the war in Vietnam.[60] He was also intensely loyal. When McCarthy, a friend of his wealthy and politically well-connected father, Joseph P. Kennedy, and consequently his first employer on Capitol Hill, died in 1957 after being censured by his colleagues for reckless allegations of communist influence in the army, Robert Kennedy went not just to the memorial service in Washington but also to the funeral in Wisconsin.

Kennedy's talent for behind-the-scenes organization shaped his involvement in presidential politics during the 1950s in ways that furthered his older brother's ambitions. When Democratic presidential nominee Adlai Stevenson surprised the 1956 national convention by asking the delegates to choose the party's candidate for vice president, Robert Kennedy organized an overnight campaign for John Kennedy, who finished a surprisingly strong second to the much better known Sen. Estes Kefauver of Tennessee. According to Schlesinger, the lessons Robert Kennedy learned from that convention stood his brother in good stead as he began preparing to run in 1960: "the importance of communications at a convention; the importance of an accurate delegate count; the importance of the rules . . . ; the importance of friendship . . . ; the unimportance of celebrated senators; the importance of uncelebrated party professionals."[61]

The 1950s planted seeds of hatred between Robert Kennedy and Lyndon Johnson that would sprout during the 1960 campaign and beyond. In the fall of 1955 Kennedy was angered when Johnson refused Joseph Kennedy's offer to finance a bid for the 1956 presidential nomination if LBJ would agree to place Senator Kennedy on the ticket as his running mate. Johnson knew he could not beat President Eisenhower and that Joseph Kennedy's real goal was to launch his son's candidacy for president in 1960. In the spring of 1960, when John Kennedy sent his brother to the LBJ ranch to discover the Texan's political intentions, Johnson outfitted Robert Kennedy with a ten-gauge shotgun for a deer hunt instead of the customary rifle. As intended, the recoil from the massive weapon knocked Kennedy to the ground, and Johnson sneered, "Son, you've got to learn to handle a gun like a man."[62] At the convention that summer, Robert Kennedy was furious at Johnson for telling the Washington State delegation that unlike Joseph Kennedy, "I never thought Hitler was right" and for standing by when India Edwards charged that John Kennedy was terminally ill and "would not be alive today if it were not for cortisone."[63] After Senator Kennedy's victory in the presidential balloting was secured, Robert Kennedy was contemptuous of Johnson's insistence on staying on the ticket after liberals expressed opposition to his selection, claiming that LBJ "burst into tears" and "just shook" when asked to consider declining the offer.[64]

At his father's insistence, the newly elected president appointed his thirty-five-year-old brother as attorney general. Robert Kennedy did not want the job. He was tired of "chasing bad men" and "thought nepotism was a problem" with his brother's choice.[65] Never had such a close relative of the president been attorney general, much less someone who had never tried a case in court. But JFK, Joseph Kennedy argued to both of his sons, needed someone who was politically "savvy" and whom he could trust completely in a cabinet of "nine strangers and a brother."[66] Father also decreed that a placeholder would occupy Kennedy's vacated Senate seat until his youngest son, Edward Kennedy, became constitutionally eligible to run when he turned thirty in 1962. As Johnson's star descended in the administration, Robert Kennedy's ascended, extending into civil rights and, increasingly, foreign affairs. Despite his ongoing supervision of Operation Mongoose, a series of covert operations aimed at disrupting Cuba's economy and removing its communist leader Fidel Castro from power, as well as his preference for military action when the president learned that the Soviet Union had installed nuclear missiles aimed at the United States in Cuba, the attorney general eventually steered his brother's much more experienced national security team on to the diplomatic course that resolved the Cuban missile crisis peacefully.[67]

Robert Kennedy was also a strong supporter of the president's inaugural pledge to "pay any price, bear any burden, meet any hardship, support any friend, oppose any foe to assure the survival and success of liberty."[68]

Specifically, he encouraged the enhancement of Special Forces counterinsurgency units in the armed services and the Central Intelligence Agency (CIA) to combat Khrushchev's "wars of national liberation" against Western-backed governments in third-world countries. He even kept a green beret behind his desk in the Justice Department and, later, the Senate.

Ever since FDR led the United States onto the world stage as a promoter of liberal values, most Democrats had been comfortable with this role.[69] Far from being what Michael Cohen calls a "Faustian bargain" meant to "protect liberalism's right flank from GOP charges of insufficient rigor in fighting the 'red threat,'" the party's assertive anticommunism was part and parcel of its activist vision of remaking both nation and world.[70] But Democrats had disliked Eisenhower's reliance on nuclear weapons as the chief means of pursuing that vision. Ground-level counterinsurgency warfare seemed much less dangerous and much better suited to winning third-world hearts and minds. On a visit to South Vietnam in February 1962, the attorney general declared: "We are going to win in Vietnam. We will remain here until we do win."[71] Slow to embrace the civil rights movement's demands for protection against violence and for strong antidiscrimination legislation, RFK eventually did so, partly out of genuine conviction and partly because he was convinced that internationally broadcast images of southern police and mobs brutally beating peaceful demonstrators were undermining American efforts to compete with the Soviet Union for the loyalty of the newly independent nonwhite nations of Africa and Asia.

Despair at his brother's death and deep resentment of the new president governed Kennedy's emotions after the assassination. For a time he was beyond rationality. "He's mean, bitter, vicious—an animal in many ways," Kennedy said of Johnson. "What does he know about people who've got no jobs, or are undereducated?" the son of wealth asked, implausibly, about the son of poverty.[72] After it became clear that Johnson had the 1964 presidential nomination wrapped up, Kennedy loyalists began urging him to name Robert Kennedy as his running mate. When thinking clearly, Kennedy knew that this was a terrible idea: "It would be an unpleasant relationship, number one. Number two, I would lose all ability to ever take any independent positions on matters."[73] But for motives of spite and entitlement, he did not discourage the efforts to pressure the president to place him in the very spot on the ticket he had tried to drive Johnson from at the 1960 convention. "The one thing Lyndon Johnson doesn't want is me as vice president," Kennedy confided in a May 1964 oral history interview. "I think he's hysterical about how he's going to try to avoid having to ask me."[74]

On July 29, 1964, Johnson met with Kennedy to tell him that he needed help in the southern and border states to defeat Goldwater in the upcoming election—help that Kennedy could not provide. He asked Kennedy to publicly state that he was not interested in being vice president. Kennedy refused, and the next day Johnson announced that he was ruling out "any member of the Cabinet" from consideration, including the attorney general. "Sorry I took so many of you nice fellows over the side with me," Kennedy wryly telegraphed his cabinet colleagues.[75] Johnson then moved Kennedy's slot on the Democratic convention calendar to the final session, after the balloting for president and vice president. Both decisions were politically astute, judging by the ecstatic twenty-two-minute ovation that greeted Kennedy at the convention, as well as by the bitterness implicit in the line in his speech that, quoting Shakespeare, urged listeners to "pay no worship to the garish sun."[76]

On the eve of the August convention, Kennedy reluctantly declared that he was running for U.S. senator from New York, his first venture as a candidate and the least bad alternative he had for staying in public office. The obstacles were great: the incumbent Republican Kenneth Keating was popular; New York Democrats were chronically divided and had lost every postwar senatorial election but one; and Kennedy was neither an experienced campaigner, an enthusiastic candidate, nor a New Yorker. Instead, he was a shy, backstage political operator who as recently as early August was registered to vote in Massachusetts.

Still the savvy political strategist, however, when polls showed him losing and Johnson winning in New York, Kennedy changed his campaign theme from "Let's put Robert Kennedy to work for New York" to "Get with the Johnson-Humphrey-Kennedy team." He invited the president to campaign with him, which he did. On Election Day Johnson carried New York by 2.5 million votes, the largest margin in history for any presidential candidate in any state at the time. Kennedy rode Johnson's coattails to a victory margin of 720,000, about one-fourth that size. Wasting no time on gratitude, however, Kennedy barely mentioned Johnson in his victory speech, infuriating the president and sealing the fate of the Brooklyn Navy Yard, which McNamara placed on a list of bases to be closed shortly after the election.[77] Nonetheless, having improved as a campaigner and demonstrated his ability to persuade people to vote for him, Kennedy could now easily imagine running for president, albeit in 1972, not 1968 when Johnson presumably would be seeking a final term.

Kennedy's assassination created not just the vacancy in the presidency that was filled by Johnson's succession, but also a vacancy in the vice presidency, which under the existing Constitution would remain unfilled until the 1964 election.[78] As soon as it became apparent that Johnson was not going to choose Robert Kennedy as his running mate, Hubert Humphrey became the widely acknowledged front-runner.

Humphrey grew up as the son of a struggling druggist in small towns in Minnesota and South Dakota. The demands of his father's store kept him from attending college until 1937, when he was twenty-six. After graduating from the University of Minnesota, Humphrey enrolled in a master's degree program in political science at Louisiana State University, en route to returning to the "U" to earn a doctorate. His master's thesis, "The Political Philosophy of the New Deal," ended with a statement of his own philosophy that prefigured the Great Society while endorsing the New Deal. Humphrey proposed six "new rights," including "the right to an adequate standard of living," "the right to the maintenance of health," and "the right to leisure and its effective use." In addition, the "shock and outrage" Humphrey felt about the racial discrimination he witnessed while living in Baton Rouge gave "flesh and blood," he later wrote, "to my abstract commitment to civil rights."[79]

Humphrey returned to Minneapolis in 1940 but for financial reasons abandoned his planned doctoral studies and took a job directing the Works Progress Administration's Twin Cities Workers Education Service. Service in government was a natural bridge into electoral politics for someone with Humphrey's exuberant personality and crusading liberalism. He ran for mayor and lost in 1943, ran and won in 1945, and ran and was reelected by the largest majority in Minneapolis history in 1947.

Statewide, Minnesota had operated for decades under a three-party system. The urban Catholic Democratic Party, the weakest of the three, split the liberal vote with the state's distinctive, largely Protestant and rural Farmer Labor Party, leaving the Republicans the largest of the three minority parties and the winner of most elections. In 1944 Humphrey worked to effect the merger that created the Democratic Farmer Labor Party, even though that meant accommodating Farmer Labor's radical Popular Front elements. Four years later, as part of his campaign to win the new party's Senate nomination, Humphrey fought hard to marginalize its left wing. With help from, among others, the young College of St. Thomas sociology and economics professor Eugene McCarthy, he prevailed in that bitter fight.

Humphrey defeated the Republican incumbent, Joseph Ball, by 243,700 votes in November 1948—the first Democrat to win a popular election for senator in the history of Minnesota.

Nationally, President Truman and other liberal Democrats were waging a similar battle for control of the party against a left-wing Democratic faction led by former vice president Henry A. Wallace. Truman had fired Wallace as secretary of commerce in 1946 for publicly defending the postwar Soviet occupation of Eastern Europe. Now Wallace was running against the president as a third-party candidate. A founding member and vice chairman of the liberal, strongly anticommunist Americans for Democratic Action (ADA) in 1947, Humphrey carried the scars and the savvy gained in Minnesota's intraparty wars into the national fight against the borderline pro-Soviet Wallaceites. The best way to beat them, Humphrey believed (somewhat ruefully, because he had been a Wallace admirer before Wallace broke with Truman), was for the Democratic Party to raise high the banner of civil rights by pledging support in its 1948 platform for the recent antidiscrimination recommendations of the President's Commission on Civil Rights. "Just as American liberalism took on the double task of using government to keep the country prosperous and the rest of the world anticommunist," Walter LaFeber has written, Humphrey "insisted on adding another dimension"—namely, civil rights.[80] The problem was that the president himself, wary of provoking an additional third-party challenge from segregationist southern Democrats, wanted the platform to mute the issue.

Humphrey persuaded 30 of the 108 platform committee members to endorse a minority plank supporting the Civil Rights Commission's report, enough to bring the issue to the full convention. Not just liberals but also, with an eye on the many black voters in their cities, northern bosses such as Chicago's Jake Arvey and the Bronx's Ed Flynn supported the plank. In the floor debate, heard by an estimated sixty million radio listeners and ten million television viewers, Humphrey's eight-minute speech was electrifying—arguably the most effective convention speech since William Jennings Bryan's much longer "Cross of Gold" oration at the 1896 Democratic convention. A 651.5 to 582.5 majority of delegates responded to Humphrey's plea to "get out of the shadow of states' rights and walk forthrightly into the bright sunshine of human rights" by approving the minority plank.[81] Humphrey's speech made him a national figure, and ADA's leaders promoted him as Truman's running mate. Truman chose Kentucky senator Alben Barkley instead, and Humphrey won his Senate election. At the start of the 81st Congress, *Time* pictured the newly elected senator on its January 17,

1949, cover with a whirlwind at his back, describing him as "a hard-working, fast-talking . . . glib, jaunty spellbinder."[82]

The conservative southern committee chairs who quietly dominated the Senate expected not to like Humphrey when he arrived in 1949: he was a liberal, a civil rights enthusiast, and, in their view, a showboater. He confirmed their apprehensions by introducing fifty-seven bills and resolutions on a wide variety of topics as a newly minted senator. Coming from a freshman ranging outside his committee specialization, none were treated seriously. He then began his second year by proposing to abolish Virginia senator Harry F. Byrd's fiscally conservative Joint Committee on Reduction of Non-Essential Federal Expenditures. The attack itself was indecorous. Compounding the offense was that Humphrey delivered it when Byrd was absent—visiting his sick mother, it turned out. Six days later, over a four-hour period, leading senators rose to attack Humphrey and then, when he attempted to defend himself, walked out of the chamber.

Humphrey realized that he had become a Senate pariah. Even strongly anticommunist speeches defending the Marshall Plan, the Truman Doctrine, and the war in Korea did him little good, although he did manage to insert a severe provision into the Communist Control Act of 1954 that provided criminal penalties for membership in the Communist Party. When Senate Democratic leader Lyndon Johnson threw him a lifeline, Humphrey grabbed it. He later recalled that LBJ invited him to become "the bridge from Johnson to my liberal colleagues," a role that would benefit Johnson by enabling him to deal more effectively with the small but growing cohort of liberal Democrats and benefit Humphrey by knitting him into the fabric of the Senate leadership.[83] During the 1950s Humphrey's stature grew both within the chamber (where he became—Johnson's term—a "whale," no longer a "minnow")[84] and among liberals, who appreciated his championing the ideas that later became the basis for the Peace Corps, the Food for Peace program, Medicare, federal aid to education, and a nuclear test-ban treaty. Nevertheless, then and throughout their association, "LBJ treated him like a staff sergeant might treat a private," said one close observer.[85]

Setting his sights on national office, Humphrey was bitterly disappointed in 1956 and 1960. He convinced himself that he was Stevenson's first choice for a running mate in 1956—an unlikely prospect, considering that both of them were midwestern liberals. Caught flat-footed when Stevenson threw open the nomination, Humphrey was devastated when the delegation from Minnesota, whose primary Kefauver had won that spring, refused to support his own candidacy. "That was the worst, that was the bitterest defeat," said his wife, Muriel Humphrey. "He felt he had been made a fool of."[86]

Four years later, when Humphrey challenged John Kennedy for the Democratic presidential nomination, his woefully underfinanced campaign was unable to compete effectively. Even the money that Johnson persuaded his own supporters to channel to Humphrey, the only nonmillionaire in the Democratic field, in hopes of snuffing out Kennedy's candidacy was nothing compared with the Kennedy family's bottomless treasury. In the West Virginia primary, the Kennedys paid Franklin D. Roosevelt, Jr., the bearer of an iconic name in the state, to cruelly attack Humphrey as a draft dodger: "He's a good Democrat, but I don't know where he was in World War II."[87] (Humphrey had tried to enlist multiple times but was classified 4-F.) Facing what turned out to be a two-to-one defeat in the primary, Humphrey bitterly complained of Kennedy: "He's the spoiled candidate and he and young, emotional, juvenile Bobby are spending with wild abandon."[88] Humphrey endorsed Stevenson at the convention, and McCarthy, now a congressman from St. Paul who had campaigned for his fellow Minnesotan in the Wisconsin primary, gave an eloquent speech nominating the former Illinois governor.

Humphrey was elected Senate majority whip after the 1960 election, a mark of acceptance by his southern colleagues, as well as an indicator of how much more liberal the Democratic caucus had become as a result of the 1958 midterm contests. As one who strongly preferred friendship to resentment, Humphrey worked faithfully to promote Kennedy's legislative program and continued to treat Vice President Johnson warmly and respectfully, even as others dismissed him as a has-been. When Johnson unexpectedly became president, Humphrey began maneuvering for the vice presidential nomination. "I want to become president," he told friends, inadvertently echoing Johnson's comment four years earlier, "and the only way I can is to become vice president."[89]

In truth, as a nationally prominent northern liberal Johnson loyalist, Humphrey was the logical choice to balance the ticket in 1964. But that did not stop the president from prolonging the agony. One motive was to create suspense at a convention that lacked it. Johnson publicly strung along two of Humphrey's fellow Democratic senators, Eugene McCarthy (elected from Minnesota in 1962) and Thomas Dodd of Connecticut. Beyond that, the president said privately that, whoever his vice president was, "I want his pecker . . . in my pocket."[90] He knew that keeping the eager Humphrey waiting would increase his craving to secure the nomination on any terms.

Longtime allies in Minnesota politics, Vice President Hubert H. Humphrey and Sen. Eugene McCarthy were rivals for the vice presidential nomination in 1964 and would become rivals for the presidential nomination in 1968. (Credit: Courtesy of Meet the Press)

When he finally made the offer, Johnson said, "I need complete and unswerving loyalty," and, Humphrey recalled, "I accepted under the conditions he had set."[91] This came as no surprise to the president. A few days before the meeting Humphrey had said on television that he believed the vice president must have "a willingness literally to give himself, to be what the president wants him to be, to be a loyal, faithful friend and servant"—disdained by one critic as "a very good description of a dog."[92]

As a final test, Johnson required that Humphrey defuse the convention eve crisis created when both the regular, segregationist Mississippi delegation and a delegation sent by the pro–civil rights Mississippi Freedom Democratic Party (MFDP) demanded to be seated. "Put a stop to this hell-raising so we don't throw out fifteen states," Johnson demanded of Humphrey.[93] Ironically, Humphrey's job was to head off exactly the kind of nationally broadcast convention battle about civil rights that had catapulted him to national fame in 1948. With help from another young Minnesota political protégé, state attorney general Walter F. Mondale, Humphrey arrived at a solution that pleased neither Mississippi faction but removed the dispute from the media spotlight, thereby accomplishing Johnson's main purpose. One enduring consequence of the settlement was that the party's rules were amended to ban racially discriminatory delegations from future conventions, starting in 1968.[94] Another, according to William Chafe, was to "convince SNCC [Student Nonviolent Coordinating Committee] members that they could not trust 'white liberals,'" laying the predicate for SNCC's turn to "black power" and even separatism two years later.[95] SNCC volunteers had provided much of the MFDP's grassroots energy, and three of them—two whites and one black—were murdered by white racists in June.

Humphrey was a popular choice when Johnson announced his selection at the convention, and he gave a rousing acceptance speech. His theme was that Goldwater was too extreme for even his Republican colleagues, much less for the nation as a whole. Eight times Humphrey declared, "Most Democrats and most Republicans in the Senate voted for" the civil rights act, the tax cut, and so on—and then rang out the refrain, loudly joined by the delegates: "But not Senator Goldwater!"[96] Humphrey continued his joyful, tireless campaigning into the fall and, as the certainty of victory in November became apparent, looked forward to serving eight years as vice president and then, at age sixty-one, to running a well-financed campaign for president in 1972.

MCCARTHY

For much of his political career Eugene McCarthy was the other Democratic leader in Minnesota and the other Catholic politician in the country. The difference was that McCarthy liked and respected Hubert Humphrey despite their temperamental differences (Humphrey boosterish and talkative, McCarthy critical and laconic) but disliked and envied John and later Robert Kennedy.

McCarthy had an intensely Catholic upbringing in rural Watkins, Minnesota. He was educated at nearby St. John's Preparatory School and then at adjacent St. John's University, both of them connected to the Benedictine St. John's Abbey from which their faculties were drawn. He was influenced by various Catholic social justice proponents, whose commitment to a noncommunist, Christian version of economic reform prevailed at St. John's when he was a student there in the 1930s. After teaching public school for several years, entering a monastery with the intention of becoming a priest or a monk (he was released for excessive intellectual pride), earning a master's degree at the University of Minnesota, receiving an instructorship at St. John's, and serving as a civilian code breaker in the War Department's

Military Intelligence Division during World War II, McCarthy accepted a faculty appointment to teach economics and sociology at the College of St. Thomas in 1946. He joined Humphrey's campaign to create the Democratic Farmer Labor Party, and in 1948, at age thirty-two, he ran for and won a seat in the House of Representatives against a one-term Republican incumbent, entering the House the same year Humphrey entered the Senate. "There are altogether too many technicians in Washington now," said McCarthy, smiling. "I guess I agree with Plato that it's the philosopher who should rule."[97]

McCarthy was an active and influential House member. In 1957 he headed a group of Democratic liberals, informally known as "McCarthy's Mavericks," that developed its own policy positions and whip system to counter the influence of the conservative southern Democrats who occupied the important committee chairs. (It evolved into the Democratic Study Group two years later.) In 1958, realizing that the voices of senators but not representatives were heard in the national media, McCarthy sought and, as part of that year's Democratic sweep, won a seat in the upper chamber, unseating Republican incumbent Edward Thye by 73,000 votes. But McCarthy was bored in the Senate, alienated from both its conservative inner circle and his fellow liberals, who came to regard him as aloof, arrogant, and lazy. "Stubbornness and penicillin / hold the aged above me," wrote McCarthy, an amateur poet.[98]

McCarthy especially disliked John Kennedy, a fellow Catholic and, born only one year after McCarthy, his contemporary. Four years after refusing to support Kennedy for vice president at the 1956 Democratic convention, McCarthy acidly told Tip O'Neill: "Actually I'm the one who should be nominated [for president]. Any way you measure it, I'm a better man than John Kennedy. I'm smarter, I'm a better orator, and if they're looking for a Catholic, I'm a better Catholic. Of course, I don't have a rich father."[99] This was in keeping with another of McCarthy's remarks in 1960: "Why don't they just nominate me? I'm twice as liberal as Humphrey, twice as Catholic as Kennedy, and twice as smart as [Missouri senator Stuart] Symington."[100] McCarthy supported Johnson for the nomination, thinking he could balance the ticket as Johnson's northern and Catholic running mate. With Johnson's permission he gave the nominating speech for Stevenson in hopes of stopping Kennedy.

Although McCarthy was as inactive on his own behalf in 1964 as he had been in 1960, he became southern Democrats' favorite candidate for vice president on the Johnson ticket. This was partly because he somewhat idiosyncratically favored the oil depletion allowance, a liberal anathema and a southern sacred cow, but mostly because they rightly feared that the strongly and, in the South, notoriously pro–civil rights Humphrey would get the nod unless they could come up with a different, less effective northern liberal whom Johnson liked. Opposition to McCarthy by Robert Kennedy, who in addition to personal dislike did not want to lose his new status as the nation's foremost Catholic politician, cut both ways with the president. Johnson toyed with the idea of naming McCarthy in order to balance the ticket both regionally and religiously. He told him that he was one of two finalists, and asked him to be available at a moment's notice during convention week—all the while knowing that Humphrey would be the more loyal vice president and thinking him more able as well. McCarthy, who along with his wife Abigail McCarthy badly wanted the nomination, figured this out during the convention and sent a telegram to the president withdrawing his candidacy. Johnson was livid. What he really wanted was to appear before the delegates with both McCarthy and Humphrey in tow and then, after milking the moment for all its drama, send McCarthy forward to nominate Humphrey. "What a sadistic son of a bitch," McCarthy said to Johnson aide Walter Jenkins when Jenkins told him why the president was upset.[101] Whatever respect, or even affection, McCarthy may have had for Johnson vanished at that moment.

WALLACE

Johnson's fear that Robert Kennedy would oppose him in one or more of the fifteen Democratic presidential primaries in 1964 did not materialize. Instead, much to his surprise, the president was challenged by an unlikely opponent who was seeking to capitalize on the national notoriety he recently had gained by resisting racial integration: Gov. George C. Wallace of Alabama.

Wallace honed his political skills and fixed his ambitions early in life in southeastern Alabama's Barbour County, where he was born and grew up. In 1935, at age sixteen, he was elected as a page by the Alabama state senate and told friends that he wanted to be governor. Although Wallace was not from a planter family in the state's black belt or a "Big Mule" industrial family in Birmingham, in 1937 he won the election for freshman class president at the University of Alabama—a traditional stepping stone to a career in state politics that almost always went to a son of the elite. He further developed his persuasive abilities the following summer by selling magazine subscriptions door to door in Georgia, North Carolina, and Tennessee, and then heading north to Kentucky, Indiana, and Michigan—hoaxing country people into believing that a new government agency, the Bureau of Recapitulation and Matriculation, was now requiring everyone to read something besides the Bible.

Soon after graduating from Alabama with a law degree in 1942, Wallace enlisted in the army air force. He declined Officer Candidate School because he "sensed that if I got back to Alabama and into politics, there would be far more GIs among the electorate than officers."[102] Using his serviceman's right to mail letters without postage, Wallace sent thousands of notes and Christmas cards to nearly every registered voter in Barbour County, where Clio and Clayton, the towns he was raised in, were located. After the war Wallace was elected to the legislature as its youngest member in 1946. Although the voters knew he had flown numerous and hazardous B-29 missions bombing the coast of Japan under the command of Gen. Curtis LeMay, Wallace was able to keep secret the "severe anxiety state (chronic)" he suffered when assigned to a high-risk training mission in California after V-J Day. From the time of his discharge in December 1945, Wallace collected a 10 percent Veterans Administration disability pension for "psychoneurosis" induced by combat.[103]

As a legislator, Wallace hitched his wagon to the star of the state's non-racist, populist governor Jim Folsom. Wallace passed a 2 percent tax on liquor to fund eight new technical and vocational schools; filibustered a bill to raise the sales tax because it penalized "the lathe operators, the brick masons, the welders, the tool and die workers"; and served as a board member of historically black Tuskegee University.[104] A statehouse reporter labeled him "the Number-One Do-Gooder in the Legislature," and the Chamber of Commerce gave him one of its lowest grades.[105] At the 1948 Democratic National Convention, Wallace was one of the few Alabama delegates not to walk out after Humphrey's strong civil rights plank was added to the platform. Two years later he was elected circuit court judge in Barbour County over state senator Preston Clayton, a lieutenant colonel during the war and bearer of the ancestral name of one of the county's main towns. "Now, all you officers vote for Clayton, and all you privates vote for me," Wallace told voters.[106] At the 1956 Democratic convention, he supported John Kennedy for vice president. This was not an unusual act for an Alabama politician of that era. Next to African Americans and Jews, poor southern whites in the 1950s "were among the nation's most liberal constituencies on nonracial economic issues" such as "full employment, improved education, and low-cost medical care."[107]

Wallace ran for governor in 1958 as Folsom's political heir, promising better roads and schools and opposing the Ku Klux Klan. He was endorsed by the state chapter of the National Association for the Advancement of Colored People (NAACP). But in the aftermath of the Supreme Court's 1954 *Brown v. Board of Education* decision and the 1955–1956 Montgomery bus boycott, Wallace lost to John Patterson, who as state attorney general had so tied up the NAACP in expensive litigation as to drive the chapter virtually out of existence. "Well, boys," Wallace said after losing the election, "no other son-of-a-bitch will ever out-nigger me again."[108] He returned to his judgeship and, seizing an opportunity to defy the federal government on a civil rights issue, refused an order from racially moderate federal district court judge Frank M. Johnson, once a close friend, to turn over Barbour County's voter registration records to the new U.S. Civil Rights Commission. "This 1959 attempt to have a second Sherman's March to the Sea has been stopped in the Cradle of the Confederacy," Wallace declared, while quietly satisfying Judge Johnson by giving the records to a grand jury, which gave them to the judge. Wallace tried to achieve martyrdom by pleading guilty to contempt of court, but Judge Johnson acquitted him, "refus[ing] to allow [this court's] authority to be bent and swayed by such politically generated whirlwinds."[109] In 1962 Wallace ran again for governor and was elected by a landslide on the slogan: "Vote right—vote white—vote for the Fighting Judge."[110] "I started off talking about schools and highways and prisons and taxes," Wallace told a newspaper editor. "Then I began talking about niggers—and they stomped the floor."[111]

One of Wallace's pledges in the 1962 campaign was to "stand in the schoolhouse door" to block any federal effort to integrate Alabama's schools.[112] A few months after declaring "segregation now, segregation tomorrow, segregation forever" in his inaugural address, he got an opportunity to do just that.[113] When a federal court ordered that two African American students be enrolled at the University of Alabama on June 11, 1963, Wallace implored white Alabamans to stay home and let him act on their behalf—he didn't want a repeat of the white riot that accompanied James Meredith's integration of the University of Mississippi in 1962. Wallace then stood in the doorway of the campus's Foster Auditorium, raised his hand, and said "Stop!" to the approaching deputy attorney general, Nicholas Katzenbach. He made a statement denouncing the Kennedy administration's "force-induced intrusion" on the university to the four hundred national and international reporters and camera operators covering the event.[114] Wallace continued blocking the door while Katzenbach and aides escorted the students to their new dormitories. His attention-getting act of mock defiance, the only one of its kind that any southern governor was able to choreograph, was a dark pastiche of Rev. Martin Luther King's recent actions during that spring's Birmingham civil rights campaign: defy the law, act out a symbolic, nonviolent drama in which a brave victim stands up for principle against overwhelming force, and in doing so "turn an apparent legal and practical defeat into a political victory."[115]

When more than forty thousand telegrams of support flooded into the governor's office, more than half from outside the South, Wallace began thinking about running for president. He had already shown the ability on national television programs such as *Meet the Press* to adopt a disarmingly reasonable and good-humored persona. Wallace dropped his racial talk in such settings and instead defended himself and his region in terms of constitutional principles such as states' rights, property rights, and judicial restraint. He also pointed to his record in Alabama of providing free textbooks to public school students and constructing new junior colleges, trade schools, and mental health facilities. Venturing north that fall to speak at Harvard University, Brown University, and Dartmouth College, Wallace had the Confederate flag and "Stand Up for Alabama" logo on his state airplane painted over and replaced with the American flag and "Stand Up for America."

Wallace's public stance of embattled intransigence in the face of certain defeat resonated not just with white southerners but also with some northerners participating in centennial observations of the Civil War, which tended to cast the South as valiant and honorable in defeat.[116] In spring 1964, in faint imitation of Robert E. Lee's decision to take the fight to the North by invading Maryland and Pennsylvania, Wallace entered three northern presidential primaries against local Johnson surrogates who were standing in for the president: Gov. John W. Reynolds in Wisconsin (April 7), Gov. Matthew Welsh in Indiana (May 5), and Sen. Daniel Brewster in Maryland (May 19). "In each campaign," Marshall Frady wrote, "Wallace met with total rejection from the state's establishment—political, religious, and journalistic."[117] But Wallace calculated that the massive northward migration of poor whites and poor blacks seeking industrial employment in recent decades had made the North more like the South.

In particular, Wallace thought that northern whites were becoming more resentful of African Americans. Campaigning in Wisconsin, Wallace discovered a new, superficially race-neutral issue—crime—that struck a chord with big-city white ethnics, especially those living near expanding black neighborhoods. "If you are knocked in the head on a street in a city today," he told rallies to massive cheers, "the man who knocked you in the head is out of jail before you get to the hospital."[118] Wallace received a surprising 33.8 percent of the Democratic vote in Wisconsin, and he followed that with 29.8 percent in Indiana. In Maryland, Wallace won 42.7 percent, including a majority of the state's white vote. Ethnic neighborhoods in Baltimore that had voted two to one for Kennedy in 1960 went strongly for Wallace.[119]

None of these showings threatened Johnson's lock on the Democratic nomination. Wallace was awarded not a single delegate and was denied a place on the convention program. On June 5 he said that he would run as an independent candidate in the general election and even got on the ballot in sixteen states. When it became clear that Goldwater would be the Republican nominee, Wallace's funding from conservative southerners dried up. An independent campaign would serve only to divide the anti-Johnson vote in the South. On the eve of the Republican convention, Goldwater, who regarded Wallace as a racist bully, spurned a private entreaty from the governor to be his vice presidential running mate, an offer conveyed by prominent Alabama Republican Jim Martin. Wallace couldn't understand why. "It must be apparent to a one-eyed nigger who can't see good out of his other eye that me and Goldwater would be a winning ticket," he said. But on July 19 Wallace ended his campaign.[120] "My mission has been accomplished," he declared, and immediately began planning for 1968.[121]

THE REPUBLICANS

The Democrats emerged from the 1964 election confident about who their candidate would be in 1968: Lyndon Johnson. The Republicans lacked not just a presumptive nominee but also, it seemed, an adequate talent pool from which to draw one. Goldwater, whose Senate term expired at the end of 1964, had no interest in serving even as the party's titular leader. When conservatives thought about who might carry his torch in 1968, no names came to mind—except, for a few, that of the actor Ronald Reagan, who unlike all previous presidents and major party nominees, had spent his entire career in show business.

The party's other recent presidential candidate, Richard Nixon, renounced politics after losing the 1962 election for governor of California—and then left his native state to practice law in New York City. Yet Nixon won points from conservatives by ardently campaigning for Goldwater, who was so grateful that at the January 1965 meeting of the Republican National Committee he pledged to support Nixon if he ever ran again. Nelson Rockefeller, as governor of New York, remained the leading figure in the party's eastern liberal wing, which expected to take back control of the GOP now that southern and western conservatives had had their electorally futile chance. But Rockefeller had been bloodied in two consecutive bids for the nomination and had little appetite for another. If not Rockefeller, then perhaps Gov. George Romney, the winner of a landslide reelection in Michigan (even as Goldwater was losing the state by two to one) but also disliked by conservatives for sitting out the campaign against Johnson. And as imperfect a talent pool as Nixon, Rockefeller, Reagan, and Romney seemed to constitute, the ranks of other well-positioned potential nominees—senators (just thirty-five Republicans, none of apparent presidential ambition and caliber), governors (sixteen, also a thin roster apart from Rockefeller and Romney), and former vice presidents (none other than Nixon)—were weaker still.

NIXON

By 1960 Richard Nixon had been on the national ballot as often as any American politician in history besides FDR (whose record he would eventually tie) and had done so at a younger age than anyone besides William Jennings Bryan. Nixon was thirty-nine in 1952, forty-three in 1956, and forty-seven in 1960. The son of a hard-luck grocer in Whittier, California, Nixon had worked his way through Whittier College. After naval service in World War II, during which he gained renown among his fellow junior officers as a talented poker player, Nixon returned to Los Angeles County as a Duke-educated lawyer and launched a career marked by political risk-taking. In 1946, at age thirty-three, he cashed in half his savings (much of it from wartime poker), challenged five-term Democratic congressman Jerry Voorhis, and was elected to the House of Representatives from California's Twelfth District with 56 percent of the vote as part of the nationwide Republican sweep. Two years later, as a member of the House Un-American Activities Committee, Nixon staked his political reputation on the veracity of Whittaker Chambers, a brilliant but eccentric *Time* editor who accused the widely respected State Department official Alger Hiss of being a Soviet agent.[122] In 1950, when that gamble paid off with Hiss's conviction for perjury, Nixon sought and won a Democratic-held open seat in the Senate against a fellow representative, Helen Gahagan Douglas, the wife of film actor Melvyn Douglas and until recently a mistress of Lyndon Johnson's.[123] Nixon's 59 percent vote led California's GOP ticket by 7 percentage points; he won by 681,000 votes in a state where registered Democrats outnumbered Republicans by 1 million. Early in that campaign, Nixon's across-the-hall House neighbor, Rep. John F. Kennedy of Massachusetts, brought him a check for $1,000 signed by his father.[124]

Nixon described himself as a "practical liberal."[125] But the thread that ran through all his successful early political gambles was fierce opposition to communism and a willingness to characterize his Democratic opponents as insufficiently anticommunist. This raised his national profile among Republicans, who blamed the Roosevelt and Truman administrations for multiple postwar failings: allowing the Soviet Union to take over Eastern Europe, standing by as communist revolutionaries overthrew the pro-American government of China, and showing insufficient concern about the presence of communists in the federal government.[126] (Nixon, unlike Joseph McCarthy, actually helped send a communist to jail.) Wanting to tap into this sentiment in 1952, former Republican presidential candidate Thomas E. Dewey and other advisers to current nominee Dwight Eisenhower, a sixty-two-year-old man who had led a wartime alliance that included the Soviets, persuaded Ike to add the young, famously anticommunist Nixon to the ticket. Nixon passed Eisenhower's one litmus test: he shared Ike's "Modern Republicanism," especially its emphasis on international engagement rather than a retreat to the isolationism advocated by Robert Taft, the Senate Republican leader and Ike's defeated rival for the nomination. "Don't get fat, don't lose your zeal, and you can be president some day," Dewey told Nixon.[127]

Nixon's candidacy was nearly derailed when the New York Post, a liberal paper at the time, ran a story on September 18 headlined: "Secret Rich Men's Trust Fund Keeps Nixon in Style Far beyond His Salary." The charge was baseless: the Nixons lived modestly and the fund was public, independently audited, raised through small donations, and used only for political expenses. But the Eisenhower campaign regarded the controversy as a damaging distraction from the presidential contest. Eisenhower's aides, and soon Ike himself, wanted Nixon to resign from the ticket. "I do not see how we can win unless Nixon is persuaded to withdraw," Eisenhower told Gov. Sherman Adams of New Hampshire.[128] But on September 23 Nixon went all in with a nationally televised speech. Declaring that "every dime we've got is honestly ours," including those that paid for his wife Pat Nixon's "respectable Republican cloth coat," he echoed FDR's wartime defense of his dog Fala by adding that there was one personal gift he would never give back: their daughters' "little cocker spaniel dog," Checkers.[129] Nixon concluded the thirty-minute program by urging viewers to wire the

Republican National Committee about whether he should step down or not. His television audience of sixty million, about 40 percent of the entire population, was the largest in history at the time. Television was still a new mass medium, no national candidate had ever made such a dramatic and personal speech, and the program aired on NBC right after the popular *Texaco Star Theatre* starring Milton Berle. Four million Americans weighed in with telegrams, letters, or phone calls, running seventy-five to one in Nixon's favor. "Laying bare his most private hopes, fears, and liabilities," wrote conservative columnist Robert Ruark, "this time the common man was a Republican, for a change," one who "suddenly placed the burden of old-style Republican aloofness on the Democrats."[130] Liberal columnist Walter Lippman demurred. "That must be the most demeaning experience my country has ever had to bear," he told a colleague.[131] But he and the rest of the "chattering class" were distinctly outnumbered.

"You're my boy," Eisenhower publicly greeted Nixon after summoning him to the Wheeling, West Virginia, airport.[132] But little love was lost between the two men from that point on. Ike was especially annoyed that in his speech Nixon said that for any candidates not to "make a complete statement as to their financial history . . . will be an admission that they have something to hide." Eisenhower, who four years earlier had gotten a special tax break that saved him $476,000 on royalties from his postwar memoir *Crusade in Europe,* had no interest in opening his records for inspection.[133] Nor had the five-star general appreciated the lieutenant commander telling him in a phone call to "shit or get off the pot" when he delayed making a decision.[134]

In 1948, GOP operatives were convinced, they had "snatched defeat from the jaws of victory" by running too high-minded a campaign against Truman. They would not make that mistake again. Nixon's main assignment, both as a candidate and, after winning the election, as the first vice president of the television age, was to campaign for Republicans and attack the Democrats so that Eisenhower could remain above the partisan fray. Perversely, however, Nixon's enthusiastic performance as attack dog, a new role for a vice president, earned not just Ike's appreciation but also his faint disdain. In eight years in office Eisenhower never invited Nixon into the White House residence. But when he tried to ease Nixon off the ticket and into a cabinet post in 1956, the president discovered that the popularity among rank-and-file Republicans that the vice president had acquired while cultivating the party's grass roots with tireless campaigning in the 1954 midterm election made such a move politically impossible. To Ike, a wider portfolio of government experience would prepare Nixon to advance through the ranks of the executive branch in the manner of a rising officer in the army. To Nixon, removal from the ticket would only be interpreted in headlines as "Nixon Dumped."[135] In the fall campaign Stevenson, once again the Democratic nominee, went after Nixon, knowing that to attack the popular Ike would get him nowhere. "The president's age, his health . . . make it inevitable that the dominant figure in the Republican party under a second Eisenhower term would be Richard Nixon," Stevenson said, alluding to Ike's heart attack in 1955 and bowel surgery in 1956.[136] "Nixonland" would be "a land of slander and scare; the land of sly innuendo, the poison pen, the anonymous phone call."[137]

Eisenhower was the first president to bump against the two-term limit imposed by the Twenty-second Amendment in 1951. A wholly unanticipated consequence of that amendment was to free second-term vice presidents to spend four years seeking the presidency without overtly offending the incumbent.[138] Nixon, who had already compiled a long list of political debts by endlessly campaigning for local candidates and raising money for local party organizations, again took advantage of this opportunity in 1958. It was his best chance to buck the historical odds—in the century prior to 1960 thirteen current or former governors of New York had been nominated for president, but not a single incumbent vice president. Rockefeller, who was elected governor in 1958 and already had a national reputation, certainly wanted the nomination, but he decided not to run after discovering that Nixon had quietly locked it up. Rockefeller then exacted a price for his support at the 1960 Republican convention. At the governor's insistence Nixon came to his New York apartment and accepted fourteen Rockefeller-dictated changes in the party platform. Goldwater branded the so-called Compact of Fifth Avenue as the "Munich of the Republican Party."[139] The 1960 Republican convention was the last at which a candidate would feel the need to appease the party's left. From then on it would be their right flank that nominees would have to guard.

Nixon's risk-taking continued in the general election campaign against Kennedy. Confident from the Checkers speech that he had mastered television (and convinced, in any event, that "television is not as effective as it was in 1952" because "the novelty has worn off"), he agreed to four debates, the first in history between presidential candidates.[140] Just by debating, Nixon yielded whatever advantage of stature he had accrued over his less experienced rival from official trips to fifty nations, including eventful and much-publicized trips to South America in 1958 and the Soviet Union in 1959, and from filling in capably when Eisenhower was temporarily disabled by health crises, which continued into his second term. On top of that, Nixon refused to rehearse, rejected wearing professionally applied makeup suitable to hot, harsh studio lights, and generally ignored the camera—and with it the television audience of eighty million. Nixon rebounded strongly in the remaining three debates but never fully recovered from his sweaty performance in the first encounter, in which he looked, sneered columnist Joseph Alsop, "like a suspect being questioned."[141] As William Rorabaugh has observed, "Nixon was both cocky and naïve about television, a lethal combination."[142]

Nixon also adopted a high-risk strategy for the overall campaign. Surprised by the large and enthusiastic crowds at late August campaign appearances in Atlanta and Birmingham, he muted his longstanding support for civil rights in an impulsive effort to carry the still solidly Democratic Deep South—completely undoing whatever he had hoped to accomplish by choosing the liberal Massachusetts United Nations ambassador, Henry Cabot Lodge, as his running mate. (He later said he wished he had chosen Sen. Thruston Morton of Kentucky.)[143] Nixon's uneasy relationship with Eisenhower, recently aggravated when the president carelessly told *Time* reporter Charles Mohr on August 24 that he would need a week to think of a specific idea he had gotten from his vice president, caused him to not ask Ike to join the campaign until just before the election. Nothing relieved Kennedy more than Eisenhower's long absence from the hustings, especially when he saw the massive and jubilant crowds that cheered the president, belatedly, during the final rallies of the campaign. Ike had not meant to disparage Nixon—he even taped a television commercial extolling his "experience, maturity, and knowledge"—but the damage was done.

Nixon's gambles did not pay off in 1960, and he lost to Kennedy by the narrowest of margins: two-tenths of a percentage point in the national popular vote. Still relatively young and politically viable, Nixon was a gracious loser, refusing to contest the election and calling off a planned postelection series of articles by *Herald Tribune* reporter Earl Mazo on fraudulent Democratic voting in Texas, Illinois, and elsewhere. He decided to run for governor of California in 1962, vowing to serve at least one full term, which would spare him from challenging Kennedy in 1964 but position him perfectly to run in 1968. Stevenson had fought a hopeless rematch with the most recent reelection-seeking incumbent, Eisenhower, in 1956. Nixon wanted to avoid a similar fate when Kennedy sought a second term.

Although early polls showed Nixon with a substantial lead over incumbent Democratic governor Pat Brown, everything went wrong from that point on. A wealthy conservative rival for the Republican nomination, state assembly minority leader Joe Shell, refused to drop out, meaning that Nixon had to wage a hard-fought and expensive primary campaign just to be nominated. Brown effectively (and accurately) argued that Nixon wanted merely to "double park" in Sacramento, using California as a launching pad for his national ambitions.[144] Nixon's memoir *Six Crises* was published in March, a best seller but, with its focus on national and international events, one that suggested to Californians that he cared little about their state. On Election Day Nixon, who had lost to Kennedy by 119,000 votes nationally while carrying California in 1960 (as he had in every one of his previous campaigns), lost to Brown by 297,000 votes. The following morning, angry and exhausted, he told a press conference, "You don't have Nixon to kick around anymore because, gentlemen, this is my last press conference."[145] Five days later ABC aired a program called *The Political Obituary of Richard Nixon*, a savagely critical documentary featuring, of all people, Alger Hiss. Six months after that, in May 1963, Nixon moved to New York and joined a law firm. "He was broke," said his friend and Eisenhower administration colleague William Rogers. "He had no future in the field he knew best. He was in Rockefeller's state and cut off."[146] "Anybody who thinks I could be a candidate for anything in any year is off his rocker," Nixon told columnist Roscoe Drummond in 1963.[147]

The Kennedy assassination caused Nixon to reassess. The case for Goldwater in 1964 was now weaker, he thought, because Johnson would undermine Goldwater's southern and western appeal in a way that Kennedy could not have. The first post-assassination Gallup Poll of Republican voters showed Nixon in the lead for the 1964 nomination. He canceled plans to sign a contract for a book chronicling the election, thinking now that he might be the subject rather than the author of such a work.[148] "I believe that any man who has become a public figure belongs to the public," Nixon said on January 9, signaling his availability, "and as long as they want him to lead, to lead."[149] But he remained on the sideline and, when write-in campaigns on his behalf in New Hampshire and elsewhere led to disappointing primary results, he decided to stay out. Knowing that many of Goldwater's delegates would be back in 1968, Nixon warmly introduced the nominee on the night of his acceptance speech at the convention as "Mr. Conservative," now "Mr. Republican," and soon "Mr. President." During the fall, Nixon made 150 campaign appearances in thirty-six states, arguably working harder for Goldwater than the unenthusiastic candidate worked for himself.

Nelson A. Rockefeller was the most politically ambitious member of the most famously wealthy family in the country. His birth in Bar Harbor, Maine, on July 8, 1908, shared the front page of the *New York Times* with news of William Jennings Bryan's nomination for president by the Democratic convention.[150] Displaying acute self-knowledge, Rockefeller later reflected that he had wanted to be president "ever since I was a kid. After all, when you think of what I had, what else was there to aspire to?"[151]

Most of Rockefeller's career as a young man was in the executive branch of the federal government rather than in electoral politics. As a heavy investor in Creole Petroleum, the Venezuelan arm of his family's gigantic main company, Standard Oil of New Jersey, Rockefeller saw firsthand that Nazi Germany was forging diplomatic and commercial alliances with the nations of South America in the late 1930s. Concerned, in 1940 he secured an appointment from President Roosevelt to a new, unsalaried position as coordinator of inter-American affairs, and four years later he became FDR's assistant secretary of state for American republic affairs. After Eisenhower took office in 1953, Rockefeller returned to government in the new Department of Health, Education and Welfare, whose creation he had recommended as chair of Ike's Advisory Committee on Government Organization. In 1954 he joined the White House staff to work on a variety of foreign policy issues.

At age fifty, Rockefeller abandoned his status as a political independent holding appointive offices and in 1958 ran as a Republican for governor of New York. Implausibly dubbed "Rocky," an average-Joe nickname for a scion of wealth, he was a natural campaigner. The sight of a Rockefeller eating blintzes on city street corners and shouting, "Hiya, fella" to everyone he saw was captivating. In an otherwise terrible year for Republicans, Rockefeller won by 573,000 votes against the Democratic incumbent, Averell Harriman. A dedicated, big-spending governor of his state even as his gaze was fixed on the presidency, Rockefeller toured the country in the fall of 1959, asking local Republicans for their support on the grounds that "Nixon can't win." The Kennedys and election chronicler Theodore H. White were among the many who thought Rockefeller would have been unbeatable in 1960. But the governor discovered on his political travels that Nixon already had the nomination sewn up. "Everyone I talked to told me I didn't have a chance," he said.[152] He announced that he would not run, then threatened to enter the race six weeks before the convention unless the Republican platform included provisions critical of the Eisenhower administration's civil rights and national defense policies. Ike was furious at Rockefeller for making these demands, especially concerning the defense plank, and irritated with Nixon for accommodating them. "Grant Surrenders to Lee" read the headline in the conservative *Chicago Tribune*.[153]

Nixon's defeats in 1960 and, especially, in 1962 when Rockefeller was cruising to a 539,000-vote reelection landslide in New York positioned the governor as the front-runner for the 1964 Republican nomination. But in 1961 he divorced his wife of thirty-one years and two years later married Margaretta "Happy" Murphy, who had divorced her husband, a friend of the governor's, and left her four children so she could marry him. Conservatives already disliked Rockefeller—his takeover of the state GOP had led to the formation of the Conservative Party in New York in 1961, and he was the main obstacle to Goldwater's nomination in 1964. Now many previous Rockefeller supporters turned against him, too, less because of the divorce than the remarriage. Sen. Prescott Bush of Connecticut lamented: "Have we come to the point in our life as a nation where the governor of a great state can desert a good wife, mother of his grown children, divorce her, then persuade a young mother of youngsters to abandon her husband and their four children and marry the governor?"[154] Rockefeller's seventeen-point lead over Goldwater among Republican voters in the Gallup Poll taken one week before he announced his engagement turned into a five-point deficit right afterward.

The wealthiest candidate ever to seek the presidency, Rockefeller entered the race for the 1964 Republican nomination anyway. He won two of fifteen primaries and lost narrowly to Goldwater in California, the final contest, after Happy bore his child, Nelson Jr., the weekend before the voting. Realizing that he could not win the nomination, Rockefeller withdrew in favor of a late entry, Gov. William Scranton of Pennsylvania. At the convention he concentrated on adding five planks to the Republican platform, especially one denouncing political extremism, which he later described as "certainly one that nobody could question."[155] Goldwater's delegates, rightly interpreting this as a veiled attack on them, drowned out Rockefeller with boos and chants of "We want Barry!" when he tried to speak. "Some of you don't like to hear it, ladies and gentlemen, but it's the truth," he bitterly told the Republican delegates. "There is no place in this Republican party for such hawkers of hate, purveyors of prejudice, such fabricators of fear."[156] Rockefeller refused to campaign for Goldwater and after the election resolved that he and other eastern liberal Republicans would regain control of the party in 1968.

George Romney was the most successful Republican candidate in the country in 1964. Two years earlier, in his first campaign for political office, Romney had been elected governor of Michigan, defeating the incumbent Democrat John B. Swainson by 81,000 votes and ending fourteen years of Democratic rule in the state. In 1964 he was reelected by 383,000 votes, even as Goldwater was losing Michigan by 1,076,000 votes. A strong supporter of civil rights, Romney earned 25 percent of the African American vote, up from 18 percent in 1962 and twelve times what Goldwater received in Michigan.[157]

Romney was born in Mexico of Mormon parents in 1907, an unusual beginning for a political figure. His mother and father were American citizens who, along with many other dissident Mormon families, migrated to Mexico because polygamy had been outlawed in the United States in 1862 and forbidden by the church in 1890. Romney's parents were not polygamists, but his grandparents, who led the migration to Mexico, were. In 1912, when George was five, the Mexican revolution drove the Romneys back to the United States, where his father moved from one poorly paid job to another in California, Idaho, and Utah. Romney, like his parents, rejected polygamy and, as an adult, strenuously opposed his church's ban on blacks serving as priests. But he was an active lifelong Mormon who served as a missionary and church leader, proudly stating during his gubernatorial years that "I am completely the product of the Church of Jesus Christ of Latter-Day Saints."[158]

Although he later became famous as a successful Detroit automobile executive, Romney spent the 1930s in Washington, initially to pursue his future wife Lenore, whose father was serving on the Federal Radio Commission. He found employment as a staff member with Sen. David Walsh, a Massachusetts Democrat, and then as a lobbyist for the large aluminum corporation Alcoa. During World War II Romney worked as general manager of the Automobile Manufacturers Association, based in Detroit but traveling frequently to Washington as the industry's chief liaison to the federal government and most prominent spokesman to Congress. Afterward Romney entered the manufacturing side as part of what became American Motors. He took over the struggling company in 1954 and decided that the only way to compete with the Big Three (General Motors, Ford, and Chrysler) was to develop a different kind of automobile. The result was the country's first mass-produced compact car, the Rambler, with Romney himself as chief salesman for the vehicle in newspaper and magazine advertise-

Ronald Reagan campaigns for Republican presidential nominee Barry Goldwater in 1964. Reagan's efforts on behalf of his fellow conservative launched his political career. (Credit: Courtesy of the Ronald Reagan Presidential Library)

ments and television commercials. The Rambler's success drove the share price of American Motors stock from seven to ninety dollars and made Romney a household name.

Romney also became an active participant in his state's civic affairs. In 1959 he spearheaded a successful campaign to write a new constitution for Michigan. He decided to run for governor in 1962, and, as with Rockefeller in New York four years earlier, the state's moribund Republican Party was happy to have a candidate whose personal popularity and wealth gave it a chance to be competitive. Narrowly elected (with active help in the campaign from his fifteen-year-old son Willard, better known as Mitt), Romney pushed unsuccessfully for a new state income tax during his first year in office. When Martin Luther King announced that he would lead a march in Detroit in June 1963, the governor declared the occasion Freedom March Day in Michigan. President Kennedy told a friend, "The one fellow I don't want to run against is Romney. . . . No vice whatsoever."[159]

In 1964 Romney toyed with the idea of entering the race for the Republican presidential nomination after Rockefeller dropped out, but he decided instead to defer to Governor Scranton and concentrate on his own reelection. His actions from that point on irritated many and confused nearly everyone. Romney opposed Goldwater at the convention, then moved that the nomination be made unanimous, and then refused to support him against Johnson. "Johnson for President, Romney for Governor," he told voters.[160] Afterward, Romney wrote to Goldwater, complaining: "Dogmatic ideological parties tend to splinter the political and social fabric of a nation, lead to government crises and deadlocks, and stymie the compromises so often necessary to preserve freedom and achieve progress."[161] But Romney's reelection, in which he ran nearly 1.5 million votes ahead of Goldwater in Michigan, instantly made him a leading candidate for president in 1968.

REAGAN

Unlike all of the other national leaders who emerged from 1964, Ronald Reagan had neither held nor run for public office. But no single event that year did more for any political figure than Reagan's nationally televised speech for Goldwater on October 27 did for Reagan himself. "A Time for Choosing"—later known among Reagan admirers as simply "The Speech"—raised more than $1 million in small donations, shattering all previous records for such an appeal. It also moved a small circle of wealthy California conservatives to urge and finance Reagan's candidacy for governor in 1966 as a way station on the road to the presidency.

Unlike the locally born Nixon, Reagan was a prototypical southern Californian, raised in the Midwest but determined to seek his fortune in the sunny climes of the fastest-growing state in the union. Born in Illinois in 1911, Reagan first achieved success by imaginatively recreating Chicago Cubs baseball games for a Des Moines, Iowa, radio station based on bare-bones wire service reports of the play-by-play. On a spring training trip to California with the Cubs in 1937 he did a screen test that led to a successful career as a film actor. In 1941 movie exhibitors voted Reagan the fifth most popular young star in Hollywood. "He has a cheerful way of looking at dames," wrote film critic Bosley Crowther in the *New York Times*.[162] Reagan became a board member of the Screen Actors Guild in 1941 and, after working as an army air force officer making training and propaganda films during World War II, was elected to the first of six consecutive one-year terms as SAG president in 1947.

Reagan's Hollywood career failed to regain traction after the war. But he became intensely involved in union and partisan politics, so much so that his wife, actress Jane Wyman, divorced him (the headline in the June 29, 1948, *Los Angeles Times* read: "Jane Wyman Divorced; Blames Rift on Politics").[163] Reagan was a strong New Deal Democrat who campaigned both for Truman and, in Minnesota, for Humphrey in 1948. He also cut a radio spot for the International Ladies' Garment Workers' Union lambasting "the 80th Congress and the National Association of Manufacturers" for "set[ting] back the cause of liberal government in the United States."[164] As president of the fifteen-thousand-member actors guild, which was investigated in 1947 by the House Un-American Activities Committee for subversive influence, Reagan defended his union's vigilance in weeding communists from its ranks without satisfying the committee's desire that he label any individual as a communist. "I detest, I abhor their philosophy," he told the committee, including Representative Nixon, "but at the same time I never want to see our country become urged, by either fear or resentment of this group, that we ever compromise with any of our democratic principles."[165]

Reagan's acting talents found a new home on television, where in 1954 he became host and occasional star of the weekly drama series *General Electric Theatre*. As part of the job, Reagan was expected to spend twelve weeks per year visiting some of GE's 139 plants, which were spread over 38 states and employed about 250,000 people. GE thought he would be telling inside Hollywood stories. Instead, absorbing the ethos of his new corporate employer and influenced by the strongly conservative views of his new wife, Nancy Reagan, and her stepfather, neurosurgeon Loyal Davis, Reagan developed and over the years perfected a probusiness speech about the dangers of big government, a version of which he eventually delivered on television for Goldwater.[166] "I suggest to you there is no left or right," Reagan said, "only an up or down. Up to the maximum of individual freedom consistent with law and order, or down to the ant heap of totalitarianism."[167]

Reagan campaigned for Nixon as a Democrat in 1960, warning about Kennedy that "underneath the tousled boyish hair is still old Karl Marx."[168] He switched parties to campaign for Nixon again in 1962, then worked even harder for Goldwater in 1964, emceeing rallies so skillfully that veteran ABC newsman Howard K. Smith told Theodore White that Reagan had missed his calling—he should have been a politician. After watching "A Time for Choosing," a group of self-made California multimillionaires led by car dealer Holmes Tuttle, oilman Henry Salvatori, and Walter Knott of Knott's Berry Farm decided that in Reagan they had found the right messenger for their conservative philosophy. In early 1965 they formed "The Friends of Ronald Reagan" and began grooming him to run for governor the following year.

CONCLUSION

The nation's resilience was tested in the year preceding the 1964 election by the assassination of a president. The challenge facing his successor—a Texan whose home state had been the scene of the crime, a southerner at a time when the civil rights movement was peaking in prominence and influence, and a scorned outsider in the administration of the slain president—was enormous. But the test of the political system posed by Kennedy's assassination was a test it had passed before. Six of Kennedy's predecessors had died in office, three of them shot to death as he had been. In every instance the vice president took over and served at least for the remaining balance of the term. As for Johnson himself, no one could have been more surefooted in dealing with the particular challenges he faced on taking office.

The resilience of the two-party system, especially in its prevailing form, also was tested in 1964. The Republicans' recent record of futility matched that of the Whig Party, whose death had been the occasion of the GOP's birth more than a century before. Like the Whigs from 1828 to 1852, the Republicans from 1932 to 1964 lost all but two presidential elections. As with the Whigs, the Republicans' only victories came when the party nominated a victorious, largely nonpartisan general—William Henry Harrison in 1840 and Zachary Taylor in 1848, Dwight D. Eisenhower in 1952 and 1956—whose personal popularity far exceeded that of his party. The Whigs had controlled one or both houses of Congress for just four years during its lifetime, the same as the GOP from FDR to LBJ. The Whigs became extinct. Could the Republicans, who after the 1964 election made up only about one-third of the House, the Senate, the governorships, and the electorate, avoid that fate? Much would depend on what happened between January 1965 and November 1966, when voters once again would go to the polls in the 1966 midterm elections.

2

PEAKS AND VALLEYS
THE PARTIES AND THE CANDIDATES, 1965–1966

The presidential candidates who emerged from 1964 cast long shadows in American political history: three presidents, three vice presidents, an independent candidate who inadvertently sparked the migration of many southern and ethnic working class whites from the Democratic to the Republican Party, the father of a future Republican presidential nominee, and two liberal leaders who helped bring down a president of their own party.

Little of this was apparent on January 1, 1965. Nor would matters be much clearer two eventful years later.

LBJ

The political wind at Lyndon Johnson's back during his first fourteen months as president was the nation's grief at John F. Kennedy's assassination and its desire to see his New Frontier initiatives realized. From the first week of his presidency, when he defined his mission with the words "Let us continue," Johnson faithfully pursued Kennedy's unfulfilled agenda, including civil rights, the tax cut, and the defense of South Vietnam. Even the War on Poverty, a Johnson project, bore a Kennedy imprint—the word *poverty*, written several times and circled on a scrap of paper at the last cabinet meeting before the president's death.

When Johnson began his full term as president in January 1965, however, the political wind at his back was his own: the landslide victory in the 1964 election, which he won by a margin of 434 electoral votes and 22.6 percentage points in the national popular vote. Johnson also extended long enough coattails to his party's other candidates to give the Democrats a 68–32 majority in the Senate and a 295–140 majority in the House of Representatives. Because the Democrats' gains had come in the North and West (they actually lost five House seats in the South), these were liberal majorities as well. And because the breadth of the Democratic victory took everyone by surprise, 1964 was perceived as a mandate election by the political community, the first of the post–World War II era.[1]

Johnson's towering political position at the start of the 89th Congress bred no sense of complacency in him—far from it. "You've got to give it all you can that first year—doesn't matter what kind of majority you came in with," he told his aide Harry McPherson. "You've got just one year when they treat you right, and before they start worrying about themselves."[2] In 1964 Johnson had introduced his vision of the Great Society but done little about it legislatively. Concerning Vietnam he had secured a congressional resolution authorizing him to "repel further aggression" but otherwise done his best to keep the war off the national docket. With the election behind him, Johnson moved aggressively on both these fronts. "I believe that we can continue the Great Society while we fight in Vietnam," he said.[3] And why not? Lighting the national Christmas tree on December 18, Johnson enthused, "These are the most hopeful times in all the years since Christ was born in Bethlehem."[4]

THE GREAT SOCIETY

On January 4, 1965, two weeks before "that first year" of Johnson's term officially began with his inauguration on January 20, the president used his state of the union address to tell Congress what he wanted it to do. In March, when it passed the Appalachian Regional Development Act to address poverty in that part of the country, Congress began to do it. A month later it enacted the first major federal aid program for elementary and secondary education in history. In June it enacted two major health care bills, creating Medicare for the aged and Medicaid for the indigent. In August Congress passed the Voting Rights Act as well as the laws that gave birth to the Department of Housing and Urban Development, the National Endowment for the Humanities, and the National Endowment for the Arts. The fall brought legislation to curb water and automobile pollution, open the borders to a much larger and more ethnically diverse population of immigrants, beautify the nation's highways, and provide massive financial support for students attending college. Nineteen sixty-six also witnessed the enactment of "hundreds of new public laws," G. Calvin Mackenzie and Robert Weisbrot have calculated, "including an Urban Mass Transportation Act, Highway and Motor Vehicle Safety acts, federal minimum wage increase, creation of a Department of Transportation, Model Cities Act, Clean Water Restoration Act, and Truth-in-Packaging and Truth-in-Labeling acts."[5]

Substantively, the Great Society marked the greatest transformation of the federal government's role in American society since the New Deal. Politically, Johnson overcame a degree of difficulty even greater than the one FDR confronted thirty years earlier. The New Deal was designed to provide a core benefit—economic security—to the great majority of voters. The Great Society's economic programs focused on the poor, who vote at a comparatively low rate, and its programs for the middle and upper classes involved quality-of-life benefits, such as more attractive highways and greater support for the arts, that addressed "the needs of the spirit" more than the checkbook. The New Deal came in response to an economic crisis that made Americans desperate for government action. The Great Society, as Johnson said in his state of the union address, was offered "in the midst of the greatest upward surge of economic well-being in the history of any nation."[6] The one clear advantage Johnson enjoyed over Roosevelt was that the Supreme Court of the mid-1960s was a bastion of liberalism, in stark contrast to the court of the mid-1930s.[7]

Johnson's promise to eliminate poverty and enhance the human spirit bespoke the confidence of liberals in the mid-1960s. The liberal assumption, which the president shared, was that every social problem has a solution, that social scientists know what the solution is, and that the solution involves creating a new program administered by the federal government. Many of the bills that constituted the Great Society came about because Johnson told his domestic policy aide Joseph Califano that "he wanted 'a program for the cities,' or an 'Asian development bank,' or 'something to help the Negro male and his family.'" Califano would then form a task force (145 in all by the end of the Johnson administration) to address the president's goal, consisting largely of social scientists inside and outside government. "You let these intellectuals get me the ideas," Johnson said. "I'll worry about the politics." He then massaged each task force's recommendations into legislation and sent a proposal to Capitol Hill, often with a small initial budget. "Congress is like a whiskey drinker," the president told Califano. "You can put an awful lot of whiskey into a man if you just let him sip it. But if you try to force the whole bottle down his throat at one time, he'll throw it up."[8] With promises, persuasion, and threats, Johnson would round up enough votes to pass each bill. His legislative skills, honed during his many years in Congress, were essential: in 1965 the average vote in the House on more than one hundred of Johnson's successful bills was only 235 to 200.[9]

Johnson's passage of the Civil Rights Act of 1964 in undiluted form had convinced most northern liberals that despite his southern origins and long congressional record of opposition to civil rights, he was strongly committed to advancing the cause of justice for African Americans. The 1964 elections revealed two additional consequences of the act. First, in combination with the Republicans' nomination of Barry Goldwater, who had voted against the bill in the Senate, it cemented the loyalty of African Americans to the Democratic Party. But second, it revealed the inability of the new law to guarantee that blacks living in the South could express that loyalty by registering and voting. Most African American adults were unable to vote in 1964 in Alabama, Georgia, Louisiana, Mississippi, North Carolina, South Carolina, and Virginia.[10]

Johnson was in no rush to introduce voting rights legislation in 1965. But in a January 15 phone conversation, Martin Luther King offered an argument that got through to the president. In the 1964 election, King said, "the only states you didn't carry in the South . . . have less than 40 percent of the Negroes registered to vote." A "coalition of the Negro vote and the moderate white vote . . . will really make the New South." "That's exactly right," Johnson replied. In February he got the Justice Department working on a voting rights bill.[11] Seizing on the public outrage that greeted the nationally televised police beatings administered to peaceful voting rights marchers in Selma, Alabama, on March 7, 1965, Johnson sent a bill to Congress providing for federal examiners to take over the registration process in any city or county that imposed a literacy test on prospective voters and in which less than half of the adult population was registered to vote. Congress passed the bill in August.[12] Black registration soared in every southern state, but especially in the Deep South where both the African American population and the barriers to voting were greatest. In Mississippi, for example, where African Americans constituted about 40 percent of the population, the black registration rate soared from 6.7 percent in 1964 to 59.8 percent by 1968.[13] In all, 740,000 more blacks in the Deep South were registered to vote in 1968 than in 1965.

For all its early success on Capitol Hill, the Great Society agenda lost momentum with the passage of time. Johnson's standing with the public, in contrast to FDR's during his first term, diminished from an average 75 percent job approval rating in 1964 to 66 percent in 1965 and 50 percent in 1966. His proposal, introduced during the 89th Congress's second session, to forbid racial discrimination in the sale or rental of housing passed in the House but failed by ten votes to secure the two-thirds majority needed to end a filibuster in the Senate, even though the bill's enforcement provisions were feeble. Ominously, the open housing bill attracted strong opposition in the North, where residential segregation was more common than in the South—a first for a civil rights measure. But for the most part these disappointments fit the pattern Johnson had predicted to McPherson: maximum support in the first year, declining support thereafter.

Johnson's more serious setbacks were less anticipated. On August 11, 1965, five days after the Voting Rights Act became law, six days of rioting erupted in the Watts neighborhood of Los Angeles—the worst race riot of the century, leaving thirty-four dead, and the first major violent racial disturbance since World War II. The following summer brought riots in Chicago, Philadelphia, Cleveland, Milwaukee, Minneapolis, and more than thirty other cities, most of them northern. "How is it possible after all we've accomplished?" a stunned Johnson asked after Watts. "How could it be?"[14] Some social scientists argued that the riots were not unexpected; instead, they were a sign, however regrettable, of the incremental progress being made by the Great Society. People in despair do not revolt, they explained. Instead, violence occurs when hopes are raised higher than reforms are able to quickly satisfy—the so-called "revolution of rising expectations."[15] Others suggested that the problems occasioned by the Great Society had been avoidable. Johnson's "singular capacity to enact so many laws and programs led him to overestimate the capacity of the government to administer and the nation to absorb so much so fast," observed Califano.[16] Nor were the new programs' design flaws merely administrative. As Mackenzie and Weisbrot have concluded, "Impatience bred sloppiness and contradiction. Ideas that had been barely tested and little debated were suddenly the policy of the land."[17] In Johnson's understandable haste to pass as many laws as possible as quickly as possible, he virtually guaranteed that mistakes of policy design and administrative feasibility would be made.

Voters had never been entirely sold on the Great Society, partly because Johnson had done so little to lay the groundwork for it during the 1964 campaign, but mainly because Americans generally believed that the poor bore most of the responsibility for their poverty. As long as three-fourths of the public thought that any able-bodied person could find a job and earn a living if he tried hard enough, there was no solid foundation of support for the War on Poverty.[18] Johnson's endorsement in a June 4, 1965, speech at

Howard University of "not just equality as a right and a theory, but equality as a fact and equality as a result" laid the philosophical groundwork for race-based affirmative action policies, feeding white voters' perception that the president cared more about impoverished racial minorities than about the working- and middle-class white majority.[19]

As for the riots, their political effect was to transform the basic public concern for law and order from an issue that worked in the administration's favor when southern white mobs were violently breaking the law into one that worked against it when the most visible lawbreakers were the intended beneficiaries of Johnson's programs.[20] Calls for "law and order" against the "sinister menace" of lynching in the South had been heard in the 1920s, and as recently as late 1963 King had employed the phrase in demanding federal protection against the Ku Klux Klan.[21] But urban riots, Omar Wasow has shown, turned the rising public support for civil rights inspired by peaceful protests into rising public support for "social control."[22] In a July 18, 1966, speech, Vice President Hubert H. Humphrey expressed sympathy for the rioters with words that played directly into critics' hands, telling the National Association of Counties that if he lived in a city slum, "I think you'd have more trouble than you have had already because I've got enough spark left in me to lead a mighty good revolt."[23] Meanwhile, as Robert Dallek has pointed out, the Johnson-sponsored community action programs, while doing little to end poverty, "were promoting greater awareness of welfare rights, which brought substantial numbers of poor onto the welfare rolls."[24] The War on Poverty, designed to get people off welfare and into jobs, seemed to be causing more people to go on welfare.

VIETNAM

From the beginning of his presidency, Johnson contemplated Vietnam with dread. He worried at first that the situation there would deteriorate to the point that it became a club in the hand of either Robert F. Kennedy or the Republicans in the 1964 election. Later, after Johnson won the election without having to say much about the war, his fear became that to keep South Vietnam from falling to the communists, he would have to increase America's military involvement to such an extent that even the popular elements of the Great Society, such as Medicare and subsidized college loans, would starve for lack of funding and attention. Johnson hated the prospect of having to sacrifice "the woman I really loved—the Great Society" for "that bitch of a war on the other side of the world."[25] Unlike Franklin D.

Roosevelt, who after Pearl Harbor willingly replaced "Dr. New Deal" with "Dr. Win-the-War," Johnson wanted to keep both of his doctors on staff.

Within weeks of taking office in November 1963, Johnson began receiving a steady stream of discouraging reports about the situation in Vietnam. "Things are not good—they've gotten worse," Secretary of Defense Robert McNamara told him in a June 9, 1964, phone call, repeating the message he had first delivered to the new president after visiting Saigon the previous December. "If we're going to stay in there, if we're going to go up the escalating chain, we're going to have to educate the people, Mr. President. We haven't done so yet." Johnson demurred, "I think if you start doing it they're going to be hollering 'You're a warmonger.'" McNamara deferred to the president's election-year judgment: "I completely agree with you."[26]

The pressures on Johnson from the administration's Kennedy alumni intensified after the inauguration. In the year that followed the December 1963 Diem assassination, South Vietnam had experienced three coups and five governments. In February 1965 National Security Adviser McGeorge Bundy returned from Vietnam and said that the war was lost unless the United States launched a sustained bombing campaign against the North, which was the main source of the men and materiel fighting to overthrow the government in the South. This time Johnson yielded, realizing that militarily the United States was in no position to negotiate an end to the war on any terms but virtual surrender. Not only would the domestic political price of abandoning South Vietnam to the communists be high, but the signal Johnson would send to the recently installed Soviet leaders, Leonid Brezhnev and Alexei Kosygin, and to the Chinese, who had just exploded their first nuclear device, would be one of weakness.

The president approved Operation Rolling Thunder, which began on March 2, 1965, and lasted with brief pauses for three years, the largest sustained air campaign in the history of warfare. Two marine battalions—combat troops, no longer mere advisers—arrived in South Vietnam six days later to guard the American air force base at Da Nang from which the bombing attacks were launched. "I'm scared to death of putting ground forces in," Johnson told McNamara, "but I'm more than frightened about losing a bunch of planes for lack of security."[27] In announcing the deployment, McNamara said the Marines would perform defensive duties only, but this promise was bound to be broken. As Tom Wicker has observed, "No American commander could be required to sit still and wait to be attacked, with all the advantages such a requirement would give to ruthless, disciplined, trained guerrillas."[28] When the South Vietnamese military installed two of their own, Nguyen Cao Ky and Nguyen Van Thieu, as a kind of dual executive in June, Johnson resolved that in the interest of stability he must buttress their authority no matter how poorly they governed.

Johnson's actions enjoyed broad initial support. Most Republicans were gung ho for escalation; they had abandoned Dwight D. Eisenhower's policy of nonintervention in Vietnam for Goldwater's bellicose anticommunism. In January 1965, for example, Nixon called for the use of air and naval power to "quarantine" South Vietnam against North Vietnamese intervention.[29] Kennedy administration Democrats, having rejected Ike's "New Look" policy of massive nuclear retaliation to deter Soviet aggression in favor of limited wars of counterinsurgency, recognized Johnson's Vietnam policy as their own. All of his decisions to increase American military involvement came at the urging of Kennedy's chief advisers—McNamara, Bundy, Secretary of State Dean Rusk, and Walt W. Rostow, who moved back and forth between the White House and the State Department. These men were, Eric Alterman and Kevin Mattson have written, "in the aftermath of the Cuban missile crisis, intoxicated by their belief in the ability of the United States to calibrate its response to any given threat to coerce its adversaries into capitulation."[30] (Johnson's own phrase to describe this incremental approach to escalation was "going up old Ho Chi Minh's leg an inch at a time.")[31] The president's incomplete knowledge of the private American concessions that had ended the missile crisis left him believing that the threat of force, not a negotiated compromise, had caused the Soviet Union to stand down.[32] Reflecting the bipartisan consensus in Washington, the public favored defending South Vietnam over pulling out by 66 percent to 19 percent in the March 1965 Gallup Poll.

Johnson hoped that the stick he was applying to North Vietnam with one hand would convince its leaders to accept the carrot he was offering with the other. On April 7, 1965, five weeks after launching Rolling Thunder, he pledged to invest a billion dollars in Southeast Asia if North Vietnam would recognize South Vietnam as an independent nation. Along with schools and medicine, Johnson promised, "The vast Mekong River can provide food and water and power on a scale to dwarf even our own TVA [Tennessee Valley Authority]."[33] North Vietnam was uninterested. With Russia and China outdoing each other to provide logistical support to the communist nation whose loyalty each was seeking, and with more than 100,000 young men turning eighteen every year, North Vietnam did not lack for resources to continue its struggle to absorb the South. The North Vietnamese economy, grounded in agriculture, was largely immune even to massive bombing. In June the American troop commitment rose above 50,000, and Gen. William C. Westmoreland, describing South Vietnam's army as near collapse, asked for 175,000 more "just to hold the fort," with additional forces likely to be needed in the future.[34] McNamara recommended that Johnson approve the field commander's request and also increase the size of the U.S. army by 375,000 through stepped-up recruitment and draft calls. The president reluctantly agreed. By the end of 1965, 184,300 American troops were stationed in Vietnam; one year later, the number had reached 385,300. For fear of triggering a Chinese assault against American forces like the one that followed the U.S. invasion of North Korea in 1950, however, Johnson was unwilling to consider a ground attack on North Vietnam.[35]

Within the White House, Vice President Humphrey initially opposed the proposed bombing campaign. Despite having a longer and closer political alliance with the president than any previous vice president in history, he paid a high price for doing so. Johnson was furious when Humphrey offered his contrary opinion at a February 10, 1965, meeting of the National Security Council and then sent the president a follow-up memo a week later, further arguing the point. Humphrey's exile, from which he would be forced to crawl back, began. Because the vice president is a statutory member of the National Security Council, Johnson could not exclude him from meetings. Instead, he stopped gathering the council and forged his Vietnam policy in informal Tuesday lunches with Rusk, Bundy, McNamara, Central Intelligence Agency director John McCone, and Gen. Earle Wheeler, the chairman of the Joint Chiefs of Staff—in other words, the council minus Humphrey. Johnson also found other ways to humiliate the vice president, ranging from not letting him take members of the Washington press corps with him on trips to stripping him of the chairmanship of the President's Council on Economic Opportunity and insisting that Humphrey say publicly that the demotion was his own idea.[36]

Johnson gave Humphrey a chance to get himself out of the doghouse in February 1966 by sending him, on one day's notice, to Vietnam. On the way home, Humphrey told aides to draft a strongly hawkish report to the president. "The Vietnam situation is a dramatized, concentrated example of what the Communists intend to do elsewhere," he instructed them to write.[37] Restored to Johnson's favor, the vice president became the administration's leading public champion of the war. "I think there is a tremendous new opening here for realizing the dream of the Great Society in the great area of Asia, not just here at home," he trumpeted in an April 19 interview

Chicago mayor Richard J. Daley's advice to the president on Vietnam was, "You put your prestige in your back pocket and you walk away." (Credit: Yoichi Okamoto, provided by the Lyndon B. Johnson Presidential Library)

with Eric Sevareid of CBS News.[38] Humphrey "cannot say something publicly without deeply believing it privately," lamented Arthur M. Schlesinger in his diary; "and when, as now, he has no choice in his public utterances, he whips up a fervency of private belief."[39] John Reilly, Humphrey's foreign affairs adviser, despaired that "desperate to get back in Johnson's good graces . . . instead of supporting the president 100 percent, he did it 200 percent. . . . He was more for Johnson's policies than Johnson."[40] Convinced though he became of the justice of the American cause, however, it was "agonizing" to Humphrey that, having earned a reputation as a champion of peace and nuclear disarmament in the 1950s, he was now becoming known as "a man of war."[41]

Mayor Richard J. Daley of Chicago gave the president different advice in 1966. When Johnson asked what he should do about the "trouble over there in Vietnam," Daley said, "Well, Mr. President, when you've got a losing hand in poker you just throw in your cards." "But what about American prestige?" Johnson asked. Daley replied, "You put your prestige in your back pocket and walk away."[42] Although frustrated by the war, walking away was something Johnson was unwilling to do. Like John and Robert Kennedy, he accepted the prevailing beliefs about the lessons of Munich and the domino theory. "We know, from Munich on, that when you give, the dictators feed on raw meat," Johnson told Senate Republican leader Everett Dirksen of Illinois. "If they take South Vietnam, they take Thailand, they take Indonesia, they take Burma, they come right on back to the Philippines."[43] He also feared the "terrible beast," his name for "the right wing. If they ever get the idea I am selling out Vietnam," he told Undersecretary of State George Ball, the one in-house dissenter he tolerated, "they'll do horrible things to the country and we'll be forced to escalate the war beyond anything you've ever thought about."[44]

Beyond those considerations, Johnson dreaded being "the first American president to lose a war."[45] For similar reasons, in May 1965 he felt compelled to send 22,000 American troops to the Dominican Republic to suppress a counterrevolution supported by communist elements but aimed at restoring moderate leftist Juan Bosch, the deposed elected president, to power. Both Republicans and Robert Kennedy, whose loathing for Fidel Castro had led him as attorney general in his brother's administration to organize Operation Mongoose, stood ready to bay at his heels if Johnson were "to sit here with my hands tied and let Castro take that island," the president claimed. "What can we do in Vietnam if we can't clean up the Dominican Republic?"[46] John Bartlow Martin, who had been President Kennedy's ambassador to the Dominican Republic and later supported Robert Kennedy for president in 1968, said after visiting the scene that he had "no doubt whatsoever that there was a real danger of a communist takeover."[47] Fortunately, with diplomatic assistance from the Organization of American States and the election in August of a moderately conservative president by Dominican voters, the crisis was resolved fairly quickly on terms satisfactory to the United States.

REPUBLICANS AND DEMOCRATS

The Republican and Democratic parties responded differently to the results of the 1964 election. The GOP knew what bad shape it was in. Despite the contrasting lessons that liberal and conservative Republicans drew from the Democratic sweep, the two groups turned their shared sense of political endangerment into a concentrated effort to rebuild the party's organizational capabilities. The Democrats, riding high and led by a president who regarded his party as potentially a rival power center, pursued a different course. As Sidney M. Milkis has argued, to the extent that Johnson and the Democratic Party had a strategy for continued political success, it was grounded in policy and administration—that is, in using the new federal programs created by the Great Society to secure the loyalties of new constituencies just as Franklin D. Roosevelt had used social security and the prolabor Wagner Act to secure the loyalties of older and working-class voters.[48] For the remainder of the decade, the Republican strategy turned out to be the better one.

Despite the massive defeat to which he led his party in 1964, Goldwater left the Republicans with two great gifts. The first was an army of about four million volunteers who had worked for him and the Republican ticket, including approximately one million small donors. In 1952 the GOP had raised 12 percent of its campaign funds in contributions of $500 or less; the corresponding figure in 1964 was 72 percent. By early 1965 the majority of funds raised by the Republican National Committee was in donations of $10 or less—"the first time this had happened in American party history."[49] Goldwater's second gift was to gracefully exit the national political stage. This was partly a matter of leaving Washington; by running for president Goldwater had forfeited his Senate seat, which was up for reelection in 1964. But it was more a matter of Goldwater forsaking the traditional claim of the defeated presidential nominee to be the party's titular leader. In particular, he did not strenuously resist the removal of the person he had installed after the convention as national party chair, the conservative Goldwater loyalist Dean Burch.

On January 21–22, 1965, the RNC took advantage of Goldwater's clean break to replace Burch with the proudly nonideological Ray Bliss, who had earned his spurs during a decade spent chairing the Ohio GOP. Bliss's entire philosophy of party leadership was summed up in his favorite phrase: nuts and bolts. During his four years as chair, the RNC sponsored frequent gatherings of state, county, and local party leaders, ultimately enrolling about twenty thousand Republican professionals and activists in workshops and seminars on candidate recruitment, voter registration, women's organizations, public relations, research, and other bread-and-butter subjects. Bliss also created the Republican Coordinating Committee, an assembly of congressional leaders, governors, and past presidential candidates whose purpose was to forge consensus positions on a wide range of policy issues that otherwise threatened to divide the party.[50]

Although Bliss was more inclined to fear the right as a potential source of intraparty schism than the left or center, those who benefited the most from his workshops were the cadres of new and relatively inexperienced

Republican workers whom Goldwater had attracted. Conservatives also benefited from Bliss's unwavering focus on party loyalty, which made Rockefeller, Romney, and other moderate and liberal Republicans who had refused to endorse Goldwater look disloyal by implication.

Moderate and liberal Republicans suffered from a lack of forums in which to develop and articulate new ideas. Unlike conservatives, who had the lively and widely circulated *National Review* and *Human Events,* moderates lost their main voice when the *New York Herald Tribune* published its last issue on April 23, 1966. The *Ripon Forum,* a publication of the recently formed and avowedly centrist Ripon Society, failed to attract a substantial readership. Yet moderate and liberal Republicans desperately needed new ideas to broaden their appeal. Historically, they had been strongest in the Northeast, appealing to voters by decrying the Democrats' dependence on corrupt big-city machines and powerful southern segregationists. These appeals were of declining value as the Northeast became relatively less populous compared to the South and West, machine politics gradually waned in most cities, and the Democrats under Johnson became the party of civil rights, not segregation.

The success of liberal and moderate Republicans, where they were on the ballot, had come to depend on being the only viable alternative if voters became unhappy with the Democrats. Conservative Republicans, however, had a new issue, or at least a new take on an old issue: "racial conservatism." "Before 1964," Edward Carmines and James Stimson have explained, "the two sides of the racial debate were progressivism and racism. Racial conservatism was a new species . . . advocated without racial bigotry and espousal of segregationist goals."[51] Goldwater himself, a longtime member of the National Association for the Advancement of Colored People (NAACP) at a time when many southern conservatives claimed that the "CP" stood for "Communist Party," was not a bigot or a segregationist; he actually had integrated his family's Arizona department stores before, not after, protests arose. Nor did he try to exploit racial fears in his presidential campaign even though, in Johnson's view, doing so offered Goldwater his only chance for victory.[52] Indeed, after a riot occurred in Harlem in July 1964, Goldwater visited Johnson in the White House to say that he would not attack the president's civil rights policies because "it could polarize the country." Goldwater also refused to air *Choice,* a powerful campaign film about urban violence, telling aides, "It's nothing but a racist film."[53] Instead, he offered voters a limited view of what the federal government should do about civil rights, grounded in constitutional theories of states' rights and property rights, along with a skepticism about Washington's ability to change racial attitudes in a way that would foster lasting progress.

The political value of racial conservatism to the GOP, Carmines and Stimson have argued, was that it gave the party an issue with which to divide the increasingly tense New Deal Democratic alliance between white southerners and northern blacks and liberals, groups whose partisan unity had been indispensable to preserving the Democrats' status as the nation's majority party. Clearly the strategy carried risks. As a result of the Voting Rights Act, hundreds of thousands of additional African Americans would now be voting in the South—and not for conservative Republicans. Depending on what was said and done in the name of racial conservatism, the strategy might even blow up in the Republicans' face among whites who supported integration. But the GOP had to try something new: "the old [New Deal] cleavage all too predictably led to Democratic victory at the polls."[54] In accenting social issues, which had been declining in political importance since the start of the Progressive Era and dormant since the New Deal, the GOP was attempting to revive a mainstay of party differences in the nineteenth century.

DEMOCRATS

Organizational vitality waned in the Democratic Party even as it waxed in the GOP. Johnson was from a historically one-party state and region where well-tooled party organization was usually superfluous to victory. His immediate concerns when he became president were to purge the Kennedy people from the Democratic National Committee and to move the locus of Democratic politics from the DNC to the White House. In the 1964 election Johnson downplayed the importance of party for the sake of appealing to independents and disaffected Republicans. When Sen. John O. Pastore of Rhode Island gave a rip-roaring keynote address lambasting the Republicans at the Democratic convention, for example, Johnson ordered subsequent speakers to lay off the GOP, whose voters he wanted, and confine their attacks to Goldwater.[55] After the election, he slashed the DNC budget to the bone, even eliminating its voter registration program. Day-to-day control of the national party mechanism shifted from the national Democratic chair, John M. Bailey, to White House political director Marvin Watson. Domestic policy development became the domain of White House–recruited academics and experts. Johnson specifically told Califano that his task forces were not to take political considerations into account.

The president's personnel policy was largely merit-based, with broad disregard for the patronage needs of his party.

Daniel Galvin has identified six things that presidents can do to build their party: "provide campaign services, build human capital, recruit candidates, mobilize voters, finance party operations, [and] support internal activities." Johnson, Galvin found, did none of them. Instead, in each of these areas except recruiting candidates, he acted as a "party predator" who took "actions that [we]re indifferent, exploitative, or meant to undercut the party's organizational capacities," including expanding the Kennedy-created President's Club for large donors in order to divert money from the party treasury into his own political account.[56] "I heard rumors you were a politician," Johnson's aide John Roche told him, "but have no evidence of it."[57] In reality, Johnson was a consummate politician, but one who wanted to personally control every lever of power from the White House. The more he allowed the DNC to do, he thought, the more dependent on it he would be. Johnson's landslide victory in 1964, the Democrats' success riding his coattails in that election, and the passage of his legislative program on Capitol Hill convinced him that the Democratic Party was doing fine as a "party in the electorate" and a "party in office" by neglecting the "party organization."[58]

Within the party, however, glimmerings of dissent and disunity began to emerge after Johnson's inauguration. On the right, the infusion of black voters into the southern Democratic electorate led to a white backlash in some states that produced rabidly segregationist nominees for governor in 1966, such as Lester Maddox in Georgia, George P. Mahoney in Maryland, and Jim Johnson in Arkansas—all Democrats. George Wallace got his wife nominated for governor when he could not persuade the Alabama legislature to overturn the term limit that barred him from running again.

On the left, a growing number of Democratic senators became outspoken critics of the war in Vietnam. On August 7, 1964, only Wayne Morse of Oregon and Ernest Gruening of Alaska had voted against the Gulf of Tonkin Resolution. But organized antiwar protests began spreading among college campuses, fueled in part by the steadily growing fears of male college students that if the war continued, they might be drafted into the army and sent to Vietnam when they graduated, flunked out, or ceased making "reasonable progress towards a degree."[59] These protesters joined the smaller, older ranks of organized peace groups: Women Strike for Peace, SANE (Committee for a Sane Nuclear Policy), Clergy and Laity Concerned about Vietnam, American Friends Service Committee, Socialist Workers Party, and later Vietnam Veterans Against the War.[60] Senate Foreign Relations Committee hearings on Vietnam in January and February 1966, organized by committee chair J. William Fulbright of Arkansas and nationally televised, raised serious doubts about the American role in the war. Among other things, Senator Fulbright placed on the national agenda the "credibility gap" between the "straight answers" he sought from the president and the answers he said he was getting from administration officials.[61] On March 1, 1966, Morse and Gruening were joined by Fulbright, Stephen Young of Ohio, and Eugene McCarthy of Minnesota in a vote to repeal the Tonkin resolution.

McCarthy's views on the war were still unformed. He mostly objected to the bombing of North Vietnam, which he regarded as militarily ineffective and feared would endanger the civilian population. On March 19, less than three weeks after casting one of the five votes to repeal the resolution, McCarthy said, "I think that the kind of escalation we now have, in which we're sending more troops, is defensible on the part of the administration." He explained that he actually disagreed with Morse's resolution but had voted with him on procedural grounds. Five weeks later, McCarthy took issue with conservative Mississippi Democrat John Stennis's statement that the United States should disengage from South Vietnam if American soldiers couldn't walk the streets of Saigon safely. "Maybe we could stay there even if there were a government asking us to leave," McCarthy said.[62] Of the roughly fifteen Senate dissenters on Vietnam by the spring of 1966, McCarthy and Robert Kennedy were among the three least outspoken and most conflicted.[63] Lifelong and devout Catholics, both of them embraced the church's form of social justice–oriented anticommunism.

Johnson was concerned about any amount of opposition among Senate Democrats, but only one preoccupied, even obsessed him: Robert Kennedy. Politically, LBJ was up and RFK down for at least three years after President Kennedy was assassinated. The scorned, scoffed-at outsider in the Kennedy administration was now the ultimate insider, while the erstwhile attorney general and presidential confidant was a mere freshman senator. And yet, said John Roche, "Not a sparrow fell from a tree but what he [the president] was convinced that it was the intervention of a Kennedy."[64] During the Watts riot, Johnson ranted privately to aides that "Bobby . . . put [Martin Luther] King on the Kennedy payroll to rile up the Negroes. That's why we had the riots. After all I've done for the Negroes. They would never have attacked me if they hadn't been put up to it."[65] Johnson especially feared that Kennedy would challenge his renomination in 1968. After all, he had underestimated John Kennedy in 1960 and now regarded his brother as an even more formidable opponent because he bore the slain president's mantle. Meanwhile, Kennedy refused to acknowledge Johnson's legitimacy as the nation's chief executive. When he said "the president," he meant his brother; Johnson was just "Johnson."

The hostility and suspicion between Johnson and Kennedy drove them apart even on matters of fundamental agreement. Both were deeply concerned about the poor—Indians, migrant workers, the hungry—and both believed that alleviating poverty was a part of President Kennedy's unfinished legacy that they had a duty to complete. "It was not politics that caused Kennedy to go to the poor," who did not vote in great numbers, wrote William vanden Heuvel and Milton Gwirtzman. "They gave him a new outlet for his old passion against injustice," which in previous years had been channeled against communist subversives, corrupt labor leaders, and organized crime.[66] Nor did politics explain Johnson's concern for poor people, which was rooted in his rural Texas upbringing and his experience as a young teacher of impoverished Mexican American children. Yet when Johnson launched the federal programs that constituted the War on Poverty and the Great Society, Kennedy reflexively began looking for a different approach. "There is not a problem or a program on which dozens or hundreds of thousands of bureaucrats are not earnestly at work," he said in veiled criticism of the Great Society. "But does this represent a solution to our problems? Manifestly it does not."[67] Kennedy's "well-publicized visits to rural and urban slums," Ronald Steel has observed, "drew attention away from the successes of LBJ's War on Poverty to its areas of failure," further infuriating the president.[68]

Similarly, Kennedy initially distanced himself from Johnson on Vietnam less because he no longer believed in the war than because Johnson's early escalation involved aerial bombing rather than the land-based counterinsurgency approach the Kennedys had championed. "The way to defeat the terrorists is to increase our ability to fight their kind of war," Kennedy intended to say in a speech drafted in January 1965 after he heard a false rumor that the president was planning to pull out of Vietnam.[69] On January 31, 1966, when Johnson ordered a resumption of the bombing after a holiday pause, Kennedy immediately condemned the attacks as ineffective. On February 19 he suggested that the Vietcong be invited to participate in peace negotiations. Rather than deal with the substance of Kennedy's criticism, Johnson and the news media treated these comments as political jabs at the president. Kennedy stopped talking about Vietnam for the rest of the year and stifled an effort at the New York Democratic convention in August to pass an antiwar resolution. But a Gallup Poll released that month showing Kennedy narrowly ahead of Johnson for the 1968 nomination among Democrats (and way ahead among independents) only fired the president's fears and hatred. "I'm afraid that by speaking out I just make Lyndon do the opposite, out of spite," Kennedy told reporter Jack Newfield. "He hates me so much that if I asked for snow, he would make rain, just because it was me."[70]

THE 1966 MIDTERM ELECTIONS

From the beginning, 1966 was a politically difficult year for Johnson. His party was gradually dividing over the war in Vietnam and his civil rights and antipoverty policies. The new community action programs were pitting liberals and minorities against big-city Democratic mayors who felt that "CAP is setting up a competing political organization in their own backyards," according to a Johnson aide.[71] Indeed, Maurice Isserman and Michael Kazin have written, "Many of the agencies launched voter registration drives to oust incumbent politicians or sponsored marches on city hall to demand improved services for poor neighborhoods."[72] In the South, the Voting Rights Act created new tensions within state Democratic Parties between the conservative whites who had always been in charge and newly registered African Americans seeking to convert the franchise into political power.

Republican vitality and unity were enhanced both by Bliss's organizational efforts and by the lack of any political imperative to do more than criticize the president. The ideological clash that divided the GOP in 1964 was happily shelved in 1966. For the time being, the party could nominate candidates in all parts of the country who were attuned to local preferences without having to decide on one candidate for president and one national platform. Every Republican could agree that inflation, which recently had doubled from 1.5 percent to 3.0 percent and rising, was Johnson's fault, along with the increase in crime and urban violence. Hawks and doves alike expressed dissatisfaction with the president's conduct of the war, which seemed to be dragging on endlessly. Johnson's approval rating dropped steadily to 44 percent by the end of 1966, almost never to rise above 50 percent again.[73]

The magnitude of the Republican victory in the midterm elections of 1966 was impressive, and it removed any doubt that the GOP had risen from the political grave in which some pundits had buried it after 1964. The Republicans gained 47 seats in the House of Representatives; they were still the minority party but by a smaller margin—248 to 187—than after any election since Eisenhower's landslide victory in 1956. Most of the new Republican representatives were conservatives. All but 20 of the 153 House candidates endorsed by the American Conservative Union won, compared with only 31 of the 87 endorsed by the Ripon Society.[74] Seven southern Democratic incumbents, all of them supporters of the Great Society, fell to Republican challengers. Not so in the Senate, where the GOP's three-seat gain was grounded in victories by liberal and moderate candidates: Mark Hatfield in Oregon, Charles Percy in Illinois, Edward Brooke in Massachusetts, and Howard Baker in Tennessee. In state elections, the Republicans gained 540 legislative seats, considerably more than they had lost in 1964, and added eight governorships to the seventeen they already had. Some of the new governors were moderates, notably Raymond Shafer in Pennsylvania, John Love in Colorado, Winthrop Rockefeller (brother of Nelson) in Arkansas, and Maryland's Spiro T. Agnew, who won 70 percent of the black vote while defeating a segregationist Democratic candidate and then declared, "I shall attempt to make Maryland a showcase of what progressive Republicanism can do."[75] Others, such as Claude Kirk in Florida, Paul Laxalt in Nevada, and John Williams of Arizona, were conservatives—as was the election's most famous gubernatorial victor: Ronald Reagan of California.

Reagan's Democratic opponent was the incumbent governor Pat Brown, who had beaten Nixon handily in 1962 and whose party enjoyed a million-vote advantage in party registration in California. Because Brown thought that Reagan's opponent in the primary—George Christopher, recently the two-term mayor of San Francisco—would be much harder to beat than the Hollywood actor and political novice, he leaked stories to the press that discredited Christopher and damaged his prospects. Reagan, whose campaign was financed by the small circle of wealthy California conservatives who had recruited him to run, won the Republican primary with 64.6 percent of the vote and immediately moved to unite the party, hiring several Christopher staff members and securing the services of the Spencer-Roberts campaign firm, which had worked for Rockefeller against Goldwater in 1964. Following their advice, Reagan hung a lantern on his inexperience, repeatedly declaring: "I am not a politician. I am an ordinary citizen with a deep-seated belief that much of what troubles us has been brought about by politicians."[76] A seasoned television performer with a genial personality,

Reagan belied Brown's charge that he was "the crown prince of the extreme right" without having to say a word, simply by his manner.[77]

Brown, like Johnson, was a big-government liberal who took pride in his state's excellent, tuition-free universities and generous welfare programs. But the combination of law-breaking demonstrations by the antibureaucratic, antimilitary, and anticapitalist Free Speech Movement on the state's flagship Berkeley campus in the fall of 1964 and the Watts riot in August 1965 had caused many Californians to doubt whether these programs were worth the high taxes needed to fund them. Even more seriously, from 1965 to 1966 murders in California rose by 14 percent, robberies by 9 percent, and rapes by 5 percent. As Matthew Dallek has observed, by successfully hammering Brown on all these matters, Reagan turned "riots, welfare, crime, student protests, and other issues into effective cudgels that could be used against liberals" throughout the country.[78] The first Republican to win a major election on a platform of law and order, Reagan defeated Brown by nearly a million votes. He thereby secured the office from which Nixon, who lost to Brown by almost 300,000 votes in 1962, had once hoped to launch his presidential campaign in 1968. Reagan's election excited many conservatives, and according to columnists Rowland Evans and Robert D. Novak, some of them had "talked to us quite seriously [in 1965] of Ronald Reagan running for president in 1968 (though some would prefer Richard M. Nixon as a sacrificial lamb against President Johnson in 1968, preserving Reagan for 1972)."[79]

Reagan won the greatest victory of any challenger in 1966, but Rockefeller, Romney, and, with his wife as a cutout, Wallace were among the incumbents who did best. Rockefeller's reelection to a third term was especially impressive. Approaching the first election since his remarriage, having broken his 1962 pledge not to raise taxes, Rockefeller's statewide approval rating in 1965 was about 20 percent. Voters assumed he had lost interest in New York and, as in 1964, would abandon them for a presidential race in 1968. The Democrats' voter registration advantage over the Republicans had more than doubled since Rockefeller last ran, from 411,000 to 876,000. But Rockefeller fought back hard.[80] In May 1966 he pledged to withdraw "completely and forever, without reservation" from presidential politics and endorsed Romney for president.[81] "I am not, will not and under no circumstances will be a candidate," Rockefeller reiterated.[82] He spent more than $5 million trumpeting his accomplishments as governor in a brilliant media campaign against a weak and woefully underfunded Democratic challenger and won by nearly 400,000 votes.[83] In Michigan Romney cruised to a third term by 527,000 votes, the second largest gubernatorial majority in the state's history. Two weeks after the election, Rockefeller and Romney met in Puerto Rico, where Rocky pledged to provide money, staff, research, and speechwriting to Romney's presidential campaign.

Wallace's victory in Alabama was technically vicarious but no less triumphant. Barred by the state constitution from seeking another term in 1966, he considered running for senator against the five-term incumbent Democrat John Sparkman. Although Sparkman's own polls showed that Wallace almost certainly would have won, the governor knew that as a freshman senator he would be "a small fish in a big pond."[84] More important, Wallace would lose the financial base among road builders, contractors, insurance companies, lobbyists, and others who did business with the state that only governors enjoy and that he needed to finance a campaign for president in 1968.[85] Wallace asked the legislature to amend the constitution so he could run again, making no bones about his intention to seek the presidency. "The liberals say George Wallace wants to be president," he said in a televised address to a joint session. "What's wrong with that?"[86] The House of Representatives agreed, but on October 22, needing a three-fifths majority, the Senate did not, despite Wallace's threat to run off any senator who voted against him—a threat he later carried out so successfully that none of the seventeen who did so were elected to another term.[87]

Wallace borrowed a page from Texas history and persuaded his wife Lurleen, on the verge of surgery for uterine cancer, to let him put her name on the ballot. In the only previous election of this kind, the impeached and ineligible Gov. James "Pa" Ferguson encouraged his wife, Miriam "Ma" Ferguson, to run and win in his stead in 1924—a unique instance of succession by a spouse and one with which Wallace was familiar. A shy woman, Lurleen Wallace's contribution to the campaign's three to five daily rallies was to read a 519-word statement asking the voters to endorse a "Wallace administration," after which her husband would rouse the crowd for an hour by tearing into the northern press, federal judges, Washington bureaucrats, and long-haired college students.[88] His implicit message to white voters was that they, not blacks, were the real victims of unfair treatment. Eleven candidates entered the Democratic primary, including two former governors, a congressman, and the state attorney general. Even though the opponent Wallace feared most, state representative Ryan deGraffenried, died in a plane crash the day after filing, Alabama's political history seemed to guarantee that in this large and strong a field no one would receive the majority needed to avoid a runoff.[89] In addition, a hundred thousand new and presumably anti-Wallace African Americans had registered to vote under the watchful eye of the federal government. But by primary day 110,000 additional whites had also registered and Lurleen Wallace received 54 percent of the vote. Jim Martin, a first-term congressman and her Republican opponent in the fall (the same Martin whom Wallace had deployed to offer his services as running mate to Goldwater in 1964), lamely argued that "we don't want any skirt for governor" but to no avail.[90] Wallace was elected in November by 538,000 to 263,000.

Of all who participated in the 1966 midterm elections, no one worked harder or was more successful than Richard Nixon, who was not on the ballot. In a prelude to 1966, Nixon had participated in the 1965 New Jersey gubernatorial campaign, nominally on behalf of Republican Wayne Dumont but actually in opposition to Rutgers history professor Eugene Genovese, who had become controversial when he called for a Vietcong victory in South Vietnam. Nixon's argument that, as a state employee, Genovese should be fired for using "the state college as a forum to, in effect, give aid and comfort to the enemy" earned him editorial scorn but buffed up the anticommunist credentials that had always been his main appeal to conservatives.[91] "It was pragmatism more than altruism that led me to take it"—*it* being "the hard, boring, and sometimes thankless work" of party building—"because I believed that whoever did would gain a significant advantage in the race for the 1968 presidential nomination," Nixon wrote in his memoirs. He was right: the December 1965 Gallup Poll, taken shortly after the New Jersey election, showed Nixon with more support for the nomination among Republicans than the next three candidates combined.[92]

Rockefeller, Reagan, and Romney were tied up with their own campaigns in 1966, which gave Nixon an open road. He concentrated his efforts in two areas: the South, home to about half of the roughly four hundred groups to which he spoke, and traditionally Republican House districts in the North and West that a Democrat had won in 1964 and were presumably ripe for the retaking. Nixon campaigned relentlessly, covering 30,000 miles, 35 states, and 82 districts. On the same day in October when he argued the case of *Time v. Hill* before the Supreme Court (superbly, by all accounts, especially that of Justice Abraham Fortas), he flew across the country to campaign in San Francisco, Oakland, and Palo Alto.

Rockefeller was worried about the friends Nixon was making on the campaign trail and pressured Bliss to stop using RNC funds to finance his travel. But what really concerned Rockefeller and the other Republican hopefuls was the positive last-minute publicity Nixon received from

Johnson. The president met with South Vietnam's prime minister, Nguyen Cao Ky, in Manila two weeks before the election, and on October 25 they issued a joint communiqué offering to withdraw American troops from South Vietnam six months after North Vietnam did the same. Nine days later, Nixon released a 2,500-word critique of the Manila communiqué charging that "Communist victory would most certainly be the result of 'mutual withdrawal'" because the Vietcong would still be in place. In August he had told the American Legion that "if Vietnam falls, the Pacific will be transformed into a Red ocean, and the road will be open to a third world war."[93] When the *New York Times* printed the text of Nixon's critique in full on November 4, Johnson lashed out at a press conference that same morning, calling Nixon "a chronic campaigner" whose purpose was "to find fault with his country and with his government during a period of October every two years."[94] "I couldn't believe it. It was too good to be true," Nixon said after the election. Both the *Times* and the president had treated him as if he were the de facto leader of the Republican Party. Johnson's attack even made Nixon a sympathetic figure.[95] In truth, the attack may have been calculated. Johnson regarded Nixon as the one Republican who could unite the Democrats behind his reelection in 1968. Romney or Rockefeller might earn votes from antiwar Democrats, Johnson reasoned, but not Nixon.

CONCLUSION

In contrast to the successful year enjoyed by Republicans Nixon, Rockefeller, Reagan, and Romney and the increasingly independent Wallace, the leading Democrats all had a hard time in 1966. Johnson's popularity sagged both within his party and among the broader electorate. The results of the midterm election were widely interpreted as a rebuke to his administration. Even before public opinion turned against the war, trust in the federal government began a decline that, in the judgment of the leading student of the subject, was caused by "public dissatisfaction with an expanding welfare state coupled with social problems that persisted."[96] Whatever small comfort Johnson may have derived from elevating Nixon above the other Republican candidates, it paled by comparison with all that had gone badly. McCarthy and Kennedy essentially sat out the campaign—at greater political cost to Kennedy, who was much more in the national spotlight—while fretting about how much to break with the president over the war. Humphrey had no such doubts. "Run on Vietnam," he advised Democrats while campaigning in thirty-seven states. His reward was to be portrayed on the cover of *Esquire*'s November issue as a ventriloquist's dummy sitting in Johnson's lap.

JOHNSON, MCCARTHY, KENNEDY, HUMPHREY

THE DEMOCRATIC BATTLE, ROUND ONE

The battle for the 1968 Democratic presidential nomination is perhaps the most storied in American history. Especially remarkable is that none of the candidates who attracted—and still attract—the most interest emerged as the nominee. President Lyndon B. Johnson, facing either defeat or a victory so bitterly secured as to render his nomination worthless, withdrew from his party's contest. Sen. Eugene McCarthy of Minnesota launched the candidacy that contributed the most to Johnson's withdrawal, but his own campaign gradually foundered. Sen. Robert F. Kennedy of New York, eager to see Johnson defeated but reluctant to challenge him and unwilling to let McCarthy claim the prize, eventually took them both on, only to be assassinated on the night of his greatest triumph. Late in the primary season and, by design, too late to contest any primaries, the eventual nominee, Vice President Hubert H. Humphrey, entered the race.

This chapter begins in early 1967, with the Republicans basking in the results of the 1966 midterm election, the economy briskly growing but troubled by rising inflation, and above all with increasing public frustration about the situation in Vietnam, where the commitment of 383,300 American ground troops and massive waves of aerial bombing generated little success in the war and much dissent at home. These developments, which continued to mark the rest of the year, raised hopes within both political parties that Johnson could be defeated in 1968. McCarthy's entry into the race, his impressive performance against the president in the New Hampshire primary, Kennedy's declaration of candidacy, Johnson's decision to withdraw,

Humphrey's late entry, the primaries war between Kennedy and McCarthy, and the assassinations of Kennedy and Martin Luther King constitute the rest of the chapter.

1967

The frustrations attending the war in Vietnam and the implementation of the War on Poverty colored Johnson's first two years as an elected president but did not overshadow his astonishing record of legislative achievement. Nineteen sixty-seven, in contrast, was nightmarish, and for the president the nightmare did not end. He actually dreamed, Johnson told Doris Kearns, recounting one of several "dreams of paralysis," that he was lying motionless in the Red Room of the White House and, as aides haggled over who would assume different parts of his job, "he could not command them, for he could neither talk nor walk. He was sick and tired, but not a single aide tried to protect him."[1] In the waking world, rioting continued in the inner cities, raising temperatures on both sides of the nation's racial divide. The president's ability to bend Congress to his will was diminished by the larger, more energetic Republican presence on Capitol Hill. The war went badly both abroad and at home. Johnson's job approval rating shrank to a late summer low of 39 percent and stayed below 50 percent for the rest of the year.

From the beginning, Johnson's course in Vietnam accorded with the advice he received from the quartet of Kennedy administration alumni who constituted his closest civilian wartime counselors: Secretary of State Dean Rusk, Secretary of Defense Robert S. McNamara, National Security Adviser McGeorge Bundy, and Bundy's deputy and successor, Walt W. Rostow. Their assumption, buttressed in general by prevailing game theories of nuclear confrontation and in particular by distorted memories of President Kennedy's success in backing down the Soviet Union in the Cuban missile crisis, was that a gradual escalation of military pressure would eventually bring the North Vietnamese to a "crossover point" at which continuing to fight cost them more than accepting South Vietnam as a sovereign nation. That assumption, underscored by continuing requests for more soldiers by Gen. William Westmoreland, the field commander, led Johnson to gradually increase the American troop commitment to 485,600—and still rising—by the end of 1967. Nearly ten thousand soldiers were killed that year, more than in all previous years combined, and twice that many were wounded.

Johnson had done everything possible to avoid a national debate on Vietnam, lest it result in irresistible political pressure to withdraw or, just as likely, to employ overwhelming force. Withdrawal, which he thought would make him "the first American president to lose a war," was unthinkable.[2] Escalation would incur costs that Johnson was certain would kill funding for the Great Society and perhaps provoke a wider war with either the Soviet Union, which already had armed North Vietnam with a sophisticated air defense system that shot down more than nine hundred American aircraft by 1968, or China, which had 170,000 Red Army personnel in the North.[3] Johnson "had a vision that maybe the Chinese would pour over the Vietnam border the way they did in North Korea" when the United States crossed the Yalu River in the Korean War, said Central Intelligence Agency director Richard Helms.[4]

The president never asked Congress for an explicit vote of support for his war policies and did not consult with legislators before launching the Rolling Thunder bombing campaign or changing the ground troops' mission from protecting military bases to hunting down the enemy in "search and destroy" expeditions. When Johnson announced new troop commitments or bombing initiatives, he did so with minimal publicity. "If you have a mother in law with only one eye, and she has it in the center of her forehead," Johnson told associates, "you don't keep her in the living room."[5] He took comfort in polls that showed a positive public response to every move he made in Vietnam, whether an escalation or a peace offer. In doing so, however, he confused the voters' short-term willingness to rally 'round the flag with long-term support for his overall conduct of the war.

In the eyes of Congress and the country, Vietnam was Johnson's war. Unfair as that judgment may have been until 1967, it had become accurate. On November 1, when the stalwart McNamara's slowly growing doubts about the war led him to send an anguished, single-spaced, nine-page memorandum to the president proposing an end to the bombing and a cap on the American troop commitment of 525,000, Johnson did not reply. "I never heard from him," McNamara said.[6] Instead, Johnson began spreading rumors that his defense secretary was cracking up and might "pull a Forrestal"—that is, kill himself as his predecessor James Forrestal did in 1949.[7] At the end of the month Johnson effectively fired McNamara by appointing him president of the World Bank.

To raise the manpower needed to carry the burden of escalation, Johnson saw the draft as a less alarming and therefore politically less risky approach than calling up the reserves or National Guard, which would have forced many married men to leave their jobs and families. The baby boom had started producing an abundance of draft-eligible eighteen-year-olds starting in 1964; besides, being drafted for two years of service had become an expected part of a young man's life after high school in the 1950s, especially the sons of working-class families who were not exempted as college students had been since 1951. But as the war escalated, those students became increasingly afraid that the draft soon would extend to them—as it did to graduate students when their exemption was lifted in 1967—either during their college years if they flunked out or right afterward if they graduated. The growth in the number of college students, from about 2,149,000 in 1952 to 7,513,000 in 1968, made this fear realistic.[8] In January 1968 the Selective Service announced that it planned to draft 302,000 young men into the army in the coming year, up from 230,000 in 1967. The application of the service's "oldest-first" policy to the large crop of graduating seniors, officials predicted, would mean that about 150,000 members of the Class of 1968 would be drafted, ten times the number from the previous year's class.

Fodder for the draft, male college students were also fodder for protest, especially those who lived on campus with lots of free time, legions of equally vulnerable peers, and supportive girlfriends. "What I wanted was to go to graduate school, get married, and to enjoy those bright prospects I had been taught that life owed me," wrote *Harvard Crimson* president James Fallows, who participated in antiwar rallies and then starved himself so that he would be disqualified from service as underweight.[9] "The draft was the best organizing tool we had," said antiwar activist Sam Brown.[10] Radical groups such as Students for a Democratic Society (SDS) saw the draft "as a handle with which to organize and educate other students about the nature of capitalism and imperialism."[11] Meanwhile, sympathetic professors were exposing students to ideas consistent with active opposition to the war and teaching them about the civil rights demonstrations that had successfully effected political change just a few years before.

More than a thousand students from northern campuses had participated in Mississippi Freedom Summer in 1964. The Student Nonviolent Coordinating Committee's (SNCC) subsequent redefinition of itself as a civil rights organization for black students left experienced white campus activists available for a new cause. Even so, the student antiwar demonstrations came as a surprise to many. The Korean War had been just as unpopular in its late stages as the war in Vietnam, but opposition remained at the level of grumbling and voting, not taking to the streets. Overlooked was that many fewer students had been enrolled in college during the war in Korea, a larger share of Korean War–era students were World War II

Marchers cross the Abraham Lincoln Bridge en route to the Pentagon in a massive protest demonstration organized by the National Mobilization Committee to End the War in Vietnam in October 1967. (Credit: Frank Wolfe, provided by the Lyndon B. Johnson Presidential Library)

veterans, and mass demonstrations had yet to prove their effectiveness as a political tactic.[12] Also overlooked was the extent to which the budding feminist movement was pushed aside for the sake of supporting civil rights for African Americans and antiwar protest on behalf of draft-age men. Young women "often ended up sitting silent in political meetings or trying to speak and being ignored," Gail Collins has written. "In general, women had no more clout in leftist student politics than they had in Congress or on Wall Street."[13] "Girls say yes to boys who say no" was an iconic wall poster of the era featuring antiwar folksinger Joan Baez and her two sisters that was sold to raise money for draft resistance.

In 1967 and afterward, unlike the early 1950s, the campuses in every region of the country but the South became hotbeds of organized antiwar activity. Johnson, who earlier in his presidency gave some of his most significant speeches to audiences at Howard University, Johns Hopkins University, and the University of Michigan, found that except for West Point and the other service academies he no longer could appear at most colleges or universities without provoking mammoth protests. On October 20–21, 1967, demonstrators left their dorms and classrooms to attend a hundred-thousand-strong march on Washington and, in particular, the

Pentagon, organized by the National Mobilization Committee to End the War in Vietnam—the "MOBE."

The president, who regarded McNamara's dissenting memo as a sign of incipient madness, looked on the protesters as either subversives or tools in subversive hands. Unwilling to accept opposition from any quarter as sincerely motivated, Johnson demanded daily reports about communist influence on the march from Federal Bureau of Investigation director J. Edgar Hoover, who gladly manufactured them.[14] Even sober-minded administration officials wondered at the nearly simultaneous outbreak of student riots and demonstrations in Paris, Rome, West Berlin, Madrid, Mexico City, Tokyo, and other major cities around the world, as well as surmising that the Soviet Union and North Vietnam would be foolish not to pour fuel on the fires of Western protest with money, advice, and other aids to active dissent. "There's a reality to the notion that the communists, the Soviets, do what they can to louse up American policy whenever they get the chance," said Bundy.[15]

Some antiwar demonstrations turned violent, but nothing compared with the 164 race riots that broke out during the first nine months of 1967, including one in Newark, where 26 died and 725 were injured between July 12 and 17, and another in Detroit, where 43 died and 467 were injured between July 23 and 27. In both cities, hundreds of homes, stores, and other buildings were destroyed by arsonists. As with the protests against the war, Johnson was convinced, according to his associate David Ginsburg, that "it was simply not possible to have so many outbreaks at the same time without someone orchestrating it"—another belief fed by Hoover, along with the president's suspicion that "the Russians think up things for [antiwar] senators to say."[16] In reality, the immediate train of causation sparking the urban riots was typically more mundane: a spell of brutally hot weather, a minor incident in a black neighborhood, excessive use of force by white police officers, an outraged reaction by witnesses of the encounter, stores looted, fires set, rocks thrown, bullets fired, and neighborhoods ruined.

In the immediate aftermath of the Newark and Detroit riots, Johnson appointed the National Advisory Commission on Civil Disorders, chaired by Democratic governor Otto Kerner of Illinois but dominated by Vice Chairman John V. Lindsay, the liberal Republican mayor of New York City. The most famous sentence in the executive summary of the commission's March 1968 report ("Our nation is moving toward two societies, one black, one white—separate and unequal") suggested that despite the 1964 and 1965 Civil Rights Acts and the Great Society, the United States was becoming more unfair to African Americans, not less.[17] The report itself called for $11.9 billion in new federal spending in urban black neighborhoods in fiscal year 1969 and double that amount by fiscal year 1971. A commercially published version of the commission report reached no. 2 on the *New York Times* best seller list, but both its verdict and its recommendation seemed counterintuitive, even bizarre, to Johnson, who was doubly outraged when the *Times* headlined its story on the report: "Johnson Unit Assails Whites in Negro Riots."[18] "There are thousands of people . . . who've worked hard every day to save up for a week's vacation or a new store," said the president, "and they look around and think they see their tax dollars going to finance a bunch of ungrateful rioters. Why, that's bound to make even a nonprejudiced person angry."[19] Many whites equated riots not with social injustice but with violent crime, which already had them worried. The disturbing 11 percent increase in serious crimes in 1966 was followed by a 17 percent increase during the first half of 1967.

Racial conservatism—the term invented by Edward Carmines and James Stimson to refer to nonracist opposition to policies branded as favorable to African Americans—gained further steam from the new style of rhetoric employed by some famous black leaders. When James Meredith was shot on a solitary protest march through Mississippi on June 6, 1966, SNCC chair Stokely Carmichael joined the mass march that followed and used the slogan "Black Power!" to outshout fellow march leader Martin Luther King's "Freedom Now!" The slogan and its logo, a raised black first, caught on. "We been saying freedom for six years—and we ain't got nothin'," Carmichael claimed. "What we gonna start saying now is 'Black Power!'" An immediate casualty of Carmichael's rhetoric was Johnson's 1966 civil rights bill, which—though "considered a fait accompli upon the shooting of James Meredith—never passed," according to Aram Goudsouzian.[20]

In danger of being marginalized within the movement, King moved leftward and attacked the war. "In a real sense," he said on April 4, 1967, in a widely reported speech at New York City's Riverside Church, "the Great Society has been shot down on the battlefields of Vietnam" by a government that has become "the greatest purveyor of violence in the world today."[21] Coming in the aftermath of his failed July 1966 campaign to integrate schools and neighborhoods in Chicago, King managed to alarm many northern whites without appeasing black militants. As the new public face of the African American political cause, Carmichael, activist H. Rap Brown (who in 1967 urged a crowd of angry blacks on Maryland's Eastern Shore to "go get your guns" because "if America don't come around, we're going to burn America down"), and rampaging urban rioters blotted out images of well-dressed, hymn-singing church people peacefully asking for basic rights in the face of violent white resistance.[22]

Johnson was politically hamstrung in his response. In public, he neither endorsed nor repudiated the Kerner Commission report, which Richard Nixon charged "blames everybody for the riots except the perpetrators of the riots."[23] When Democratic voting expert Richard M. Scammon warned Johnson's close aide, Harry McPherson, about a burgeoning "social issue" through which "voters were becoming quietly enraged by crime and disorder and by what they regarded as permissiveness by institutional authority," McPherson followed Scammon's advice to "get [Johnson] photographed with a man in blue." But as McPherson pointed out, if the president, beleaguered in his party by opposition to the war in Vietnam, "was to retain the support of the national Democrats—by and large a liberal army—he would have to remain a liberal at home, talking less of stopping crime than of its causes."[24]

Tempering these unsettling events at home and in Vietnam, the economy boomed throughout 1967. The gross national product grew by about 4 percent and unemployment fell below 4 percent. But in August rising inflation, the declining dollar, and a projected $29 billion budget deficit for fiscal year 1968—roughly the amount the United States was spending annually on the war—forced Johnson to ask for a 10 percent surcharge on corporate and personal income taxes that would last "for so long as the unusual expenditures associated with our efforts in Vietnam require higher revenues."[25] As Maurice Isserman and Michael Kazin have pointed out, "Defense spending increases personal income but not the amount of consumer goods on which such income can be spent—a classic formula for inflation."[26] For the first time, the president was telling all Americans to make a wartime sacrifice.

Unconvinced by a request for which Johnson had not prepared them, 73 percent of voters said they would rather see federal spending reduced than pay higher taxes.[27] Rep. Wilbur Mills, the dominating chairman of the tax-writing House Ways and Means Committee, insisted on $5 billion in immediate spending reductions and another $20 billion of cuts in future obligations, conditions the president was unwilling to accept.[28] Johnson's long-standing concern that he would have to forsake the Great Society—"the woman I really loved"—for "that bitch of a war on the other side of the world" was in danger of being fulfilled.[29] Indeed, none of the president's major legislative initiatives—the tax increase, a crime bill, civil rights, East-West trade, and executive branch reorganization—was enacted in 1967. He did take pleasure in congressional passage of an "anti-nepotism" statute forbidding the president from appointing relatives to government positions, which was widely and accurately interpreted as a post facto rebuke of Robert Kennedy's appointment as attorney general.

Johnson's political position as the year drew to a close was uncertain. His main advantage on the eve of the campaign was the unthinkability, at least among members of the political community, of denying a reelection-seeking president the nomination of his party. The last time an incumbent had faced a serious intraparty challenge was more than a half century before, in 1912, when former president Theodore Roosevelt's campaign to unseat President William Howard Taft as the Republican nominee both failed and doomed their party to defeat in the general election. Only about 40 percent of the delegates to the 1968 Democratic convention would be from primary states, and not many of those were bound by law or party rules to vote for the winner of their state's primary. The rest, in the bleak assessment of Robert F. Kennedy supporters William vanden Heuvel and Milton Gwirtzman, would be southern (about 20 percent), labor or labor-controlled (about 30 percent), or among the "good share of the rest [who] would be controlled by party leaders with ties to the president."[30] Johnson's approval rating rose modestly toward the end of 1967, in part because of a spontaneous, hope-giving summit meeting that he arranged with Soviet premier Alexei Kosygin on the campus of New Jersey's Glassboro State College on June 23–25 and in part because of a well-orchestrated "Success Offensive" that he and other administration officials launched that fall to persuade the country that the war was finally being won. Both of these activities exemplified the president's ability to engineer foreign policy events that instantly boosted his popularity.

Yet the party whose nomination Johnson would be seeking in 1968 was severely divided and organizationally weak. The Great Society and the civil rights acts were unpopular among conservative Democrats, and opposition to the war was intense and growing among Democratic liberals. Kennedy and his family's loyalists smoldered with resentment and disdain toward Johnson, and LBJ feared that RFK would just as readily attack him from the right as from the left if he sensed vulnerability on that flank. On May 3, for example, Kennedy cosponsored a bill to prohibit "the desecration or improper use of the flag of the USA" with conservative Democrat Alan Bible of Nevada.[31] As for the Democratic National Committee, Johnson's efforts to emasculate it as a potential rival power center had been all too successful.

"The Democratic National Committee is not staffed or equipped to conduct a successful presidential election," reported Postmaster General Lawrence O'Brien, a political professional whom Johnson asked to draw up a plan for reelection. Matters were no better in the states, O'Brien added: "Many of the state organizations are flabby and wedded to techniques which are conventional and outmoded."[32]

Nor was Johnson's enthusiasm for another campaign and another term as president undiluted. Even as he assigned O'Brien to begin planning for the election, he was telling his cabinet, his secretary, and close Texas associates such as Gov. John Connally that he probably would not run again. In the past, whenever Johnson had talked about quitting a race, Lady Bird Johnson had cajoled him out of it. This time she strongly urged him not to run, underscoring his own concern that he might not survive another four years as president.[33] Johnson himself noted that both his father and grandfather had died of heart failure when they were sixty-four, the age he would reach in August 1972.[34]

THE SEARCH FOR AN ANTIWAR CANDIDATE

"We know who our nominee will be," said DNC chair John M. Bailey on January 8, 1968. "The Republicans have all their bloody infighting to look forward to."[35] Bailey's statement perfectly expressed the conventional political wisdom of the day. It also turned out to be wrong.

The search for an antiwar candidate to oppose Johnson began in the spring of 1967, when Allard Lowenstein and Curtis Gans, two young liberal activists with Americans for Democratic Action (ADA), canvassed prominent antiwar Democrats in search of a challenger and won public support from ADA's president, Harvard economist John Kenneth Galbraith. Although the GOP was the only party guaranteed to have an open nominating contest in 1968 and Gov. George Romney of Michigan, a leading candidate, was a critic of the war, Lowenstein, an ADA board member, and Gans, a staff member, confined their search to fellow Democrats. In one instance, they approached retired general James M. Gavin, a World War II hero who had publicly described the Vietnam War as "a tragedy."[36] But they lost interest when he told them he was a Republican. Lowenstein and Gans wanted to end the war, but they also wanted to remake the Democratic Party. Arthur Schlesinger urged Galbraith to run, only to learn that he was constitutionally ineligible because he had been born in Canada.[37]

Kennedy was every antiwar activist's first choice, especially after he called for a bombing halt in a March 2, 1967, speech on the Senate floor, his first serious public break with the president. Johnson immediately escalated the bombing, prompting Kennedy to order his speechwriters not to include any more references critical of the president because they were counterproductive. Instead, five days after the Senate speech, Kennedy said on the *Today* program, "I'm going to support President Johnson" in 1968 and would be "glad to campaign."[38] On June 3, two weeks after privately asking Schlesinger, "How can we possibly survive five more years of Lyndon Johnson? Five more years of a crazy man?" Kennedy introduced the president at the annual New York State Democratic dinner by praising "the height of his aim, the breadth of his achievements, the record of his past, and the promise of his future."[39]

Kennedy knew from the reaction to his March 2 speech that every public disagreement with Johnson on the war or any other issue would be portrayed in the media as the latest installment in their personal rivalry. He also feared that because Johnson's hatred was so great, calling for the president to do something might provoke him to do the opposite—such as when Johnson increased the bombing rather than ending it. Kennedy thought that the president probably could beat him for the nomination, "but if I really challenge him, he cannot win the election."[40] All Kennedy would accomplish by poisoning the well for Johnson, as well as for the congressional and other down-ballot Democratic candidates who would suffer with him, would be to bring down the wrath of the party and jeopardize his own planned presidential campaign in 1972. Two strongly antiwar Senate Democrats who were running for reelection in 1968, Oregon's Wayne Morse and Joseph Clark of Pennsylvania, urged Kennedy to stay out of the race lest he divide the party so badly as to cost them their seats.[41] If he ran now, Kennedy himself said, "I'll be at the mercy of events Johnson can manipulate to his advantage."[42] "Suppose in the middle of the California primary, when I am attacking him on the war, he should suddenly stop the bombing and go off to Geneva to hold talks with the North Vietnamese?" he asked Schlesinger. "What do I do then?"[43]

On September 23, meeting at his Hickory Hill home in northern Virginia, Kennedy told Lowenstein to find someone else to challenge Johnson, noting that if he ran, "people would say that I was splitting the party out of ambition and envy. No one would believe that I was doing it out of how I feel about Vietnam and the poor."[44] But Kennedy remained torn, and on October 8 he authorized political aide Joseph Dolan to sound out Democratic leaders around the country. Dolan did, and their strong negative reactions to Kennedy's potential candidacy "made him feel as though he was engaged in a secret conspiracy to overthrow the government."[45] When Schlesinger and young Kennedy Senate staffers such as Jeff Greenfield, Adam Walinsky, and Peter Edelman kept up the pressure to run, Kennedy convened another meeting on December 10. President Kennedy's closest adviser, Theodore Sorensen, and Sen. Edward M. Kennedy rebutted the staffers' arguments by saying that if RFK challenged Johnson for the nomination and lost, which they thought he would, he would ruin his chances for 1972.[46] Pollster Louis Harris, who had worked for John F. Kennedy's campaign in 1960, told Robert F. Kennedy he had no chance.[47]

Kennedy fought back, arguing that to wait five years would just mean casting more controversial votes in the Senate and thereby alienating more interests, but in the end he accepted the old hands' advice over that of the young Turks. Besides, who knew what might come of Eugene McCarthy's challenge to Johnson, which he had announced on November 30? Kennedy disliked McCarthy, but if his candidacy revealed weaknesses in the president's political standing, Kennedy could no longer be accused of dividing the party if he decided to run.

McCarthy was not Lowenstein and Gans's second choice to take on Johnson, much less their first. Despairing of Kennedy's reluctance, they approached Sen. George McGovern of South Dakota. McGovern said their cause was worthy but that he could not run because he was up for reelection. With them in his office, he opened the *Congressional Directory*, looked down the list of senators, and saw that every antiwar Democrat was on the ballot in 1968 except McCarthy and Lee Metcalf of Montana. McGovern recommended McCarthy, who as a Catholic would perhaps be less vulnerable to the charge of being soft on communism.

As it turned out, McCarthy had been thinking since early that year of challenging Johnson in some primaries as a protest candidate, much as Gov. George C. Wallace of Alabama had done from the right in 1964. On August 17 McCarthy stalked out of a Senate Foreign Relations Committee hearing when Undersecretary of State Nicholas Katzenbach testified that the president had all the authority he needed under the Gulf of Tonkin Resolution to conduct the war in Vietnam without any further declaration by Congress. "Someone's got to take them on," McCarthy told a *New York Times* reporter who caught him outside the committee room. "And if I have to run for president to do it, I'm going to do it."[48] When Lowenstein and Gans visited McCarthy on October 23, he agreed to run. A few days before his November 30 announcement in the Senate Caucus Room, McCarthy met briefly with Kennedy, whose private reaction to the news was distress that someone else was acting more boldly and courageously than he. Kennedy did not promise to stay out of the race indefinitely.

McCarthy's announcement speech foretold a candidacy that would be low-key and liberal. He did not say he was running for president but rather that he would "challenge the president's position and the administration's position" and "would enter the Democratic primaries in four states: Wisconsin, Oregon, California, and Nebraska," along with, perhaps, Massachusetts and New Hampshire.[49] His statement focused on Vietnam, where he called for an end to the bombing; negotiations that included the National Liberation Front (NLF), or Vietcong; a coalition government; and a phased, not an immediate, withdrawal of American forces. At his initial campaign appearance on December 2 before the Chicago convention of the Lowenstein and Gans–formed National Conference of Concerned Democrats, a gathering of 450 people from forty-two states, McCarthy gave a muted, almost scholarly speech opposing both the war and the expansive view of presidential power shared by Johnson and the Kennedys. The speech drained from the hall the energy that had been roused by Lowenstein's rip-roaring, anti-Johnson introduction. The event left Lowenstein and McCarthy mutually disappointed, McCarthy because of Lowenstein's heated rhetoric (which left the senator "visibly pissed," according to Lowenstein lieutenant Gary Hart) and Lowenstein because of McCarthy's seeming lack of enthusiasm.[50]

The press praised McCarthy for his courage in taking on the president but scorned his chances of success—the word *quixotic* appeared in many published reports. In the White House, said O'Brien, "McCarthy's candidacy was not taken seriously by anyone around the president. It was regarded as a joke, an annoyance."[51] Only with reluctance did McCarthy decide on January 3, 1968, ten weeks before the voting, to enter the March 12 New Hampshire primary. A late January Gallup Poll showed that after two months of desultory campaigning ("I'm not really a morning person," he said while scratching several scheduled predawn factory-gate appearances from his schedule), McCarthy no longer trailed Johnson nationally by three to one. The margin was now four to one.[52]

And then came Tet.

TET IN VIETNAM, A PRIMARY IN NEW HAMPSHIRE

Tet is the variously dated start of the New Year in Vietnam; in 1968 it fell on January 30. Violating a planned holiday cease-fire, during which half of South Vietnam's army went home to visit their families, about 85,000

North Vietnamese and Vietcong troops attacked thirty-six of South Vietnam's forty-four provincial capitals, five of its six autonomous cities, and multiple military bases. Saigon was hit the next day, and parts of the American embassy compound were occupied for several hours.

Militarily, Tet was a failure for the communist forces.[53] The offensive did not spark a domestic uprising, was beaten back with massive casualties, and resulted in severe permanent damage to the NLF. To Americans watching the news on television, however, the attacks seemed catastrophic. Johnson, Humphrey, Westmoreland, and Ambassador Ellsworth Bunker had just finished their late 1967 "Success Offensive" to convince the public that the war was finally going well. "We are beginning to win this struggle," the vice president said in a mid-November appearance on *Today*. A few days later Westmoreland told the National Press Club that the communists were "unable to mount a major offensive. . . . I am absolutely certain that whereas in 1965 the enemy was winning, today he is certainly losing. . . . The end comes into view."[54] Johnson's Gallup approval rating had risen accordingly, from 38 percent in October to 48 percent in January. Yet never before Tet had the communists been able to carry the fight to South Vietnam's cities, much less invade its capital. And no matter how weak the Vietcong became, North Vietnam was able and more than willing to take up the slack. From the beginning, 1968 was shaping up to be what it became: the bloodiest year of the entire war for American soldiers, who suffered more than a hundred thousand casualties by December, including 14,594 deaths.

"Only a few months ago we were told that 65 percent of the population was secure," said McCarthy. "Now we know that even the American embassy is not secure."[55] On February 13, the ADA board, responding to massive pressure from state and local chapters, voted 65–47 to endorse McCarthy over Johnson, overcoming strong opposition from the United Auto Workers, United Steelworkers, and other unions. Labor representatives on the board argued fiercely that McCarthy was a "one-issue man" whose record on domestic policy was far inferior to the president's, and the heads of three major unions resigned their seats after the vote.[56] Their protests did not matter: to most ADA members Vietnam outweighed everything else put together. "No one cared that McCarthy was awful on domestic affairs," recalled ADA leader Joseph Rauh. "He was right on the war and the war was everything."[57] In reality, McCarthy had the voting record of a mainstream liberal on most social and economic issues but not the passion that union leaders expected of their heroes.

Two weeks later, after visiting Vietnam, the respected CBS news anchor

Walter Cronkite made a rare editorial comment during a prime-time news special called *Report from Vietnam*. "To say that we are closer to victory today is to believe, in the face of the evidence, the optimists who have been wrong in the past," said Cronkite, calling for steps toward a negotiated withdrawal.[58] Whether, as has often been repeated, Johnson reacted to the broadcast by saying, "If I've lost Cronkite, I've lost Middle America" (or in another version, "I've lost the war") is uncertain, but losing the support of such a widely known and trusted figure could not help but be politically damaging.[59] Beyond that, all three networks, whose presentation of the war on their evening news programs had generally been positive until Tet, became much more critical in their coverage.[60] On February 28, Joint Chiefs of Staff chairman Earle Wheeler told a war-weary president that to stave off disaster Westmoreland needed 105,000 more troops by May 1 and an additional 100,000 by December 1.

On January 30, the same day the communists launched Tet, Robert Kennedy met with the Sperling breakfast, a regular gathering of about fifteen Washington reporters, to declare once again that he was not going to run. Reiterating his usual argument that his candidacy would merely "split the Democratic party, and Democratic candidates would be beaten all over the country," Kennedy said, "I would not oppose Lyndon Johnson under any conceivable circumstances"—softened slightly to "foreseeable circumstances" before he cleared the quote for publication. For McCarthy, opposing the war was reason enough to enter the race; for Kennedy, there was no point running unless he could win. But in staying out Kennedy showed no inclination to support McCarthy—just the opposite. "Gene McCarthy hasn't been able to tap the unrest in the country," he told the Sperling group, adding, "McCarthy has hurt me by his taunting, and he hasn't helped himself. He's made it impossible for Kennedy people to work for him."[61] Kennedy's reaction when he later learned about Tet was to ramp up his antiwar rhetoric, declaring on February 8 that "a military victory is not in sight and . . . it probably will never come."[62] But he let the deadlines pass for entering the New Hampshire and Massachusetts primaries and told the Nebraska secretary of state not to put his name on the ballot because he definitely was not running.

McCarthy's decision to enter New Hampshire was reluctant because the state had no organized peace movement and was a Republican stronghold whose economy was booming on the strength of war-related defense contracts. He would have preferred starting in his home-state neighbor, politically progressive Wisconsin, whose primary was on April 2. But McCarthy's campaign was going nowhere in December and January, and supporters were beginning to lose interest, including the major donors he was counting on to finance his candidacy. These included Stride Rite shoe company president Arnold Hiatt; Dreyfus Corporation's Howard Stein and Jack Dreyfus, Jr.; Singer Sewing Machine heiress Anne Peretz and her husband Martin, a lecturer at Harvard; Clark Thread family member Blair Clark (who doubled as McCarthy's campaign manager); and, eventually, General Motors heir Stewart Mott, who had started out as a major donor to Republican Nelson A. Rockefeller.

McCarthy's first foray into New Hampshire on January 25 was encouraging. Because it was a small state with relatively few Democrats, low-key face-to-face campaigning worked better than stirring oratory, which played to McCarthy's strength. Johnson, still obsessed with Kennedy, did not take McCarthy seriously, choosing to rely instead on Gov. John King's organization to campaign on his behalf—roughly the approach he had taken against Wallace in 1964. Early press attention was focused on the Republican primary, which initially seemed more likely to offer a real contest.

The Tet offensive energized opposition to the war and with it McCarthy's candidacy. Most college students could not vote—except in Georgia, Kentucky, Alaska, and Hawaii the minimum voting age was still twenty-one—but, free of family and career responsibilities, they could volunteer.[63] Students came from more than a hundred colleges, mostly from Dartmouth College and various Boston-area campuses. The longhairs worked on mailings and other behind-the-scenes activities in a basement room at campaign headquarters. The "straights"—those who were willing to shave their beards (or bob their hair), "wear a coat and tie and 'nice pants'" (or a skirt—but "no miniskirts"), and generally be "Clean for Gene"—were sent out to canvass voters door to door, reaching nearly all of them by primary day.[64] "Being Clean for Gene was a door opener . . . part of the broad strategy to show that young Democrats who were wearing neckties, coats, and were clean shaven with short hair could be against the president," said Sam Brown.[65] What all the volunteers had in common—about two thousand laboring full-time and five thousand on weekends toward the end of the campaign, including Wellesley College student Hillary Rodham—was that they hated the war but believed the system could be made to work. By primary day, McCarthy had "the biggest and best field organization ever assembled for any political campaign," according to Richard Goodwin, who worked for Johnson and Robert Kennedy before joining McCarthy.[66] McCarthy roused himself to a good effort once he realized things were going well, reviving the political skills he had demonstrated as an undefeated candidate in Minnesota. Even McCarthy's reserved manner worked in his favor among laconic New Hampshirites. Nothing about the way he spoke or looked seemed radical either in person or on television.

McCarthy said he began to think he had a chance "when I realized that you could go into any bar in the country and insult Lyndon Johnson and nobody would punch you in the nose."[67] Responding to what he and his volunteers were hearing from the voters, his campaign became much more about opposition to the president, whom people disliked for multiple and varying reasons, than about ending the war. McCarthy's clean-shaven canvassers emphasized character and leadership, and his campaign ads said nothing about whether he was for or against the war. "Vote for a man you can believe in" appealed to voters who opposed Johnson on any grounds.

When Romney dropped out of the Republican race on February 28, the media spotlight began to shine on the Democratic primary, in which McCarthy was campaigning but Johnson was absent. Romney's withdrawal also meant that McCarthy was the only antiwar candidate in either party. Nearly all the coverage McCarthy received was good. As Richard Strout, author of the *New Republic*'s TRB column, observed, "Mr. McCarthy is the pet of the reporters because he is everything that a presidential candidate is supposed not to be and so he is fun to watch: witty instead of shrill, composed instead of noisy, talking sense instead of nonsense."[68]

Johnson's campaign was hapless, in part because his willful neglect of the DNC and other party organs had percolated down to statewide Democratic organizations. Democratic senator Thomas McIntyre predicted that the president would get all but about 10 percent of the vote, setting the bar absurdly low for McCarthy to exceed expectations. Governor King's organization sent every Democratic voter a pledge card with an identification number and three perforated sections: one to keep, one to send to the local party organization, and one to send to the White House. The cards struck many voters as alien to the principle of the secret ballot; McCarthy shrewdly compared them to a Texas cattle brand. King also allowed two candidates pledged to Johnson to run for each delegate slot, treating places on the ballot like patronage favors. The president even permitted himself to be outspent by three to one.

Two days before the primary, the *New York Times* revealed the Pentagon's request for 205,000 more troops in Vietnam, which would have raised the total above three-quarters of a million, including the 150,000 reserves who would have to be called up. Johnson realized what was happening in New

Sen. Eugene McCarthy's presidential campaign caught fire after his surprisingly strong showing in the New Hampshire primary. Here he campaigns in New Haven, Conn. (Credit: Minnesota Historical Society)

Hampshire, but only at the last minute. On the eve of the voting he told aide John Roche that McCarthy would "get 40 percent, at least 40 percent. Every son of a bitch in New Hampshire who's mad at his wife or the postman or anybody is going to vote for Gene McCarthy."[69]

New Hampshire Democrats cast two votes on primary day, one in a nonbinding "beauty contest" and one for actual delegates. Johnson won the beauty contest with 27,520 votes—all of them write-ins since his name was not on the ballot—to McCarthy's 23,263 in the Democratic primary. In the Republican primary, an additional 5,511 voters wrote in McCarthy and 1,778 wrote in Johnson. Depending on how one counted, Johnson prevailed by 4,257 votes (a 7.7 percentage point margin) or 521 votes (less than 1 point). Either way he won, but McCarthy did extremely well. In the delegate contest, McCarthy's victory was unambiguous. With King's candidates splitting the pro-Johnson vote among themselves, twenty McCarthy delegates were elected and only four pledged to the president.

Like the campaign, the vote in New Hampshire was less about peace in Vietnam than about unhappiness with Johnson. In a survey conducted during the primary but not published until after the election, political scientists at the University of Michigan found that for every two McCarthy voters who wanted to get out of Vietnam, three wanted the president to use more force. A plurality of those who supported McCarthy in the primary said at the time that they preferred George Wallace in November.[70] McCarthy ran a superb campaign, and the money poured in—he eventually spent about $11 million, more than Kennedy ($9 million) and Vice President Hubert H. Humphrey (about $4 million).[71] But it was not clear that either he or the cause that motivated him to run would be its chief beneficiary.

KENNEDY GETS IN

McCarthy's New Hampshire–sparked viability left Kennedy with two choices: support McCarthy or enter the race himself. Both were unpalatable but not equally so. "Eugene McCarthy is not competent to be president," Kennedy told McGovern, whom he phoned "in great distress, great anxiety" when he heard that McCarthy was going to run.[72] Beyond that, Kennedy hated that McCarthy had become the new hero of college students, even in his home states of Massachusetts and New York, and he feared that McCarthy might emerge from 1968 as the liberal front-runner for the 1972 nomination. In every political niche that Kennedy thought he should occupy, he found McCarthy.

Kennedy pretty much decided to run five days before the New Hampshire primary, but aides talked him out of announcing lest the write-in votes he inevitably would attract from potential McCarthy supporters hand Johnson a landslide. Kennedy did tell Goodwin to get word to McCarthy that he planned to declare, to which McCarthy replied, "Why don't you tell him that I only want one term anyway? Let him support me now, and after that he can have it." When Goodwin demurred, McCarthy added, "The presidency should be a one-term office. Then the power would be in the institution. It wouldn't be so dependent on the person."[73] Kennedy found this unbelievable, as it would have been for himself or the great majority of politicians. He also had little time to wait: the deadline to file for the California primary was March 18, less than a week after the returns from New Hampshire were in.

On March 13, while McCarthy and his supporters were still celebrating their victory, Kennedy said that he was "actively reconsidering the possibilities that are available to me," a particularly graceless and, but for the imperatives of the political calendar, ill-timed statement.[74] A student volunteer in the McCarthy campaign despaired, "We woke up after the New Hampshire primary, like it was Christmas Day. And when you went down to the tree, we found Bobby Kennedy had stolen our Christmas presents."[75] Liberal columnist Jack Newfield called Kennedy "a ruthless political opportunist." Murray Kempton, who in 1964 had written that, because of "his wound so great" from his brother's assassination, "we owe him nothing smaller than election to the Senate," now wrote that RFK "confirmed the worst things his enemies have ever said about him."[76] Historians Lee Benson and James Shenton organized the placement of an ad in the *Times* stating that intellectuals "must choose between morality and amorality, between McCarthy and Kennedy."[77] Older, devoted supporters of Adlai Stevenson, the Democratic presidential nominee in 1952 and 1956, reminded each other that Robert Kennedy headed the organization that steamrolled their hero at the 1960 convention, in sharp contrast to McCarthy, who gave a famously excellent speech placing Stevenson's name in nomination.

Later that day Johnson further complicated RFK's decision with a phone call to Theodore Sorensen. On March 11 Sorensen had suggested that the president create a blue-ribbon commission on Vietnam, with Kennedy as a leading member. Now Johnson told Sorensen that he was interested in pursuing the idea, which put Kennedy on the spot. If he agreed to serve, he would have to sideline himself politically. If he refused, he risked being accused of putting ambition ahead of peace. Kennedy finessed his way off the hot seat by going to the Pentagon with Sorensen the next day and presenting Clark Clifford, who had become secretary of defense on March 1, with a dove-stacked list of nominees for the commission and a demand that the president "issue a statement that the time had come to reevaluate, in its entirety, our policy in Vietnam." That night Johnson decided not to go forward on the grounds that to appoint a commission on those terms "would give comfort to Hanoi," "usurp presidential authority," and give every appearance of being a "political deal."[78] "I guess Bob will run now," Sorensen told White House staff member DeVier Pierson, whom Johnson had instructed to convey his decision.[79]

Kennedy scheduled his announcement for Saturday, March 16, in the same Senate chamber where McCarthy and, eight years earlier, JFK had declared their candidacies. At 2:00 that morning, Edward Kennedy met secretly with McCarthy in Wisconsin to convey his brother's offer to divide up the remaining contests between them, including a promise to campaign for McCarthy in Wisconsin's April 2 primary. RFK's other message, his brother later recalled, was that "if McCarthy was going to talk about the cities and urban policies as much as about the war, he wouldn't get in." McCarthy "was just basically completely uninterested" and "rather disdainful," Kennedy recalled. "He was on his high. It had all moved for him. He was in the catbird seat."[80] In particular, McCarthy already had Wisconsin sewn up. A few hours later Schlesinger, who had been urging Kennedy to run for months, told him that if his candidacy divided the antiwar vote and enabled Johnson to win the primaries, liberals wouldn't forgive him. "Why not come out for McCarthy?" Schlesinger said, arguing that it was just a matter of time until McCarthy flamed out. "Every McCarthy delegate will be a potential Kennedy delegate. He can't possibly win." "I can't do that," Kennedy replied. "It would be too humiliating. Kennedys don't act that way."[81] In truth, McCarthy not only had supplanted Kennedy but was taunting him. "He plays touch football," McCarthy said of Kennedy. "I play football. He plays softball, I play baseball. He skates in Rockefeller Center, I play hockey."[82]

Kennedy's announcement speech, written by Sorensen, was stuffed with the sort of grandiose rhetoric ("At stake . . . is our right to moral leadership of this planet") that suited his late brother much better than him.[83] RFK argued that because New Hampshire had shown that the Democratic Party was already deeply torn, his previous unwillingness to run and thereby divide the party no longer applied. Reluctant to give up on the division of labor his younger brother had proposed to McCarthy hours before, Kennedy said that he would enter primaries in Nebraska, Oregon, and California and wished McCarthy well in Wisconsin, Pennsylvania, and Massachusetts. "In no state will my efforts be directed against Senator McCarthy," he said, not explaining how that would work since McCarthy had already announced he would contest all the primaries Kennedy was entering. In response to questions Kennedy said that his position on Vietnam was to deescalate the American involvement, including a bombing halt, and allow the Vietcong a role in the "future political process of South Vietnam"—a position indistinguishable from McCarthy's.[84]

The challenges facing Kennedy were enormous. Not only were Johnson and McCarthy opponents and even enemies of his, but many customary Kennedy supporters now wondered if there really was a "new Kennedy" different from the reputed ruthless, clannish "bad Bobby" of old. "It was going to reaffirm a view about Bobby being particularly aggressive and ruthless and letting nothing get in his way," recalled Edward Kennedy. "Those were some of the characteristics that he had, and this played into that. . . . Because this would fall into that definition of ruthless, ambitious, power hungry."[85]

RFK's entry into the race came two or three months later than made sense for a candidate planning to assemble a primaries-based, grassroots campaign organization. Still worse, he had spent little of the previous year laying the groundwork for such a campaign by touring the country to raise money for his party and discreetly recruit local supporters. Organizationally, Kennedy would have to settle for "second-level Democrats" in many states because Johnson and McCarthy already had signed up the top tier. Internally, Kennedy said, "The worst problem I am going to have is putting together the men who were with my brother with the men who have been with me"—that is, blend the experienced politicos from JFK's 1960 campaign with RFK's young Senate staffers, who were certain to resent being relegated to a secondary role because they were the ones who had been right all along about his running.[86] Like JFK's campaign organization, RFK's "was top-down rather than grassroots."[87] Unlike JFK's, it lacked a Robert Kennedy to keep its disparate elements working together.

Kennedy's lack of preparation led him to wildly overestimate the extent of his appeal to state and local Democratic politicians. He thought many would rally to him as the logical alternative to a politically damaged Johnson and a personally quirky McCarthy. Kennedy learned how wrong he was when, right after entering the race, he pitched hard for Mayor Daley's support, knowing that Daley thought the war was a mistake. Daley turned him down flat, auguring the response he received from other party professionals around the country. "Even the Lord had skeptical members of his party," Daley said, implicitly comparing Johnson to Jesus Christ and Kennedy to Peter, Doubting Thomas, or even Judas Iscariot. "One betrayed him, one denied him, and one doubted him."[88] None of the AFL-CIO's twenty-nine international unions endorsed Kennedy; nor did the United Auto Workers.[89]

Kennedy's strategy then became to win enough primaries to drive McCarthy out of the race and impress the delegates that he was the party's best hope in November. "We have to write off the unions and the South now, and replace them with Negroes, blue-collar whites, and the kids," he said.[90] But because the first primary he could enter was on May 7 in Indiana, nearly two months away, Kennedy frantically took to the road to show party leaders that he at least could attract big crowds. In the second half of March alone, Kennedy campaigned in sixteen states. He hit Johnson hard at an early appearance in Los Angeles, accusing the president of "calling on the darker impulses of the American spirit." But after getting that out of his system Kennedy ran a mostly upbeat, positive campaign.[91] He used some of his brother's rhetorical flourishes ("We can do better") but for the most part accented issues he had become passionate about as a senator: Vietnam, of course, but also hunger, the exploitation of migrant labor, the plight of Native Americans, law and order, racial justice, and finding nonbureaucratic solutions to poverty—none of which he credited McCarthy or Johnson with caring about. A late March Gallup Poll showed that even though Democratic voters preferred Johnson to McCarthy by 59 percent to 29 percent, they backed Kennedy over the president by 44 percent to 41 percent.[92] Yet on March 24, the *New York Times* reported that McCarthy and Kennedy combined had a projected 790 delegates while Johnson had a projected 1,725—413 more than the 1,312 he needed for the nomination.

JOHNSON GETS OUT

Johnson enjoyed being president when Congress, the press corps, and the public supported him. The rejection from all these quarters that marked 1967 and promised to continue through 1968 made the job miserable. "I frankly did not believe in 1968 that I could survive another four years of the long hours and unremitting tensions I had just gone through," he later wrote.[93] Johnson's family history of short-lived men and his personal history of coronary ailments—two heart attacks in the 1950s—made him fear another attack that would kill him or, even worse, a stroke that would leave him incapacitated like Woodrow Wilson during his final eighteen months as president.

Nor did Johnson relish the prospect of campaigning all year long. Eight years earlier, he had refused to fight for the nomination, even though that meant he had no chance of winning. As president he was even less willing to campaign strenuously, especially knowing that his public appearances would be plagued by noisy protests and perhaps violence. "The president still traveled about the country," his aide Harry McPherson observed, "but from military bases to [American] Legion and farm conventions, using these like stepping-stones in a torrent."[94] If he won the nomination and the election, as Johnson thought he would, governing would be difficult because he would have to divert time from Vietnam and probably make dovish concessions, even some he thought would be militarily disastrous. Johnson convinced himself that not running would enable him to govern with bipartisan support and, taking the long view, would be the historically proper thing to do. "No other president who has served for part of a term, then for a full term, has ever succeeded himself for another full term," he began pointing out.[95]

Johnson was nonetheless torn about not running for reelection. Despite the relentless attacks on him from critics in the media, the Senate, JFK alumni, and the campuses, he "knew—I simply knew—that the American people loved me. After all that I'd done for them and given to them, how could they help but love me?"[96] He dreaded the thought that his most hated enemies—RFK, Richard Nixon, and Ho Chi Minh—would think they had beaten him. He asked longtime aide Horace Busby to write a withdrawal statement to append to his January 17, 1968, state of the union address, then pocketed it. "It just didn't fit," he explained to an aide. "I couldn't go in there and lay out a big program and then say, 'Okay, here's all this work to do, and by the way, so long. I'm leaving.'"[97] Two weeks later the Tet offensive began, further postponing any withdrawal lest it appear that the communists had him on the run. Johnson suffered from the postponement because once New Hampshire voted and Kennedy entered the race in mid-March, his withdrawal was bound to be interpreted as the result of his being driven out.

Not that this interpretation would be groundless. Johnson himself later said that Kennedy's entry was "the final straw. The thing I feared from the first day of my presidency was actually coming true. . . . And the American people, swayed by the magic of the name, were dancing in the streets. The whole situation was unbearable for me."[98] The whole situation included the primary in Wisconsin, where O'Brien told the president he would be "badly defeated" by McCarthy by "sixty-forty. Maybe two to one."[99] For that matter, the prospect for victory in any primary looked dubious, and in Nebraska and Oregon, which like Wisconsin automatically put the names of candidates on the ballot, there would be no masking the personal nature of the rejection by relying on a write-in campaign or running a local surrogate in his place. On March 30 Johnson learned that the next Gallup Poll would show him with a 35 percent approval rating, the lowest of his presidency. On that same day Busby pointed out that if he waited until Wisconsin voted just three days later, "it would look bad to quit after a defeat."[100]

Johnson also knew how precarious his policy toward Vietnam was. Wheeler and Westmoreland's request for 205,000 additional troops at the end of February had triggered a month-long review of the entire war in March. A task force headed by Clifford and composed of the administration's military and civilian national security leaders concluded that despite the ongoing bombing campaign and the crippling of the Vietcong ground forces, North Vietnam was infiltrating three to four times as many troops southward as it had the year before. The Joint Chiefs admitted that even if the president approved the generals' troop request, they had no plan for victory except to invade North Vietnam, which Johnson believed would pro-

On March 31, 1968, President Lyndon B. Johnson stunned the nation by announcing his withdrawal from the election at the end of a nationally televised speech on Vietnam. (Credit: Yoichi Okamoto, provided by the Lyndon B. Johnson Presidential Library)

voke China and the Soviet Union to enter the war. Sending 205,000 more troops to Vietnam meant adding another 306,000 to the ranks of active duty armed forces for support purposes, entailing a $10 billion addition to the fiscal 1969 budget.[101] Clifford wanted the United States to negotiate its way out of Vietnam, not get further involved, but with Rusk and Rostow dug in against him, he needed more leverage.

On March 25 Clifford, with the president's permission, assembled the same group of fourteen high-ranking foreign policy officials from recent administrations—the so-called wise men—that in November 1967 had strongly endorsed the president's conduct of the war. "Mr. President," recent national security adviser McGeorge Bundy said in a meeting the next day, "there has been a very significant shift in most of our positions since we last met." Former secretary of state Dean Acheson then spoke for a majority of the group, saying, "We can no longer do the job we set out to do in the time we have left, we must take steps to disengage."[102] For these men and the corporate leaders they moved among, national security was not just military but economic. Spending, especially on the war, was driving up prices to the extent that exports were down, considerable sums were being sent abroad, and the nation's trade balance with the booming economies of Western Europe was in free fall. Gold still backed the dollar, which made it the international currency of choice. But with gold flowing out of the country, the dollar's soundness was in question. Inflation, which had averaged 1.3 percent from 1961 to 1965, rose to 3.8 percent in the second half of 1967 and 4.4 percent in the first months of 1968. The dollar teetered in global markets and both the American and global economic systems with it. Only skillful maneuvering by the Treasury Department averted an immediate breakdown. Clearly reductions, not increases, in federal spending of all kinds, as well as a tax increase to slow the demand for imports, were needed to prevent "the most serious economic crisis since the Great Depression."[103] In June, after a legislative end run around Ways and Means chair Mills, Johnson finally got the tax increase he had requested the previous fall.

Johnson initially resisted the wise men's advice on the war, but then succumbed—if he lost this group, he could not hope to rally the nation for an escalation. He scheduled a televised prime-time address on Sunday, March 31, to announce a unilateral halt of the bombing in most areas of the North and to appoint Averell Harriman as his "personal representative" to "any forum, at any time, to discuss the means of bringing this ugly war to an end."[104] He asked Busby to add a passage announcing his withdrawal from the election and stopped by Humphrey's apartment that morning to tell the vice president, who was en route to Mexico, what might be coming. "Even if I should run and be reelected," Johnson told the weeping Humphrey, "I most likely would not live out my term."[105]

This time, unlike in January's state of the union address, Johnson stuck to his plan, knowing that if he did otherwise his peace offer would be dismissed as a political ploy aimed at the Wisconsin primary electorate. At the end of his forty-minute address Johnson declared that he "should not permit the Presidency to become involved in the partisan divisions that are developing in this political year" and then—changing "would not" to "will not"—added, "I shall not seek, and I will not accept, the nomination of my party for another term as president."[106] His poll ratings shot skyward and on April 3 Hanoi expressed a general willingness to negotiate. The early glow of optimism wore off, however, when negotiations bogged down in procedural haggling over matters such as where the parties would meet, who would participate, and even the shape of the negotiating table. Infuriated with the North Vietnamese, and with public attention still focused on his bombing halt, Johnson sent an additional fifty thousand troops to

Vietnam, raising the total to 536,000 by late summer. Nearly ten thousand Americans were killed in combat during the first six months of 1968, a few more than died in all of 1967. B-52 bombing missions tripled in 1968.

WISCONSIN AND THE KING ASSASSINATION

Like nearly everyone else, Robert Kennedy was surprised by and un-prepared for Johnson's announcement. What was the purpose of his cam-paign now that the president had withdrawn, the bombing had stopped, and peace negotiations seemed to be on the horizon? Kennedy's immediate reaction was that with the president out of the race he might be able to sew up the nomination by securing endorsements from Daley, Gov. Richard Hughes of New Jersey, Pittsburgh mayor Joseph Barr, and other big-state party leaders. He found once again that he was wrong—they were waiting on Humphrey to declare. Not a single governor and hardly any congress-men endorsed Kennedy, and only two of his Senate colleagues did: Joseph Tydings of Maryland and Stephen Young of Ohio. Fence-sitting antiwar vot-ers who might have backed Kennedy if they thought he was the only one who could beat Johnson now had no reason not to support McCarthy.

McCarthy, although just as surprised and unprepared as Kennedy, had two advantages over him. First, McCarthy was the giant killer, the one po-litical leader who had the courage to challenge the president when he ap-peared unbeatable and the war when it seemed unstoppable. "We could not believe that we, a group of young, inexperienced students, had helped engi-neer the downfall of the world's most powerful politician," said McCarthy supporter Ben Stavis—but led by McCarthy they had.[107] Second, McCarthy was on the ballot in Wisconsin, where the extent of his triumph would be confirmed by the electorate.

McCarthy had three weeks to campaign in Wisconsin after his victory in New Hampshire, and he took advantage of every day. His organization in the state was, if anything, even better than in New Hampshire. Volunteers canvassed about 1.3 million homes. McCarthy later claimed, rightly, that "there has never been a campaign in the history of this country in which persons below the voting age were as extensively and directly and effec-tively involved as they were in the campaign of 1968."[108] Volunteer leaders, who were older than the student workers, were similarly concentrated in schools and on campuses: one national survey found that 31 percent were college professors or administrators, and another 14 percent were elemen-tary or secondary schoolteachers or administrators.[109]

Wisconsin's Democratic primary, unlike New Hampshire's, was open—

Republicans and independents could vote in it. When Rockefeller announced on March 21 that he was not running for the Republican nomination, McCarthy urged Rocky's supporters to cross over and vote for him. The one discordant note for McCarthy involved black neighborhoods, especially in Milwaukee, the state's largest city. McCarthy was reluctant to campaign in them, knowing that all the other candidates—Johnson, Kennedy, and Humphrey if it came to that—had stronger claims on African American voters than he did. When some of his supporters objected (press secretary Seymour Hersh actually quit in protest), McCarthy rhetorically swung to the opposite extreme, using uncalibrated language in a speech condemning "white racism."[110] Even then, he appeared passionless, due as much to his temperament and demeanor as to any lack of commitment.

McCarthy lost Milwaukee's black wards to Johnson by two to one, while winning the primary 412,160 to 253,696—56.2 percent to 34.6 percent, with 46,507 write-in votes (6.3 percent) for Kennedy. He swept fifty-two of Wisconsin's sixty delegates. It was a strong victory, but perhaps not as strong as if Johnson had stayed in the race. In any event Johnson's withdrawal meant that McCarthy gained no momentum from winning. More to the point, McCarthy's days as a protest candidate were over. From this day forward, voters would be evaluating him as a potential president and, as with Kennedy, wanting to hear what he had to say about issues other than Vietnam and presidential overreach.

McCarthy's political difficulties were compounded and Kennedy's eased by the April 4 assassination of Martin Luther King in Memphis, where the civil rights leader had traveled to support sanitation workers in their strike against the city government for more pay and safer working conditions. In recent months King had been working to organize a cross-racial "poor people's march on Washington," and as William H. Chafe has pointed out, in the Memphis strike, "class and race operated together, dramatically illustrating the principal objectives of the entire Poor People's campaign."[111] King's murder took the steam out of the campaign, which wilted in midsummer.

The assassination triggered several days of rioting in 110 cities. "Now that they've taken Dr. King off," said Stokely Carmichael, "it's time to end this nonviolence bullshit."[112] All told thirty-nine died, about 2,500 were injured, and substantial swathes of black neighborhoods were burned to the ground. The worst disturbances were in Baltimore and Washington, where rioters came within two blocks of the White House.[113] The Secret Service held Vice President Humphrey's plane in New York because it could not guarantee safe passage to his office either in the Capitol or adjacent to the

White House, where, for the first time since the Civil War, soldiers were deployed in a ring of defense.

All of the candidates for president except Wallace issued statements of tribute and regret and attended King's funeral in Atlanta—even Nixon, whom King had described as a "tragic choice" for the GOP nomination weeks before his death.[114] But only Kennedy faced and addressed a black audience on the night of the assassination. The combination of racial injustice and rampant law-breaking that King's assassination represented was not one that McCarthy had much to say about. But it gave Kennedy the issues he needed to explain why he was still running for president in the first primary of his career.

"THE POLITICS OF HAPPINESS, . . . THE POLITICS OF JOY"

Humphrey's initial reaction when Johnson told him he wasn't running for reelection was fear that he would be out of a job. McCarthy's candidacy did not worry him. But "there's no way I can beat the Kennedys," Humphrey said, and he dreaded becoming "a punching bag for Kennedy, only to be humiliated and defeated in the convention."[115] Humphrey was still thinking about 1960, when he had no choice but to enter primaries and his campaign was woefully underfinanced because even his natural allies in labor thought his chances were minimal against John Kennedy and Lyndon Johnson.

But 1968 was dramatically different. AFL-CIO president George Meany and I. W. Abel, president of the United Steelworkers, endorsed Humphrey right away, as did several prominent Jewish leaders and Democratic businessmen, mayors, governors, congressmen, and party officials. "Never before," observed David Broder, "has the national labor federation become so openly involved at so early a stage in the fight for the Democratic presidential nomination."[116] Even southern Democrats embraced Humphrey as, if nothing else, the alternative to Kennedy. John McKeithen, the conservative white governor of Louisiana, and Carl Stokes, the African American mayor of Cleveland, both rallied to Humphrey—like him and the president, they were establishment Democrats. Money poured in from business, labor, and the South—this time it was a Kennedy who was gasping for funds, at least for the moment. (His father, Joseph P. Kennedy, bankrolled JFK's campaign in 1960, but was incapacitated by a permanently disabling stroke a year later.) "Bob Kennedy was not going to run away with the nomination," a delighted Humphrey realized after making and receiving dozens of phone calls from politicians in Washington and around the country.[117]

Nor did Humphrey have anything to gain by entering primaries this time around, a fact that was brought home when McCarthy won the April 23 Pennsylvania primary with 71.7 percent of the vote but received only twenty-one of the state's 103 delegates. The rest, many of whom had already been chosen, supported Humphrey at the urging of Mayor Barr of Pittsburgh and Mayor James Tate of Philadelphia. With no need to rush, Humphrey had ample opportunity to build a strong organization and develop a sound strategy. Unfortunately he did neither of these things. Unlike Kennedy and McCarthy, Humphrey had given no thought to running for anything other than reelection as vice president and, because his role in the campaign would have been determined entirely by the president, he devoted little thought even to that. Not realizing that he had no chance of luring young voters away from McCarthy and Kennedy, Humphrey appointed two junior senators, Walter F. Mondale of Minnesota, forty, and Fred Harris of Oklahoma, thirty-seven, as cochairs of his national campaign. Neither of them was young, cool, or antiwar enough to appeal to youth; neither was experienced in national elections; neither liked sharing the job with the other; and both had full-time responsibilities in the Senate.

The result was an organizational void that was filled by old Humphrey friends such as Max Kampelman, Orville Freeman, Robert Short, and Edgar Berman, who feuded endlessly among themselves. Humphrey's vice presidential staff was not much help. "One of the problems Humphrey had," said George Ball, "was that he had a lot of second-rate people around him. It's almost implicit in the job of vice president that he can't get good staff because he really has nothing important to do."[118] Nor did it help matters that even though Humphrey told Mondale that he and Harris had "carte blanche," he also said he would "meddle . . . as much as necessary" and had, according to Mondale, "about 800 informal campaign managers."[119]

Humphrey's basic strategic dilemma was whether—and, if so, how—to put some distance between himself and Johnson. Any incumbent vice president seeking the presidency faces this quandary in some form. Separating oneself from the president appears unattractively disloyal, but binding oneself to the president prevents one from displaying the qualities of strength and independence that voters value in the presidency.[120] In addition to the intrinsic institutional dilemma, Humphrey had Lyndon Johnson to deal with. In an acutely perverse manifestation of the age-old tension between mentors and protégés, Johnson wanted Humphrey to succeed him in the abstract but not in any practical sense. When Johnson heard that Secretary of Agriculture Freeman had endorsed his old friend and fellow Minnesotan, for example, he ordered Califano to tell the entire cabinet to "stay out of the race or get out of the government."[121] Johnson also hoped that, perhaps because of a breakthrough in Vietnam, the Democratic convention, timed to coincide with his birthday in late August, might turn to him. Such an event would spare Johnson the pains of a nomination campaign while launching him triumphantly into the general election.

Johnson had grown used to Humphrey's uncritical and enthusiastic championing of the administration's policies in Vietnam and made clear that even the smallest deviation from that approach, the most modest suggestion that he might do things differently, would bring down the president's wrath. In truth, both Humphrey, who had always been a staunch anticommunist, and the groups supporting his candidacy already supported the war, especially labor leaders and southerners. For reasons of conviction and politics, Humphrey dismissed a suggestion from Gov. Harold Hughes of Iowa and Vermont governor Philip Hoff that he resign as vice president so he could speak his own mind. Humphrey did not understand why Johnson was doing nothing to help him, not even in private, but he thought he had no choice—and most of the time, wanted none—other than to bind himself to the president and his policies at least until the convention.

Humphrey had to announce his candidacy sometime, and he eventually decided on April 27, well past the filing date for any primary. After delivering a polished, effective announcement speech to an enthusiastic crowd at Washington's Shoreham Hotel, Humphrey got caught up in the exultation of the moment and ad-libbed: "Here we are, the way politics ought to be in America, the politics of happiness, the politics of purpose, the politics of joy."[122] In the month of King's assassination and the post-assassination riots, with Americans dying in Vietnam at a rate of 315 per week, this remark, which was pure Humphrey, struck exactly the wrong note. As the *New Republic*'s Richard Strout, who regarded Humphrey as a "warmhearted, likable man," observed, "Sometimes he wows audiences and then won't stop. . . . He is like a mad vending machine: insert a dime and you get your peanut bar, and then another, and another. There is no stopping it. It rains peanut bars."[123]

None of this prevented Humphrey from becoming the instant front-runner for the Democratic nomination. In April and May, he won delegate caucuses and conventions in Delaware, Arkansas, Hawaii, Arizona, Maryland, Nevada, New Jersey, Missouri, Maine, and Vermont, with unions providing most of the organizational muscle. A *Newsweek* survey showed him with 1,280 delegates, only 32 fewer than he needed to be nominated, and

CBS News estimated that he had 1,483, which was 171 more than required. *Time* reported in early May that Humphrey enjoyed a four-to-one majority among his party's members of Congress. Both the Gallup and Harris Polls showed Humphrey in the lead with Democratic voters.[124] Equally encouraging, the personal animosity McCarthy and Kennedy felt toward each other and toward the president did not extend to Humphrey, despite his support for the war. "The worst thing about all this," said Kennedy, "is that we're in a fight with Hubert Humphrey. He's a great guy."[125] Kennedy's benign opinion of the vice president was not reciprocated; Humphrey was still mad about "bad Bobby's" treatment of him in 1960. But Humphrey clearly regarded Kennedy as the more serious rival for the nomination, and even urged some of his financial supporters to quietly give money to the McCarthy campaign in Oregon and California to undermine Kennedy.

INDIANA

Johnson's original plan for the May 7 Indiana primary was the same as in 1964: have the governor of the state—Matthew Welsh then, Roger Branigin now—appear on the ballot as his surrogate so that he could remain at least nominally above the political fray. The plan worked well enough in 1964, insulating Johnson to some extent from the embarrassment attending Wallace's success in winning 29.8 percent of the Democratic primary vote. In 1968, however, Johnson's withdrawal left Branigin on the ballot as neither fish nor fowl—not a presidential candidate or even a favorite son in the usual sense, but not a stand-in for someone else, either. Branigin was widely assumed to be for Humphrey, but the vice president did not campaign for the governor's slate and the governor did not endorse him. Branigin stayed in the race because he was already on the ballot, did not want to see an antiwar candidate prevail, and hoped that by winning he might earn himself the vice presidential nomination. Indiana was "the mother of four vice presidents and could be the mother of a fifth," he declared.[126] The *Indianapolis Star*, the state's largest morning paper, ran a totally inaccurate piece saying that Humphrey was seriously considering Branigin as a running mate.

In addition to whatever excitement attended the prospect of a Vice President Branigin (not much, even if people believed it), support from the *Star*, owned along with the evening *Indianapolis News* by the conservative Republican Eugene Pulliam, was one of two advantages the governor enjoyed against McCarthy and Kennedy. The other was the state Democratic organization, one of the last in the country whose seven thousand patronage appointees were each responsible for kicking back 2 percent of their government salary to the party. These advantages were worth less than met the eye, however. Branigin had neglected the party organization, not repaying favors in the expected way, and because he was term-limited in 1968, he was about to become yesterday's news. Pulliam, supportive as he was, was more interested in stopping Kennedy than promoting Branigin. "I think whenever Senator McCarthy comes to Indiana that we should give him as full coverage as possible," Pulliam told his editors, "but that does not apply to a man named Kennedy."[127]

McCarthy did not list Indiana as a primary he planned to enter when he announced his candidacy in November. Riding the momentum of his triumphs in New Hampshire and Wisconsin and wanting to defeat Kennedy head to head as soon as possible, he changed his mind. In addition to respectful coverage by the Pulliam newspapers, he had quiet financial support from pro-Humphrey unions, who shared his desire to smother Kennedy's candidacy in its crib. McCarthy's attacks on Kennedy were mostly indirect. In New Hampshire he had criticized the government's Vietnam policy since 1963—that is, since Johnson became president. In Indiana he began focusing his attacks on the preceding three years, stressing the origins of the Vietnam War in the Kennedy administration. "Any man who played a prominent role in developing the policies of the early sixties, I think, can be called upon to explain his role in those policies," he charged. This represented not just a change in tactics but also in opinion for McCarthy, who earlier had said that America was "approaching the ideal in the years from '62 and '63," having "mastered the problems of the economy" and "begun . . . to develop a kind of restrained attitude toward the rest of the world."[128] McCarthy also repeatedly promised to fire J. Edgar Hoover, a promise he assumed Robert Kennedy could not make because Hoover knew too much about President Kennedy's sexual relationship with Judith Campbell, a lover he shared with Mafia boss Sam Giancana.

But McCarthy did not adapt well to Johnson's withdrawal. Except for obliquely incorporating the Kennedys into his indictment of the war, he did not adjust his stump speech to the fact that Johnson was no longer running. With the president out of the race, student volunteers no longer flocked to the McCarthy campaign in the same numbers or with the same urgency. Instead of concentrating on Indiana's suburbs, where his natural appeal to educated reform Democrats was greatest, McCarthy followed an oddly rural strategy in scheduling his appearances. Even in small towns, his campaigning was desultory and a bit disdainful. "They kept talking about the poet out there," McCarthy later said. "I asked if they were talking about Shakespeare or my friend Robert Lowell. But it was [the once-popular 'Hoosier Poet'] James Whitcomb Riley. You could hardly be expected to win under those circumstances."[129] Some staff members, including organizer Ben Stavis, began wondering "whether we really wanted Eugene McCarthy to be president," considering the lack of interest he showed in his own effort and its degeneration into "essentially an anti-Kennedy campaign."[130] Jeremy Larner, a speechwriter, found "even more disturbing . . . McCarthy's tendency to single out those campaign people who shared the propensity to grovel" and to shut out those who spoke frankly to him.[131]

Like McCarthy, Kennedy did not originally plan to compete in Indiana but became convinced that he needed to engage his opponent quickly and directly. Once in, however, he realized, "Indiana is the ballgame. This is my West Virginia"—that is, a conservative, Protestant, heartland state like the one whose primary his brother won in 1960 on similarly uncongenial political terrain.[132] Kennedy's first appearance in Indiana was at a scheduled rally in a black neighborhood in Indianapolis on what turned out to be the night of the King assassination. Kennedy had his own reasons to fear assassination—"There are guns between me and the White House," he once said—but refused to succumb to them.[133] Ignoring advice from Mayor Richard Lugar and the chief of police to cancel the rally, Kennedy went anyway, his wary police escort peeling off at the edge of the ghetto.

Many in the crowd had not heard what happened to King; they got the news only when Kennedy told them. In a remarkable, spontaneous six-minute speech, Kennedy said,

> For those of you who are black—considering the evidence there evidently is that there were white people who were responsible—you can be filled with bitterness, with hatred, and a desire for revenge. . . . Or we can make an effort, as Martin Luther King did, to understand and to comprehend, and to replace that violence, that stain of bloodshed that has spread across our land, with an effort to understand with compassion and love.

He then said, "I had a member of my family killed"—something he almost never mentioned in public—and, from memory, quoted Aeschylus. "He wrote: 'In our sleep, pain which cannot forget falls drop by drop upon the heart until, in our own despair, against our will, comes wisdom through the awful grace of God.' . . . Let us dedicate ourselves to what the Greeks wrote so many years ago: to tame the savageness of man and to make gentle

A campaign poster for Sen. Robert F. Kennedy, who won all but one Democratic primary before being assassinated on June 4, 1968. (Credit: Poster produced by Posters, Inc., 214 Maple St., Holyoke, Mass. 01040, www.postersinc.com)

the life of this world."[134] More than a hundred cities rioted when King died, and across the country 21,000 federal troops and 34,000 National Guardsmen were called out, the largest military deployment for a civil emergency in the nation's post–Civil War history. But in Indianapolis the crowd somberly, peacefully dispersed.

With Johnson no longer a candidate and McCarthy as opposed to the war as he was, Kennedy stressed two other issues inspired by the King assassination and ensuing riots: racial justice and his record as a law-enforcing attorney general, a record that seemed all the more impressive when wedded to his apparent ability to forestall violence in Indianapolis. Kennedy had the black vote sewn up, but he still insisted on talking about issues of race, poverty, and hunger to well-to-do audiences. When an Indiana University medical student asked him, "Where are you going to get all the money for these federally subsidized programs you're talking about?" Kennedy replied, "From you. . . . You sit here as white medical students, while the black people carry the burden of the fighting in Vietnam."[135] Speaking to the Civitan, a business club, in Vincennes, Kennedy talked about "*American children, starving in America,*" and asked, "Do you know there are more rats than people in New York City?" Laughter erupted, and Kennedy turned on his audience: "*Don't. Laugh.*"[136]

Kennedy was willing to preach but eager to win. White voters "don't want to listen to what the blacks want and need," he told reporter Jules Witcover. "You have to get them listening by talking about what they're interested in before you can persuade them about other matters."[137] Kennedy cut his shaggy hair—the source of thousands of complaints to his campaign—and stressed the law-and-order half of his message, which had the added advantage of implicitly contrasting his service as attorney general with McCarthy's complete lack of executive experience. Three new campaign advisers—Richard Goodwin, who left the McCarthy campaign on April 7; Lawrence O'Brien, who resigned from Johnson's cabinet to work for Kennedy on April 10; and John Bartlow Martin, a Hoosier and former Stevenson campaign aide—urged Kennedy not just to mention but to stress his record as "chief law enforcement officer of the United States"—so much so that in California Republican governor Ronald Reagan quipped that Kennedy was "talking more and more like me."[138]

Kennedy developed an argument in Indiana that the nation's ghettos could be revitalized through "tax incentives to harness the vast resources of private enterprise," a phrase he used repeatedly in speeches.[139] This represented a nonbureaucratic approach to fighting poverty that Kennedy had long believed in and ardently promoted in Brooklyn's Bedford-Stuyvesant neighborhood—in contrast to the New Deal and Great Society liberals of his party who reflexively equated private enterprise with selfishness and government with nobility. It also carried the political advantage of appealing to African Americans interested in black self-determination, businessmen interested in tax breaks, and whites wanting ghettos to prosper so that blacks would stay there. Asked by British interviewer David Frost to name "the historical character . . . you most admire," Kennedy listed four, all Republicans: Abraham Lincoln, Theodore Roosevelt, Herbert Hoover, and Charles Lindbergh.[140]

The results of the Indiana primary were both heartening and disheartening for Kennedy. He outpolled Branigin by 42.3 percent to 30.7 percent, an 89,418-vote margin, with McCarthy trailing at 27.0 percent. He also earned the votes of fifty-six of Indiana's sixty-three delegates on the first ballot. Kennedy received 86 percent of the state's black vote. According to a postprimary instant analysis by political columnists Rowland Evans and Robert D. Novak, he even carried the blue-collar white vote in Gary, a conclusion touted by Kennedy staffers as evidence of his ability to bridge racial divisions and accepted by the *New York Times,* which said that Kennedy had assembled "an unusual coalition of Negroes and lower income whites."[141]

In truth, Robert Kennedy's victory in Indiana was more like John Kennedy's 1960 win in Wisconsin than in West Virginia: a decision, but not a knockout. McCarthy treated Indiana as if he had won, claiming that in November any Democrat would carry the blacks and blue-collar workers who voted for Kennedy but that only he could pull educated, middle-class suburbanites away from the Republicans.[142] *Times* columnist Tom Wicker wrote that McCarthy had "done the most to advance his own cause" because he and Branigin had held Kennedy below 50 percent.[143] Kennedy could not believe it—"He finished last!"[144] Nor could he fathom McCarthy's concession speech, in which he claimed that speaking one's mind was more important than winning. "That's not the way I was brought up," Kennedy said. "We were brought up to win."[145] Even less heartening for Kennedy was the follow-up analysis of the results that showed he actually carried only eleven of Gary's seventy white precincts. Worst of all, Indiana's delegates were pledged to him for just one ballot. Chosen by Branigin's organization, they were inclined to break for Humphrey as soon as they could.

Kennedy's first-place finish in Indiana was joined with a victory that same day in the District of Columbia, where he defeated a slate pledged to Humphrey, who refused to compete, by 62.5 percent to 37.5 percent. McCarthy had won on the previous two Tuesdays in Pennsylvania (April 23) and Massachusetts (April 30), but only the latter earned him many delegates. Kennedy took his campaign to Nebraska the week after Indiana. Although by law McCarthy's name also was on the ballot, he did not take the bait, preferring to make his stand in Oregon on May 28 in hopes of gaining momentum for the California primary one week later. On May 14 Kennedy polled 51.7 percent in Nebraska, his first majority victory and in a state that was only 2 percent African American. McCarthy received 31.2 percent but because he had made no effort, his showing was once again interpreted by the press corps as better than expected.

OREGON

Except for Wisconsin, every contested primary from March 12 to May 14 was in a Republican state: New Hampshire, Indiana, Nebraska. The final two primaries would take place in competitive and, in the case of California with its forty electoral votes, strategically important states in the general election.

Everything went wrong for Kennedy in Oregon, mostly because of his own mistakes and miscalculations, starting with the appointment of Rep. Edith Green to run his campaign there. Eight years earlier, when her energy level and political connections were greater, Green had been John Kennedy's point person in Oregon; this time around she was one of the very few members of Congress to support Robert Kennedy. When Green volunteered to run things again, Kennedy offhandedly accepted the offer. Thinking that momentum from Indiana and Nebraska would see him through in Oregon, he also sent his best political staff to California or New York, which kept him from realizing how poorly organized he was in Oregon until too late.

Oregon was a fundamentally weak state for Kennedy. One percent black and 10 percent Catholic, with few Latinos or even ethnic whites, its middle-class, well-educated population was perfectly suited for McCarthy. "There were no bloc votes," said McCarthy, meaning no large ethnic, racial, religious, labor, or other traditionally Democratic groups in Oregon.[146] "This state is like one giant suburb," was Kennedy's unhappy assessment.[147] Yet, foolishly, he doubled down instead of writing off Oregon as McCarthy had written off Nebraska. Kennedy campaigned intensely and a week before the primary said, "If I get beaten in a primary, I'm not a very viable candidate. . . . I have to win in Oregon."[148] Three days later, columnist Drew Pearson published a story, which was leaked to him by Johnson, reporting that as attorney general Kennedy had authorized the FBI to "bug" Martin Luther King. Kennedy's press secretary, Pierre Salinger, denied it, and technically he was correct: what Kennedy approved was wiretapping King's phones, not bugging his rooms. To most voters this was a distinction without a difference.

Kennedy continued to play into McCarthy's hands, refusing to debate for fear of elevating him to Kennedy-level stature. This may have been a shrewd ploy in most places, but it offended Oregon's educated voters, who expected candidates to debate. On May 25 McCarthy went to the Portland Zoo in anticipation of Kennedy's scheduled arrival in order to press his demand for a debate in person. When Kennedy arrived and found that McCarthy was just fifty yards away, he said, "Let's get out of here" to an aide and beat a hasty retreat.[149] Before he could escape his car was temporarily blocked by three McCarthy staffers shouting "Chicken! Coward!" allowing television cameras to record the whole episode. For Kennedy, who placed such a premium on physical courage, the spectacle was mortifying. On primary day, McCarthy prevailed by 44.0 percent to 38.0 percent, the first defeat at the polls ever suffered by a Kennedy after twenty-seven consecutive victories and, as Kennedy aides despaired, a guarantee that no matter what happened in California McCarthy would remain in the race all the way to the convention.

CALIFORNIA

As drama, California was for Democrats in 1968 what the state had been for Republicans in 1964: the last confrontation between the two remaining primary candidates and the one with the largest prize—174 delegates, winner-take-all, more than had been at stake in all the preceding primaries combined. Arguably, however, the California primary was a sideshow shoved onto center stage. As McCarthy and Kennedy fought for the allegiance of California's Democratic voters, Humphrey continued to lock up the great majority of delegates chosen outside the media gaze, in local conventions and small gatherings of state party leaders. To be sure, a slate originally pledged to Johnson and then to Humphrey was on the California ballot, headed by state attorney general Thomas Lynch. Union money was raised and spent on Humphrey's behalf instead of being channeled at his direction to McCarthy, as was the case earlier in the primary season. But Humphrey did not campaign in California, any more than he did in Indiana, Nebraska, or Oregon. Instead, confident that he had the nomination in hand, Humphrey now hoped for a decisive Kennedy victory, which he expected would dry up McCarthy's financial and volunteer support and force him to drop out of the race. Humphrey was convinced that Kennedy would campaign for him in the fall, thereby reuniting the party. He had no such confidence in McCarthy.

Kennedy looked at California differently, counting on victory there to propel him to the nomination. Except for eight days in Oregon, Kennedy had been campaigning full-time in California since May 11, spending part of each day in northern California and part in the south in order to attract daily television coverage throughout the state. As in Indiana, he benefited from strong backing in the African American community. What was different about California was the large number of Latino voters, who were especially drawn to Kennedy by his enduring support for Cesar Chavez, the leader of the United Farm Workers, the union of migrant laborers. Open-car motorcades through city streets in minority neighborhoods attracted frenzied crowds of admirers, who tore off Kennedy's ties and cuff links—even his shoes—and rubbed his hands raw in their zeal to touch him. Kennedy, never one to eschew support from party regulars when he could get it, relied on California assembly speaker Jesse Unruh to mobilize his effective Los Angeles County Democratic organization on primary day.

For weeks the polls had shown Kennedy with a strong lead in California. Unlike McCarthy, he had run and won a tough race in a large state in 1964, when he had been elected to the Senate from New York. But McCarthy gained momentum from his victory in Oregon just seven days before the primary. As in other states, McCarthy relied on California's college students, educators, and suburban liberals; he also enjoyed considerable support in deep-pocketed Hollywood. He gave two major speeches in California designed to sharpen the distinction between him and Kennedy. Concerning foreign policy, McCarthy argued on May 21 in San Francisco that the war in Vietnam was the culmination of policies long supported by John Kennedy, Robert Kennedy, and Hubert Humphrey. "We did not wake up one morning and find ourselves with half a million men in that part of the world, just by chance," he said. "It was no departure from the kind of diplomacy which we had been following up to that time."[150] On domestic policy, McCarthy argued a week later at the University of California at Davis that Robert Kennedy's proposal "to offer programs for the ghetto alone is another form of paternalism. . . . The ghetto may have a few more factories and a few more jobs, but it will remain a colony."[151] Kennedy's tireless campaigning meant that he was on television more than McCarthy, which was crucial in a state where voters learned much more about candidates from the media than from grassroots organizations. But McCarthy's cool, reasonable demeanor when he did appear on news programs may have done him more good than footage of Kennedy being mobbed by wild-eyed crowds.

As in Oregon, McCarthy challenged Kennedy to a televised debate. This time Kennedy had no choice but to agree. "Conditions have changed," he explained. "I'm not the same candidate I was before Oregon and I can't claim that I am."[152] The candidates appeared together on June 1, the Saturday before the primary, on a special nationally televised evening edition of the ABC News Sunday morning program *Issues and Answers*. Kennedy prepared intensively, McCarthy barely at all, and during the debate McCarthy was so subdued that he appeared less cool than cold, even indifferent. The crucial exchange between the candidates came when McCarthy, once again trying to make up with strong rhetoric for his lack of affinity with black voters, said, "We have to get [ghetto dwellers] out into the suburbs. . . . Otherwise, we are adopting a kind of apartheid in this country." Kennedy pounced: "You say you are going to take 10,000 black people and move them into [suburban] Orange County."[153] Kennedy's long-standing position was, as he said in early 1966, that it was "important that the vast majority of Negroes be enabled to achieve basic financial and social security where they live now," with the unemployed put to work rebuilding their neighborhoods.[154] But in this context he was clearly appealing to white suburbanites who did not want blacks moving any closer. McCarthy let Kennedy's distortion of his statement pass, and by a two-to-one margin voters who saw the debate thought Kennedy won it.

Kennedy was desperate to prevail in California and thereby persuade McCarthy's supporters "that I'm the only candidate against the war that can beat Humphrey." "Humphrey's running around the country picking up delegates," he told aides with understandable impatience. "My only chance is to chase Hubert's ass all over the country."[155] As the returns came in on primary night, it was clear that although McCarthy carried northern California—the part of the state closest to and most like Oregon—Kennedy won everywhere else. In the final tally, Kennedy received 46.3 percent of the 3,181,753 votes that were cast; McCarthy 41.8 percent, 142,865 fewer than Kennedy; and the pro-Humphrey Lynch slate 12.0 percent. Victory was sweet, but not reaching 50 percent was a disappointment: it neither relegated McCarthy to the sidelines nor sent a clear message to state party leaders that Kennedy was a better choice than Humphrey.

Worse for Kennedy, the New York primary loomed on June 18. The primary was a byzantine affair: delegates were elected by district, and nothing on the ballot told voters which candidates for delegate supported which candidates for president. Victory in the state Kennedy represented in the Senate was by no means assured. Kennedy had spent as little time with New York's Democratic politicians as possible, and because of Johnson's animus, "his power to recommend appointments was more severely limited than any Democrat in the Senate."[156] "There's a general feeling among the pols," O'Brien reported to the other leaders of the Kennedy campaign, "that Bob has paid little attention to them."[157] As for reform Democrats and their favorite newspaper, the earnestly liberal *New York Post,* they had signed on early with McCarthy, fondly recalling that he supported their hero, Adlai Stevenson, in 1960 while Kennedy was pushing Stevenson aside. "I don't want to stand on every street corner in New York for the next two weeks," Kennedy lamented.[158]

As the votes were counted in California, Kennedy told Goodwin to tell McCarthy that "if he withdraws now and supports me, I'll make him secretary of state."[159] He then declared victory to a joyous crowd of followers in the Embassy Room of the Ambassador Hotel in Los Angeles. Kennedy also was excited that he handily won that day's primary in South Dakota, drawing massive support from the state's Indian reservations. "And now on to Chicago!" he cried, wishing away both New York and the nearly three-month slog until the convention.

Kennedy normally exited election-night ballrooms through the crowd, and that is where his bodyguards began clearing a path as soon as he concluded his remarks in the Embassy Room. But on this night he cut through the kitchen, taking the quicker route to the area where he planned to meet the press. While in the kitchen passageway, Kennedy was shot by Sirhan Sirhan, a twenty-four-year-old Palestinian immigrant who resented Kennedy's support of Israel. Wounds from a .22 caliber revolver usually are not fatal, but one of the three bullets that hit Kennedy crashed through the soft tissue behind his right ear and lodged fatally in his brain. Kennedy was pronounced dead at 1:44 a.m. PDT on Thursday, June 6. Johnson's bitterness extended to asking Secretary of Defense Clifford why Kennedy's family thought they could bury him—neither a president nor a war hero—in Arlington National Cemetery, near his brother. Clifford said that the president had the authority to make that call, and Johnson grudgingly acquiesced.

Would Kennedy have been nominated if he had lived? Philip Converse and colleagues are among those who think he could have won—and been elected in November. They argue that the public's broadly positive feelings about the candidate "suggest that Robert Kennedy might have won an election over Richard Nixon, and perhaps with even greater ease than he would have won his own party's nomination."[160] Converse's poll was taken after Kennedy was killed; surveys taken while he was still campaigning are inconclusive about what the public would have wanted. In May Gallup and Harris both polled the three-way contest between Humphrey, Kennedy, and McCarthy and found Humphrey ahead of Kennedy by either 9 (Gallup) or 11 (Harris) percentage points and Kennedy ahead of McCarthy by either 12 (Gallup) or 2 points (Harris).[161] On June 2 Gallup reported that Humphrey led Kennedy among Democratic county chairs by 70 percent to 16 percent. (McCarthy had 6 percent.) None of these polls reflected the results of the California primary, which surely would have boosted Kennedy, and no poll could gauge what might happen during the twelve weeks between the primary in early June and the convention in late August.

In any event, delegates, not voters, still nominated the presidential candidates in 1968. A memo prepared by Kennedy's staff on the day of the California primary reveals how steep a climb he faced.[162] The memo is a state-by-state analysis of where each convention delegation stood and where things needed to end up in order to secure the nomination for Kennedy. Currently, it estimated, Humphrey led with 994 delegates to Kennedy's 525.5 and McCarthy's 204, with 872 undecided. By most media accounts, this tally severely underestimated Humphrey's support, which generally was thought to be close to or above the 1,312 needed for nomination. The memo also assumed that Kennedy already had 132 of New York's 190 delegates, which, considering McCarthy's strength and Kennedy's weakness in the state, was optimistic bordering on fanciful. But even taking the tally at face value, it showed that to win the nomination, Kennedy would need nearly all of McCarthy's delegates, about ninety of Humphrey's, and more than 70 percent—all but 150—of the undecided. Possible? Yes, especially if polls started showing conclusively, which they had not yet come close to doing, that Humphrey would lose to Nixon and Kennedy would beat him. Likely? No. The convention's three main power bases—labor, the South, and the state party organizations—were all strongly for Humphrey and strongly against Kennedy.

REAGAN, ROMNEY, NIXON, ROCKEFELLER
THE REPUBLICAN BATTLE, ROUND ONE (AND WALLACE)

The Republican Party emerged from the 1966 midterm elections not just confident of its survival but strongly optimistic about its chances for regaining control of the White House in 1968. Within the GOP, moderates and liberals emerged from the elections equally optimistic about their chances for regaining control of the party.

Moderates were hopeful about 1968 for three reasons. One was their certainty that Republicans had learned their lesson from Sen. Barry Goldwater's landslide defeat and would ruefully return to the traditional eastern-dominated nominating process that had produced an unbroken line of centrist presidential nominees during the previous two decades: Wendell Willkie in 1940, Thomas E. Dewey in 1944 and 1948, Dwight D. Eisenhower in 1952 and 1956, and Richard Nixon in 1960. A second cause for optimism among moderate Republicans was how well their candidates had done in statewide elections in the midterm. With the exception of Ronald Reagan, the newly elected governor of California, all of the most frequently mentioned contenders for the presidential nomination who arose from the election were moderates or liberals: Nelson A. Rockefeller, the reelected governor of New York; George Romney, who won his second consecutive landslide reelection as governor of Michigan; Charles Percy, victorious over three-term incumbent Democratic senator Paul Douglas of Illinois—even potential favorite son candidates for president such as governors James Rhodes of Ohio and Raymond Shafer of Pennsylvania.

Finally, most moderates and liberals, led by Rockefeller, were ready to unite behind a single candidate: the attractive, energetic, successful Governor Romney. So, too, at least initially, were many Republican voters. In the first Gallup Poll taken after the midterm elections, Romney led with 39 percent, trailed by Nixon (31 percent), Reagan (8 percent), Rockefeller and Percy (tied with 5 percent), and Mayor John V. Lindsay of New York City (2 percent). In the Harris Poll conducted two weeks after the election, Romney led Lyndon B. Johnson 54 percent to 46 percent. No other Republican even came close. Nixon and Rockefeller both trailed Johnson by 8 percentage points and Reagan trailed him by 34 points. A March 1967 Gallup Poll confirmed Romney's eight-point lead while showing Nixon tied with the president.

Nixon's strength, as in 1960, was less ideological than organizational. A spring 1967 survey of Republican county chairs placed him well ahead of the other contenders in every region of the country. By campaigning for Republicans of all ideological stripes in 1966, he had buttressed his support among party regulars who cared above all about winning elections. Nixon's defeat by John F. Kennedy in 1960 and, especially, by Pat Brown in 1962, however, meant that he had much to prove about his viability as a candidate. He needed, Nixon acknowledged, to "enter all the primaries to prove that I *could* win," knowing that even one or two losses might cause Republican professionals to turn away from him as unelectable.[1] Using a baseball analogy, he told former Kansas congressman Robert Ellsworth, his campaign manager at the time, that he needed a good fielding average, not a good batting average—closer to 1.000 than to .300.[2] Still, the local pros' hearts were with Nixon; they were rooting for him to do well.

Nixon entered 1967 concerned about Romney, whom he regarded as "even money to get the nomination" because he was well financed and running strongly in the polls, but worried about Rockefeller.[3] "From my point of view," Nixon later wrote, "the most interesting question about Romney was whether Nelson Rockefeller was using him as a stalking horse for his own candidacy."[4] But, politically astute as he was, Nixon disregarded as too inexperienced and too conservative the political figure who in the end would pose the greatest threat to his nomination, Ronald Reagan. He also dismissed the hazard to his election posed by Gov. George C. Wallace of Alabama, whose own triumph in 1966—the election of his wife as governor in his stead—had launched his independent candidacy for president.

REAGAN

"There is no second level of national leaders on the right," wrote Robert J. Donovan in the aftermath of the 1964 election, "no obvious successor to the Goldwater mantle."[5] Reagan's smashing victory against Brown in 1966 changed that. It made him Goldwater's heir. The question was when, not whether, Reagan would seek the Republican presidential nomination.

Reagan repeatedly pledged during his campaign for governor that he would not run for president in 1968 but refused to rule out accepting a draft. During most of his first year in office he did nothing to discourage conservatives who were inclined to issue such a call. In February 1967 Reagan announced that he would be California's favorite-son candidate at the Republican convention, locking up all eighty-six of its delegates, second only to New York's ninety-two. His stated purpose was to avoid a divisive Republican primary fight like the one between Goldwater and Rockefeller in 1964, but when the secretaries of state of Wisconsin, Nebraska, and Oregon said they intended to place him on their states' 1968 primary ballots he said it would be "arrogant" to tell them not to. In June Reagan addressed the Young Republican national convention in Omaha, where the meeting hall was plastered with "Reagan in '68" banners, posters, and bumper stickers. Responding to invitations, he made extensive speaking tours through the Mountain West, Midwest (including primary states Wisconsin and Nebraska), and South, raising about $1.5 million for the party. In California Reagan governed from the center on most issues, including a massive increase in sales, income, corporate, and excise taxes that he signed into law in 1967. But he fed rhetorical red meat to the right, decrying the typical campus protester at Berkeley and elsewhere as someone "who dresses like Tarzan, has hair like Jane, and smells like Cheetah."[6]

Reagan was surefooted before any audience, anywhere. His out-of-state appearances as governor simply continued what he had been doing for the previous fifteen years: traveling the country as a spokesman for General Electric and a leading crusader for the Goldwater campaign and other conservative causes. His main subject had always been national, not California, issues. On May 15, 1967, Reagan bested Sen. Robert F. Kennedy so thoroughly in a prime-time nationally televised debate on Vietnam that afterward Kennedy wheeled on an aide and demanded, "Who the fuck got me into this?"[7] But Reagan's strategy of remaining open to a presidential campaign without committing to one was derailed on October 31, when investigative columnist Drew Pearson charged that for six months Reagan had tolerated the presence of a "homosexual ring" in the California governor's office—in contrast to President Lyndon B. Johnson, Pearson added, who had removed his closest aide, Walter Jenkins, from the White House staff in 1964 as soon as he was arrested for soliciting sex from another man. Pearson's charge was a wild exaggeration. Reagan's chief of staff, Phil

Battaglia, had been identified by other aides as homosexual and had hired a young scheduler who was also gay, but that was it. Reagan dismissed them shortly after being told about the situation in late August.[8] But in the political climate of the day, as intolerant of homosexual relations as it was tolerant of heterosexual promiscuity, Reagan's immediate presidential hopes suffered from what would have been a national scandal if he had chosen to run.[9]

ROMNEY

Moderate and liberal Republicans were convinced that they erred in 1964 by not uniting behind a single candidate. Rockefeller, former senator and vice presidential nominee Henry Cabot Lodge, and Sen. Margaret Chase Smith of Maine had divided the votes of Republicans opposed to Goldwater, allowing him to sail to the nomination on a strong conservative tailwind. In 1968 these Republicans intended to rally behind one candidate, a task made easier by Rockefeller's strong disavowal of interest in running. As the early poll results indicated, they had reason to believe that they had found the right person in Romney.

Romney's greatest political virtues contrasted nicely with the less attractive qualities that many voters associated with Nixon. The Michigan governor's integrity, sincerity, and moral uprightness shone brightly against the backdrop of Nixon's "Tricky Dick" reputation, as well as making Johnson's growing "credibility gap"—the divide between what the president said and what voters believed was true—seem wider. Unlike Nixon, Romney was a seasoned executive who in the private sector had saved American Motors and in the public sector had governed Michigan adroitly. Romney also had shown an ability to win votes from Democrats, an essential component of victory in strongly Democratic Michigan and, for that matter, in the Democrat-leaning United States, where Republicans had won only two of the previous nine presidential elections. As was the case with Reagan in California, Romney's success in passing a state income tax in 1967 was regarded by most conservatives as a responsible alternative to big government–style fiscal irresponsibility. And unlike Rockefeller, whom conservatives loathed for running against Goldwater, Romney was merely disliked for not endorsing him against Johnson.

Johnson thought Romney was the Republican with the best chance to beat him and looked for ways to undermine the governor. During the July 1967 riot in Detroit he found one. Romney stubbornly refused to ask the president to send troops to quell the six-day disturbance because to do so

A campaign poster for Gov. George Romney, the early frontrunner for the Republican nomination. (Credit: Courtesy of the Library of Congress)

would mean admitting that the city was in a state of insurrection that he as governor had failed to quell. The two front-runners for their parties' presidential nominations fiddled while Detroit burned, to the detriment of both. Johnson finally dispatched ten thousand soldiers, ending the rioting. In announcing his decision on national television, he noted seven times that Romney had "been unable to bring the situation under control."

Inflexibility was a Romney weakness, but not the only one. He was an earnest but plodding orator who frequently misspoke or, especially when discussing Vietnam, vacillated between contradictory positions. Reporter Jack Germond said he wished his typewriter had a key that spelled out "Romney later explained" with one stroke.[10] He was a Mormon whose polygamous grandfather had led the family to Mexico, where Romney was born. Some questioned whether he was constitutionally qualified to be president. Did the "natural born Citizen" requirement in Article II, section 1, mean that the president had to be born on American soil or simply, as most scholars argued, be born of American parents?[11] Romney's extended family, spawned by his grandparents' many children, included 237 cousins. Finally, even though he had worked with labor leader Victor Reuther to desegregate housing in Detroit after a previous round of rioting in 1943, made

American Motors the only major employer in the state to push for fair employment legislation, and marched with Martin Luther King, Romney was politically tainted by his devout membership in a church that despite his efforts still banned African Americans from the priesthood.

Nixon was not the only one wondering whether Romney was merely a stalking horse for Rockefeller. Swearing that he was not a candidate, Rockefeller both endorsed Romney and provided him with much of the $1.5 million he eventually spent on his campaign, as well as with top-level staff (including foreign policy adviser Henry Kissinger), mailing services, and research. These were valuable assets but attached to a chain that Rockefeller could yank at any time.[12] Some speculated that Rockefeller's support was aimed not at helping Romney but at pricing other, younger moderate prospects out of the race—notably Senator Percy, Mayor Lindsay, and Sen. Mark Hatfield of Oregon, each of whom Rockefeller may have thought would be harder to push aside than Romney if he decided to run after all.

As a governor Romney knew he would have to establish credentials in foreign policy, an area in which Nixon and Johnson were experienced and he was not. In August 1967 he broke from Nixon as well as the president by calling the Vietnam War a "tragic mistake" and indicating that he would run as a peace candidate in 1968. This represented a major shift from Romney's previously steadfast support for the war, including a statement on April 7 that "it is unthinkable that the United States withdraw from Vietnam."[13] On August 28, the *Detroit Free Press* praised Romney's antiwar conversion in a full-page editorial headlined "Romney Starts to Emerge from the Vietnam Tangle." Saluting the governor for his change of mind, the editors noted in passing, "He appeared to be brain-washed by the military during his 1965 trip to the front."[14]

Three days later, on August 31, Romney videotaped an interview with Detroit television talk show host Lou Gordon to be aired on September 4, the debut of Gordon's new *Hot Seat* program. "Well, you know, when I came back from Vietnam in 1965," Romney said in answer to a question about the war, "I just had the greatest brainwashing that anybody can get when you go over to Vietnam. . . . And since returning from Vietnam . . . I have changed my mind in that particular. I no longer believe it was necessary for us to get involved in South Vietnam."[15] Gordon, who was eager to get his show into national syndication, sent a transcript of the interview to the *New York Times*. As Jonathan Alter has observed, Romney's comment was especially debilitating "in the wake of the novel and the movie *The Manchurian Candidate*, which depicted brainwashing of an American by North Koreans."[16]

National political reporters already doubted that Romney was up to the intellectual challenges of the presidency, but the canons of journalistic objectivity meant they could not simply say so in print or on the air. Armed with a statement that could be interpreted as evidence of guilelessness or even stupidity, however, they shined a bright spotlight on Romney's change of mind and portrayed it unfavorably instead of favorably, as the *Free Press* had done.[17] On September 5 the *Times* ran a story headlined "Romney Asserts He Underwent 'Brainwashing' on Vietnam Trip," and other news organizations picked up the item and spun it the same way. As part of the general mockery, Democratic senator Eugene McCarthy said, "I would have thought a light rinse would have done it."[18] The *Free Press*'s in-town rival, the *Detroit News*, noted that Romney had continued to support the war for two years after his 1965 trip and wondered, "How long does a brainwashing linger?"[19] The *News* called on him to "get out of the presidential race" in favor of Rockefeller.[20] Romney's support for the Republican nomination sank in the Gallup Poll from 24 percent in August to 14 percent in September. "I've never seen anything like it in all my years in politics," Nixon marveled. "One minute he's the frontrunner, the next he's down. Words are so very, very important."[21]

Refusing to be deterred, Romney formally announced his candidacy for president in Detroit on November 18, with Rockefeller still avowedly in his corner. "I don't want to be president," Rockefeller claimed after *Time* ran a cover story in its October 20, 1967, issue pitching a Rockefeller-Reagan ticket.[22] Attending a December meeting of Republican governors in December, however, Rockefeller let slip that he would accept a draft—a willingness that he repeated in February 1968 after headlining a Romney fund-raiser in Detroit. Much to Rockefeller's chagrin, Romney was quickly proving inadequate to the task of stopping Nixon. Much to Romney's disappointment, the flow of money, staff, and other promised resources from Rockefeller slowed to a trickle. "The day that Romney made that brainwashing remark," recalled one aide, "Kissinger packed up and . . . went out of there like a shot."[23]

NIXON

After being judged the big winner of the 1966 midterm elections because of his success as a campaigner for Republican candidates of all political stripes, as well as Johnson's backhanded anointing of him as the de facto leader of the GOP, Nixon shrewdly did the unexpected. Instead of continuing to dominate the Republican stage, he took a leave of absence from it. Losing elections in 1960 and 1962 had not been part of any master plan, but in 1967 and early 1968 Nixon was able to find the virtue of that defect. "I am going to take a holiday from politics for at least six months," he announced almost as soon as the midterm results were in, "with no political speeches scheduled whatsoever."[24] Nixon showed great restraint during this period, ceding the spotlight to Romney and gambling that the governor, being inexperienced in the national political arena, would suffer rather than benefit from his status as the undisputed front-runner. "Let 'em chew on Romney for a while," Nixon told speechwriter Pat Buchanan.[25]

Nixon's political advantages in the presidential campaign were subtle. He had done this before, a huge edge for any candidate but especially one who, like Nixon, was willing to honestly evaluate what went wrong and what needed to be done differently. As someone who had been out of office for eight years, he had not had to cast any controversial votes or make any divisive decisions, a luxury that neither Romney, Rockefeller, Reagan, Percy, nor any other Republican officeholder enjoyed. Freed of public responsibilities, Nixon also was able between March and June 1967 to polish his foreign policy credentials by making extended tours of Europe and the Soviet Union, Asia, Latin America, and Africa and the Middle East, where his meetings with world leaders were covered by the foreign bureaus maintained by leading American newspapers, magazines, and television networks at the time. As familiar a figure overseas as he was on the national scene, Nixon, at fifty-three, actually was younger than his Republican rivals.

Meanwhile, back home, the absence of scrutiny from the national political press allowed Nixon to take his time assembling a staff, developing a strategy for both the nomination and the general election, and packaging his return to politics as the "new Nixon," a man made wiser and more statesmanlike by defeat at the polls, exile from office, reflection on the great issues of the day, international travel, and intense self-examination. Written off as a loser, he was initially covered by junior reporters, who did not remember much about his earlier career and with whom he was "accessible in those days, reasonably friendly."[26] Judging from a *New York Times* profile by thirty-one-year-old Robert Semple in January 1968, the packaging sold the product. Semple described Nixon as "a walking monument to reason, civility, frankness," "humor," "tranquility," and "candor."[27]

Nixon learned a great deal from his loss to Kennedy. He had envied Kennedy's young and capable staff in 1960 and decided to emulate him when putting together his own campaign organization for 1968. Nixon's new

After losing elections for president in 1960 and governor of California in 1962, Richard Nixon had to prove that he could appeal to voters in 1968 in order to secure his party's presidential nomination. (Credit: Richard Nixon Presidential Library)

team included a talented trio of writers: Buchanan, an ardently conservative polemicist with the *St. Louis Globe-Democrat*; William Safire, a public relations executive and a centrist; and Raymond Price, an editorial writer for the liberal Republican *New York Herald Tribune* until it folded in August 1966. His team also featured a bright group of media advisers, including television executive Frank Shakespeare, who took a leave of absence from CBS to work on the campaign; advertising executive Harry Treleaven; and, eventually, Roger Ailes, the producer of the popular syndicated *Mike Douglas Show*, who told Nixon that he was wrong to think television was a gimmick and would lose again if he did not realize this. The team also included aides whom Nixon assembled from the Nixon, Mudge, Rose, Guthrie, Alexander, and Mitchell law firm, including Leonard Garment and, on his advice, John

Sears, Tom Evans, and senior partner John Mitchell. This new staff not only brought the energy of youth to the Nixon campaign but also, by its mere presence, buttressed the argument that he really was a new man.

Nixon admired Kennedy's adroit use of television and was readily persuaded not to underestimate its importance in 1968. "In 1960, I felt the big speech was the most important and I had to be up for it," he reflected. "Meeting committees and politicians was next, then press conferences, and then TV. Now we've reversed the order. Now television and the press conferences are the most important, and that's why I won't do them on the run."[28] Reviewing multiple hours of videotape, Ailes, Garment, Shakespeare, Price, and Evans realized that filmed stump speeches, the mainstay of Nixon's television campaigns in the past, displayed him at his worst: overwrought in spoken language and herky-jerky in body language. Informal question-and-answer sessions, however, revealed Nixon at his best: calm in speech and manner, masterful in his command of the material. The five of them devised and, as the campaign unfolded, increasingly relied on a new-style television campaign for Nixon: a series of live, regionally broadcast thirty-minute programs in which citizen panelists, both friendly and (within limits) unfriendly, asked him questions in front of a supportive studio audience. Nixon stood before the panel without notes or podium, looking to all the world like Daniel in the lion's den. Although few questions dealt with matters with which he was unfamiliar, he did not know what he would be asked. The programs had a kind of controlled spontaneity; the lions were real but toothless. In further contrast to 1960, Nixon was well lit (the advent of color television helped) and professionally made up. The television studios were kept chilly enough to prevent him from sweating.[29] As Nixon did better and better in the primaries, reporters' access to the candidate grew less and less.

Apart from refashioning his image, Nixon faced the challenge of repositioning himself within a Republican party that was in ideological flux. This was no easy matter. To be sure, the GOP had nominated moderates for president in seven of the previous eight elections. But the one exception, when the party moved dramatically rightward, was the most recent. In 1960 Nixon had cruised to the nomination riding both moderate and conservative tides. He had spent eight years as the vice president in a moderate Republican administration and on some issues, notably civil rights, was more liberal than President Eisenhower. But his conservative credentials also were strong: he was a crusading anticommunist during his six years in Congress and, as vice president, gave raucously partisan speeches that made him anathema to liberal Democrats. Republican conservatives judged him in part by his liberal enemies.

Nixon renewed his ties to the Republican right by campaigning ardently for Goldwater in 1964, thereby earning the conservative icon's pledge of support in January 1965. Phyllis Schlafly, arguably the leading conservative activist in the country, supported Nixon because of his strong anti-Soviet credentials, which Reagan, focused as governor on domestic policy, could not yet match.[30] Nixon's midterm campaigning had been nationwide but with a southern accent—he spoke numerous times in all eleven states of the South in 1965 and 1966. This enabled him to cultivate support among the region's leading Republicans, including Sen. John Tower of Texas and, especially, Sen. Strom Thurmond of South Carolina, whose deep gratitude Nixon won by praising him as "no racist" but rather "a man of courage and integrity."[31] Nixon secured an endorsement from William F. Buckley, Jr., the founder and editor of conservatives' favorite periodical, the *National Review*. As long as Reagan was a possible candidate, however, Nixon knew that he would never be conservatives' solid first choice, any more than most liberals would prefer him to Romney or Rockefeller.

Faced with this challenge, the identity Nixon forged in preparation for the 1968 election was a curious but shrewd mixture of two elements that transcended conventional ideology. One was his claim to foreign policy statesmanship, which was something that none of his real or potential gubernatorial opponents could match; only Rockefeller came close. This claim was of general appeal during the Cold War, when voters feared the prospect of nuclear conflict and communist expansion and, starting in 1948, invariably turned to experienced Washington hands in presidential elections. It was of particular appeal because it enabled Nixon to mute the Vietnam issue by promising to a secure a "victorious peace" without explaining how he would accomplish that goal. When Nixon said that to be more specific about his approach to the war would be poor statesmanship because it would show his hand to the North Vietnamese, he could reasonably expect that many voters would respect his judgment. Nixon remembered that in 1952 Eisenhower had been able to finesse discussions of the equally unpopular Korean War by simply promising, "I will go to Korea." He hoped to pull off something similar in 1968, while privately telling his future son-in-law Edward Cox that, if elected, "I'm going to Moscow and Peking."[32]

The other main element of Nixon's political identity entering 1968 was a kind of cultural populism, the rousing of grassroots resentment not of an economic elite but of an academic, governmental, and media elite. The steadily growing postwar economy had sucked much of the oxygen out of political attacks on Wall Street and big business, but changing race relations and the questioning of traditional values on college campuses were breeding other resentments. In contrast to professors, bureaucrats, and influential media figures, who seemed chiefly concerned with celebrating youthful protesters and sympathizing with assertive racial minorities, Nixon claimed to represent the "silent center"—that is, "the millions of people in the middle of the American political spectrum who do not demonstrate, who do not picket or protest loudly" but who do work hard, carry a mortgage, pay their taxes, and do their best to send their children to college.[33] In addition to feeling disrespected on the campuses and in the media, this hardworking majority, including many blue-collar workers, Catholics, white southerners, and other mainstays of the New Deal Democratic coalition, also worried about "crime and lawlessness," which in late February 1968 ranked for the first time ever as the public's leading concern in the Gallup Poll. Never in American political history had a presidential nominee raised crime as a significant issue. Four years earlier, Goldwater had refused campaign aides' advice to do so. In 1968, both responding to and aggravating public concern about the problem, Nixon and Wallace did.

Nixon was no stranger to the politics of resentment. In the face of eastern liberal disdain, he had taken on establishment favorite Alger Hiss in 1948 and put his family's bare-bones finances on display in the 1952 Checkers speech. He still chafed at being spurned by New York law firms after earning his bachelor's degree at Whittier College and law degree at Duke University, both of them well off the beaten path to Wall Street, which at the time led through New England boarding schools and Ivy League universities.

In October 1967 Nixon published two articles that, taken separately, manifested the two prongs of the statesman-populist appeal he hoped would draw votes from the left and especially the right and middle wings of the party in the primaries. With help from Raymond Price, Nixon wrote the first article, a dramatic call to "come urgently to grips with the reality of China" and not "leave China forever outside the family of nations," for *Foreign Affairs,* the journal of the Council on Foreign Relations and the ultimate establishment organ.[34] For the second he turned to Buchanan. "What Has Happened to America?" lamented the nation's recent riots, drug epidemic, and campus disorders and blamed "opinion-makers"—specifically, "teachers, preachers, and politicians"—for "promoting the doctrine that when a law is broken, society, not the criminal, is to blame." It ran in the mass-circulation *Reader's Digest*.[35]

Just as Nixon's appeal was two-pronged, so were its political advantages. Both elements—foreign policy statesmanship and cultural populism—reflected critical aspects of who Nixon authentically was. He could deliver both messages with genuine conviction. Beyond that, both elements rested on Nixon's main insight into what voters in a period of turmoil at home and war abroad valued above all: calm, security, and order.

NEW HAMPSHIRE

"If I can't establish in these miserable primaries that I am the strongest possible candidate, then I am through," Nixon said with cold realism.[36] Goldwater had won the nomination in 1964 because his supporters cared more about being right than about winning the election. Nixon did not have that luxury. He would have to prove that even though he had not been elected on his own since 1950, he was a winner.

Of blessed relief to Nixon, his and Romney's decision to concede the primaries in California, Ohio, Florida, and a few other states to favorite son candidates meant that he only needed to focus on four contests: New Hampshire on March 12 followed by the three states in which candidates were placed on the ballot involuntarily, by judgment of the various secretaries of state: Wisconsin on April 2, Nebraska on May 14, and Oregon on May 28. Because all four primaries were in northern or coastal states, Nixon's challenge was to win without making pledges that would alienate southern and western voters, most of them conservatives whose hearts were with Reagan even if their heads were with Nixon.

Although Nixon worried about the "cranky" and therefore unpredictable character of New Hampshire's rural voters, he was popular there.[37] In 1956 Sen. Styles Bridges had countered a move to drop Nixon from the national ticket by organizing a write-in campaign in which the vice president won 82 percent of the vote for renomination. Campaigning personally in 1968, Nixon would bring up the "new Nixon" theme without waiting to be asked about it. "Is there a new Nixon?" he would say. "The answer is yes—of course there's a new Nixon. I've changed, just as America changed, just as we've all changed over the course of years. But on the basic things—on matters of character, of conscience—that has not changed."[38] The February 29 release of the Kerner Commission report on the urban riots supplied ammunition for his campaign's law-and-order theme. "It, in effect, blames everybody for the riots except the perpetrators of the riots," he charged on

March 6.[39] With an eye less to winning black votes, a tiny share of the GOP primary electorate in New Hampshire, Wisconsin, Nebraska, and Oregon, than to assuring moderate whites that his emphasis on crime and lawlessness did not imply a lack of commitment to civil rights, Nixon offered a plan to foster "black capitalism" with tax credits. "Black ownership would mean black pride, black jobs, black opportunities, and yes, black power," he said.[40]

Facing rising pressure to be more specific about what he would do in Vietnam, Nixon punted. "Our disagreement on the war in Vietnam is not about the goal," he said in a February 2 press conference accompanying his formal declaration of candidacy in Manchester. "Our disagreement is about the means to achieve that goal . . . and I will be spelling out ways and means that that can be accomplished during the course of the campaign."[41] This was the source of the charge that Nixon claimed to have a "secret plan" to end the war, and of the continuing demands that he reveal it. As a rule, though, Nixon stuck to calls for "new leadership that will end the war and win the peace." In fact, his general theme was that "it is time America had new leadership."[42]

For Nixon, the January 30 Tet attacks were less politically meaningful than the event that preceded them by a week: North Korea's capture on January 23 of an American naval intelligence ship, the *Pueblo*. The North Koreans charged that the vessel was not only spying on them, which was true, but doing so in their sovereign waters, a dubious claim. Not just the ship but the captain and eighty-two crew members were held captive, and both officers and men were mistreated and humiliated. The standoff between Johnson and North Korean leader Kim Il-sung lasted until December 23, more than a month after the election, when the United States apologized and the captain and crew, but not the ship, were released. Nixon never made clear what he would do differently in the crisis, but he worked the incident into his general indictment of President Johnson's (and by implication, Vice President Humphrey's) weak leadership. "When respect for the United States of America falls so low that a fourth-rate military power like North Korea will seize an American naval vessel on the high seas, it is time for new leadership," Nixon said, invariably to loud applause.

Romney ended his candidacy on February 28, two days after an internal poll showed him trailing Nixon in New Hampshire 75 percent to 10 percent and about two weeks before the primary. Nixon was disappointed because to "defeat an opponent" was "the reason I had decided to enter the primaries in the first place."[43] But Romney felt he had no choice. His support in the national polls had been spiraling downward ever since his "brainwashing" remark and, despite diligent campaigning in New Hampshire, he was doing no better there.

Rockefeller's refusal to rule out a draft and unwillingness to fulfill his promise to continue funding Romney's campaign left bitterness in its wake. Some speculated that one reason Romney's campaign manager, longtime Rockefeller operative Leonard Hall, steered Romney toward the exit was to deny Nixon the sort of meaningful victory that would make it harder for Rocky to catch him if he decided to enter the race. Hall's divided loyalty aside, he and his coterie of campaign veterans and Romney's younger Michigan staff were constantly at war with each other, whipsawing the candidate from faction to faction.[44] In fact, of all the candidates in 1968, Nixon was the only one to successfully forge a cohesive, smoothly running organization that melded younger staffers with older ones, loyalists with specialists, and insiders with outsiders.

Even with Romney out of the running, Nixon's 80,666 votes in the primary were impressive—the most that any candidate had ever received in a New Hampshire primary and more than all of the other votes cast that day for candidates of both parties. (He even finished third in the Democratic primary with an additional 2,532 write-in votes.) But Nixon's victory was overshadowed by McCarthy's strong showing against Johnson in the Democratic contest. The morning-after speculation among Democrats that Robert Kennedy would enter the race was matched by speculation among Republicans that with Romney out, Rockefeller would get in—a prospect that roused the same sort of insecurities and resentments in Nixon that the prospect of Kennedy's entry triggered in Johnson. The difference was that Nixon thought he could beat Rockefeller, and to prove his electability he wanted someone to beat.

ROCKEFELLER STAYS OUT, ROCKEFELLER GETS IN

Right after winning a third term as governor of New York in 1966, Rockefeller not only endorsed Romney for president but said: "I am not, will not, and under no circumstances will be a candidate again."[45] Later, explaining why he had abandoned his long quest for the presidency, Rockefeller waxed philosophic. "Something happens in life and you lose ambition because you have a sense of fulfillment," he told a reporter. "I just don't have the ambition or the need or the inner drive—or whatever the word is—to get in again."[46]

A growing number of cynics shared Nixon's suspicion that Romney was unwittingly walking the point for an eventual Rockefeller candidacy. At the first sign of faltering, they believed, Rockefeller would pull the financial plug on Romney and enter the race. When Romney not only faltered but fell, speculation hardened into conventional wisdom: Rockefeller would announce his candidacy after the New Hampshire primary was over and the list of candidates on the Nebraska primary ballot was fixed—that is, after March 15—but before the Oregon ballot was similarly set on March 22. The presumption was that Rockefeller would write off Nebraska as Nixon territory but approach Oregon, which he carried in 1964, as a state whose primary he could win. "I believe Rocky when he says he's lost his ambition," said former Johnson aide Bill Moyers. "I also believe he remembers where he put it."[47] Rockefeller fed the speculation with a March 1 statement that he was "not contending for the nomination, but I am ready and willing to serve the American people if called."[48]

On March 19 the *New York Times* reported that Rockefeller would become a candidate the next day. Gov. Spiro T. Agnew of Maryland, who was elected in 1966 against a segregationist Democrat on a civil rights platform, was a fervent Rockefeller admirer who created a draft Rocky organization in Maryland in January 1968 and took it national in mid-March. So confident was Agnew that Rockefeller would declare his candidacy that he invited a group of statehouse reporters to watch the live broadcast of the announcement with him on the morning of March 20. But Rockefeller's private soundings had shown that he had even less support among state and local Republican leaders than when he first thought of running in 1960. Many of those grassroots leadership positions were now held by Goldwater Republicans. Pressure on Nebraska's secretary of state from both the Nixon campaign and Robert Kennedy, who entered the Democratic race on March 16 and wanted to be on the state's primary ballot, meant that Rockefeller would have to be on it as well, setting up a sure defeat in his first primary. Without the courtesy of a phone call telling Agnew what to expect, Rockefeller allowed his loudest supporter to suffer the humiliation of learning that he would not enter the race at the same time as the rest of the country—and, even more embarrassing, as the room full of reporters.

Nixon's reaction to Rockefeller's declaration was complicated: disappointment that he still had no credible opponent against whom to demonstrate his electability mixed with relief that he would not have to compete against his massively self-financed and supremely energetic rival. Agnew's reaction was not complicated at all: he was angry. Nixon hastened to set up a meeting with Agnew on March 29, and the two men were mutually impressed. "All Agnew did was tell him what an asshole Rockefeller was," said John Sears. "That got rid of the ice in the conversation very quickly."[49] Agnew was the sort of man Nixon frequently fell for: tall, good-looking, self-confident. "There is a mysticism about men," Nixon later ruminated. "There is a quiet confidence. You look a man in the eye and you know he's got it—brains. This guy has got it."[50] In addition to being personally impressive, part of what Agnew had was a life story not unlike Nixon's. Each was the son of a small grocer, worked his way through college and law school, and served in World War II—and each had been humiliated by Rockefeller.

Within weeks of Rockefeller's decision not to enter the race, the political world turned upside down. On March 31 Johnson announced that he was withdrawing from the election to pursue peace negotiations with North Vietnam. This enabled Nixon to cancel a speech in which, responding to pressure to be specific about what he would do in Vietnam, he planned to call for more bombing, less ground fighting, and an attempt to persuade the Soviet Union to apply diplomatic pressure to North Vietnam to recognize South Vietnam's sovereignty.[51] Johnson's announcement, a relieved Nixon now declared, meant that candidates "should avoid anything that might even inadvertently cause difficulties for our negotiators."[52] Recognizing the widespread public hope for a peaceful settlement that the president's speech aroused, however, Nixon did change the stock phrase defining his goal for Vietnam from a "victorious peace" to an "honorable peace."[53]

Johnson's withdrawal made Rockefeller think he could persuade Republicans that he, not Nixon, would be the party's strongest candidate, especially against Kennedy. Martin Luther King's assassination four days later and the ensuing riots convinced Rockefeller that the voters would insist on electing a president who had dealt constructively with urban problems. In the altered political environment, he believed, his ten-year gubernatorial record of creating new programs for public housing, student loans, minimum wage increases, consumer protection, and other purposes offered just what independent voters and disaffected Democrats would be looking for in November. Party regulars might not want to nominate him, but they would be convinced to do so by public opinion polls showing that he was the only Republican who could be elected.

Nixon, along with Rockefeller's erstwhile champion, Governor Agnew, interpreted the new developments differently. When King's assassination sparked massive rioting in Baltimore and Washington, Agnew summoned local civil rights leaders to an April 11 meeting and lectured them severely about their alleged tolerance of black militants—at which point most of them infuriated him further by walking out. Adding to the general sense of mayhem, at Columbia University a month of demonstrations began in late March against the university's plan to raze part of a Harlem neighborhood in order to build a new gymnasium. Black and white student protesters united in opposition to the university but divided among themselves. Blacks occupied Hamilton Hall, the administration building, and then banished their white peers, who in turn occupied Low Library. Prefiguring the riots that accompanied the Democratic convention four months later, on April 30 New York City police violently removed all of the students in an assault that left about 150 injured and more than 700 under arrest. "The police," Mark Kurlansky has written, "working-class people, resented these privileged youth who would not support the war that working-class children were fighting."[54]

Nixon's cultural populism, made manifest in his vow to restore law and order by appointing a new attorney general—a routine action by any new president that Nixon made sound dramatic—resonated more strongly than ever with Republican voters who saw discord and violence where the cultural elite saw healthy protest against a sick society. As part of his appeal to Democratic blue-collar whites, on May 8 Nixon issued a position paper espousing strong anticrime policies that borrowed its title from Franklin D. Roosevelt's 1941 "Four Freedoms" speech: "Toward Freedom from Fear." Three days after Johnson withdrew, Nixon swept the Wisconsin primary with 79.7 percent of the vote—dramatically higher than second-place finisher Reagan, whose name had been placed on the ballot by Wisconsin's secretary of state and who received only 10.4 percent.

Rockefeller dismissed Nixon's Wisconsin victory as quickly dated by events and attributable, in any case, to the absence of active competition and a flukishly strong organizational effort by John Mitchell, a state and municipal bond lawyer who had worked with local officials in the state. In truth, Rockefeller's ability to command the services of talented aides, partly by supplementing their official salaries out of his own pocket, led him to disregard how capable and well organized the Nixon campaign was. Rockefeller's memory was of the hapless 1960 effort, when Nixon tried to be his own campaign manager, making every decision himself, often in a state of exhaustion. But, as with television, Nixon had learned from experience that he needed to find good people and delegate responsibility to them. In Wisconsin he recognized Mitchell's unique combination of campaign management skills and political connections—"he knew all the politicians in America," marveled Leonard Garment. Soon Mitchell was running Nixon's national campaign, overseeing activities such as fund-raising, volunteers, and relations with state and local party officials.[55] Meanwhile, H. R. Haldeman, a young veteran of Nixon's California campaigns with a strong background in advertising, ran the candidate: his schedule, speeches, and media appearances. Haldeman emphasized pacing: why maintain a six-speech-per-day routine, six days per week, when the television networks would broadcast only one story each day that would reach a much larger audience? Traditional campaigning, Haldeman argued, left the candidate "punchy . . . with no time to think."[56]

Rockefeller's organization, although filled with stellar individuals, was not nearly as effective as Nixon's. For one thing Rockefeller's decision to enter the race on April 30, just six weeks after unexpectedly announcing he would not run, caught his staff by surprise. For another, he organized them badly, each with his own fiefdom, and allowed them, grateful as they were for his financial patronage, to treat him sycophantically rather than give him frank advice. With no one to tell him differently, Rockefeller assumed that he could turn 1968 into a rerun of his 1966 campaign for governor: start out way behind but win by spending "Babylonian sums" to advertise his way to victory through a paid media campaign.[57] Like Kennedy in 1960, Rockefeller needed to convince reluctant party leaders that only he was popular enough to win the general election. Unlike Kennedy, however, he would have to do so by driving up his poll numbers, rather than by winning primaries. Rockefeller won the Massachusetts contest on the day he announced his candidacy with a write-in campaign that earned him 30.0 percent of the vote against Nixon's 25.8 percent (also write-ins) and 29.5 percent for favorite-son candidate Gov. John Volpe, the only one on the ballot. But the deadline already had passed for entering other primaries, including Oregon, where Rockefeller eschewed the write-in route that had just worked so well in Massachusetts.

Rockefeller's strategy for pumping up his poll numbers rested on an advertising campaign that included 42 television spots per week on 100 stations in 30 cities and weekly full-page ads in 54 large-circulation newspapers in 40 cities. The spots and ads were concentrated in 13 states, which collectively had 60 percent of the nation's population.[58] Texas aside, Rockefeller ignored the South: the only Rockefeller for President organization in the whole region was in New Orleans, where Tulane University graduate student Newt Gingrich opened one on his own initiative. In truth, Rockefeller knew so little about the South that he sometimes confused Arkansas, where his brother Winthrop was governor, with Alabama.[59]

Rockefeller's ads, along with his speeches and rallies, focused on his plan to create New York–style big spending programs for the nation's cities and his newfound desire to end the war. He had been virtually silent about Vietnam since making several hawkish speeches in 1964 but now called for the war to be "de-Americanized" because there was "no purely military solution." This opened the door for Nixon, without naming names, to call on all who were running for president to "not destroy the chances for peace with a mouthful of words from some irresponsible candidate. Put yourself in the position of the enemy. He is negotiating with Lyndon Johnson and Secretary [of State Dean] Rusk and then he reads in the paper that . . . a potential president of the United States will give him a better deal than President Johnson."[60] Without entering a single primary, Rockefeller spent about $8 million on his campaign, only $1 million less than Nixon. Two-thirds of it—about $5.5 million—came from Rockefeller and his family.[61]

Rockefeller was optimistic about his chances because, unlike Nixon, he had a history of winning votes from Democrats and Democratic-leaning independents. He urged Republican delegates to look not at primary results or surveys of Republican voters but rather at polls matching him and Nixon against Humphrey and Kennedy, one of whom (probably Kennedy, Nixon assumed) would be the Democratic nominee. But even if Rockefeller could persuade delegates to cast their votes at the convention on that basis, it would not be enough for the polls to show Rockefeller beating the Democrats. They also would have to show Nixon losing to them.

NEBRASKA AND OREGON

California's June 4 primary was the last one on the Republican calendar, but in contrast to 1964 the state was not a political battlefield between warring armies of conservatives and liberals. With Nixon's acquiescence, Reagan was alone among the candidates on the ballot as the state's favorite son. Unopposed, Reagan received 1,525,091 votes, which along with the 171,279 votes he picked up in other primaries enabled him actually to outpace Nixon in the national primary vote by 16,727. This impressed Reaganites but no one else. The third-place finisher was another favorite son, Gov. James Rhodes of Ohio, who received 614,492 votes in his state's May 7 primary.

In the month before California voted, Reagan's supporters also launched serious efforts in Nebraska, which held its primary on May 14, and Oregon, which voted on May 28. In both states Reagan was placed on the ballot by the secretary of state and refused to withdraw, claiming that his place on the California ballot meant he could not sign a statement saying that he was not a candidate without "committing perjury"—even though he repeatedly said he was not one, not really.[62] Nebraska was Nixon territory, his strongest state against Kennedy in 1960 with 62.1 percent of the vote, and he was the only candidate to campaign there in the primary. Rockefeller ran numerous ads on Nebraska television and radio stations but to little avail; he received only 5.1 percent of the vote. Reagan supporters ran commercials for him, earning the Californian 21.3 percent. Nixon swept Nebraska with 70.0 percent, but the press played up Reagan's showing. Ward Just observed in the *Washington Post* that Nixon "must be America's only major political figure who can win 70 percent of a state's vote and still have the analysts talk about his opponent's 23 [*sic*] percent."[63] Nixon seethed at this disparate treatment. "What the hell are we supposed to do?" he complained to Buchanan. "Paint our asses white and run with the antelope?"[64] But the truth is that national political reporters always want to keep a contest going so that they will still have a story to cover. They also like seeing a fresh face emerge, and Reagan was that. From May 2 to May 22, he conducted a five-state fund-raising tour for the GOP, carefully avoiding the primary states.

Reagan's supporters made their biggest effort in Oregon, spending about $200,000 on television—more than one-fourth of the $750,000 that was spent on the entire Reagan campaign.[65] They had seen his vote double from Wisconsin to Nebraska. At that rate, they calculated, Reagan might win in Oregon with 44 percent and, after California voted just a week later, enter the convention with genuine momentum.[66] What they hoped for, Nixon dreaded, and he campaigned harder in Oregon than in any other state against the opponent whom NBC evening news anchor David Brinkley described as "the biggest spending non-candidate in history."[67] This mattered to Oregon's voters—in 1964 Rockefeller had won the primary on the slogan, "He cared enough to come." In any event, the hopes of Reagan backers probably were in vain even if he did campaign: Oregonians resented wealthy, sunny California and also tended to support liberal Republicans such as Hatfield, its recent governor and current senator. Nixon reached out to these voters with a speech on May 16 called "A New Alignment for American Unity." In it he proposed to forge a coalition among five groups that he thought could be united by their shared resentment of government: traditional free enterprise Republicans, new-style liberals seeking "participatory democracy," the South, black militants, and the silent center. "At one and the same time," observed Allen Matusow, "Nixon expressed compassion for the oppressed, acquiesced in segregation, endorsed black power, and preached the virtues of free enterprise."[68] As with his "black capitalism" appeal, the speech was Nixon's way of persuading moderate Republicans such as the ones who dominated Oregon that he wasn't a racist or right-winger even though he was ardently pursuing southern support.

Nixon swept Oregon with 65.0 percent of the vote. He had won every primary he entered. The victories yielded him only 112 delegates, miles short of the 667 he needed to be nominated. But they made his point: he was once again a winner, at least among Republican voters. Reagan finished second in Oregon with a disappointing 20.4 percent. Instead of continuing to increase geometrically (or even arithmetically) from primary to primary, he actually dropped a percentage point from his performance in Nebraska. Rockefeller received 11.6 percent from write-in votes. If he had campaigned hard in Oregon, as he did in 1964, he surely would have done much better.

Rockefeller was playing a different game, one in which the scoreboard was the polls and victory was measured by how much he surpassed Nixon in matchups against the leading Democratic candidates. The initial results were promising: a Gallup Poll released on May 12 showed Nixon leading Humphrey by 3 percentage points while Rockefeller was 7 points ahead. Similarly, Nixon led Kennedy by 10 points compared with Rockefeller's 14-point lead, and Nixon led McCarthy by 2 points, considerably less than the 9 points by which Rockefeller led him. Gallup trial heats released on June 23 showed Rockefeller leading Humphrey by a point while Nixon trailed the vice president by 5 points. This was the ideal outcome for Rockefeller and one he counted on to persist until the convention in early August.

Meanwhile, Reagan's leading supporters, led by backstage campaign impresario F. Clifton White, dismissed the results of Nixon's primary victories, all of them in the North, and concentrated their efforts on southern delegations. White had engineered Goldwater's nomination in 1964 and the South had been Goldwater's strongest region. Reagan owned the affection of southern Republicans; Nixon's challenge was to get them to follow their leaders—including Goldwater himself—and vote for him rather than someone who had held public office for little more than a year.[69] To that end Nixon traveled to Atlanta on May 31 for a meeting with southern state party chairs organized by Senator Thurmond, who was typical of Nixon's supporters in the South: he was inclined to endorse Nixon but said of Reagan, "I love that man. He's the best we've got."[70]

Nixon buttressed the South Carolinian's support by promising to raise import tariffs to protect the state's textile industry and to create an antiballistic missile defense program, which Thurmond had promoted vigorously as ranking minority member of the Senate Armed Services Committee. Nixon also pledged to the state chairs that he would take into account white southern sensibilities concerning school integration, specifically promising to oppose busing to achieve racial balance, which a unanimous Supreme Court had opened the door to on May 27 in *Green v. County School Board of New Kent County*.[71] Nixon operatives asked southern Republicans to consider that with Wallace in the race as an independent candidate, Reagan probably could not carry the Deep South. Nixon's appearance in Atlanta stopped the bleeding of southern support to Reagan, not by healing the wound but by stitching it; he could only hope the stitches would not come loose.

Whether anyone else was using the polls to keep score the way Rockefeller wanted them to, and whether southern affection for Reagan would become southern votes at the convention, were still unclear. But if either or both of Nixon's rivals could peel away enough votes to deny him a first-ballot nomination, all bets were off.

WALLACE

Like nearly all southern politicians of the era, George Wallace was a lifelong Democrat and in 1964 competed in three Democratic presidential primaries against President Johnson. That experience exhilarated Wallace while it lasted, but from his perspective, it did not last long enough. From April 7, 1964, when he made a strong showing in the Wisconsin primary, until May 19, when he ran even better in Maryland, Wallace was in the national spotlight—and then, nothing. The Democrats denied him a place on the program at their convention in August, nominated Johnson by acclamation, and left Wallace on the sidelines for the rest of the year.

On January 17, 1967, the day after Lurleen Wallace was inaugurated as governor of Alabama—a figurehead-style queen, with her husband as prime minister—Wallace's aides persuaded him to run in 1968 as an independent candidate instead of once again challenging Johnson for the Democratic nomination. Their arguments seemed strong, even those that were undone by later developments: Johnson had the Democratic nomination locked up, an independent candidacy would keep Wallace in the race and in the news all the way to November, Goldwater supporters disillusioned with their party's return to the political center would be more willing to vote for Wallace as an independent than as a Democrat, and Wallace might win enough electoral votes to deny either major party nominee a majority, thereby creating a situation in which he could try to negotiate concessions

A campaign poster for former governor of Alabama George C. Wallace, who after contesting three Democratic primaries in 1964 ran as an independent candidate in 1968. (Credit: Courtesy of the Library of Congress)

from one of them in return for his support.[72] Wallace even entertained the possibility of winning the election. He frequently pointed out that eleven presidents had been elected without a national popular vote majority, including three who received fewer votes than their opponents. "Lincoln was a plurality winner, and I'll be a plurality winner," Wallace liked to say.[73] Unlike every other nationally significant third-party or independent candidate since the American Party—the so-called Know Nothings—nominated former president Millard Fillmore in 1856, Wallace would be running against both major parties from the right.

Wallace's aides told him that he would have to get started right away because the effort required to secure a place on all fifty state ballots would be herculean. The Democratic and Republican Parties enjoyed duopoly status in most states. Comfortable competing with each other, they wrote election laws designed to discourage any other parties or candidates from entering the political market. Ohio, for example, required signatures equal in number to 10 percent of the total vote in the most recent gubernatorial election—433,100 in 1968—and the signatures had to be submitted by February 7, 1968, nine months before the presidential election. In California, Wallace would have to persuade 66,059 voters to fill out a two-page form registering them as members of a new political party. New York demanded only 12,000 signatures, but they had to include at least 50 from each of the state's 62 counties, some of which had populations under 4,000. Signatures in every state would be scrutinized by hostile Republican and Democratic election officials and ruled invalid for the smallest of reasons— leaving off (or inserting) a middle initial that was in (or not in) the existing registration record, for example, or not knowing the number or address of the precinct one lived in.

Wallace accepted and met these challenges. His New York supporters gathered not 12,000 but 107,000 signatures. He spent the last six weeks of 1967 giving more than a hundred speeches in California and even formed a political party with which his supporters could register. In most states, including California, the party appeared under his preferred name—the American Independent Party—but for reasons of varying state law it ended up with six different names, including the Courage Party in New York and the George Wallace Party in Connecticut.[74] Wallace had no desire to form a new party with a platform, a national committee, a convention, and a roster of candidates for other offices—but if that was what California and some other states required, he would jump through their hoops. In the end, more than a hundred thousand Californians filled out the required form and registered as AIP members. In Ohio the secretary of state ruled Wallace's petitions invalid because they were filed after the deadline, but in October 1968 the Supreme Court decided by a 5–4 vote in *Williams v. Rhodes* that, on equal protection grounds, the state must grant him a place on the ballot.[75] Wallace's campaign to get on all fifty state ballots cost time and money that the major party nominees did not have to spend a minute or a nickel on, but in the end it succeeded, with the exception of the majority-black District of Columbia. All told, his supporters gathered 2.7 million signatures on petitions, of which about a million were ruled invalid, mostly on technicalities.[76]

From June 1967, when Lurleen Wallace was severely weakened by cancer, until May 6, 1968, when she died, Wallace's ability to campaign nationally was limited by his need to be with her in Montgomery or Houston, where she was seeking treatment. Her death, which elevated Lt. Gov. Albert Brewer to the governorship, reduced Wallace's fund-raising ability in Alabama, much of which hinged on controlling the state's contract-writing purse strings from the governor's office. Brewer, once a Wallace ally, was now concerned with getting elected governor in his own right in 1970.[77] The severing of Wallace from his financial base posed a serious problem. Advertising, travel, and other campaign expenses aside, the drive to get on state ballots alone cost the campaign about $2.5 million. Wallace solved the problem by hosting $25-a-plate dinners and passing around yellow plastic buckets at his rallies. Like the tedious, expensive ballot drive, this dollar-and-change form of fund-raising was not what Wallace preferred, but it had the effect of giving many of his supporters a sense of ownership in his campaign through their investment of time collecting signatures or money placed in the bucket. About one-third of those who attended Wallace's rallies made a donation.

Wallace also used 1967 to develop the themes and stock applause lines that would carry him through 1968. More than most southern politicians of his generation, he was adept at cloaking his references to race in non-racial language. "There isn't any backlash among the mass of American people against anybody because of race," he said on *Meet the Press* in April. "There's a backlash against big government in this country." In October he told a Mississippi audience:

> You can put LBJ in the sack. You can put HHH in the sack. And you can put Robert "Blood-for-the-Vietcong" Kennedy in the sack. You can put . . . the left-wing Governor Romney and Nelson Rockefeller, that socialist governor, in the sack. Put 'em all in the same sack, shake 'em up. I don't care which one comes out, you stick him back in—because there isn't a dime's worth of difference in them.[78]

Reagan was a "sissy actor," Wallace said, and as for Nixon, he was "the general at Little Rock when they put the bayonets in the backs of southerners," a reference to President Eisenhower's enforcement of court-ordered school integration in the Arkansas capital in 1957.[79]

The stormiest applause came when Wallace laid down a marker to protesters, always portrayed as spoiled, unwashed, long-haired college students: "If any demonstrator lies down in front of my car when I'm president, that'll be the last car he lays down in front of."[80] He also attacked both welfare recipients as ungrateful drains on the treasury and "multibillion-naires like the Rockefellers and the Fords and the Mellons and Carnegies who go without paying taxes."[81] In that sense, Wallace was a throwback to the producerist ideology expressed in the 1892 Omaha Platform of the People's Party, fanning workers and farmers' resentments of the nonproductive classes both at the top and the bottom of the economic ladder.[82]

Wallace's speeches always included a long list of his kind of people, "the average man on the street: the pipe fitter, the communications worker, the fireman, the policeman, the barber," and so on through the "beautician," the "oil worker," the "bus driver, the truck driver," and all the rest.[83] Liberals talked about the white working class in general. Wallace knew it in all its particularities.

Wallace's supporters were, like those attracted to the extreme left wing of the antiwar movement, convinced that the political system was controlled by a small elite that scorned their values and neglected their concerns. "People always say that George Wallace just appeals to the crackers, the peckerwoods, and the rednecks," Wallace declared. "Well, George Wallace says there's an awful lot of us rednecks in this country—*and they're not all in the South!*"[84] Nor did they hold conservative positions on all issues. Wallace's supporters opposed welfare and busing to achieve school integration, but they also wanted national health insurance, social security, price controls, and a government guarantee of a job for everyone.[85]

Wallace officially declared that he was running for president on February 8, 1968. His support as an independent candidate in the Gallup Poll registered at 11 percent. On the eve of his inauguration as governor in 1963, when Ku Klux Klan bombings and shootings were the issue, Wallace had said he was "sick and tired of . . . too much hollerin' about law and order."[86] The urban violence of the next five years, culminating in the King riots in April, enabled him to talk about law and order as a way of playing on racial fears and resentments, and his support rose to 14 percent in early May. As a former Alabama state senator said of Wallace, "He can use all the other issues—law and order, running your own schools, protecting property rights—and never mention race. But people will know he's telling them, 'A nigger's trying to get your job, trying to move into your neighborhood.'"[87] "The rioters and the looters," wrote NAACP president Roy Wilkins, were Wallace's unwitting "little helpers."[88] Through the first nine months of 1968, Wallace rode a steep upward trajectory that eventually peaked at 21 percent, doubling his support from when he announced. Spared any need to compete in primaries, he was free to campaign against both the Democrats and Republicans all year long, with an eye on November.

As Wallace's campaign gained steam, political strategists of all persuasions looked at the electoral map with furrowed, sometimes sweaty brows. If, as seemed quite possible, Wallace won the 174 electoral votes in the nation's sixteen southern and border states, the Republican or Democratic nominee would have to win 270 of the nation's remaining 364 electoral votes—that is, 73 percent of them—to keep the election from going into the House of Representatives or, better still from Wallace's perspective, into a bargaining process in the electoral college. Electors in eight of the states he hoped to carry were not bound by state law to vote for the candidate who carried their state, and these clearly would be free to cast their votes for whichever major party nominee Wallace designated. As for electors from the other strong Wallace states, the laws that bound their votes generally carried no penalty and in any event were of dubious constitutionality.

5

THE CONVENTIONS

National party conventions were still important political events in 1968. When the Republicans gathered in Miami Beach on August 5 and the Democrats assembled in Chicago on August 26, more was at stake for each party than simply staging a four-night, carefully scripted infomercial for the television audience. Although the last multiballot presidential nomination had been in 1952, the memory of suspense-filled, sometimes brokered conventions was relatively fresh. Floor fights over the credentials of competing state delegations, provisions of the party platform, and rules of the convention still served as tests of power for the contending candidates. Multiple state delegations entered conventions pledged to favorite-son candidates in the hope that they might gain concessions from the eventual nominee in return for throwing him their support. The vice presidential nomination remained unsettled until after the balloting for president, often in the wee hours of the next morning. The three television networks—CBS, NBC, and ABC—covered the conventions live and gavel-to-gavel, usually for more than ten hours per day.

The 1968 Democratic convention was famously event-filled. To be sure, the assassination of Sen. Robert F. Kennedy on the night of his victory in the June 4 California primary left Vice President Hubert H. Humphrey the strong front-runner for the nomination. Richard Nixon, for one, had been convinced that Kennedy was going to be the Democratic nominee. As the results came in on primary night, Nixon told aides, "It sure looks like we'll be going against Bobby."[1] Even with that possibility ended, albeit in circumstances that all of Kennedy's rivals sincerely mourned,

Sen. Eugene McCarthy still had little hope of mounting a successful challenge to Humphrey. McCarthy was weakened by his defeat in all but one of the primaries he entered against Kennedy and remained acidly estranged from the Kennedy retinue. But the prospect of last-minute candidacies by Sen. Edward M. Kennedy of Massachusetts or even by President Lyndon B. Johnson shadowed the convention. Riots in the streets and parks of Chicago and fierce battles within the convention hall about rules, credentials, and, especially, the platform plank dealing with Vietnam complicated Humphrey's effort to unite the party in support of his candidacy. Uncertainty attended his choice of a running mate until the morning of the convention's fourth day.

The Republican gathering in Miami Beach, the first GOP convention ever held in a southern state, was less eventful but more suspenseful. A race riot broke out on the eve of the convention in which three died, which was three more than died in all the rioting that occurred in Chicago during the Democratic gathering. But the riot was in the all-black Liberty City neighborhood of Miami, not in Miami Beach, a man-made island separated by Biscayne Bay from the city and, more important in terms of media coverage, from the networks' television cameras. Inside the hall, no fights over rules, credentials, or the platform enlivened the proceedings. In these ways the Republicans skirted the sort of controversies that plagued the Democrats. But concerning the main business of the conventions, the nomination for president, greater uncertainty attended the proceedings in Miami Beach than in Chicago. Both Gov. Nelson A. Rockefeller of New York and Gov. Ronald Reagan of California had hopes for the nomination that depended on each coming up with enough votes so that, together, they could deny Nixon a first-ballot victory. After that, they believed, much of Nixon's support would melt away. Finally, as in Chicago, the selection of the vice presidential candidate was an early morning affair.

THE RUN-UP TO THE REPUBLICAN CONVENTION

Nixon emerged from the primaries as the clear front-runner for the Republican nomination. He had done what, months before, he had gritted his teeth and resolved to do out of political necessity: belay his loser image by taking on all comers in the primaries and defeating every one of them. In the course of doing so, Nixon made no missteps that would alienate the party regulars who chose delegates in the nonprimary states. Nor did he say or do anything that could come back to haunt him in the general election campaign. His effort to persuade the political press that there was a "new Nixon" was remarkably successful. "The Nixon of 1968 was so different from the Nixon of 1960," wrote election chronicler Theodore H. White, a longtime Nixon critic. "There had indeed come to be a new Nixon . . . competent, able, . . . a firmer, wiser, thoroughly mature man."[2] Novelist Norman Mailer, a supporter of Robert Kennedy, rhapsodized that the *new* Nixon" was "a man who had risen and fallen and been able to rise again, and so conceivably had learned something about patience and the compassion of others."[3]

Doing everything right did not guarantee Nixon the nomination. He was still the two-time loser from 1960 and 1962 who had not won an election on his own in nearly twenty years. He was an old face in a year marked by novelty and change in the nation's culture and politics. He lacked fervent support from any of the GOP's ideological camps.

During the two months leading up to the Republican convention, Nixon faced different challenges from each of his two opponents. The challenge from Rockefeller was his avowedly superior ability to win the general election for the party. It was grounded in two related premises: that preconvention polls would indicate that Rocky was the only Republican who could beat the Democrats in November, and that delegates would care so much about winning that they would hold their noses and choose the liberal governor of New York as their party's standard bearer. In contrast, the challenge to Nixon from Reagan involved winning the nomination itself—in particular, on persuading conservative Republicans not to yield control of the party whose presidential nomination they had captured in 1964. Reagan's challenge also was based on the twin presumptions that conservatives, especially from the South and West, were powerful enough to seize control of the convention if they chose to do so, and that they were sufficiently dissatisfied with Nixon that they could be persuaded to make that choice.

ROCKEFELLER

The threat from Rockefeller proved easier for Nixon to deflect. In 1960, when Rockefeller made last-minute demands to change the platform, Nixon had to prostrate himself to the governor because the greatest danger to his nomination lay on his political left. By 1968 that was no longer the case. In the party that nominated Goldwater in 1964, the more serious threat to a candidate trying to stake out the middle ground lay on the right.

Rockefeller, who had been booed off the stage at the 1964 Republican convention, knew that the party had changed. But he campaigned ardently for its nomination. Starting on April 30, the day he announced his candidacy, Rockefeller traveled to forty-five states and spoke with more than a thousand Republican delegates. He even went to New Orleans on May 19 to meet with the southern Republican state chairs, a futile expedition but one that he hoped might pry loose a few delegates for himself and, even more important, spark a southern migration toward Reagan that would drain votes from Nixon.

For all Rockefeller's personal efforts, his campaign centered on the ads he ran in newspapers and on radio and television in the most populous states and cities. Rockefeller thought that Kennedy's assassination had opened a door for him to appeal to the young and African American voters who constituted the core of RFK's support. To that end, his ads stressed liberal themes with a conservative twist. One sixty-second commercial showed a black man walking out of the shadows on a dark city street while Rockefeller's voice was heard talking up the need to create employment programs for ghetto dwellers. The point seemed to be that the best way to keep black criminals at bay was to get them jobs—a liberal response to a conservative concern. As proof that the whole purpose of the Rockefeller campaign was to pump up his poll numbers in the general election trial heats, his ads stopped running on July 23, the day Gallup completed its final preconvention poll.

By then, however, things had started going seriously wrong for Rockefeller. Sen. Mark Hatfield, a popular moderate Republican from Oregon, endorsed Nixon on June 20. Former president Dwight D. Eisenhower, recovering from his fifth heart attack in Walter Reed Hospital, added his own endorsement on July 18. Rockefeller's effort to rouse support from his fellow governors at the annual meeting of the Republican Governors Association in mid-July fell flat. Although most state executives were Republicans and most Republican governors were moderates, Rockefeller was endorsed by only one: Raymond Shafer of Pennsylvania. George Romney of Michigan and Spiro T. Agnew of Maryland, each nursing feelings of betrayal by Rockefeller, were conspicuous nonendorsers.

The worst news for Rockefeller came on July 30, when Gallup released its final preconvention poll with the headline—in capital letters—"NIXON OVERTAKES HUMPHREY AND MCCARTHY; ROCKY RUNS EVEN AGAINST BOTH DEMO-CRATS." The poll showed Nixon leading McCarthy by five percentage points and Humphrey by two points, a reversal of Nixon's two- to six-point deficit against Humphrey in the three previous Gallup Polls conducted since late May. Rockefeller merely tied Humphrey and led McCarthy by only a point. The Harris Poll, published the next day, had a very different result: Rocky led Humphrey by six points while Nixon trailed him by five points,

Rocky can win.

New York governor Nelson A. Rockefeller's late campaign for the Republican nomination was based on the argument that, in contrast to Richard Nixon, "Rocky can win." (Credit: Courtesy of the Library of Congress)

about the same as he had in other recent Harris Polls.[4] Against McCarthy, Rockefeller led by six and Nixon trailed by eight. But the damage was done. Rockefeller needed the polls to speak clearly about his superior electability. Instead, their results, taken together, were ambiguous. What's more, the Gallup Poll, which was generally more respected than the Harris Poll, was released first.

Rockefeller took his campaign to the convention, which began on August 5, five days after the polls were published. But his fortunes now lay entirely in events beyond his control. All of the favorite-son candidates—a considerable number, controlling substantial blocs of delegates—would have to stay in the race rather than climb on the Nixon bandwagon. Reagan would have to declare his candidacy and spark an exodus of Nixon delegates from the South and West. In sum, the party's left and right, despite their massive differences and history of mutual hostility, would have to forge a temporary alliance against the center.

REAGAN

Rockefeller's hopes of becoming the Republican nominee for president were forlorn. Except in parts of the Northeast, he was anathema to the vast majority of the party's delegates and voters. But his hopes of denying Nixon the nomination were less unrealistic, especially if Reagan got into the race.

Approaching the convention, Nixon was particularly vulnerable among the delegations of the Deep South, whose size had grown markedly since 1964. The Republicans' delegate allocation formula had long included a six-vote bonus for each state that supported the party's nominee in the previous presidential election. Aside from Arizona, a conservative stronghold in its own right, that bonus went in 1968 to Alabama, Mississippi, Georgia, Louisiana, and South Carolina—and no other states. Moreover, Nixon's strategy for the general election involved winning the Outer South states of Virginia, North Carolina, Tennessee, Florida, and possibly Texas while conceding nearly the entire Deep South to former Alabama governor George Wallace. This did not sit well with those states' party leaders, who believed that with Reagan heading the ticket they had a reasonable chance to sweep the entire South. Southern support in 1968 represented a bigger prize at the Republican convention than at any time in the party's history. Since 1952 the southern and border states' share of delegates had risen from 19.0 percent to 26.7 percent. Nixon's best region, the Midwest, had declined from 30.8 percent to 26.4 percent, and Rockefeller's East had contracted from 30.8 percent to 26.6 percent.

Whatever prospects Reagan had for winning the nomination were hurt by his own lackadaisical performance during the run-up to the convention. Inexperience limited his efforts in two ways. One was that Reagan, unversed in national politics, was slow to realize how much could be accomplished in June and July even though the primaries were over and the convention had not yet begun. The other was that he had genuine doubts about his qualifications for the presidency after only eighteen months in public office. He "wasn't ready to be president," Reagan told more than one confidant.[5] When he met on May 19 in New Orleans with the same group of southern state party chairs that rebuffed Rockefeller, he dimmed their enthusiasm by giving every indication that he would not be a candidate. "He killed the idea dead," one southern chairman told columnists Rowland Evans and Robert D. Novak.[6] In South Carolina party chair Harry S. Dent's judgment, "had he asked for support in the atmosphere of that occasion, charged with his presence, the Californian would have received it from us then and there."[7]

Nixon, in contrast, impressed the group twelve days later in Atlanta with conservative answers to all their questions about Supreme Court appointments, busing to achieve public school integration, national defense, and his willingness to work through the party chairs in awarding federal patronage in their states. On June 19 Goldwater, who a year earlier at the Bohemian Grove had advised Reagan not to run because the Democrats would take him apart on the issue of experience, sent a letter urging him to abandon his favorite-son candidacy and "release your delegates together with a statement that your vote would go to Dick."[8]

Despite Nixon's ardent wooing and Reagan's seeming standoffishness, southern delegates' ardor for the Californian remained undimmed. In late June, when the South Carolina delegation met, all twenty-two preferred Reagan. It took every bit of Senator Thurmond's considerable influence to keep them from busting out of the corral. "I am laying my prestige, my record of forty years in public life, I am laying it all on the line this time," Thurmond told the delegates, whose state party owed much of its success to the senator's conversion from Democrat to Republican in 1964. "Believe me, I love Reagan, but Nixon's the one."[9]

Reagan's competitive juices finally started flowing, spurred by reports from former Goldwater organizer F. Clifton White, whom the governor's core group of California supporters had hired to work on Reagan's behalf, that southern delegations were poised to break his way. Starting on July 17, three weeks before the convention, Reagan met with Republican delegates from around the South at gatherings in Texas, Arkansas, Mississippi, Indiana, Kentucky, Alabama, North Carolina, Maryland, and, by invitation, California. "If nominated," he said, "I won't be a reluctant candidate. I'll run like hell."[10] He won a pledge of second-ballot support from Texas and South Carolina. Kentucky said it would be with him on the third ballot. But winning pledges was not Reagan's main purpose—not yet. At every stop he merely asked delegates not to commit to any other candidate until the convention.

THE REPUBLICAN CONVENTION

On the face of it, Nixon had every reason to be confident when he arrived in Miami Beach on Monday, August 5. Reagan and Rockefeller's presence in the race made him the candidate of the party's center, the one best positioned to receive Rockefeller's delegates if Reagan made a serious run at the nomination and Reagan's delegates if Rockefeller's star somehow ascended. Of these two possibilities, the latter was the less likely but also the one that Nixon feared more. This was partly because he knew Rockefeller to be a formidable political figure with deep pockets and a strong record, in contrast to Reagan, whom Nixon dismissed as untested both as a governor and a candidate for national office. Rockefeller also might benefit, Nixon worried, from the fact that despite the rising importance of the South at the convention, the GOP's delegate allocation formula still favored the industrial states of the North whose delegations received bonus votes for electing congressmen, senators, and governors in large numbers in 1966. All of these states had been on the receiving end of Rockefeller's media barrage. Nixon fretted that their delegates might regard Rockefeller as the candidate most likely to carry their home states.

Rockefeller's strategy hinged on persuading five northern favorite-son candidates to stay in the race: Gov. James Rhodes of Ohio, who controlled his state's 58-member delegation; Governor Romney of Michigan, who led his state's 44 delegates; Governor Agnew of Maryland, with 26 delegates; Sen. Clifford Case of New Jersey (40); and, of course, Reagan, who had California's 86 delegates. Added to the other favorite sons—senators Frank Carlson of Kansas (20 delegates) and Hiram Fong of Hawaii (14) and governors Walter Hickel of Alaska (12) and Winthrop Rockefeller of Arkansas (18)—these 316 delegates, plus the roughly 350 that Rockefeller expected to support him, plus the 150–200 that he thought Reagan would be able to add to his California base from the South and Mountain West would be enough to deny Nixon the 667 votes he needed for a first-ballot nomination.

Rockefeller predicted that he would win a fourth or fifth ballot victory, but in truth he had little hope of benefiting even if Nixon faltered. Outside the Northeast, Rockefeller had virtually no second-choice support in any delegation except his brother Winthrop's Arkansas. The convention's conservative character was demonstrated on Monday night, when the delegates greeted Goldwater, Rockefeller's nemesis in 1964, with tumultuous applause and cheered his speech exuberantly. At that point it became clear that Rockefeller's one chance—the longest of long shots—would be to revive *Time* magazine's old idea of persuading Reagan to run as his vice president. But Reagan's response to suggestions that he serve as running mate on anyone's ticket was, "Even if they tied and gagged me, I would find a way to signal by wiggling my ears."[11] At the start of the convention, Agnew took his revenge on Rockefeller for leaving him at the altar in March by endorsing Nixon.

Reagan had plans of his own. On Monday of convention week, the California delegation passed a resolution asking him to shed his favorite-son cloak and become "a leading and bona fide candidate for president." "Gosh," said Reagan, who was the first contender to arrive in Miami Beach, "I was surprised. It all came out of the clear blue sky."[12] Others were less astonished. Asked to comment, Gov. David Cargo of New Mexico said, "It's like a woman who's eight and a half months pregnant announcing she's going to have a baby."[13]

On the day of his announcement Reagan met with the Kansas, Nebraska, Iowa, and Minnesota delegations, but it was clear that the lowest-hanging fruit as he tried to create a sense of momentum lay in North Carolina, Georgia, Mississippi, Florida, Louisiana, Texas, and Alabama, which together had 218 votes. Although most of these delegates had reconciled themselves to voting for Nixon, they were a hair trigger away from jumping to Reagan at the slightest excuse. On the eve of the convention Nixon nearly gave them one. For weeks he had been dangling the vice presidential nomination in front of multiple moderate and liberal Republicans, partly as a way of securing their support and partly because of his misplaced sense that his vulnerability lay on the left, with Rockefeller. The Nixon campaign leaked the names to the press, as did some of those whom he sounded out. Public speculation centered on Mayor John V. Lindsay of New York City and senators Charles Percy of Illinois, Edward Brooke of Massachusetts, and Mark Hatfield of Oregon. On Monday, August 5, the *New York Times* ran a story saying that Nixon was going to choose a liberal in order to balance the ticket. Clif White believed that several southern delegations, especially those from Florida, Mississippi, and South Carolina, were just one or two conversions away from swinging to Reagan.

Nixon thought that he had locked up the South when he met with the southern state party chairmen on May 31, but now he had to fight for it all over again. Even southern party leaders who strongly supported Nixon, such as Dent of South Carolina, Howard "Bo" Calloway of Georgia, William Murfin of Florida, and Clarke Reed of Mississippi, liked having Reagan in the race so they would have something to bargain with. As Reed said, "The harder Nixon had to fight, the more the South stood to gain. So we wanted a nice open convention" at which Nixon would prevail.[14] "I'd rather he owe us than the liberals" for his nomination, Reed added.[15] A deeper concern for Nixon was that the southern party chairs would abandon him if their delegations stampeded to Reagan.

On Monday night Thurmond told Nixon that all the southern delegates needed to hear him as their leaders had in May and Thurmond himself had in personal conversations. The next day Nixon appeared before two groups of delegations, first those from the Deep South plus Texas and Kentucky and then those from the Outer South plus South Carolina. The meetings were closed to the press but at the request of a *Miami Herald* reporter a Florida delegate snuck a tape recorder into the second meeting. Based on the questions they asked, the three issues that most concerned the southerners were busing to achieve school desegregation, the liberal Supreme Court, and the vice presidential nomination. Nixon assuaged their concerns on all of these matters in adroitly measured, uncontroversial language. He supported integration but opposed sending "a child that is two or three grades behind another child into a strange community" just to "try to satisfy some professional civil rights group," a veiled way of saying that inner-city black children would not be bussed into white suburban schools.[16] Regarding the Supreme Court, he pledged to appoint justices who would "interpret the law and not make the law" in the manner of the Warren court. As for the vice presidency, Nixon promised, "I am not going to take, I can assure you, anybody that is going to divide the party."[17] (Translation: he would not choose a liberal.)

The *Herald* printed Nixon's remarks. The story did Nixon no harm in the North while fortifying his support in the South, where his promises were now on the record. Goldwater, Thurmond, and Sen. John Tower of Texas solidified whatever gains Nixon made in these appearances by visiting southern delegations in their state caucuses. Thurmond warned, "A vote for Reagan is a vote for Rockefeller."[18] Goldwater kept talking up the

Californian for vice president, forcing an exasperated Reagan to repeatedly say he would not accept the nomination under any circumstances.

Reagan spent Tuesday meeting with the delegations from Mississippi, Alabama, and Texas. But it was too late. Even more than they wanted a nominee who could carry their states, Deep South delegates wanted someone who would win the election. Only a Republican president could move the courts in a more conservative direction and stave off the pressure for school desegregation from the Departments of Justice and Health, Education and Welfare—and only a Republican president indebted to the South for his nomination would be inclined to do so. Nixon could win in November, most of them believed, but not the inexperienced Reagan. By Tuesday night, CBS News estimated, Reagan's support had declined to 181 delegates, down eleven from the night before. Largely on the strength of the Arkansas delegation, whose governor, Winthrop Rockefeller, endorsed his brother while preserving his own favorite-son status, Rocky gained seventeen votes, raising his total to 260 in the CBS estimate.

Nixon remained stuck at 628, up just one vote from Monday night and still thirty-nine shy of the nomination. Even if the South continued to hold firm, he needed to break open at least one of the large northern favorite-son delegations: Rhodes's Ohio, Romney's Michigan, or Case's New Jersey. On Tuesday night, New Jersey cracked. At Nixon's urging, Bergen County Republican chair Nelson Gross told CBS that he and his suburban county's other four delegates intended to urge their colleagues to abandon Case at the delegation's meeting on Wednesday morning. Gross predicted that Nixon would receive thirty of the state's forty votes, twelve more than he actually ended up getting. But even with just eighteen New Jersey votes, Nixon was essentially over the top. So confident of a first-ballot victory did New Jersey's defection make him that he told his supporters in the other favorite-son delegations to honor their commitments—a gesture that Rhodes, Romney, Carlson, and the others appreciated. According to Reagan campaign adviser Stuart Spencer, even the California delegation "had a back-up position for Richard Nixon" if Reagan faltered on the first ballot, which Spencer had negotiated with California's lieutenant governor Robert Finch, a close ally of Nixon.[19]

Tuesday's evening session of the convention was uneventful, which was exactly what national party chair Ray Bliss had intended when he created the Republican Coordinating Committee in 1965. In three years of regular meetings, the party's leading governors, senators, representatives, and past presidential nominees produced a series of policy papers that laid the foundation for most of what went into the platform. "Our goal is peace and understanding, at home and abroad," intoned House Republican leader Gerald Ford of Michigan, the convention chair. "No more platitudes," he added unselfconsciously.[20]

Ford's Senate counterpart, Everett Dirksen of Illinois, presented the platform to the convention, concluding his remarks with a call-and-response recitation of the Pledge of Allegiance that roused the delegates to a frenzy. (He also said, "Never has the sanctity of life been so scorned," referring not to abortion, which was not a partisan issue at the time, but rather to the rising murder rate.) Dirksen's main goal as platform chair—and Nixon's as the front-running candidate—was to avoid floor fights of the kind that severely divided the party in 1964. When Rockefeller objected to a draft of the Vietnam plank that basically endorsed Johnson administration policy, Dirksen, a skilled legislative leader who knew the value of accommodation, altered the language to reflect Rockefeller's emphasis on reaching a negotiated settlement. The platform's domestic policy provisions accepted certain liberal goals but proposed conservative means of achieving them, largely through state and local rather than federal action. The convention adopted the platform by a voice vote, with little or no audible dissent.

Wednesday brought a new complication for Nixon: a story by Don Oberdorfer in the *Herald*, distributed at Clif White's direction to all delegates in their seats, claiming that he had decided on Hatfield as his running mate. Although Hatfield added to Nixon's woes by saying, "I wouldn't turn it down," Senator Tower dismissed the story as "a plant" by the Rockefeller or Reagan campaign for the purpose of driving conservative delegates away from Nixon. Rockefeller turned up the heat in a different way in his visits to state delegations, attacking Nixon for the first time in his campaign as someone who had not won an election in eighteen years. But Rockefeller's repeated declaration that "there will be no first ballot nomination, and this will be an open convention" sounded increasingly hollow.

Wednesday's session offered traditional convention fare—a seemingly endless series of nominations, seconding speeches, and demonstrations culminating in the first ballot. At 5:45 p.m. EDT, CBS anchor Walter Cronkite interrupted California state treasurer Ivy Baker Priest's nominating speech for Reagan to report that his network's tally now showed Nixon with 676 votes, a nine-vote majority. At 10:13 p.m. Agnew ascended the podium to nominate Nixon. His forceful manner belied by his cracking voice, Agnew's intonation was so uneven that the first big cheer arose halfway through this sentence: "At this moment of history the Republican Party has the duty to put forward a *man* [cheers], a man to not only match this moment but to master it." Agnew's speech was preceded by nominations for Reagan, Rockefeller, Hickel, Fong, Carlson, Winthrop Rockefeller, and Romney, and was followed by nominations for Case, Rhodes, Thurmond (who withdrew in favor of Nixon, but only after a nominating speech and four seconding speeches), and perennial also-ran Harold Stassen, now making his fifth bid for the presidency. Stassen was "the most misunderstood and underestimated man in America," according to nephew J. Robert Stassen, who nominated him. Not until 1:14 a.m. on Thursday did the balloting begin, and then only after convention chair Ford drew boos and groans by announcing that "This Is My Country" would first be performed.

Stassen's prediction of a sixth-ballot nomination went unfulfilled, as did Rockefeller's confident statement that Nixon's momentum had been stopped in its tracks. The states were called alphabetically, and when Florida cast 32 of its 34 votes for Nixon, all hope vanished that Reagan would steal the southern delegations from him. In the end, Nixon swept the South by more than four to one over Reagan: 228 to 53, with Rockefeller trailing with 6. Nixon also dominated the Midwest 150 to 28 (Rockefeller) to 6 (Reagan) and the border states 81 to 19 (Rockefeller) to 10 (Reagan). On the strength of his support in California, Reagan won the Pacific states 92 to 44 (Nixon) to 4 (Rockefeller), but Nixon bested him in the Mountain West 100 to 15, with Rockefeller receiving 9 votes. Rockefeller won only in the Northeast, far outpacing Nixon by 205 to 87.[21] Reagan received just one vote in the region. In all, Nixon received 692 votes, twenty-five more than required for nomination. Although he had votes in reserve if he needed them in Ohio, Kansas, and other favorite-son states, he also risked losing much of his southern support if he did not make it over the top on the first ballot. Dent was able to hold South Carolina for Nixon, for example, only by promising that on the second ballot the delegation would be free to vote for Reagan.

The roll call ended at 1:56 a.m., and when the chair of the California delegation asked permission for Reagan to address the convention, Ford ruled him out of order, leaving the governor standing awkwardly on the podium. Reagan's turn came when he moved to make the nomination unanimous in a one-minute speech; the motion passed with no audible dissent. Reagan may "have another shot at the presidency," observed Cronkite, "but it seems unlikely," given his age. (He was fifty-seven.) Rockefeller was less gracious in defeat. Asked why he lost, he replied, "You ever been to a Republican convention?" Rockefeller did place a congratulatory call to Nixon, who did not offer him a place on the ticket. "Don't spend the time," Rockefeller had already told a journalist who was trying to ask him if he would accept the vice presidential nomination. According to Nixon, Rockefeller said that "Ron didn't come through as well as he thought he would."[22]

Nixon took questions from reporters, surrounded by his family in their hotel suite. Asked to explain his comeback, he gave a clinically political answer. "Looking at it as a political observer," he said, "the vacuum that occurred in the Republican Party as a result of the defeat of '64, the fact that I was the major campaigner for the party in 1966, the fact that we had the development in foreign affairs which put great effect and great interest in foreign policy." With an eye on November, Nixon said he had made no effort to poach delegates from the large-state governors who were favorite-son candidates because he wanted their enthusiastic support in the fall, unleavened by resentment or hurt feelings.

Nixon then turned to the vice presidential nomination. To be sure, this was a matter he had been thinking and even polling about for some time. One poll was of three hundred party leaders, whom he wrote to ask three questions:

Who would be the best running mate to provide geographical and
    philosophical balance?
Who would be the best campaigner?
Who was best qualified to be president?

The letters were gestures, a show of respect to the Republican officials whose opinions Nixon pretended to be soliciting. The other poll was of voters to see which of several prospective vice presidential candidates would help the ticket. None of them did. John Sears said that after seeing the results, "Actually we wanted to run without a vice president."[23]

Nixon had been a running mate in 1952 and 1956 and had chosen one in 1960. He wanted someone in his own vice presidential image: loyal, hardworking, and willing to attack the opposition relentlessly so that he could take the high road and appear presidential. He did not want to repeat his mistake in 1960, when he chose United Nations ambassador Henry Cabot Lodge, a lazy campaigner who occasionally embarrassed Nixon with off-message remarks, such as promising to appoint "a Negro in the cabinet"—a promise that Kennedy denounced as "racism in reverse" while pledging to appoint the best people on a color-blind basis.[24] Nixon almost certainly would have chosen an African American for his cabinet, but as his party's candidate for president, it was his prerogative to decide whether and when to make such a promise.

After dismissing the press from his suite shortly before 3:00 a.m. on Thursday, Nixon convened a series of four meetings with varied groups totaling about fifty party leaders, members of his own staff, and other supporters, including Rev. Billy Graham. When no one brought up Agnew's name in either of the first two gatherings, Nixon tried to prime the pump by saying that Agnew had given "a hell of a nominating speech."[25] This remark went unechoed because Agnew's speech had been a dud. After the second meeting, with a group of mostly congressional and state leaders, Nixon took Goldwater aside and asked, "Could you live with Agnew?" Goldwater, who had made the notoriously bad choice of an obscure House member, William Miller of New York, as his vice presidential candidate in 1964 because "he drives Johnson crazy," said, "Hell, yes. He's the best man you could have. He's been firm, and so what if he's not known? No vice president ever is."[26]

After that same meeting, Thurmond gave Nixon three lists, one with his preferred candidates—Reagan, Tower, Rep. Rogers Morton of Maryland, Rep. George Bush of Texas, Sen. Howard Baker of Tennessee, and Sen. Robert Griffin of Michigan; one labeled "unacceptable" that listed Hatfield, Lindsay, and Rockefeller; and one headed "no objections," scribbled during the meeting when he heard Nixon mention Agnew and Gov. John Volpe of Massachusetts, another Nixon favorite and, like Agnew, an "ethnic" Republican who had been elected governor in a Democratic state. "You have nothing to worry about," Nixon told Thurmond. "You will be pleased."[27] But when Agnew's name again failed to come up in the third of Nixon's morning meetings, he gathered a small group of close aides and associates and asked two of them, first Robert Finch, the popular lieutenant governor of California and a longtime friend, and then Representative Morton, his convention floor manager, if they would consider running with him. Knowing that the offers were born of jitters, both men refused. Bush's appeal was that he was young and from Texas in a year when Nixon feared losing the youth vote and the Lone Star State. Nixon "decided against it," the first-term representative wrote to a friend, "because of my short service in the House."[28]

Nixon clearly wanted Agnew. "Agnew's a tough, shrewd Greek," he told speechwriter William Safire. "He *wears* well. He wears *well*."[29] Also, as Nixon later wrote in his memoir, with Wallace in the race, Agnew "fit the bill geographically," which Volpe did not. Nixon knew that, with the exception of Thurmond's South Carolina, he would lose the Deep South to Wallace and therefore needed to win "the entire rimland of the South," to which Maryland was a bordering state.[30] Nixon asked Senator Tower, who was at the final meeting, to call Thurmond and ask if he wanted Agnew or Volpe. It was a way to flatter Thurmond while knowing what he would say. In addition to preferring a border state candidate to a New Englander, Thurmond read the Washington newspapers and knew about Agnew's confrontation with Maryland's civil rights leaders in April, which he heartily approved. No one ran background checks on prospective running mates in this era, so Nixon did not know until the fifth year of his presidency that Agnew had regularly taken bribes from Maryland contractors as a local official, as governor, and later as vice president.[31]

Nixon announced his selection of Agnew at 12:40 p.m. on Thursday. The instant press reaction was surprise—"Spiro who?"—and hostility. Agnew was an obscure figure to most national political reporters. In a book published several months before the convention, Stephen Hess and David Broder had assessed fourteen likely vice presidential candidates.[32] Agnew was nowhere on the list. What most reporters did know was that Agnew had switched to Nixon after being embarrassed by Rockefeller in March and that he had attacked his state's civil rights leaders. The instant media consensus was that Nixon chose Agnew partly as payback for defecting from Rockefeller and partly to appeal to racist voters, not just in the South but also in the white working-class neighborhoods of the northern cities. Nixon's effort to pass off Agnew as an urban expert was scoffed at. Before becoming governor Agnew had been the elected chief executive not of Baltimore but of suburban Baltimore County. His solution to urban problems, like that of most of the city's whites, had been to move to the suburbs as soon as he could afford to. In that sense, Agnew fit an electorate that, for the first time in history, was more suburban than urban or rural.[33]

Liberal Republicans, mildly disappointed by Nixon's nomination, were furious about his selection of Agnew. Gov. John Chafee of Rhode Island, former Pennsylvania governor William Scranton, and Rep. Charles Goodell of New York tried to persuade Lindsay to let them nominate him for vice president at the convention's Thursday evening session. But Lindsay had national ambitions of his own and was not about to do what Rockefeller so self-destructively did in 1964: split the party. He not only refused to contest Agnew's nomination but agreed to make a seconding speech endorsing his candidacy. Chafee, Scranton, and Goodell then turned to Romney, who impulsively agreed to run. Romney received 186 votes to Agnew's 1,119. He won half of Arkansas's delegates, a majority of votes from Delaware,

Michigan, Minnesota, Oregon, and Rhode Island, and scattered support in fifteen other delegations—and that was it.

The time required to beat back Romney's challenge pushed Nixon's acceptance address to nearly 11:00 p.m. It was a well-honed, well-polished version of the speech he had been giving since 1966. Nixon's theme was general: America has serious problems at home and abroad; therefore, "It's time for new leadership in the United States of America!" He praised "the great majority of Americans, the forgotten Americans, the non-shouters, the non-demonstrators" who "work and they save and they pay their taxes and they care." Nixon once again promised to appoint "a new attorney general of the United States of America!"—one of the few specific pledges he made. His main flourishes were rhetorical, long anaphoric refrains offered in the manner of Martin Luther King. Contemplating the bicentennial of American independence in just eight years, Nixon offered a vision of "our nation at peace and the world at peace," of a people "once again proud of their flag," of cities free of "the problems of slums and pollution and traffic," and of a "rural America [that] attracts people to the country"—with each dream introduced by the phrase "I see a day." He organized his inspirational peroration on the theme, "I see a child." "I see the face of a child . . . living in poverty and hopelessness," he said. "I see another child," one who grew up with help from good parents and inspirational teachers, coaches, and ministers. "Tonight he stands before you nominated for president of the United States of America," Nixon said, to long and heartfelt applause. "For most of us . . . the American dream has come true," he concluded. "And what I ask you to do is help make that dream come true for millions to whom it's an impossible dream today."[34]

Nixon knew he was playing on emotion and proud that he did it so well. "I'd like to see Rocky or Romney or Lindsay do a moving thing like that 'impossible dream' part where I changed my voice," he bragged to Safire. "Reagan's an actor, but I'd like to see him do that."[35] The speech was among the best Nixon had ever given, second only to his Checkers speech in 1952. Cronkite said he was "spellbound." "Obviously there's a new Nixon," added CBS's main commentator, Eric Sevareid, the latest to join that chorus. "There's an air of solidity about this man that wasn't there some years ago, a great air of a kind of natural authority about him. . . . He is, it seems to me, a more solid man, surer afoot."

With the minor exception of Agnew's nomination, which provided the convention's sole discordant note, Nixon left Miami with a united Republican Party, in stark contrast to 1964. Rockefeller, Reagan, and all the favorite sons had been treated with proper professional courtesy. Neither they nor their supporters left feeling disregarded or disrespected. In the days following the convention Nixon spent hours phoning Rockefeller, Reagan, Romney, Rhodes, Scranton, Lindsay, senators Brooke of Massachusetts and Jacob Javits of New York, and governors John Love of Colorado and Dan Evans of Washington to seek their advice and stroke their egos. The platform walked a fine line between liberals and conservatives on domestic policy and, after Rockefeller's minor suggestions were incorporated, between hawks and doves on Vietnam. (Unlike Humphrey, Nixon faced no serious pressure from within his party to take a particular stand on the war.) His speech had been uplifting and uncontroversial. The massive television audience for the convention witnessed a party that had its act together. Nixon's postconvention "bounce" in the Gallup Poll lifted him from a two-point lead over Humphrey in July to a sixteen-point lead—45 percent to 29 percent, with the still-soaring Wallace at 18 percent—in the poll taken August 8–11, right after the convention.

The failure of the convention, like the failure of Nixon's campaign for the nomination, was more subtle. Neither the candidate nor his party stood for anything that would alienate voters, but what did it stand for that would excite or even attract them? The GOP was energized, but mostly by the prospect of winning the presidency, not by anything that it planned to do once in office. "Nixon had always acted as the bubble in the plumber's level," Geoffrey Kabaservice has observed, "seeking the dead center of the GOP."[36] But the center as he and, at his direction, the Republican platform presented it in 1968 was defined more by what it was not—neither too far left nor too far right—than by what it was. The broader electorate, indifferent to which party would win the spoils of victory, was impressed in the short term but presumably would want to know more about what Nixon and the GOP intended to do besides offer new leadership and appoint a new attorney general.

THE RUN-UP TO THE DEMOCRATIC CONVENTION

Robert Kennedy's assassination left Eugene McCarthy the only candidate in the race for the Democratic presidential nomination who opposed the war in Vietnam. He was also the only surviving candidate to have drawn a significant number of votes in the primaries. Indeed, of all the votes cast in Democratic contests in 1968, McCarthy won the most: 38.7 percent to Kennedy's 30.6 percent, with Johnson trailing at 5.1 percent and Humphrey at 2.2 percent.

Despite his reluctance to campaign in New York, McCarthy added to his total in the state's June 18 primary. All but 67 of New York's 190 delegates to the Democratic National Convention were chosen in the primary, with each of the forty-one congressional districts allotted three delegates. Uniquely among the primaries, in New York only the names of those running for delegate appeared on district ballots, not the names of the candidates to whom they were pledged. The primary placed a premium on grassroots organization to educate voters about which unfamiliar names to mark if they supported a particular presidential candidate. Kennedy had dreaded the New York primary because McCarthy was better organized there, the result of his being the first candidate to raise the antiwar banner against Johnson, and also because Kennedy had neglected the state party while he was in the Senate. On primary day, sixty-two McCarthy delegates were elected and thirty who ran as Kennedy loyalists. Humphrey won twelve, and the rest were uncommitted.

MCCARTHY

For Kennedy's core supporters—family, friends, and political aides—McCarthy's status as the surviving antiwar candidate compounded the cruelty of the assassination. The intense rivalry between the two men—each convinced that he was both the leading Catholic politician in the country and the party's most effective critic of the war—had warped into personal hostility in the heat of the campaign. McCarthy's victory in New York, Kennedy's home territory, posthumously aggravated the problem. So did his response when new gun-control legislation was introduced in Congress after the assassination. However defensible his position may have been as prudential lawmaking, McCarthy's June 16 comment that "you really ought not to try to put through legislation under panic conditions" rubbed the raw nerves of RFK's core supporters.[37] "He could not have chosen anything better calculated to alienate Kennedy people," wrote McCarthy speechwriter Jeremy Larner.[38]

Organizationally, the McCarthy campaign had always been a mess at the top, plagued by competing power centers (campaign manager Blair Clark, founding organizer Curtis Gans, McCarthy's Senate staff, his wife Abigail) and the candidate's preference for sycophants and artistic hangers-on. McCarthy was right to think that "we may not be very well organized at the top, but we're the best organized campaign at the bottom that there's ever been in the history of the country."[39] That worked beautifully in the primaries. But heading into the convention the challenge was both clear and different.

McCarthy needed to ardently woo Kennedy loyalists and convince them to put aside all differences in the service of their shared opposition to the war. He also needed to reach out to party regulars who were not firmly committed to Humphrey by pointing to polls showing that the vice president was hopelessly behind Nixon but that McCarthy was competitive against him. The final Gallup Poll released before the convention, for example, showed Humphrey trailing Nixon by 16 percentage points and McCarthy behind by only 5 points.

Instead, McCarthy did none of these things, nor much of anything else. He essentially stopped campaigning after the California primary, and when he did visit state delegations, he refused to tell them what they wanted to hear—namely, that he would loyally support the nominee of the party against Richard Nixon. Meeting with the California delegation on August 12, McCarthy deigned to mention the name of Robert Kennedy, to whom these delegates were devoted. Leaders such as Walter Reuther, the head of the United Auto Workers, and Harold Hughes, the governor of Iowa, made clear that all they needed from McCarthy was a phone call asking for their support. McCarthy made no such calls. He was "sleep-walking" through the final stage of the campaign, said Clark, and "had obviously quit."[40] Sen. George McGovern of South Dakota, who the previous fall had steered candidate-seeking antiwar Democrats to McCarthy, was "astounded" when McCarthy told him in early July that he was not going after Kennedy's delegates. "The nomination is already sewed up," McCarthy said. "Hubert's got it."[41]

MCGOVERN

In fall 1967 McGovern had been Allard Lowenstein and other antiwar activists' second choice after Kennedy as the candidate to challenge Johnson for the Democratic nomination. The son of a Methodist minister in Mitchell and other small South Dakota towns and, at age twenty, a decorated bomber pilot in World War II, McGovern earned a doctorate in American history at Northwestern University funded by the GI Bill and began teaching at his alma mater, Dakota Wesleyan University. His dissertation was on the Colorado coal miners' attempt to unionize in 1914, the "revolt against capitalism" that led to the Ludlow massacre organized by the mine owners.[42] McGovern supported the left wing third-party candidacy of Henry Wallace against President Harry S. Truman in 1948 but, four years later, campaigned for Democratic nominee Adlai Stevenson. Restless in academe, McGovern became executive secretary of the South Dakota Democratic Party in 1953 and built a statewide organization essentially from scratch.

At the urging of some of Robert F. Kennedy's supporters, Sen. George S. McGovern of South Dakota entered the Democratic nominating contest after Kennedy was assassinated. (Credit: AP Images)

So effective was McGovern at grassroots organizing that the party, which in 1952 had secured only two of 110 seats in the state legislature, was able to elect him in 1956 to one of South Dakota's two seats in the U.S. House of Representatives—the first time the state had sent a Democrat to Congress in twenty years. In 1960 McGovern narrowly lost a bid to unseat incumbent Republican senator Karl Mundt while also campaigning for John F. Kennedy for president. Grateful for his efforts, JFK and his campaign manager, Robert Kennedy, saw to it that McGovern was appointed to head the Food for Peace program. In 1962 he was elected by 597 votes to an open seat in the Senate. His need to campaign for reelection six years later dissuaded McGovern from accepting the antiwar activists' request to challenge Johnson.

As a senator, McGovern's relationship with Robert Kennedy was strong. He persuaded the Senate to create the Select Committee on Nutrition and Human Needs, a cause dear to Kennedy's heart that also served the agricultural interests of their states. Although he voted for the Gulf of Tonkin Resolution in 1964, McGovern became an outspoken critic of the war just one year later and in spring 1967 called the bombing campaign "a policy of madness."[43] On June 8, 1968, riding RFK's funeral train from the memorial mass at St. Patrick's Cathedral in New York City to burial in Arlington National Cemetery near Washington—an intensely emotional eight-hour journey—some young Kennedy aides urged McGovern to pick up the slain candidate's fallen torch and enter the race for the nomination. In late July McGovern sought assurances from Kennedy's brother-in-law and close adviser Steve Smith that Sen. Edward Kennedy did not intend to run in his brother's stead.

Smith gave a green light and McGovern announced his candidacy on August 10, two days after the Republican convention. "I believe deeply in the twin goals for which Robert Kennedy gave his life," McGovern said in his announcement speech, "an end to the war in Vietnam and a passionate commitment to heal the divisions in our own society." Kennedy aides Pierre Salinger and Frank Mankiewicz joined McGovern's campaign staff. Many of Kennedy's delegates rallied to McGovern, some because they were irreconcilably alienated from McCarthy and others who would have gone with McCarthy for the asking but were never asked. Liberal opinion was divided about McGovern's entry. The *New York Times* condemned "sore-head elements in the party's Kennedy wing" for not uniting all of the Democrats' antiwar factions behind McCarthy, but the *Progressive* magazine argued that without McGovern in the race Kennedy's delegates would vote for Humphrey. Nearly all of Kennedy's black supporters shifted to Humphrey anyway, having known him much longer and therefore trusting him much more than either McGovern or McCarthy.

HUMPHREY

The initial flow of delegates from Kennedy to Humphrey was rapid and extensive. By June 10, less than a week after the assassination, the *New York Times* estimated (overestimated, it turned out) that Humphrey would pick up 400 of Kennedy's delegates, with McCarthy gaining 75 and the 174 members of the Kennedy-pledged California delegation remaining uncommitted. Kennedy's absence from the race and McCarthy's passivity spared Humphrey what promised to be bruising fights at the state Democratic conventions in Ohio and Michigan.

But nothing about Humphrey's status as the front-runner was secure during the preconvention months of June, July, and August. The loyalty of the new Humphrey delegates was uncertain, especially if Edward Kennedy or, as it turned out, a Kennedy proxy such as McGovern got into the race. Humphrey's funding sources dried up. As he later wrote, "A large share of the money pledged to me came from New York business leaders who feared and distrusted Bob [Kennedy]. With his death their interest in me waned"—indeed, most of their subsequent donations went to Nixon.[44] As a consequence, Humphrey had to cancel a planned preconvention advertising campaign and lay off members from his campaign staff.

More than anything, Humphrey was plagued by his support for Johnson's war policy. His speeches drew sparse and unenthusiastic crowds, and were interrupted by hecklers chanting "Dump the Hump" and other less G-rated epithets. "Why Change the Ventriloquist for the Puppet?" read one protester's sign, reviving memories of the November 1966 *Esquire* cover that depicted Humphrey as a dummy sitting on the president's lap. Meanwhile, Johnson's hope that stopping the bombing and withdrawing from the election would lead to productive peace negotiations was proving forlorn. Johnson thought his terms for ending the bombing of North Vietnam, which he had resumed on July 1, were reasonable: North Vietnam must respect the demilitarized zone between north and south, end its shelling of southern cities, and express its willingness to sit down with the government of South Vietnam.[45] North Vietnam's behavior changed not a whit, either on the battlefield or in the Paris negotiations, such as they were. "I halt, and then Ho Chi Minh shoves his trucks right up my ass," fumed Johnson. "That's your bombing halt."[46] South Vietnam refused even to send a delegation to Paris.

Just as the great hope that led Johnson to extend an olive branch to the communists on March 31 had been undone by events, so had his great fear of a Kennedy challenge. Much of the motivation for Johnson's withdrawal from the election had been the prospect of a brutal nominating contest with Kennedy that the president either would lose or would win at the cost of a fatally divided party. With Kennedy gone, the greatest source of pressure on Johnson to make further concessions to North Vietnam was gone as well. So was the nightmare of being denied renomination by his hated rival. As the summer wore on and Humphrey languished in the polls against Nixon, Johnson toyed with the idea of reentering the race. He was sure he could beat the Republican, who he frequently said was "like a Spanish horse who runs faster than anyone for the first nine lengths and then turns around and runs backwards."[47]

Although the responses he received from the southern governors, whom he had asked Texas governor John Connally to canvass, were strongly discouraging, Johnson did not give up. He sent out chief political aide Marvin Watson, recently appointed to fill the traditionally partisan role of postmaster general, to make his own soundings. He reminded his most loyal donors not to send money to Humphrey, and he kept firm control of the convention machinery, including the schedule of events and the communications equipment in the convention hall. All of the convention's officers—permanent chair Carl Albert of Oklahoma, the House majority leader; keynote speaker Daniel Inouye, a senator from Hawaii; rules committee chair Samuel H. Shapiro, the governor of Illinois; credentials committee chair Richard Hughes, the governor of New Jersey; and platform committee chair Hale Boggs, a congressman from Louisiana—were Johnson men. All of the delegations seated near the podium, including Texas and Illinois, were dominated by party regulars. New York, California, Wisconsin, and the rest of the insurgents were banished to the rear of the hall.[48]

Humphrey was angry at Johnson. "The president didn't run because he knew he couldn't make it," he fumed to aides on June 19. "And he clothed me with nothing." But Humphrey also was stuck. Break with Johnson, as some aides were advising, and offer his own plan for Vietnam? Sometimes, as in a June 20 comment, Humphrey hinted that he might do exactly that. "Hubert Humphrey as vice president is a member of the team," he told the National Press Club. "Hubert Humphrey as president is captain of a team."[49] Some advisers even counseled quitting the team—that is, resigning as vice president so that he would no longer be constrained by the loyalties demanded of the job.

But to break with Johnson carried risks that Humphrey was not prepared to take, not least of them the president's reentry into the race. Humphrey would appear not only disloyal but also hypocritical if he distanced himself from Johnson. For two years the vice president had been the administration's most ardent public defender of the war. Most recently, at the Oklahoma state Democratic convention, he had said, "Anyone who would repudiate a government and a policy of which he has been a part in order to gain votes is not the kind of person you can trust to keep the promises he makes in a campaign."[50] Three of Humphrey's four main groups of supporters—southern delegates, labor leaders, and big-city party regulars—were prowar. Only his African American backers would cheer a declaration of independence, and even then not too loudly for fear of antagonizing the president.

Humphrey finally decided to try to "break out of the cocoon without repudiating my father," a metaphor no less clear for being mixed.[51] In late spring he created a task force of distinguished academics to help him construct a major statement on Vietnam. Led by Edwin Reischauer, Samuel Huntington, and Zbigniew Brzezinski, the group advised him to call for a

As late as the Democratic convention, President Lyndon B. Johnson entertained hopes that, despite his withdrawal from the election, the party would ask him to run. (Credit: Yoichi Okamoto, provided by the Lyndon B. Johnson Presidential Library)

de-Americanization of the war and a halt to the latest round of bombing. Meeting with them on July 25, Humphrey seemed to agree. "I would favor an immediate halt in the bombing," he planned to say, based on a continuing "decline in the infiltration rate from North Vietnam." But, he added, "I'll have to show it to the president."[52]

Humphrey headed to the White House that evening. Johnson had met with Nixon the day before and gratefully received the Republican candidate's pledge that "as long as the administration did not soften its position [in Vietnam], he would not criticize us."[53] When Johnson saw Humphrey's draft statement he told the vice president that by issuing it he would "endanger American troops like his sons-in-law [Charles Robb and Patrick Nugent, the husbands of Johnson daughters Lynda Bird and Luci Baines, respectively] and cost lives. I would have their blood on my hands," Humphrey recalled Johnson saying. "He would denounce me publicly for playing politics with peace."[54] Nixon pledged "not to undercut my negotiating position," the president added, with a between-the-lines threat that even if he could not deny Humphrey the nomination, he could withhold his support in the general election. "I've eaten so much of Johnson's shit that I've grown to like the taste of it," Humphrey fumed to an aide after the meeting.[55] He later wrote, "The president was impossible on the war. Such a fury when I showed him my task force report on Vietnam. . . . I had a choice. Break with the president and be denounced as irresponsible. Or muddle through. Really no choice if I wanted to be president. And I do, how badly I do."[56] When intelligence reports arrived showing that North Vietnam was preparing to launch another major offensive, Humphrey at least had a face-saving reason to back down.

Humphrey's bootless quest for a formula that would allow him to place some distance between himself and Johnson without alienating the president continued. On August 9 he showed Johnson a draft of a call he wanted to issue to end the bombing if North Vietnam reciprocated. Johnson again refused: "If you just let me work for peace, you'll have a better chance for election than by any speech you're going to make."[57] Ten days later, addressing the annual convention of the Veterans of Foreign Wars, Johnson declared, "We are not going to stop the bombing just to give them a chance to step up the bloodbath."[58] The president's August 19 speech coincided with the first day of meetings by the Democratic platform committee, whose responsibilities included writing the Vietnam plank. Johnson was laying down a marker to the committee as well as to the vice president.

As the August 26 opening of the convention approached, Humphrey asked that it be moved to Miami Beach. In October 1967 Daley had persuaded Johnson to have the convention in Chicago in order to keep Illinois's twenty-six electoral votes from going Republican in the November election. He sweetened the pot by offering $750,000 in cash subsidies and $150,000 in city services to the Democratic National Committee and promised that Johnson's vote tally in Cook County would exceed the 65 percent Daley had turned out for him in 1964. This was no idle boast: Daley carried every ward in the city when he ran for a fourth term in 1967, earning 74 percent of the vote. Daley also pointed out that, unlike Newark, Detroit, and other cities, Chicago had experienced no race riots during the fabled "long, hot summer" of 1967.[59] By July 1968, however, race riots had occurred in the city, and Humphrey was concerned that planned strikes by Chicago's electrical workers and taxi and bus drivers would hobble the convention. Even more, he worried about "detailed reports of meetings of such SDS [Students for a Democratic Society] radical factions as the Weathermen" and other "professional radicals" at which plans were laid to "organize local blacks in protest, stirring racial strife, and then to organize the students for a confrontation with the police." But Johnson refused to move the convention: "He had given his word to Daley and he wasn't going to back down."[60]

Humphrey's concerns were exaggerated but not groundless. Since organizing the massive march on the Pentagon in October 1967, the National Mobilization Committee to End the War in Vietnam had been planning a similarly large and peaceful protest at the Democratic convention. The MOBE was led by longtime pacifist David Dellinger and his young lieutenants Tom Hayden and Rennie Davis, just returned from a visit to Czechoslovakia where they turned over their draft cards to a representative of South Vietnam's communist National Liberation Front. The three targeted the Democrats because they could only afford to organize for one convention and at the time plans were made everyone believed that the Democrats would renominate Johnson. Meanwhile, in a separate effort, the small but publicity-savvy Youth International Party announced plans for more dramatic acts of disruption. "Yippie" leaders Abbie Hoffman and Jerry Rubin vowed to put LSD in Chicago's water supply, disguise cars as taxis and drive unsuspecting Democratic delegates to Wisconsin, and deploy attractive men to seduce the delegates' wives and daughters.

Were the Yippies kidding? Their nomination of a pig for president should have been a clue. But Daley—who, after the riots following King's assassination in April, complained that the police had not been ordered to "shoot to kill any arsonist" and "shoot to maim or cripple . . . any looters"—

did not think so.[61] What's more, the mayor conflated the peaceful MOBE with the anarchic Yippies. Fearing that 100,000 protesters were headed to his city to wreak havoc, he placed the 11,900-member Chicago police force on twelve-hour shifts and, acting through Governor Shapiro and President Johnson, called up 5,600 National Guardsmen and had 7,500 army troops on standby at bases in Texas, Oklahoma, and Colorado. Daley also severely restricted the parade permits issued to antiwar groups and refused them permission to stay overnight in the city's parks. The one permit granted to the MOBE authorized a rally in Grant Park, just east of the downtown convention hotels, on August 28, the day the Democrats would nominate their candidate.

Daley's fears were unrealistic. The MOBE was not the Yippies. Johnson's withdrawal in March, along with McCarthy's instruction to his supporters to stay home, meant that many fewer than the feared (or hoped-for) hundred thousand demonstrators were coming to Chicago. The "see-you-in-Chicago crowd . . . want to tear it all down," said McCarthy aide Sam Brown, who wanted nothing to distract from the effort to nominate McCarthy or at least get a peace plank into the party platform.[62] At their peak, the demonstrators numbered fewer than ten thousand, with only about one-fifth of those from outside the Chicago area.[63] For example, a New York peace group that sent fifty busloads to the Pentagon march in 1967 needed only five for the Chicago trip. Humphrey wrote to Daley urging that more parade permits be issued, but he received no reply.

Humphrey arrived in Chicago on Saturday, August 24, dreading the worst—a last-minute Johnson candidacy, a Kennedy draft, a disorderly city, a bitter platform fight—but hoping for the best. "I'd like to feel that when I went to Chicago that there were enough delegates in hand so that we had some degree of security, so that I could be a serene and pleasant man while I'm there," Humphrey said.[64] The preconvention Harris Poll showed that he had widened his lead over McCarthy among Democratic voters from 6 percentage points in July to 18 points in August: he led 56 percent to 38 percent. Convention-eve surveys by *Newsweek* and the *New York Times* gave him nearly 1,250 delegates—only sixty to seventy short of the 1,312 needed for nomination and several hundred more than McCarthy's 800 in the *Newsweek* survey or 619 in the *Times* survey. If Humphrey could emerge from a relatively harmonious convention as the nominee of his party, he might receive the same sort of bounce in the polls that Nixon got from the Republican conclave.

THE DEMOCRATIC CONVENTION

Nothing about the convention-eve gathering of Democrats in Chicago augured the sort of peaceful, unified assembly that Humphrey craved. The delegates were an admixture: from the nonprimary states, white, male, middle-aged or older party regulars chosen, in many cases, more than a year in advance in "secret caucuses, closed slate-making, [and] widespread proxy voting"; and, from the much smaller number of primary states: academics, peace activists, feminists, and other party outsiders elected as McCarthy and Kennedy supporters. As the Democrats' postelection Commission on Party Structure and Delegate Selection—the McGovern-Fraser Commission—concluded in 1969, overall the "nominating process was dominated by party wheel horses, entrenched office holders, and local bosses."[65] In contrast, the McCarthy-pledged Wisconsin delegation included nine professors (but no farmers), and among his Connecticut delegates were actor Paul Newman, playwright Arthur Miller, and cartoonist Jules Feiffer. Prolonging the preconvention agony (and shortening the postconvention period of wound-licking and peacemaking), the Democrats scheduled their assembly later on the election-year calendar than any major-party convention in more than a century.[66] In setting the date the previous fall, Johnson had wanted his renomination to coincide with his sixtieth birthday on August 27. In the end, Johnson did not even attend the convention, the first president to skip the event since Franklin D. Roosevelt in wartime 1944.

On a host of issues, John Soule and James Clarke found, Democratic delegates were much more divided in their views than Republican delegates were at their convention. Asked about three foreign and six domestic policies, Democrats were able to achieve at least 70 percent agreement on only two: the rightness of civil disobedience and the wrongness of denying foreign aid to countries less anticommunist than the United States. In contrast, at least 70 percent of Republican delegates shared the same position on seven of the nine issues, all but foreign aid and civil liberties. Democratic delegates were more liberal on average than Republican delegates but less united in their liberalism than the Republicans were in their conservatism.[67]

It helped the assembled Democrats not a bit that Chicago's convention hall, the International Amphitheatre, was in one part of town—the old stockyards, where flies still buzzed everywhere, including around the speakers' podium—and the hotels for delegates, alternates, the media, and other attendees were in another part of town, about five miles away. Daley had barbed wire–topped fences erected around the amphitheater—soon dubbed "Fort Daley"—and told city workers to gather up loose rocks and paving stones and to seal manhole covers with tar for several blocks in all directions. Concessionaires in the convention hall were instructed not to put ice in the drinks they sold. Like rocks outside, ice cubes inside could be dangerous projectiles. At midnight on Sunday, August 25, the eve of the convention, the police violently evicted a couple hundred Yippie-led protesters from Lincoln Park, two miles north of the convention hotels and nearly seven miles north of the amphitheater. After similar confrontations on Monday and Tuesday nights, police grudgingly allowed the uprooted, sleep-deprived crowd to migrate southward and stay overnight in Grant Park, across the street from the hotels and closer to the action.

Humphrey's immediate worries had to do with events within the convention hall rather than around it. Would President Johnson run?[68] "How fervently Johnson hoped he would be drafted by the convention in 1968," John Connally marveled in his memoir.[69] Johnson's allies and acolytes fed this hope. "You know your husband is going to be nominated, don't you?" Sen. James Eastland of Mississippi told Lady Bird Johnson two weeks before the convention.[70] "This convention is going to draft the president if there is the slightest indication the draft will be accepted," Johnson operative Jake Jacobson fawningly reported from Chicago on the Saturday before the opening session. Jacobson also quoted Daley as saying, "If Lyndon wants this nomination, he has got our delegation," which the mayor offered more as a pleasantry than a pledge.[71] "Ninety percent of Humphrey's delegates are Johnson delegates," claimed Connally, although he also recognized that there was "no way" his fellow southern governors would try to draft Johnson at this late date.[72]

All of these judgments but the last were wildly off the mark, but they fueled Johnson's dream of making a dramatic surprise appearance in the convention hall on Tuesday night, his birthday, and stampeding the delegates into nominating him. Only when platform committee chair and Johnson loyalist Hale Boggs told the president that morning that he might get a bad reception did Johnson realize how hopeless his cause was. "Your enemies will stir things up," Boggs warned. Carl Albert, the convention chair, "worried" that "if he himself had come out there, he might have been killed—the president."[73] Johnson had already been forced to abandon what he hoped would be a game-changing announcement in his convention speech: a summit meeting in Moscow with Soviet premier Alexei Kosygin and Communist Party leader Leonid Brezhnev. Upsetting that plan, on the night of August 20 a quarter million Soviet and Eastern European troops had begun marching into Czechoslovakia to suppress freedom demonstrations. The president told Boggs, "I've never felt lower in my life. How do you think it feels to be completely rejected by the party you've spent your life with, knowing that your name cannot be mentioned without choruses of boos and obscenities?"[74] Johnson "probably didn't want the nomination," his chief White House aide, Joseph Califano, concluded. "By now he was becoming concerned about his health and fearful of another heart attack. But he certainly hoped it would be offered."[75]

Humphrey also worried that Edward Kennedy might enter the race, igniting not just his late brother's supporters but also the legions of party regulars who, based on the polls, believed that Humphrey was a sure loser in November. On July 26 the grieving Kennedy had issued a statement withdrawing from consideration for the vice presidency. But he said nothing about the presidency, and shortly before the convention Daley, who did not think Humphrey could carry Illinois, told Kennedy, "If you want to have the nomination for president of the United States, you could have it . . . by acclamation."[76] On August 23, the Friday before the convention, Kennedy dispatched Steve Smith to find out if a draft was possible. When Smith told Daley that Kennedy might be interested, the mayor agreed to postpone his planned Sunday endorsement of the vice president for forty-eight hours. On Monday, the first day of the convention, Smith reported to Kennedy that if he allowed himself to be nominated, he would receive enough votes to deny Humphrey a first-ballot victory. That evening, Kennedy told Arthur M. Schlesinger that although he probably should bow out, "it is true that we have a hell of an investment in 1968. Bob's efforts to change the policies and directions and the rest—I want to follow that up in every way I can."[77] According to Kennedy aide Milton Gwirtzman, Kennedy "was absolutely not ready. He had just been through such a trauma. . . . [But] if they were going to make him their nominee for president, I don't think he would have turned it down."[78]

On Tuesday afternoon, August 27, at McCarthy's initiative, he met with Smith and Richard Goodwin, who had worked on both the McCarthy and Robert Kennedy campaigns after leaving the Johnson White House. Varying accounts of that meeting have appeared, but all agree that McCarthy offered to withdraw his candidacy after his name was placed in nomination and then urge his delegates to vote for Kennedy. "I could never have done this for Bobby," McCarthy reportedly added, exactly the sort of remark that drove Kennedy intimates up the wall and made them doubt that he would do what he promised.[79] Meanwhile, the talk of a Kennedy draft, along with the growing unlikelihood of a late entry by Johnson, spurred most of the southern favorite-son candidates to endorse Humphrey on Tuesday, including Sen. George Smathers of Florida and governors Connally of Texas, Buford Ellington of Tennessee, and Robert McNair of South Carolina. Humphrey's estimated delegate count soared from 1,295 on Monday night to 1,503 twenty-four hours later, according to CBS News. McCarthy remained frozen at 523 and McGovern rose slightly from 50 to 57, with California expected to lift him well above 100 when it caucused.

In addition to not trusting McCarthy to make good on his offer, Kennedy now realized that Humphrey had the nomination locked up. To go forward and lose would make it all the harder for him to turn down the vice presidential nomination that Humphrey had already offered him once in a meeting at Kennedy's McLean, Virginia, home and was certain to offer again.[80] "If I indicated an interest in going for the number one job," Kennedy recalled, "I couldn't turn the party down for the number two job. If I was able to, willing to, risk my family and risk the kind of violence and other possibilities in running for the first one . . . you couldn't very well say no to number two."[81] And even if he somehow won his party's presidential nomination, the thirty-six-year-old Kennedy said, "How could I conscientiously combat allegations by Nixon—and we had to anticipate he would make them—that I was too young, that I had no record in public life to recommend me for the high office of president, that perhaps I was trying to trade on my brothers' names."[82] On Tuesday night, Daley made Kennedy's decision for him. With his forty-eight-hour postponement about to expire, he phoned Kennedy to say that he was endorsing Humphrey. The next morning Daley announced that the Illinois delegation would vote 112 for Humphrey, 3 for McCarthy, and 3 for McGovern.

Humphrey was winning but winning ugly. The southern governors who endorsed him did so without enthusiasm. Humphrey would be a weak candidate in their states, but, they reasoned, any Kennedy would be weaker. They also were upset with Humphrey because of concessions he made to northern reform delegates on issues of convention rules and credentials. The McCarthy and McGovern campaigns were determined to pick multiple fights on these matters in the hope that by winning some of them, they would check Humphrey's momentum and place his nomination in jeopardy. Humphrey was determined not to let this happen. His strategy was to give ground wherever he reasonably could, partly to avoid losing test votes and partly to appease the McGovern and McCarthy delegates whose support he would need in the fall campaign.

Calibrating when to yield and when to stand firm was no simple matter. Under the procedures of the Democratic convention, rules, credentials, and platform fights were easy to start: if your side lost in committee, it took only 10 percent of the committee's members—eleven people—to bring a minority report to the full convention that would then be debated and voted on, all on national television. During rules committee meetings the week before the Democratic convention, Humphrey ducked one fight by sending a letter to Governor Hughes of New Jersey, the chair of the committee, accepting a McCarthy-initiated motion, supported by McGovern, to abolish the unit rule "at this convention."

Humphrey's gesture of appeasement infuriated his southern supporters. Southern and border state delegates constituted a gradually shrinking minority at Democratic conventions—28.9 percent in 1968, down from 33.2 percent in 1952—and lived in quadrennial fear that the party would nominate a presidential candidate who was unacceptably liberal. Until 1936, when FDR insisted that the rule be changed, the Democrats had required a two-thirds majority for nomination, which gave the South a de facto veto over objectionable candidates. Since then, eleven southern and border state delegations had relied on the unit rule, which allowed each state to cast its vote unanimously for whichever candidate or position a majority of delegates from the state favored, thereby giving southern leaders maximum bargaining power at the convention. Now Humphrey was offering to give the unit rule away, for what struck southerners as merely short-term tactical reasons. "Hell, I wish I hadn't written that sentence," Humphrey lamented when Connally squawked.[83] But it was too late. On Monday night the convention voted down the Texan's motion to postpone abolition of the unit rule until 1972.

Humphrey also yielded to McCarthy-McGovern forces on the rules committee on the question of how delegates to future conventions would be chosen. The McCarthy campaign in particular was angry that even in primaries its candidate won, the rules allowed state party leaders to stack their delegations with Humphrey supporters, many of them chosen in unpublicized meetings held before the campaign began. In Pennsylvania, for example, McCarthy won 71.7 percent of the primary vote but only 20.9 percent of the delegates. In advance of the convention, McCarthy supporters formed the ad hoc Commission on the Democratic Selection of Presidential Nominees, chaired by Governor Hughes of Iowa, to propose new rules requiring more open and participatory procedures for delegate selection.[84] To give the commission an air of disinterestedness, Rep. Donald Fraser of

Minnesota, an early Humphrey supporter, was recruited to serve as vice chairman.

As part of the same report in which it proposed immediate abolition of the unit rule, the rules committee included a recommendation to create an official party commission for "investigating the advisability of rules changes" in advance of the 1972 convention. The credentials committee made a similar recommendation on the first night of the convention, and it passed unanimously. On the convention's second night, McCarthy supporters on the rules committee offered a minority report instructing the new party commission to focus on banning the unit rule "at any stage" of the delegate selection process, not just at the national convention, and to require that "all feasible efforts have been made to assure that delegates are selected through primary, convention, or committee procedures open to public participation within the calendar year of the national convention." Humphrey took no position on the motion. "Our objective was to get a nominee," said Max Kampelman, a close adviser. "This was unimportant."[85]

Lack of guidance from the Humphrey campaign left his delegates confused, and in states such as Maryland and Missouri, many of them ended up voting for the rules committee's minority report. Historians, political scientists, and political activists all know that the main consequence of adopting the minority report—which the convention did by a vote of 1,351.25 to 1,209—was to create the party commission, headed first by McGovern and then by Fraser, that transformed presidential nominations into the primaries-based competition that has characterized the process ever since. But at the time most delegates focused on the unit rule part of the motion. When Albert called for a vote, he said the motion was for "abolition of the unit rule in all Democratic conventions down to the local level." After the motion passed, Cronkite dismissed it as "pretty much of a technical matter." Most newspaper reports did not mention the vote at all.

Humphrey fought back harder against most of the challenges to his delegates' credentials. Unlike rules for the future, these concerned votes he might need right now. In resolving the dispute over the credentials of the segregated Mississippi delegation at the 1964 Democratic convention, the national party had decided that, starting in 1968, state parties must form their delegations "regardless of race, color, creed, or national origin." Led by Joseph Rauh, their chief credentials strategist, McCarthy's supporters filed challenges with the credentials committee against fifteen mostly southern delegations. Humphrey's supporters on the committee conceded Rauh's challenge to the Mississippi delegation, whose violations of the nondiscrimination rule were especially egregious. "For the first time," Timothy Thurber has noted, "a delegation had been excluded from the convention on grounds of racial discrimination."[86]

Humphrey also agreed to divide the Georgia delegation equally between party regulars and insurgents. Rauh rejected the arrangement and on Monday night brought challenges to the Georgia as well as the Texas and Alabama delegations to the convention floor. He and other McCarthy advisers hoped that by forcing Humphrey to side with the South on questions of racial fairness, they could draw off enough of his northern supporters to prevail. But Humphrey's delegates stayed sufficiently united to deny McCarthy even symbolic victories on these matters. The Texas challenge failed by a 411.5-vote margin and the Alabama challenge by 726.5 votes, leaving both states' regular party delegations intact. Although the Georgia challenge lost by 371.9 votes, that left the Humphrey-supported compromise delegation in place. Gov. Lester Maddox, a rabid segregationist who had declared his candidacy for president on August 17 and then dropped out when none of his fellow southern governors endorsed him, led the Georgia regulars out of the convention in protest.

Winning the credentials votes was satisfying for Humphrey, but the main preliminary bout—the fight over the platform plank on Vietnam— still loomed. Previous conventions had experienced fierce platform battles, most recently the 1964 Republican convention, but almost never over foreign policy. Humphrey did everything possible to avert this one. Meeting with representatives from the McCarthy and McGovern campaigns in advance of the convention, Humphrey adviser David Ginsburg indicated that the vice president would accept virtually any plank that did not call for an "unconditional" halt to the bombing, refer to the Vietnam conflict as a "civil war," or propose the "imposition" of a coalition government on South Vietnam. On August 23, the McCarthy-McGovern doves, joined by Kennedy loyalists, yielded on the latter two points but not on the first: the bombing, they insisted, had to stop—period. The next day Ginsburg arrived at a formulation that Humphrey thought would be acceptable to all: "Stop the bombing of North Vietnam. The action and its timing shall take into account the security of our troops and the likelihood of a response from Hanoi."[87]

As he had promised the president he would, Humphrey ran this language by Secretary of State Dean Rusk, who said, "We can live with this, Hubert." On his own initiative, Humphrey showed it to National Security Adviser Walt W. Rostow, who also had no objections.[88] Johnson, however, insisted that the plank read: "Stop all the bombing of North Vietnam when this action would not endanger the lives of our troops." Humphrey pleaded with the president: "when" instead of "taking into account" would kill any prospect for a deal. Johnson erupted. "This plank just undercuts our whole policy," he insisted, "and, by God, the Democratic Party ought not to be doing that to me, and you ought not to be doing it; you've been part of this policy."[89] The president's frustration with North Vietnam's unwillingness to treat the Paris negotiations as anything other than a propaganda forum had steadily hardened his position on the war since the talks began in May.

Johnson's adamancy and Humphrey's acquiescence brought the effort to find a compromise solution to an end. On Wednesday afternoon, August 28, faced with a choice between the McCarthy-McGovern-Kennedy plank and the Johnson (and, reluctantly, the Humphrey) plank that had been approved by the platform committee by a vote of 62 to 35, the delegates concluded a three-hour debate by voting 1,567.75 to 1,041.25 for the administration's version. Numerous Humphrey delegates from New York, Michigan, and Mississippi, where the delegation that replaced the ousted regulars was highly liberal, endorsed the peace plank. Humphrey's preferred version—the one calling for an end to the bombing "taking into account" other considerations—was never introduced, much less voted on. The perverse consequence was that the Democratic platform ended up more hawkish on Vietnam than the Republican platform, which at least called for a "de-Americanization" of the war. Nixon had been pulled leftward by Rockefeller and Humphrey tugged rightward by Johnson to the point that, at least for the moment, they moved past each other on this issue.

Humphrey wrote in his memoir, "I should have stood my ground" against Johnson; "I should not have yielded." But he immediately added: "Having said that, I feel it is highly questionable whether I could have succeeded. President Johnson, enraged, would have become a formidable foe, causing troubles that I probably could not have overcome." Was Humphrey correct to think that by doing what he thought was right he would have guaranteed his defeat? To be sure, Humphrey's main supporters at the convention—Connally on behalf of the South and AFL-CIO president George Meany on behalf of organized labor—were Johnson men who wanted him to support the war. And, as Humphrey often pointed out, "the vice president has very few guns in a battle with the presidential artillery."[90] But Humphrey vastly underestimated how remote the prospect of a Johnson candidacy had become by the third day of the convention. He also misjudged how much the power balance between him and Johnson would shift away from the lame-duck president when Humphrey became the nominee of the Democratic Party, especially if its major dissident wing had been wooed and won.

Wednesday's evening session was meant to be all about nominating speeches, celebratory demonstrations, and the balloting that would officially anoint Humphrey as his party's candidate for president. But Wednesday was also the day of the MOBE's scheduled demonstration in Grant Park, the one event for which it had a permit from the city. The crowd of about ten thousand that gathered there was in a confrontational mood—angry that the police had made the violent eviction of demonstrators from Lincoln Park a nightly event and even madder that the convention rejected the peace plank and was about to nominate Humphrey. Police who warned the crowd to stay in Grant Park were greeted with insults, bottles, and rocks. When a demonstrator climbed a pole in the park to remove an American flag, helmeted officers waded in, swinging billy clubs.

That night Dellinger led about five thousand members of the crowd out of the park, crossing an unguarded bridge before being hemmed in by police at the intersection of Michigan and Balbo Avenues. The protesters' plan was to march five miles south to the amphitheater. A line of several hundred police and National Guardsmen met them and, from about 8:00 to 8:30 p.m. CDT, launched tear gas grenades and then attacked, wielding mace and clubs. As demonstrators chanted "The whole world is watching" and "Sieg heil," the Nazi salute to Hitler, more than a hundred people were injured in the bloody melee, including twenty-five police officers. It was Abbie Hoffman's dream come true: "We want to fuck up their image on TV . . . the image of a democratic society being run peacefully and orderly."[91] More to the point politically, the nation saw two Democratic Party constituencies—peace activists and public employees—literally at each other's throats. "A ballet of purgatory," said McCarthy, looking out his hotel room window.[92]

A strike by the International Brotherhood of Electrical Workers against the Illinois Bell Telephone Company prevented the networks from televising the riot live, but at about 9:00 p.m. they began showing film of the event, cutting away from Cleveland mayor Carl Stokes's seconding speech for Humphrey. "That instrument just recruits trouble," fumed Humphrey, pointing at a television. "I'm going to be president someday. I'm going to appoint the FCC [Federal Communications Commission]—we're going to look into all this."[93] Some delegates even brought portable televisions into the hall, and word rapidly spread about what was happening near the intersection of Michigan and Balbo. Sen. Abraham Ribicoff of Connecticut threw out his nominating speech for McGovern and roared, "With George

Mayor Richard J. Daley reacts strongly to Connecticut senator Abraham Ribicoff's declaration at the Democratic convention that "with George McGovern as president, . . . we wouldn't have to have Gestapo tactics in the streets of Chicago." (Credit: Library of Congress, U.S. News and World Report Magazine Photograph Collection)

McGovern as president, . . . we wouldn't have to have Gestapo tactics in the streets of Chicago." The cameras cut to Daley, shaking his fist and, as Norman Mailer put it, telling Ribicoff "to go have carnal relations with himself." "How hard it is to accept the truth," roared Ribicoff, smirking down at the mayor.[94]

Pandemonium ensued in the convention hall. Shortly after Ribicoff was done speaking, the networks showed the riot footage all over again. "Almost universally," Cronkite narrated, "the bystanders have been horror-stricken by the action of the police," including "people of substance in the community [and] some delegates who were downtown." He and the demonstrators assumed that the public agreed with them. In contrast Humphrey, whose hotel room on the twenty-ninth floor of the Conrad Hilton hotel was penetrated by tear gas from the street below, quickly released a statement: "They don't represent the people of Chicago. They've been brought in from all over the country. We knew this was going to happen. It was all programmed."[95]

The balloting for president commenced late on Wednesday night. McGovern received 146.5 votes, about half of them from South Dakota (24) and California (51). McCarthy had been barely active at the convention; at a joint appearance with Humphrey and McGovern before the California delegation, he wearily said, "I do not intend to restate my case. . . . The people know my position."[96] He received 601 votes, more than half of them from Massachusetts (70), New York (87), California (91), Wisconsin (49), and Oregon (35). Rev. Channing Phillips, a Kennedy delegate from the District of Columbia, received 67.5 votes from twenty-six states, making him the first African American ever nominated at a major party convention. Humphrey, who dominated every region of the country except the Pacific coast, which he lost to McCarthy, and New England, where he and McCarthy essentially broke even, received 1,759.25 votes, almost 450 more than he needed. When Pennsylvania put Humphrey over the top and the television cameras showed his wife Muriel seated in the vice president's box at the amphitheater, Humphrey popped up from his chair in the hotel room, danced a jig, and kissed the screen. In the convention hall the boos that greeted the nomination were almost as loud as the cheers. McGovern and Kennedy quickly endorsed Humphrey and pledged to campaign for him. But McCarthy said, "I could not support a Democratic candidate whose views do not come close to mine."[97]

The first three days of the convention had dug a deep hole for Humphrey. To the national television audience, Tom Wicker has observed, "the Democrats became the party of violence in the streets *and* the party of police repression."[98] But Humphrey still had the vice presidential nomination and his acceptance speech to try to gain back some lost ground. He put both to good use.

Humphrey's first choice for vice president, Edward Kennedy, had already turned him down and also scotched another appealing possibility: Kennedy's brother-in-law Sargent Shriver. Shriver had been the founding director of both the Peace Corps for President Kennedy and the Office of Economic Opportunity for President Johnson, whom he now served as ambassador to France. A Catholic and a Kennedy by marriage, the ebullient Shriver would add to the ticket if the Kennedys supported him but detract from it if they did not. They did not. If anyone in the family ran for national office, it would be Ted; besides, some Kennedys were mad at Shriver for not resigning from the Johnson administration to campaign for Robert Kennedy.[99]

That left Humphrey with the list he had been mulling for weeks. It had three names on it, but only one that was a real possibility: Governor

Hughes of New Jersey (anathema to Connally because of his work as chair of the credentials committee), Sen. Fred Harris of Oklahoma (too young at thirty-seven), and Sen. Edmund Muskie of Maine—an ethnic like Agnew (Polish rather than Greek), a Catholic like Kennedy and Shriver, and a "quiet man" (unlike Humphrey, who admitted, "I talk too much," and who "wanted someone who makes for a contrast in styles").[100] Muskie had been elected both governor and senator in Maine, a state that until 1964 had voted Republican in every presidential election. A minor psychological bonus of the Muskie nomination for Humphrey was that Johnson disapproved, wondering "what political good this can do for you" and suggesting he choose Gov. Terry Sanford of North Carolina instead.[101] But Humphrey, who had noted the widespread press and public disapproval that greeted Nixon's selection of Agnew, thought that choosing a running mate with "quality, character, and ability" would give him an edge he could exploit in the fall campaign.[102]

In the anarchic spirit of the convention, Julian Bond, a twenty-eight-year-old black state senator from Georgia, also was nominated for vice president, even though he fell seven years short of the Constitution's minimum age requirement. In general, though, Muskie's nomination was well received, and so was Humphrey's acceptance speech, which was considerably better than Johnson's in 1964 or Kennedy's in 1960 and almost as good as Nixon's speech earlier that month. The streets of Chicago were quiet, albeit uneasily, on Thursday night, and the galleries were packed with Daley supporters who could be counted on to cheer lustily. No distracting cutaways to street violence marred the evening's television coverage; in fact, in a twenty-three-minute live interview, Daley so dominated Cronkite that the anchor ended up praising "the politeness and the genuine friendliness of the Chicago Police Department." In preparing his speech, Humphrey once again prudently resisted a suggestion—this time from Democratic operatives Lawrence O'Brien and Joseph Napolitan, as well as from Jeanne Kirkpatrick and some of Humphrey's other political scientist friends from his University of Minnesota days—that he announce his resignation as vice president and declare independence from Johnson. "It would not look like an act based on principle or conviction; it would look like a gimmick," Humphrey said. "It would seem strange. And it will enrage the president."[103]

Humphrey's speech was earnest, emphatic, and fervent. After soberly expressing regret about the week's violence, he made a virtue of necessity by celebrating the vigorous debates that had taken place at the convention.

Humphrey invoked the Democratic pantheon of FDR, Truman, Stevenson, and JFK to rouse the crowd, and then he praised Johnson, who "accomplished more of the unfinished business of America than any of his modern predecessors." For the first time at the four-day convention, Johnson supporters were invited to cheer for their man and did. But Humphrey's main theme was peace. After reciting the Prayer of St. Francis near the beginning of his speech ("Where there is hatred, let me sow love"), he declared, "I shall do everything within my power . . . to bring a prompt end to this war," and then added: "The policies of tomorrow need not be limited by the policies of yesterday." Developing the theme of peace, Humphrey said, with real passion: "We must end the [nuclear] arms race before it ends us. . . . There is no more urgent task than ending this threat to the very survival of our planet, and if I am elected as your president I commit myself body, mind, and soul to this task." Unlike Nixon's speech, Humphrey's did not end with a stirring peroration, but it did the job.[104]

Johnson's birthday-based scheduling of the convention left Humphrey no time to rest or prepare for the general election. Labor Day, the traditional start of the fall campaign, was four days away. "I desperately needed time to heal wounds, build party organization, raise money, outline our advertising," wrote Humphrey—but there was no time.[105] The challenge of healing wounds was complicated by a violent dawn raid that police made on McCarthy's headquarters on the Hilton's fifteenth floor on Friday, provoked by the bags of urine and fecal matter that they thought were being thrown on them from the rooms. McCarthy, whose support Humphrey needed, had watched Wednesday's riots somewhat impassively, but this shook him. He later said, "It was really a kind of fascist-run convention." Johnson "wanted a fascist takeover of the convention."[106]

Humphrey also backed and filled in his public comments about Daley's handling of the demonstrations, which by week's end had resulted in 668 arrests and hundreds needing medical treatment for wounds inflicted by—and in some cases against—the police. "We ought to quit pretending that Mayor Daley did something that was wrong" was soon followed by a disclaimer that he did not "condone the beating of those people with clubs."[107] An August 30 Sidlinger poll showed that 71 percent of Americans supported Daley's actions. Humphrey could not win: side with Daley and further alienate his party's already disgruntled left wing or criticize the mayor and alienate both him and the public.

Still, Humphrey's selection of Muskie and his acceptance speech had done him some good. To be sure, his postconvention bounce was nominal. The early September Gallup Poll showed him up 2 percentage points and Nixon down 2: he now trailed the Republican by 43 percent to 31 percent, with Wallace up a point to 19 percent. Considering the week's events, to be in even slightly better shape than before it began was more than might have been expected.

6

THE GENERAL ELECTION

Back-to-back presidential elections often present roughly similar electoral maps. This simplifies the calculations candidates make about where to spend their time, money, and other resources during the two months that separate Labor Day, long the traditional start of the fall campaign, from its conclusion on Election Day. In 2012, for example, President Barack Obama carried twenty-seven states, including the District of Columbia, and Republican challenger Mitt Romney carried twenty-four states. All of Obama's states had also supported him in 2008, and Romney won all twenty-two states that Republican nominee John McCain carried in that election. In fact, thirty-four states—fully two-thirds of them—voted for the same party's presidential candidate in all six elections from 1992 to 2012. Even in 2016, when the election transferred control of the White House from Democrat to Republican, forty-four states voted as they had four years earlier.

Nothing remotely similar can be said about the 1964 and 1968 elections. As a guide to where to campaign, the 1964 map was virtually useless to Richard Nixon and Hubert H. Humphrey four years later. Republican candidate Barry M. Goldwater carried just six states in 1964: his home state of Arizona and the five states that constitute the Deep South. With George C. Wallace running as an independent four years later, Nixon was sure to lose at least four of these states, all but Arizona and perhaps South Carolina. Similarly, of the forty-five states that Democratic president Lyndon B. Johnson carried in 1964, a large number were highly unlikely to vote for Humphrey or any other Democrat in 1968, including virtually the entire Mountain West, Outer

South, and rural Midwest. The 1952 and 1956 elections, in which Republican nominee Dwight D. Eisenhower swept the map almost as completely as Johnson did eight years later, were equally useless benchmarks for 1968. Only the 1960 election, narrowly fought between Nixon and John F. Kennedy, provided any sort of a guide, but 1960 had lacked a strong third-party candidate. More than most major party nominees, Nixon and Humphrey would have to make some fairly speculative decisions about which states they could count on, which states were hopeless, and which states were competitive and therefore deserved their attention.

Enjoying nearly a month of leisure after the Republican convention ended on August 8, Nixon was able to sort through the electoral confusion and develop a careful strategy for winning the November election. In 1960 he had rashly promised in his acceptance speech at the Republican convention to "carry this campaign into every one of the fifty states," a decision that left him exhausted before his first debate with Kennedy and obliged him to visit Alaska on the weekend before the election.[1] The visit enabled Nixon to win a state that he otherwise probably would have lost (he carried it by only 1,043 votes). But Alaska's three electoral votes paled by comparison with those of several large states where he could more profitably have campaigned instead, all of which he ended up losing by less than 1 percentage point: Illinois (27 electoral votes), New Jersey (16), and Missouri (13).

Nixon would not make that mistake in 1968. Instead he developed what amounted to a three-tiered version of the electoral map. The first tier, in which he intended to spend most of his time and money, consisted of the seven largest states: New York (43 electoral votes), California (40), Pennsylvania (29), Illinois (26), Ohio (26), Texas (25), and Michigan (21). Of these seven, Nixon had carried only California and Ohio in 1960, but he thought that all except New York were winnable this time around. If he was right, he would earn as many as 167 electoral votes from these six states alone, putting him more than halfway to the 270 needed to win the election. The advantage of targeting the Empire State, even if he lost there, was that doing so would force Humphrey to commit a great deal of time and money to defending it.

The second tier of states, nearly all of them medium-sized and competitive, would receive lesser but still significant amounts of the campaign's resources. Nixon carried four of these states in 1960: Wisconsin (12 electoral votes) and the Outer South states of Florida (14), Virginia (12), and Tennessee (11). Others had gone for Kennedy but, Nixon calculated, were now within his grasp: New Jersey (17 electoral votes), Missouri (12), North

Carolina (13), Agnew's Maryland (10), neighboring Delaware (3), and South Carolina (8), the only Deep South state he thought he could win from Wallace, largely because of Sen. Strom Thurmond's towering influence there. Sweeping these ten states would add another 112 electoral votes to Nixon's total, bringing him to 279, enough to win the election.

The third tier was Nixon's insurance policy. It included all the states that he carried handily in 1960 and assumed he could count on carrying again without spending a minute or a dime there: Mountain West states Colorado (6 electoral votes), Arizona (5), Utah (4), North Dakota (4), South Dakota (4), Idaho (4), Wyoming (3), and Alaska (3); Midwestern Indiana (13), Iowa (9), Kansas (7), and Nebraska (5); border states Kentucky (9) and Oklahoma (8); and, in New England, traditionally Republican New Hampshire (4) and Vermont (3). Even without Maine, where Nixon got 57 percent of the vote in 1960 but which came off the 1968 list when Humphrey chose native son Edmund Muskie as his running mate, the sixteen third-tier states had 91 electoral votes. These could either carry Nixon to a landslide victory with 370 electoral votes or, failing that, provide a cushion in case he failed to sweep the first two tiers. And with Nixon leading Humphrey by 12 percentage points in the Labor Day Gallup Poll, longshot states such as Washington (9 electoral votes) and Connecticut (8) might be within his grasp. If Nixon could keep states like these in play, were 400 or more electoral votes attainable?

Perhaps not. But political campaigns, like military campaigns, always look different, and almost always worse, in the field than on the map. Each of Nixon's rivals also started out with a group of states he could probably count on winning. For Wallace, the list was regional: the Deep South states of Georgia (12 electoral votes), Alabama (10), Louisiana (10), and Mississippi (7), for a total of 39 electoral votes. Humphrey's base was scattered across the northern half of the country. It included his and Muskie's home states (Minnesota, with 10 electoral votes, and Maine, with 4), Massachusetts (14), West Virginia (7), Rhode Island (4), Hawaii (4), and the District of Columbia (3)—seven states, 46 electoral votes. In addition, depending on how things went in the campaign, both of Nixon's opponents could become competitive in a much wider range of states. None of Nixon's electoral vote–rich first-tier states were beyond Humphrey's reach; nor were his second-tier states of New Jersey, Wisconsin, Missouri, and Maryland. Adding all of these states' electoral votes to Humphrey's 46-vote base would bring the Democrat to 307, 37 more than he needed to win. Wallace, who scored 19 percent in the Labor Day Gallup Poll, just 12 points behind Humphrey, had a chance to sweep the South and penetrate the border states, racking up as many as 174 electoral votes, almost all of which would come at Nixon's expense.[2]

To be sure, Nixon's chances of executing his strategy were greater than either Wallace's or Humphrey's. The Nixon fund-raising operation was a juggernaut. "Ours was by far the most expensive campaign ever," said finance director Maurice Stans, "and I never once had to go to him to ask him to do anything to raise money."[3] Stans's team, which had raised $9 million to win the nomination, eventually procured $24 million more for the general election. In addition to tapping large, business-oriented donors eager to back a Republican nominee who seemed likely to win, Stans benefited from the large pool of small donors that Goldwater developed in 1964 and Ray Bliss sustained during his tenure as Republican National Committee chair.[4] Wallace continued to live off the land, raising approximately $7 million, about 20 percent from large donors such as right-wing oil man Bunker Hunt, who gave an estimated quarter million dollars, and the other 80 percent in donations of $50 or less that Wallace secured through direct-mail solicitations, inexpensive fund-raising dinners, and passing the bucket at his rallies.[5] In a year when "people power" and "participatory democracy" were slogans of the antiwar left, this was the real thing. As Michael Kazin observed, "Wallace was the first serious presidential candidate in the twentieth century who identified himself as a working man."[6]

Humphrey eventually raised about $11 million, which was $4 million more than Wallace raised. But very little of it was available at the outset of the fall campaign. The disastrous Democratic convention and the adverse early September polls dissuaded the large donors on whom the party had become dependent from contributing. The labor unions initially held back, unsure whether their best strategy was to follow their hearts and support their old friend or follow their heads and concentrate on saving Democratic governors and members of Congress from being swept out of office in the expected Nixon landslide.

President Johnson was no help—just the opposite. When Humphrey's chief fund-raiser, Robert Short, asked if he could tap into the President's Club's $600,000 fund, much of which Humphrey had raised as vice president, or the $700,000 the Democratic National Committee still had from its sale of corporate ads in a 1965 LBJ puff book called *Toward an Age of Greatness,* Johnson refused. Johnson also denied Humphrey the use of his fund-raising team.[7] Neither wealthy antiwar liberals, Democratic businessmen, nor, observed Lawrence O'Brien, the sort of "'fat cats' . . . who, in a close election, give to both parties, insuring that whoever wins, they'll have a foot in the door" were opening their checkbooks for Humphrey.[8] Begging O'Brien to come back for the general election after stints with Johnson and Kennedy and promising him "full control in all areas" was the one good organizational move Humphrey made in the entire campaign, even though it meant allowing O'Brien to be both campaign manager and DNC chair.[9]

"We had no money [after the convention]," said one aide. "We had no organization. . . . We did have a media plan, but we didn't have the money to go with it."[10] Humphrey's advertising was designed by an ad hoc group assembled by media director Joseph Napolitan, whom O'Brien brought in to replace the expensive Madison Avenue firm Doyle Dane Bernbach. But Humphrey was able to run virtually no radio or television ads in September. No major party candidate in history had been as underfinanced as he was during the first half of the general election campaign. To make matters worse, his campaign team was a mess, filled with personal friends who got along with Humphrey but not with each other, posing a never-ending challenge to both him and, despite the promise of full control, O'Brien. "For reasons that have never been clear," wrote David Broder, "Humphrey and his staff had devoted little thought to the general election campaign—not even after [Robert] Kennedy's murder made it virtually certain that Humphrey would be the nominee."[11] Humphrey's preconvention concern that Johnson or Edward Kennedy would make a late entry into the race is one such reason. Another is Humphrey's organizational incompetence.

While Humphrey scrambled to break out of the vicious cycle in which poor polls led to low donations, a weak campaign, more poor polls, and so on, Nixon began to translate money into organization, media, and the other costly components of a national campaign. The Nixon organization ran with "crisp, mechanical efficiency," deploying every new form of campaign technology.[12] These ranged from computers that printed out individualized four-paragraph letters from the candidate on sixty-seven different issues to a three-wave series of monthly panel polls in thirteen critical states. Knowing that the news media would grant roughly equal daily coverage to all the candidates no matter what they did, and wanting to avoid running Nixon ragged, which brought out the worst in him, the campaign scheduled only one or two rallies per day. To screen out hecklers, these usually were ticketed events; for those who made it inside, Nixon sometimes had campaign staffer John Ehrlichman arrange for "flying goon squads" to "rough [them] up."[13] To make sure the rallies made it onto the nightly network news programs, they were scheduled early enough in the day (and often close enough to an airport) so that the footage could be flown to New York in time to be spliced into stories on that evening's show. Events began on time, the halls were full, and if Republican elephants were present they were given enemas beforehand to deny camera operators embarrassing shots. Money paid for Nixon's large and talented organization, but that was not the whole story. Unlike Humphrey and Wallace, Nixon had campaigned for votes all year. His organization was battle-hardened, having been "tested in the primaries, with most of the personality conflicts long since resolved."[14]

Apart from limited, highly scripted public events, which were designed to give the national media only one story per day to focus on, Nixon did numerous live interviews with local television anchors, whose excitement at appearing with a presidential candidate could be counted on to overwhelm any inclination or ability to ask probing questions. He also continued the practice of buying blocks of regional television time for "Ask Nixon" events. In these thirty-minute programs, Nixon would answer questions from a diverse-looking panel of citizens. The questions were unscripted but hardly taxing for an experienced candidate, especially in a setting that included a cheering studio audience. To viewers, "the image," according to Gabriel Sherman, "suggested a candidate bravely facing threats from all sides without a podium or teleprompter to defend him."[15] Nixon generally avoided interviews with national news anchors and political reporters, but on September 16 he found time to appear on the popular NBC television program *Rowan and Martin's Laugh-In*. His single line, an endlessly recurring one on the show that had already worked its way into the national vernacular, was: "Sock it to *me?*" The message was subliminal: Nixon is a regular guy with a sense of humor. Erring on the side of dignity, Humphrey declined an invitation to appear on the show and regretted it later.

Nixon's image makers were good: Harry Treleaven, Frank Shakespeare, Roger Ailes, H. R. Haldeman, and other experienced and talented hands from the worlds of television and advertising. His issues staff was even better, with Alan Greenspan guiding domestic and economic policy and Richard Allen overseeing foreign policy. But of the two teams Nixon leaned more heavily on the former than the latter. In an era when the use of sixty-second campaign ads as well as half-hour paid broadcasts seemed shocking both to seasoned political observers such as election chronicler Theodore H. White and newer ones such as Joe McGinniss, who wrote a book about Nixon's media campaign called *The Selling of the President*, Nixon made heavy use of the format.[16] Some of the ads involved his talking directly to the camera, usually without a script. For others, Treleaven recruited Gene Jones, a documentary filmmaker who understood television from his years as a producer of the *Today* show. Jones made eighteen ads for Nixon, the first of which flashed arresting still photographs of scenes from the war in Vietnam over a jarring drumbeat. The viewer did not see Nixon but heard his voice decry the ineffectiveness of the war effort and promise "new leadership—not tied to the policies and mistakes of the past."[17] Nearly half of Nixon's campaign treasury—$11 million—was spent on advertising, and more than $6 million of that went to television.[18] To an unprecedented (and, in subsequent elections, unsurpassed) degree, the leading topic of both his positive and negative ads was crime.[19]

Sitting on a large lead and facing a disorganized, underfunded Democratic opponent, "Nixon was playing not to lose," according to speechwriter William Safire.[20] Like his commercials, Nixon's basic campaign speech was essentially unaltered since the primaries. Day after day, he articulated voter frustration with the war and the breakdown of law and order—and then proposed little that was more specific than "new leadership" as the solution. Offering himself as that leader, Nixon would tell audiences:

> My friends, I was vice president for eight years, and I am proud of the fact that I served in an administration that ended one war and kept the nation out of other wars. . . . And, my friends, I am proud that I served in an administration in which we had peace in the United States, in which we did not have this problem of violence and fear which pervades this nation and its cities today.[21]

Nixon's rhetorical style was direct and unadorned. His "view . . . [was] that campaign rhetoric should be a weapon, not an ornament" observed William Gavin, another of his speechwriters.[22] To the extent that Nixon would get specific, it was usually in the service of promises to do things that any president would do: "pledge a new attorney general," form a cabinet of "big men with big responsibilities," choose Supreme Court justices who would "interpret the law and not make the law."[23] His appeal to the voters was personal: our country is in a ditch, and "Nixon's the one" (the campaign's slogan, along with "This time vote like your whole world depended on it") to pull us out. Nixon even urged Haldeman to stress the theme that he was "'the man for the times.' The Churchill analogy is probably appropriate. Churchill was 'in the wilderness' as he put it during the 'thirties but was called back to lead his country in a period of crisis."[24]

In 1960 Nixon had faced a real strategic dilemma: try to build on the 39 percent of the African American vote that Eisenhower received in 1956, or

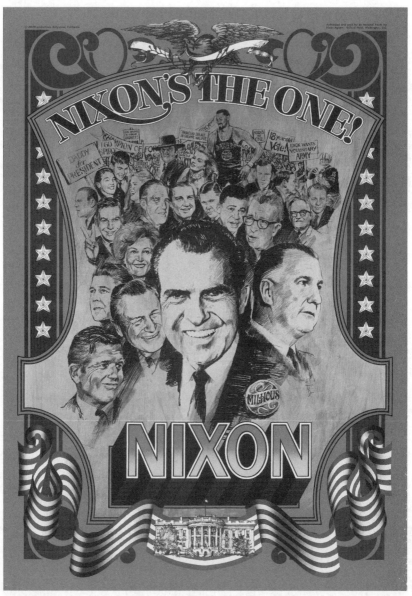

A campaign poster states the theme of Richard Nixon's presidential campaign: "Nixon's the One!" against a backdrop of other Republican leaders. (Credit: Courtesy of the Library of Congress)

direct his appeal to white voters in the South? In 1968 this was no dilemma at all. Goldwater had driven away all but 6 percent of the black vote in 1964. Nixon needed to get twice that in order to govern effectively as president, he told Harrison Salisbury of the *New York Times,* and for this reason he kept fellow Republican Edward Brooke of Massachusetts, the only African American in the Senate, close by him on the campaign trail.[25] Nixon also endorsed the Johnson administration's largely symbolic open housing bill after King was assassinated. It became law in April but, for the first time in the history of civil rights legislation, with less support in Congress from Republicans than Democrats.

Nixon realized that trying to get many black votes against Humphrey, the Democrats' leading champion of civil rights for twenty years, would be politically pointless. Even to make the effort would mean forfeiting the entire South to Wallace and abandoning or at least drastically recasting his law-and-order theme. "I am not going to campaign for the black vote at the risk of alienating the suburban vote," Nixon said privately.[26] Publicly, he cast his lot with "the Forgotten Americans, those who did not indulge in violence, those who did not break the law, people who pay their taxes and go to work, who go to their churches, people who are not haters, people who love this country."[27] To listeners it went without saying, as Nixon never did, that the faces of America's forgotten were white.

Humphrey's strategy for winning began with digging himself out of the deep hole in which he found himself after the Democratic convention. "The Democratic Party had broken in two before the eyes of a nation," wrote Norman Mailer, "like Melville's whale charging right out of the sea."[28] No less vividly, Humphrey told his wife Muriel, "It's as if we've been pushed off the rim of the Grand Canyon, and now we have to claw our way up the sides."[29]

In addition to lack of funds, Humphrey faced the problem of a still-divided party. Johnson stood aloof from the campaign, ready to pounce if the vice president deviated in any way from the administration's Vietnam policy. On September 9, for example, Humphrey told a Philadelphia audience, "Negotiations or no negotiations, we could start to remove some of the American forces in early 1969, or late 1968."[30] Secretary of State Dean Rusk immediately demurred and Johnson dismissed any idea of withdrawing troops or ending the bombing in a speech the next day to the American Legion. "No man can predict when that day will come," Johnson told the Legionnaires, "because we are there to bring an honorable and stable peace to Southeast Asia, and no less will justify the sacrifices that we and our allies have made."[31] Asked in Houston about the president's rebuke, Humphrey pointed to a headline in the *Houston Post*—"Marine Regiment Heads Home from Vietnam War"—not realizing that another regiment was being rotated to Vietnam to replace it. "Wonder why Johnson shot me down when I said that troops would be withdrawn in 1969," Humphrey later wrote. "I got the information from the White House. Ruined my credibility, made me look like a damned fool."[32] Taking advantage of Johnson's unhappiness with Humphrey, on September 15 Rev. Billy Graham carried a private message from Nixon to Johnson: Nixon "will never embarrass him after the election" and "will seek his advice continually."[33] Johnson disliked Nixon, but this message was one of several that softened his attitude for a time.

Even as Johnson sniped at Humphrey on Vietnam from his right, Eugene McCarthy worried him on his left. In an early September meeting convened privately by the senator's former press secretary, Seymour Hersh, McCarthy and several other critics of the war discussed the possibility of his reentering the race as an independent candidate. Richard Goodwin said that raising money from deep-pocketed antiwar Democrats would be no problem, and McCarthy fancifully mused, "I guess we could win New York, California, Oregon, Minnesota, and maybe even Wisconsin." "If the election were thrown into the House of Representatives—as some people believed it could be," McCarthy later wrote, "these states might have constituted the balance of power."[34] But McCarthy decided not to run, instead heading off to Europe for several weeks.[35] When he returned he spent the first ten days of October covering the World Series between the Detroit Tigers and St. Louis Cardinals for *Life* magazine.

Relieved as Humphrey was that McCarthy was not still running, he needed more than that: an endorsement to mute the opposition of his party's antiwar wing. At early campaign appearances that opposition was both angry and noisy, sometimes drowning out Humphrey with the now familiar chants of "Dump the Hump," "Sell-Out," and "Sieg Heil." His underfunded, disorganized staff was incapable of keeping hecklers away, and Humphrey was incapable of handling hecklers skillfully when they showed up. At a September 18 rally in Boston at which Humphrey and even Massachusetts senator Edward Kennedy were shouted down, the red-faced candidate said, "Your actions here are going to disgust the American people and injure the cause of peace."[36] "These are not just hecklers," he charged angrily at a September 24 news conference after another week of disrupted rallies. "These are highly disciplined, well-organized agitators, many of them anarchists . . . determined to destroy the effectiveness of the Democratic party and indeed to destroy the country."[37] "You know," the normally exuberant Humphrey told his friend and physician Edgar Berman early one morning, "the toughest part of the day is right now—just getting out of bed to face the music."[38] Underfunded to a historic degree, Humphrey also was treated more disrespectfully by audiences than any previous major party nominee.

As these early appearances indicated, Humphrey could not wait until he and his campaign had "claw[ed] our way up" before deciding on a strategy. They were forced to develop one on the fly. One element was to secure labor's enthusiastic support, which is why Humphrey reluctantly allowed AFL-CIO president George Meany to drag him to New York City to march alongside the union leader in what predictably turned out to be a lethargic, poorly attended Labor Day parade on September 2. Nearly 19 million workers, representing 23 percent of the total labor force, belonged to unions in 1968—a higher number, although not a greater percentage, than at any time in history.[39] Humphrey needed the unions' national executives to deploy their considerable funds and local leaders to turn out the rank and file on his behalf. All Democrats relied on the unions to get their members to the polls. But Humphrey had two particular needs. One was for labor to provide the grassroots muscle that neither the Democratic Party, enervated by Johnson's neglect and the bitter nomination contest, nor the severely underfunded Humphrey organization had. The other was to keep union members and their families from voting for Wallace. Union leaders were especially alarmed when one of the United Auto Workers' largest locals— Local 326 in Flint, Michigan—voted overwhelmingly on September 10 to endorse Wallace.[40]

Another basic element of Humphrey's developing strategy was to energize black voters to turn out in great numbers, partly by reminding them of his long support for civil rights, but mostly by raising fears of what a Nixon or Wallace presidency would mean for African Americans. "We're faced on the one hand with third-party extremism," Humphrey said in an early speech, referring to Wallace. "And we're faced on the other . . . with the age-old coalition of the conservative Republicans and the Dixiecrats, the Nixons and the Strom Thurmonds."[41] Humphrey also relied on strong support from Jewish voters, whom he worked to attract by reminding them of his unwavering support for Israel and his long-standing commitment to social justice. When Nixon and Wallace talked about law and order, Humphrey's unvarying response was: "Civil peace is made up of two equal parts: order and justice," which struck many blue-collar whites as a diluted commitment to law and order.[42] O'Brien and even Humphrey's friend, political scientist Evron Kirkpatrick, pushed him to be less "soft" on the issue.[43] But, as Jeremy Mayer has pointed out, "Humphrey was constrained . . . because for many blacks and white liberals, even the phrase 'law and order' was anathema."[44]

Humphrey's greatest political asset was that the Democrats were still the country's majority party. According to the University of Michigan's Survey Research Center, self-identified Democrats outnumbered Republicans 55 percent to 37 percent in 1968.[45] They had won all but two of the nine most recent presidential elections, and except for national heroes Herbert Hoover in 1928 and Dwight D. Eisenhower in 1952 and 1956, no Republican had been elected since 1924. The Democrats had controlled both houses of Congress for thirty-two of the last thirty-six years. But with Nixon and Wallace dominating the Democratic South and threatening the party's support among northern blue-collar voters, Humphrey's hope of winning the election required more than just shoring up the support of the Democrats' most loyal constituencies. Absent funding and organization, he needed to make a compelling case to a broader audience to have any hope of turning things around.

Feeling his way along, relying on trial and error, Humphrey developed three specific appeals. One was to remind voters of how well the economy had done during the administration in which he served and under Democratic administrations generally. After seventy straight months of economic growth and low unemployment, the longest period of prosperity in the nation's history, Humphrey would ask audiences, why change parties? A "growing, expanding economy" would fund an "increase [in] Social Security by 50 percent across the board," he promised.[46] Even more than the candidate, supportive labor unions hit hard on growth and employment issues in their efforts to rouse enthusiasm for Humphrey among their members, especially those who seemed inclined to vote for Wallace. When mid-September polls conducted by the unions showed that Humphrey would be lucky to get 50 percent of the labor vote, UAW president Walter Reuther put aside his disagreement with the candidate about Vietnam, swung his union's executive board squarely behind him ten days after the Democratic convention, and, on September 19, came out swinging. In a speech to his members, Reuther spent a few words praising the vice president and a lot of words attacking Wallace, whom he charged was "building on fear" and "will destroy America."[47]

A second Humphrey argument, first used by President Harry S. Truman to great effect against Thomas E. Dewey in 1948, was that the Republican candidate was offering the voters little more than a "program of platitudes and generous generalizations" instead of addressing the issues facing the country.[48] "Nixon's firm positions would make an ad for Jello look like concrete," Humphrey said dismissively.[49] In particular, he made hay of Nixon's unwillingness to debate him on national television. Like Johnson in 1964, Nixon had no intention of debating his opponent: he was way ahead in the polls, could buy all the television time he wanted, had unhappy memories of his 1960 debates with Kennedy, and was not about to give Humphrey a free, prime-time, nationally televised forum in which to attack him.

Nixon dodged the debate challenge in various ways, arguing publicly that he would be glad to debate Humphrey if Wallace was not included while privately (and successfully) urging congressional Republicans to stifle Democratic efforts to change the existing "equal time" law that guaranteed third-party candidates the right to share the stage with the major party nominees on any televised news program. "Self-interest determined my position on the debates," Nixon wrote ten years later. "Humphrey was still far behind me in the polls, and would therefore be the beneficiary of any debate."[50] Humphrey kept the issue alive for the length of the campaign. "Where is he? Where is The Shadow?" he would ask crowds, comically peering about the hall.[51] He even offered to buy network time for the sort of head-to-head debate Nixon claimed he wanted if Nixon would promise to show up. In truth, Humphrey liked having the issue almost as much as he wanted an actual debate.

Humphrey's third argument, which he made more and more with the passage of time, was that his running mate, Edmund S. Muskie, was a much worthier candidate for vice president—and a much safer bet to stand the proverbial "one heartbeat away" from the Oval Office—than the Republican vice presidential nominee, Spiro T. Agnew. Wallace, for his part, had no running mate at all as late as the beginning of October. An August agreement with A. B. "Happy" Chandler, the seventy-year-old former governor of Kentucky and commissioner of baseball, foundered on Chandler's unwillingness to temper his views on racial integration. As baseball commissioner Chandler had overseen Jackie Robinson's debut as the first black player in the major leagues, and as governor he had integrated his state's public schools soon after the Supreme Court's 1954 ruling in *Brown v. Board of Education*. Aides to Wallace argued that Chandler agreed with him on every other issue, would help defuse the charge that his candidacy was motivated by racial hatred, and was popular enough to tip the balance to Wallace in Kentucky and neighboring Tennessee. Wallace initially agreed but when news of Chandler's looming selection leaked in early September, several delegations of Wallace-pledged electors told him they would resign if he went through with the nomination. Equally important, Bunker Hunt and other large donors called Wallace to object. He backed off.

Nixon had assigned Agnew a specific and narrow role in the campaign: to shore up the border states and Outer South against Wallace. But as a candidate for national office, Agnew found himself in a bright media spotlight for which he was utterly unprepared. Offhand comments of a kind that had gone unremarked during Agnew's years as a local politician were suddenly the stuff of national news. One gaffe followed on the heels of another, starting with his charge that Humphrey was "soft on inflation, soft on communism, soft on law and order," the middle phrase a brutal epithet from the Joseph McCarthy era whose connotations of treason Agnew seemed totally unaware of. "When I am moving in a crowd," he said soon afterward, "I don't look and say, 'Well, there's a Negro, there's an Italian, and there's a Greek, and there's a Polack,'" using an offensive term for Polish Americans in the course of asserting his indifference to race and ethnicity. "What's the matter with the fat Jap?" Agnew asked reporters on his campaign plane two days later, referring to the sleeping correspondent of the *Baltimore Sun,* Gene Oishi, with what he meant as a teasing pleasantry. This prompted a Humphrey commercial in which Frank Sinatra decried "a man who has a strange habit of calling people Japs and Polacks."[52] Then, in an effort to defend his depth of knowledge about urban problems against the charge that he seldom campaigned in poor neighborhoods, Agnew said, "If you've seen one city slum, you've seen them all. . . . I don't think it's imperative that I conduct showboat appearances through ghetto areas to prove I know something about the problems of the cities." In the otherwise well-oiled Nixon campaign machine, Agnew was grit in the gears.[53]

Muskie initially looked good merely by comparison to Agnew. His low-key campaigning attracted little attention from either the media or the bands of hecklers who plagued Humphrey's appearances. His speeches and interviews were thoughtful and gaffe-free but made little news. On September 25, however, Muskie became a national star.

Speaking to an outdoor crowd in Washington, Pennsylvania, Muskie faced severe heckling from an antiwar band of Washington and Jefferson College students. Instead of lashing out, he told them, "You pick one of your number to come up here right now, and I'll give him ten minutes of uninterrupted attention."[54] In return, the hecklers would have to listen to his own speech right afterward. Utterly disarmed, the students agreed. The

The only man qualified to be Vice President. **MUSKIE**

CITIZENS FOR HUMPHREY MUSKIE, 1025 Connecticut Avenue, N.W., Washington, D.C. • Hon. Terry Sanford, Chairman

More than in any other election, Democrats featured their vice presidential candidate, Sen. Edmund S. Muskie of Maine. (Credit: Courtesy of the Library of Congress)

speeches given first by Rick Brody, their chosen representative, and then by Muskie were unmemorable. "I hope that we are on the threshold of an era in which the individual citizens will drop the apathy of the past and become concerned not on a one-shot basis, but a continuing basis," Muskie blandly argued.[55] What caught the nation's attention was the poise with which he turned an all-too-familiar scene of disorder and generational conflict into one of calm, reasoned, and respectful discourse. News outlets hastened to run admiring profiles of the senator, providing the campaign with its first favorable coverage all month. Reporters let statements pass that, if Agnew had made them, would have been ridiculed. For example, speaking to rural audiences, Muskie would frequently quote Thomas Jefferson's observation that if people were jammed together in cities, "they would begin to eat one another."[56]

Humphrey made the most of his comparative advantage in running mates. As soon as he could afford to, he began running a television commercial showing the words "Agnew for Vice President?" over a soundtrack of hysterical laughter. After ten seconds of this, a printed message appeared on the screen: "This would be funny if it weren't so serious."[57] A radio ad opened with the *thump-thump, thump-thump* of a beating heart, followed by an incredulous voice saying: "Imagine Spiro T. Agnew a heartbeat away from the presidency."[58] In speeches, Humphrey praised Muskie so fulsomely that comedians joked that he was the first candidate for president to promise to die in office. More seriously, the assassination of John F. Kennedy in 1963 and the recent murders of Robert F. Kennedy and Martin Luther King had made voters more than usually aware that the election of not just the president but also the vice president was a matter of consequence. As for Wallace, his erratic efforts at vice presidential recruitment foundered through September. Wishing he could run without a running mate, he was compelled by multiple state laws to find one in order to appear on their ballots.

A booming economy, Nixon's unwillingness to debate, and a superior candidate for vice president all helped Humphrey gain some traction in the weeks that followed the Democratic convention, but not nearly enough. His crowds were small, and state and local Democratic candidates kept their distance; only bands of hecklers could be counted on to show up at his rallies. McCarthy remained on the sidelines, still withholding his endorsement. The fund-raising picture remained bleak. Without the unions, Humphrey would have had almost no organized grassroots support at all.

In the face of these impediments, and with Nixon and Wallace campaigning effectively, none of Humphrey's progress as a candidate registered immediately in the polls. The Gallup Poll taken on September 20–22 actually showed slippage in his support from the survey taken about two weeks earlier. Nixon, who taunted Humphrey to name one policy on which he disagreed with President Johnson, remained steady at 43 percent. Wallace rose from 19 percent to 21 percent, and Humphrey lost 3 points, declining from 31 percent to 28 percent. Other than among Jews and African Americans, Humphrey trailed or ran only slightly ahead of Nixon among every traditionally Democratic group in the electorate. On September 23 a CBS News report on the state of the race found Humphrey to be in last place: Nixon, 333 electoral votes; Wallace, 39; and Humphrey, 33.

In late September a desperate Humphrey crossed a bridge he had wanted but feared to cross at least twice before. At the Democratic convention, he had pursued the idea of adding a compromise peace plank on Vietnam to the party platform. In early September he publicly embraced troop withdrawals. On both occasions, Johnson bared his teeth and Humphrey shrank back. Realizing the folly of campaigning as a champion of the war but unwilling to anger the president, Humphrey was left with virtually nothing meaningful to say on the issue. On September 23, for example, he told a Toledo audience:

> It is my intention when I become the president . . . to reassess the Vietnamese situation in light of the amount of assistance that is required from the United States, particularly in combat forces, as the army of South Vietnam improves, as they become more combat effective, it would be my policy, after a reassessment of the situation in Vietnam, on the ground and the political situation, to move towards a systematic reduction in American forces, keeping in mind the safety of South Vietnam, and I think we can do it.[59]

Nixon, who was no more specific than Humphrey about what he intended to do in Vietnam, could at least decry the administration's failures there. That option was closed to the vice president.

What kept Humphrey from placing daylight between the policy of the Johnson administration and the policy he wanted to pursue as president? Long experience with Johnson had habituated Humphrey to yield when they disagreed; their history included no instances of defiance. As a candidate, Humphrey rationalized his deference with various arguments, especially the loyalty that he felt a vice president owes to the president and the political price he was sure Johnson would exact if he strayed from the administration line. In addition, Humphrey "constantly felt optimistic about a major breakthrough on Vietnam," said O'Brien. "He was given to understand there would be a major breakthrough."[60]

All of these arguments had been unpersuasive to nearly everyone around Humphrey for weeks. He was, after all, the presidential nominee of the nation's largest political party. As for the deeply unpopular Johnson, there was little he could do for Humphrey and even less that he actually was doing. "You're not your own man," O'Brien told Humphrey in mid-September. "Unless you change direction on this Vietnam thing and become your own man, you're finished."[61]

Only in the face of looming political disaster and personal humiliation did Humphrey realize that he had no choice but to chart a different course on Vietnam. Scrambling to raise the $100,000 needed to purchase a half hour of prime time on NBC, O'Brien scheduled a speech for the evening of Monday, September 30, from Salt Lake City, where Humphrey was campaigning. As a symbol of independence, Humphrey did not display the vice presidential seal during the speech—or ever again.

Humphrey's actual proposal was modest: "As president, I *would* stop the bombing of the North as an acceptable risk for peace. . . . If the government of North Vietnam were to show bad faith, I would reserve the right to resume the bombing."[62] But the country was impressed that at long last he had shown evidence of being his own man. The media played the story as "Humphrey Breaks with Johnson on Vietnam," in part because George Ball, his new foreign policy adviser, who had just quit his job as Johnson's United Nations ambassador, led other aides in privately briefing reporters that the real meaning of the speech could be found between the lines: "What he's really saying is that he'd pull the troops out and try to end the war January 21, 1969."[63] Within a few days, Humphrey began aligning his rhetoric with Ball's spin. "What did I say at Salt Lake City?" he asked a mid-October crowd in Kansas City. "I said I would stop the bombing as an acceptable risk for peace—period. . . . No comma or semi-colon."[64]

Johnson was angry about Humphrey's speech and McCarthy feigned indifference, dismissing it as "good openers for twenty-five cent poker."[65] But the Democratic Party was energized and many in its antiwar wing were placated. As recently as September 28, two days before the speech, Humphrey had faced his worst day of heckling at an appearance in Seattle. From October 1, the day after the speech, until the end of the campaign he almost never faced serious heckling again. A sign at a rally read: "Former Hecklers for Humphrey"; another declared: "If You Mean It, We're with You."[66] Local candidates "were suddenly clustered about" his appearances, which

Humphrey rightly interpreted as "one of the best bellwethers" of how the campaign was going.[67]

Money started to pour in: about $250,000 in small donations averaging $14 each in direct response to the speech, followed by a steady stream of large checks from deep-pocketed donors persuaded that Humphrey's candidacy was no longer hopeless. In all, fewer than thirty individuals accounted for one-third or more of the $11 million that Humphrey ultimately raised for his campaign, including wealthy Minnesota friends such as agribusinessman Dwayne Andreas ("the major source of fundraising," according to O'Brien) and three members of the United Artists board spurred on by company president Arthur Krim, a Johnson fund-raising mainstay whom the president finally turned loose for Humphrey.[68] As for the candidate, said O'Brien, "The most important thing about the speech was the effect on Humphrey himself. He felt good about it, he was his own man."[69]

The final Gallup Poll in September, taken during the four days prior to Humphrey's speech, obviously reflected none of this. What it did show, in addition to Nixon's fifteen-point lead, unchanged from the week before, was the breadth and persistence of the support for Wallace, who had risen steadily throughout the year and leveled off at about 20 percent. Wallace was thriving on the campaign trail, where large and enthusiastic crowds not only showed up wherever he went but also filled the yellow buckets that "Wallace Girls" passed around with $1 and $5 and $10 bills, even quarters and dimes. Audiences craved hearing his familiar lines like concertgoers cheering a band's greatest hits. "The Supreme Court of our country has handcuffed the police," Wallace invariably said, reprising a line from his 1964 Democratic primary campaign, "and tonight if you walk out of this building and are knocked in the head, the person who knocks you in the head is out of jail before you get in the hospital, and on Monday they'll try a policeman about it."[70] He made hecklers part of the show ("that's all right, honey—that's right, sweetie pie—oh, that's a he"), so much so that staff members sometimes distributed tickets to protesters, seating them in a side balcony close to the stage so the audience could see them taunting Wallace and Wallace putting them down. "These are the kind of folks that people are sick and tired of in this country, all over the United States," he told a Milwaukee audience, gesturing toward about five hundred noisy protesters led by the antiwar priest Father James Groppi. "And all I can say is that the anarchists in this country better have their day now because after November 5, you're through."[71]

As September unfolded, Nixon consistently hammered southern audiences with the argument that for conservatives to vote for Wallace would only help elect Humphrey. Nixon's chief southern supporter, Strom Thurmond, was featured in a series of regionally broadcast ads explaining that Wallace was not wrong; he just could not win. Fortunately for Nixon, he relied on Thurmond in southern matters rather than an otherwise savvy campaign aide, the New Yorker Kevin Phillips, who suggested running ads with a country music character called "Hank Snerd" urging southerners not to "waste yer vote / On a man cain't win."[72]

Democrats had their own concerns about Wallace, whose support among blue-collar workers in the industrial states continued to drain votes from Humphrey. The UAW and AFL-CIO launched a massive campaign among their members. A leaflet widely distributed by the Committee on Political Education (COPE), the AFL-CIO's deep-pocketed political action committee, headlined the theme of the anti-Wallace effort: "WALLACE'S ALABAMA RANKS 48TH AMONG STATES IN PER-CAPITA ANNUAL INCOME," "WALLACE'S ALABAMA RANKS 48TH AMONG STATES IN PER-CAPITA PUPIL EXPENDITURES IN PUBLIC SCHOOLS," "WALLACE'S ALABAMA HAS ONE OF THE HIGHEST ILLITERACY RATES IN THE NATION," and so on.[73] COPE had a computer with 13 million names that ran nonstop, pumping out mailings about Alabama's hostility to unions, high sales tax, and substandard school system. "Do you want Alabama wages and Alabama working standards in Michigan, in Pennsylvania, in Ohio?" asked COPE director Al Barkan.[74]

Both Nixon and Humphrey were desperate to convince Wallace supporters that they would be wasting their votes by casting them for him. But Humphrey had the intrinsically better argument. Because there was virtually no chance that Wallace would carry any northern state, it was widely understood that none of his popular votes in that region would translate into electoral votes. In contrast, Wallace was at least competitive in every southern and border state, bringing any or all of their electoral votes within his grasp. In fact, the mid-September Gallup Poll showed Wallace leading Nixon by 7 points in the South, a region defined by the pollster as the eleven states of the old Confederacy plus Kentucky and Oklahoma.

Except for occasional flights of fancy ("Just think," he said one day, gazing from an airplane window, "someday I'll be president of all that"),[75] Wallace knew he had no chance of winning the election. But his frequent campaign trips outside the South continued to give him enormous pleasure. He loved demonstrating again and again that many northerners were just as upset as southerners about a federal bureaucracy bent on imposing racial integration, a criminal-coddling legal system, and whiny, pampered college students who had nothing legitimate to complain about. More important, the positive responses Wallace got up north helped certify his seriousness as a candidate to voters in the South and border states.

The mid-September Gallup Poll showed Wallace leading in the Deep South with 52 percent to 20 percent each for Nixon and Humphrey but trailing narrowly elsewhere in the region: Nixon, 37 percent; Wallace, 33 percent; Humphrey, 24 percent. Wallace calculated that with enough southern and border state support he could deny either major party candidate a majority of electoral votes. Carrying states outside the Deep South and winning a substantial number of popular votes in the North would also distinguish him from Thurmond, the Dixiecrat nominee in 1948, whose 2.4 percent of the popular vote and 39 electoral votes were confined almost entirely to the four Deep South states he carried.

FORTAS

Strategies and tactics aside, politically relevant events occurred outside the control of the candidates and their campaigns. Tet, the King assassination and ensuing riots, and the Soviet invasion of Czechoslovakia were among them. So was the announcement of two vacancies on the Supreme Court at a time when Nixon and Wallace were both regularly attacking the court's liberalism on the campaign trail.

The two vacancies were triggered by one man's action. On June 13 Chief Justice Earl Warren privately informed President Johnson, in a face-to-face meeting and in writing, of his "intention to retire as Chief Justice of the United States, effective at your pleasure." In a letter sent nearly two weeks later, Johnson formally replied that he would "accept your decision to retire at such time as a successor is qualified"—that is, nominated by the president and confirmed by the Senate. Johnson's decision to appoint Justice Abraham Fortas, whom he had added to the Court in 1965, to be chief justice and Fifth Circuit Court of Appeals judge Homer Thornberry to replace Fortas as associate justice turned Warren's retirement into two nominations. Both nominees were close friends of the president, Thornberry since childhood and Fortas since Johnson became a member of Congress in 1937. Thornberry actually represented the president's Texas district in Congress.

Warren was seventy-seven years old when he decided to step down. His reasons were clear: he did not think judges should serve much beyond age seventy-five; he was convinced, after the assassination of Robert Kennedy, that Nixon would win the election; and he did not want Nixon to be the president who named his successor.[76] Nixon had accumulated many ene-

When Lyndon B. Johnson nominated longtime friend Justice Abraham Fortas to be chief justice, critics charged that Fortas had remained too close to the president while serving on the court. (Credit: Yoichi Okamoto, provided by the Lyndon B. Johnson Presidential Library)

mies during his twenty-two years in public life, but none who had despised him longer and in greater detail than Warren. As the liberal Republican governor of California, Warren had watched Nixon's political debut in his fiercely anticommunist race for Congress in 1946, and he "disliked the type of campaign that unseated Congressman Jerry Voorhis" for its "attack without proof or documentation."[77] Warren had nothing good to say about Representative Nixon's investigation of Alger Hiss and felt that his attacks on Democratic rival Helen Gahagan Douglas in the 1950 Senate election were "grotesquely unfair."[78]

Worst of all, Nixon had undermined Warren's hopes of emerging from the 1952 Republican convention as the party's compromise nominee for president. On the California delegation's train ride to Chicago, Nixon, who was publicly committed to Warren but angling to impress Eisenhower, spread the word that Ike was a sure thing and Californians should not risk missing the bandwagon. He persuaded sixty-two of the state's seventy delegates to vote with Eisenhower in a series of important credentials votes, which assured Ike the nomination. One of Warren's law clerks on the Court said later that when the chief justice talked about Nixon, he would use "terms that ordinarily would be reserved for someone who had proved to engage in serious violations of criminal law and ethical conduct."[79]

Johnson welcomed Warren's decision. He feared that Humphrey's defeat would result in Nixon appointing conservative justices who would overturn Great Society legislation just as an earlier court for a time thwarted FDR's New Deal. The conditionality of both Warren's resignation ("effective at your pleasure") and Johnson's acceptance ("at such time as a successor is qualified") meant the worst that could happen would be for Warren and Fortas to remain on the court in their current capacities—or so Johnson thought.

During the thirteen days the president kept the matter secret, he confidentially secured for his two nominees the endorsement of the American Bar Association's Standing Committee on the Federal Judiciary and, more importantly, of Richard B. Russell of Georgia, the Senate's most influential southern Democrat, and Everett Dirksen of Illinois, the Senate Republican leader. Russell was a duck-hunting buddy of Thornberry, who had won Johnson's seat in the House of Representatives when Johnson was elected to the Senate in 1948. He assured the president: "I will support the nomination of Mr. Fortas, but I will enthusiastically support the nomination of Homer Thornberry."[80] Dirksen's friendship was with the president, whom he believed had the right to expect Senate confirmation of any nominee who was professionally qualified, as Fortas manifestly appeared to be.[81] Johnson was confident that the combination of southern Democrats who would like the moderate Thornberry, northern Democrats who already liked the liberal Fortas, and Dirksen's Republicans would easily put both nominees over the top. On June 26 the president announced Warren's retirement, Fortas's promotion, and Thornberry's appointment.

The network evening news programs carried Johnson's announcement and Nixon's response while campaigning: "It would have been wise for the president to ask Chief Justice Warren to serve in the [court's] fall term, thereby leaving selection of new justices to the next president."[82] Based on rumors of Warren's impending retirement, Sen. Robert Griffin of Michigan, a first-term Republican, had already collected eighteen of his GOP colleagues' signatures on a petition urging that the next chief justice "should be designated by the next president."[83] News coverage took note of the outgoing president's close friendship with both nominees, and the words "lame-duck" and "cronies" quickly entered the public debate. Nevertheless, Johnson's legislative aides assured him the day after he announced his nominations that Fortas already had at least sixty-seven votes, enough to impose cloture if Griffin and his allies tried to defeat him by filibuster—as Senate Judiciary Committee chair James O. Eastland of Mississippi told the president they would. Johnson also was convinced that Nixon would not actively oppose the appointment of the first Jewish chief justice in history, especially one, as Fortas reminded the president, who had been so fulsome in his praise of Nixon's argument before the court in the 1967 case of *Time v. Hill*.[84]

History was working both for and against Johnson. On the one hand, no Supreme Court nominee had been rejected by the Senate since John J. Parker in 1930, and Fortas himself had been confirmed *viva voce* as an associate justice when Johnson nominated him just three years earlier. Nor had any sitting justice ever been denied confirmation as chief justice. On the other hand, ten of seventeen previous Supreme Court nominations made by presidents in their final year had not been confirmed, a failure rate of 59 percent, more than five times the 11 percent failure rate (15 out of 131) for nominations made in earlier years of their tenure. Clearly the safest course for a president in Johnson's situation would be, as Secretary of Defense Clark Clifford had advised, to pair Fortas with a nonpolitical Republican nominee such as Albert Jenner, a prominent Chicago attorney.[85] Instead Johnson, with just half a year left in his presidency, chose the riskiest possible course by nominating two close personal and political associates.

Contemporary developments were even more damaging to the president's cause. Like a series of tumbling dominos, one unfortunate event followed another. First, Johnson prevaricated in responding to his mentor Russell's strong endorsement of Alexander Lawrence for a federal district court judgeship in Georgia. Johnson's claim that Attorney General Ramsey Clark was refusing to sign off on the nomination was true but, in Russell's view, irrelevant: Johnson, not Clark, was the president. On July 2 the offended Russell, who felt he was "being treated as a child or a patronage-seeking ward heeler," wrote to Johnson serving notice that he no longer felt bound to support Fortas and Thornberry.[86] Johnson chewed out Clark and sent Lawrence's nomination to the Senate, where it was approved. But Russell was unmoved, unwilling to appear to be trading his vote for an appointment.

Second, confident of his ability in such settings, Fortas broke all historical precedent for both sitting justices and nominees for chief justice by agreeing to testify at his confirmation hearings. From July 16 to July 19, he was raked over the coals by members of the Senate Judiciary Committee on a range of subjects. Taking their cues from a number of published reports, senators grilled Fortas about his alleged willingness, on a regular and frequent basis, to advise his friend Johnson on matters that ran the gamut from appointments to legislation, executive actions, and the war in Vietnam. Fortas dissembled, and even lied at times, in the course of minimizing or denying his activities. Worse, he did so unpersuasively. In truth, he had held 145 meetings with the president while on the court, not counting their many hundreds of phone conversations.[87]

Among other activities, Justice Fortas helped write the 1966 state of the union address and other speeches, drafted Johnson's response to Gov. George Romney's reluctant request for troops to put down the Detroit riots in 1967, participated regularly in White House discussions of the Vietnam war, made multiple recommendations concerning judicial appointments, and even discussed a pending case involving the Penn-Central railroad merger with the president before writing the Court's majority opinion.[88] None of this was known in detail, but all of it and more was suspected, in part because over the years Fortas had freely implied that he was a major player in the administration, even bragging that he knew and used all the underground entrances to the White House from adjacent buildings.[89] Those familiar with Fortas's activities were stunned by his testimony, which according to White House chief of staff Joseph Califano "was so misleading and deceptive that those of us who were aware of his relationship with Johnson winced with each news report of his appearance before the Senate committee. Cronyism was now the least of the charges some of us feared."[90]

When that subject was exhausted, Senator Thurmond challenged Fortas to defend a number of unpopular Warren court decisions concerning the rights of accused criminals and pornographers—echoing campaign attacks that Nixon was regularly making against the court even as he consistently withheld specific public comment on Fortas. In one prominent obscenity case, Fortas had been the only justice to vote in favor of allowing a porn flick called *Flaming Creatures* to be shown in theaters.[91] Thurmond arranged private screenings of it and what Louisiana Democrat Russell B. Long called the other "Fortas films."[92] Fortas's frequently restated refusal—by one count he demurred fifty-nine times during two hours of questioning by Thurmond—to discuss these rulings on "separation of powers" grounds rang hollow in light of the many hours the justice had spent at the White House advising the president.[93] Nixon's silence in public did not prevent him from privately urging Republican and southern Democratic senators to oppose the nomination.[94] "Nixon wanted the Fortas nomination killed," wrote campaign aide Pat Buchanan, "but did not want our fingerprints on the murder weapon."[95]

From the campaign trail, Humphrey launched a blistering attack against Nixon, whom he charged on September 13 had "made a deal with Strom Thurmond to undermine Fortas. He could have Mr. Fortas confirmed in a week if he'd say the word, because it's his troops in the Senate, his supporters, that are blocking that confirmation."[96] But clearly the last thing Humphrey needed, after nine months in which violent crime rose 21 percent over the same period a year ago, was a nomination that drew attention to the court's unpopular rulings broadening the rights of criminal suspects and defendants, most of which Fortas had endorsed as an associate justice.[97] Still refusing to state a position on the nomination, Nixon defused the issue. "I don't oppose Fortas," he said in reply to Humphrey's charge. "I don't support him. I oppose a filibuster. I oppose any filibuster."[98]

Meanwhile, Johnson used every wrench and hammer in his political toolbox on Fortas's behalf, rallying business executives such as Henry Ford II and Coca-Cola president Paul Austin to lobby their senators, mobilizing Jewish and African American organizations to defend a Jewish nominee with a strong record on civil rights, and appealing to liberals in general to support their fellow liberal. But the final blow came when committee hearings resumed in mid-September and it was revealed that Fortas had been taking money for activities that, however worthy, had been paid for by former corporate clients likely to have at least occasional business before the court.

Fortas's income had gone down substantially when he left private practice to become a justice, but not his lifestyle. In 1966 he signed an agreement with Louis Wolfson, embroiled at the time in a Securities and Exchange Commission investigation, to provide advice to the Wolfson Family Foundation in return for an annual lifetime payment of $20,000 to Fortas or, if he died first, to his wife. Fortas cashed the check for the first year's payment and kept the money for eleven months before acknowledging the impropriety of the arrangement and returning it (Wolfson was by then under indictment by the SEC). The following year Fortas accepted $15,000—about seven times the amount that was customarily paid—to teach a summer seminar at American University's Washington College of Law. The seminar was paid for with money raised by Fortas's former law partner, Paul Porter, from five friends and clients of the firm. Taken together these payments nearly doubled Fortas's $39,500 salary as a Supreme Court justice, and both posed potential conflicts of interest.[99]

On September 17 the Judiciary Committee reported Fortas's nomination to the Senate by a vote of eleven to six, withholding any recommendation on Thornberry, whose appointment would be rendered moot if Fortas was not confirmed as chief justice. Democratic committee members supported the nomination by eight to three and Republicans divided evenly, three to three. Republican senators began filibustering the nomination as soon as it reached the Senate floor on September 25, and two days later Dirksen, whose support for Fortas had placed his leadership of the by now strongly anti-Fortas Senate GOP in jeopardy, said he would not vote for cloture and was only "neutral" on the nomination itself.[100] As an intended kindness to Fortas, Johnson insisted that the Senate vote on a cloture motion before he withdrew the appointment. Johnson thought he had fifty-seven votes, not enough to end the filibuster but a strong endorsement nonetheless. "With a majority on the floor for Abe," Johnson told his staff liaison to the Justice Department, Larry Temple, "he'll be able to stay on the Court with his head up. We have to do that for him."[101] The vote on October 1, less than a week before the court was scheduled to begin its 1968–1969 term, was well short of two-thirds and barely favorable: 45 to 43, with twelve senators (nine of them Democrats) absent. Democratic senators from outside the South voted for cloture by 33 to 4, but of the seventeen southern Democrats present, only two supported the motion. Ten Republicans, all of them northern, supported cloture, but twenty-four voted against it, including all three southerners. Later that day, at Fortas's request, Johnson withdrew his name and, a week later, decided not to submit any further nominations.

7

THE GENERAL ELECTION
OCTOBER AND NOVEMBER

Richard Nixon faced the same fundamental political challenge in the general election as in the nomination campaign: to fend off one opponent on his right (Ronald Reagan then, George C. Wallace now) and another on his left (Nelson A. Rockefeller then, Hubert H. Humphrey now). By the end of September, Nixon's year-long strategy of downplaying issues for the sake of offering himself as the remedy for the Johnson administration's failures of leadership appeared to be working as well against the Democrats as it had against his fellow Republicans. Every poll showed him with a substantial lead. Humphrey's sense of desperation had led him at last to put aside his fear of alienating the president and propose a different course of action in Vietnam. His nationally televised September 30 speech from Salt Lake City energized his campaign. But whether the political costs of breaking with Johnson would exceed the benefits remained to be seen. And to the extent that Humphrey's speech succeeded in gaining him the lead in more states, the likelihood of Wallace winning enough electoral votes to deny either major party nominee a victory on Election Day grew.

As October began, Wallace's strategy seemed plausible. A recent *Newsweek* survey found him leading in nine states with eighty-nine electoral votes: the Deep South states of Alabama, Georgia, Louisiana, Mississippi, and South Carolina; the Outer South states of Arkansas, Florida, and North Carolina; and the border state of Kentucky.[1] *Newsweek*'s analysis accorded with both the Nixon and Humphrey campaigns' assessment of Wallace's strength. If he carried all nine states, then Nixon would need not 51 percent of the 538 electoral votes to win, as in a two-party contest, but rather 60 percent: 270 of the remaining 449. With Humphrey at last on the move, the chances increased that no candidate would secure an electoral majority—exactly the outcome for which Wallace hoped.

Even as Wallace was nursing dreams of using his electoral votes to become the national power broker, however, he stood on the verge of a decision that would bring down his candidacy from its peak of popularity as surely as Humphrey's speech on the war had turned his own campaign's trajectory upward.

Wallace ended September plagued by indecision over a matter that he cared almost nothing about but could not avoid: the choice of a nominee for vice president. Weeks earlier he had backed away from his preferred candidate, former Kentucky governor and senator Happy Chandler, in the face of strong opposition to Chandler's moderate civil rights record by various Wallace-pledged electors and donors. Lacking a political party, inattentive to organizational matters for which he had a "vague contempt," and with a national campaign staff consisting almost entirely of trusted Alabama associates, Wallace had allowed his state campaign organizations to become dominated by self-nominated extremists from groups such as the right-wing John Birch Society and Minutemen in the North and the segregationist White Citizens' Council in the South.[2] He sometimes said that the American Independent Party should be called the Squirrel Party because it had all the "nuts."[3] But in choosing a running mate, Wallace now realized, he would have to satisfy them as well as himself.

Wallace considered possible nominees as varied as former secretary of agriculture Ezra Taft Benson and Kentucky Fried Chicken founder Col. Harlan Sanders. In the end he decided on former air force general Curtis LeMay, celebrated for his leadership of the Strategic Air Command but notorious for his expansive views on the use of nuclear weapons, which made him the model for the nuke-loving Gen. Jack D. Ripper in the 1964 Stanley Kubrick film *Dr. Strangelove, or: How I Learned to Stop Worrying and Love the Bomb.*[4] LeMay appealed to Wallace because he was widely admired by Goldwater-style anticommunists, a group that Wallace thought he could steal away from Nixon. Wallace appealed to LeMay because his policy on Vietnam was that he would ask the Joint Chiefs of Staff what to do and then do it.

The selection of LeMay was a dubious proposition from the outset. Wallace's basic appeal, dating back to his earliest campaigns in Alabama, had always been to enlisted men who were used to grousing about officers. LeMay had been a four-star general. In addition, he was devoid of political experience and completely unprepared to be shoved onto the brightly lit stage of a national campaign. Not surprisingly, the October 3 press conference in Pittsburgh at which Wallace unveiled his new running mate was an unmitigated disaster. Asked how he would fight the war in Vietnam, LeMay ruminated, "Well, we seem to have a phobia about nuclear weapons. . . . I think there are many occasions when it would be most efficient to use nuclear weapons." As for the fear that such weapons would cause long-term damage, LeMay said that on the Bikini atoll, site of many nuclear tests, "the land crabs were a little bit 'hot,'" but the rats "are bigger, fatter, and healthier than they ever were before." A frantic Wallace rushed to the microphone to intervene, telling the reporters, "General LeMay hasn't advocated the use of nuclear weapons, not at all. . . . He's against the use of nuclear weapons, and I am too." Resisting rescue, LeMay said, "If I found it necessary I would use anything we could dream up—including nuclear weapons if it was necessary." Then, sensing that things were not going well, he concluded: "I'll be damned lucky if I don't appear as a drooling idiot whose only solution to any problems is to drop atomic bombs all over the world. I assure you I'm not."[5]

The prospect of LeMay as vice president sobered many voters who previously had been inclined to think of Wallace as a serious candidate, not just someone whose rhetoric appealed to them. Equally important, the choice placed Wallace, who had been gleefully on the attack all year, uncomfortably on the defensive. Nixon remained cautious in his response to LeMay's press conference, but Humphrey pounced: "It would be disastrous if anyone who spoke as General LeMay did this morning should come into a position of high responsibility."[6] Both candidates were pleased that LeMay had reinforced their message that Wallace was unpresidential. Wallace responded by sending LeMay to South Vietnam on a "fact-finding mission." "That's the last you will ever hear from him," Wallace told columnist Robert D. Novak in an off-the-record interview. "Nothing more! Not a word!"[7] When the general returned from Vietnam, he was dispatched to remote locations and urged to confine his speech-making to topics such as "Preserving Our Natural Resources for the 21st Century," a subject for which he had great enthusiasm and about which he was thought to be safely uncontroversial until, in answer to a question about overpopulation, he said, "There are many cases where abortion is proper."[8]

Choosing a running mate was not the only thing Wallace had to do to satisfy the trappings of a presidential candidacy. On October 13, campaigning in San Francisco, he released a platform. The document was hastily cobbled together and drew heavily from his speeches. Twice, it advertently used the first-person singular pronoun. Substantively, it was a generally conservative document but, like its author, offered some liberal economic proposals, including a 60 percent increase in Social Security benefits, broader Medicare coverage, a "job training" and "public works program," mass transit, and "an aggressive campaign at all levels of government to combat the serious air and water pollution problem."[9] On September 16 Wallace had held a modest convention of the Texas American Independent Party in Dallas to satisfy state ballot requirements, but he avoided holding a national convention "out of fear that too many members of openly racist organizations would show up."[10] In general, Wallace was loath to spend time cultivating support from other politicians, even those who might have been favorably disposed to his candidacy.

In broad outline, the story of the campaign in October and early November was simple. Nixon's support remained level at about 43 to 45 percent, as it had ever since the Republican convention. Wallace's declined from about 20 percent to about 13 percent, losing more than one-third of his support in all regions of the country. Humphrey's share of the electorate rose substantially, from about 30 percent to near parity with Nixon. Gallup estimated that an average of 200,000 votes per day were flowing to Humphrey during the final five weeks of the campaign.[11]

These broad trends masked some churning in the numbers. Even as he was losing votes to Humphrey in the North, Nixon was gaining more than three million previous Wallace supporters. They were persuaded not only by Nixon's (and, in the South, Thurmond's) relentless "don't-waste-your-vote" message but also by Humphrey's rise in the national polls, which meant that sticking with their favorite might deprive Nixon of so many votes as to swing the election to the Democrat. Humphrey wooed away more than two million erstwhile Wallace supporters, virtually all of them in the North. They were scared off by LeMay's seemingly casual attitude toward nuclear war and, especially, by criticisms of Wallace's record as governor of Alabama, which the unions were relentlessly bringing to the attention of their members and families. In addition, Humphrey virtually swept the 7 or 8 percent of voters who began October undecided; he also won from Nixon another couple million voters who until Humphrey's September 30 speech thought that the Republican probably offered the best hope for ending the war.

These developments occurred not suddenly but slowly, and even then only after events such as Humphrey's Vietnam speech and Wallace's choice of a running mate had time to work their way into most voters' consciousness—a classic example of the two-step flow of political information and

Some talk change.
Others cause it.

Humphrey

After staking out an independent position on the war in Vietnam, Democratic nominee Hubert H. Humphrey gained ground in October by arguing that only he would bring about real change. (Credit: Minnesota Historical Society) advice from newsmakers to local opinion leaders and only then to relatively inattentive average voters.[12] An October 6 story in the *New York Times,* based on interviews with hundreds of politicians across the country, reported that Nixon still led with 380 electoral votes to Wallace's 66 and Humphrey's 28. "He Drops Further Behind" was the subhead bearing on Humphrey, who was credited with leading only in Hawaii, Minnesota, Rhode Island, West Virginia, and the District of Columbia.[13] A few days later the Gallup Poll showed merely a modest change in the race since its survey two weeks before: Nixon, 43 percent; Humphrey, 31 percent; Wallace, 20 percent.

As October unfolded, however, the enthusiasm-money-polls cycle that had spiraled downward for Humphrey since the Democratic convention finally began to spiral upward. His zest on the campaign trail inspired large, excited crowds. "What has Richard Nixon"—occasionally "Sir Richard the Chicken-Hearted" because of his unwillingness to debate—"ever done for old folks? . . . for schools? . . . for the working man?" Humphrey would ask crowds. The call-and-response style refrain: "Nothing!"[14] As for Wallace, Humphrey told voters at a labor rally in Detroit, "If you want to feel damn mean and ornery, find some other way to do it, but don't sacrifice your country. George Wallace has been engaged in union-busting whenever he's had the chance."[15] Taking advantage of Sen. Edmund S. Muskie's popularity, Humphrey pledged, "I really will give Ed responsibility. He'll run the domestic end, and I'll get us out of Vietnam."[16] Even before he had enough money to launch a television campaign, Humphrey's message began to get through. In 1968 the daily audience for the three major network evening news programs was about 60 million (there was nothing else on television to compete with them) and the average length of the candidate's sound bites in the stories that appeared on these programs was relatively long: 42 seconds, compared with less than 8 seconds by 2004.[17] News reports had worked against Humphrey when the typical story was about his responding angrily to hecklers. They worked for him when the words and pictures combined to show an exuberant candidate and cheering audiences.

Endorsements soon followed. Johnson, perhaps impressed that Humphrey had finally stood up for himself, gave a national radio address on October 10 attacking Wallace as "a false prophet of fear" and Nixon as "the one who said Medicare would do more harm than good."[18] The broadcast, with cameras present so excerpts could be shown on the evening news, was paid for by the International Ladies' Garment Workers Union. Johnson also organized a massive rally for Humphrey emceed by Frank Sinatra on the final weekend of the campaign in Texas, perhaps the one state where the president's endorsement could still do a candidate considerable good. In giving the go-ahead for the rally, which drew a capacity crowd to the Houston Astrodome, Johnson sent word to John Connally that "We can't be embarrassed by having this son of a bitch Nixon carry the state."[19] Connally's previous role in the campaign had been to put Nixon in contact with major Texas donors, with no objection from the president.

Endorsements also came Humphrey's way from the left. To be sure, McCarthy did little for Humphrey, breaking his postconvention silence on October 8 merely to demand that, as the price of his support, Humphrey commit to elections in South Vietnam with full Vietcong participation. When, despite Humphrey's demurral, McCarthy endorsed him anyway three weeks later, his statement was tepid. Humphrey's "position with reference to the war in Vietnam and the demilitarization of American foreign policy, as well as the matter of the draft . . . and also the reform of the Democratic party's internal processes—his position falls short, really, of what I wish it were," said McCarthy. "However, the choice is now between Vice President Humphrey and Richard Nixon and, as between those two, I support the vice president."[20] But other party leaders who had strenuously opposed Humphrey's nomination, such as Sen. Abraham Ribicoff of Connecticut, ten pro-McCarthy Democratic House members, and, by a 71–16 vote of its executive board on October 5, Americans for Democratic Action, flocked to endorse him. Even McCarthy, loath as he was to praise Humphrey, was happy to attack Nixon, "the kind of guy who, if you were drowning twenty feet from shore, would throw you a fifteen-foot rope and tell you he's meeting you more than halfway."[21]

Support for Humphrey rose from 31 percent in the October 3–12 Gallup Poll to 36 percent—just 8 percentage points behind Nixon and 21 points ahead of the fading Wallace—in the poll taken October 17–21. Money by now was pouring into Humphrey's treasury. Donations and loans, including $240,000 each from Hollywood mogul Lew Wasserman and Prohibition-era gangster John ("Jake the Barber") Factor (which were never repaid), came in at such a pace that during the final two weeks of the campaign Humphrey was able to match Nixon ad for ad on radio and television, helping narrow Nixon's overall advantage in media spending to 2 to 1 on television, 4 to 1 on radio, and 2 to 1 in newspapers.[22] As the nominee of the majority party, Humphrey's spots, unlike Nixon's, almost never featured the candidate's face or voice. Instead they focused on "all the things the Democrats have done for you, including aid for education, summer jobs for kids, a higher minimum wage, Social Security, and Medicare."[23]

The unions redoubled their efforts on his behalf. By one estimate, they registered 4.6 million new voters, distributed 115 million pieces of campaign literature, dispatched 72,000 canvassers to knock on doors, and, on Election Day, rallied 94,000 volunteers to serve as babysitters, ride givers, poll watchers—whatever it took to get Democrats into the voting booth.[24] Unions spent about $7 million on the election, nearly double the amount they spent in 1964.[25]

Humphrey's zestfulness on the campaign trail was matched by Wallace's growing testiness, born of declining support in the polls and, at one point, sheer exhaustion. Antiwar protesters, tired of being props at Wallace rallies, adopted a new approach: dress neatly, wear Wallace hats and buttons, and offer mock cheers at inappropriate moments or chant disorienting right-wing slogans such as "Kill the commies!" to throw him off his stride. Wallace would respond angrily, not deftly, sometimes touching off fights within the crowd that dominated the news coverage. According to *Los Angeles Times* reporter Jack Nelson, "an atmosphere of hate permeated almost every political rally."[26] Wallace's law and order theme seemed wildly out of sync with these images of lawlessness and disorder. At a rally in Detroit, a brawl featuring fists, chairs, and sticks actually broke out during the playing of the National Anthem. On October 16, at a particularly rowdy event in El Paso in which Wallace pointed at a heckler and shouted, "You're a little punk," the Secret Service told camera operators not to shine their lights on him for fear of assassination. "He looked haggard and at times even frightened," NBC correspondent David Burrington reported. Wallace canceled the next day's events and returned to Montgomery to rest for a few days. An aide cited "complete exhaustion."[27]

Nixon's campaign continued steadily, unflappably on its course. His rallies were well advanced and virtually all alike: bands, cheerleaders, a balloon drop, and a large supportive crowd. His speech remained substantially unchanged: "Over the last four years we've had the worst crime wave in the history of America. Over the last four years we haven't had one moment of peace abroad. Over the last four years we've had the worst inflation we've ever had in this country over the last twenty-five years." His anodyne solutions: "Let in the sun and remove the darkness," "I believe we must go forward," and above all, "We need new leadership."[28]

Nixon could be specific. He spoke in support of the oil depletion allowance and space program in Texas, the textile industry in the Carolinas, the Tennessee Valley Authority in Tennessee, and the steel industry in Pennsylvania. He also could be substantive, albeit inconspicuously. To rebut the charge that he was not saying much of anything, he decided on October 12 to deliver a series of ten nightly fifteen-minute speeches on education, NATO, labor, conservation, and other topics during the last two weeks of October—but on radio, with no cameras present. "Give 'em substance until it runs out of their ears," he told Haldeman, referring to the media, "and then they'll quit their bitching."[29] His most noteworthy October radio speech called for replacing the draft with a volunteer army. This had been a cause among some conservative Republicans since Barry M. Goldwater proposed ending conscription on libertarian grounds in 1964. It also was a direct pitch to "our young people" and if instituted, Nixon believed, would cut off the oxygen that stoked antiwar protests.[30]

Asked if Nixon's campaign lacked "passion," campaign manager John Mitchell replied, "I don't know what passion has to do with it. . . . I think our operation has been, as you put it, without passion because we have planned it and programmed it and had the time to carry it out."[31] Nixon himself told his speechwriters, "Be very careful not to reflect on Johnson. . . . Let's not get too biting."[32] For all its advantages, problems attended such an approach. It was temperamentally misaligned with the candidate. Nixon was trying to avoid mistakes in order to protect his lead even though he was most comfortable on the attack, as in his earlier elections to the House of Representatives, the Senate, and the vice presidency. It was politically misaligned with his status as the nominee of the party out of power, whose job it was to convince voters that the incumbent party had failed. And as a by-product of his decision to remain above the fray on Vietnam, Nixon was hardly talking at all about foreign policy, which was substantively his strongest suit. According to Stephen Ambrose, Nixon mentioned China only once, and Cuba not at all, during the fall campaign.[33] "We were like a basketball team sitting on a lead," lamented speechwriter Pat Buchanan, "taking no risks, freezing the ball, running out the clock."[34]

The Nixon organization's superficial calm masked two growing concerns as Humphrey moved up in the polls. The first was that, between them, Humphrey and Wallace would win enough electoral votes to deny Nixon a majority. Not wanting to confront even the possibility of having to bargain with Wallace for his electors after the results were in, Nixon called on Humphrey to join him in a pledge to support whichever candidate won the most popular votes. Humphrey demurred, saying he would "stand by the constitutional process."[35] Both Nixon and Humphrey could read the Twelfth Amendment to the Constitution, which said that if no candidate received a majority of electoral votes, "then from the persons having the highest numbers not exceeding three on the list of those voted for as President, the House of Representatives shall choose immediately, by ballot, the President. But in choosing the President the votes shall be taken by states, the representation from each state having one vote . . . and a majority of all the states shall be necessary to a choice." Both candidates also knew that in the House, the Democrats currently dominated "the representation" of twenty-eight state delegations—two more than the required majority of twenty-six—and the Republicans controlled only eighteen. Wallace, having no party, controlled none, although Democratic House members from any Deep South state he carried in November would be hard-pressed not to support him, at least initially. Only a Republican victory in the House elections could reverse this imbalance. But no one expected such an outcome, and if it somehow occurred it would be the by-product of a massive Nixon landslide that would make any House intervention unnecessary.[36]

If Nixon won a plurality but not a majority of electoral votes, he planned to bring pressure to bear on Democratic House members in states or districts that he carried to vote for him. By mid-October, a handful of southern Democrats had already pledged to vote for the candidate who won their district, and others may have as well if the occasion arose. In the meantime, Nixon worried about the possibility but liked the issue. He told Safire, his speechwriter, to "bang away at how Humphrey was afraid to meet the people in the primaries, and now he's afraid to accept the decision of the majority of the people today."[37] Humphrey's decision not to defer to the popular vote gave Nixon a weapon to hit back with when the Democrat slammed him for not agreeing to debate. The two candidates spoke about these matters in the language of principle, but it was straight political interest that animated their positions.

The other matter that concerned Nixon was what President Johnson was up to in Vietnam.

VIETNAM

Nixon's approach to Vietnam throughout the entire year had been to decry the sorry state of the war and offer himself as the leader who could end it on satisfactory terms. He justified his decision not to propose any specific plan on the ground that the country has one president at a time and that nothing said by a presidential candidate should encourage the enemy to think that it would be better off waiting for a change in leadership. On October 1, the day after Humphrey's speech calling for a bombing halt, Nixon responded: "It is possible that the men in Hanoi could interpret this particular statement as offering them a concession in January that they could not get now."[38] But Humphrey had astutely cleared his proposal with Averell Harriman and Cyrus Vance, the lead American negotiators at the Paris peace talks, which enabled him to brush off Nixon's objection as misinformed.

Nixon's great fear was that Johnson would unveil an election-eve breakthrough in the long-stalled negotiations that would trigger a last-minute surge of support for Humphrey, whose defeat, for all his and Johnson's differences, would represent an adverse verdict on the president. In mid-September Nixon learned from Henry Kissinger, a Harvard professor who was privy to the negotiations, that Johnson was considering a bombing halt in hopes of motivating North Vietnam to negotiate seriously. Kissinger was well wired within the foreign policy circles of both parties; Richard Holbrooke, who was part of the American negotiating team, said that "Henry was the only person outside of the government we were authorized to discuss the negotiations with."[39] Angling to be national security adviser no matter who won the election, Kissinger made another call to John Mitchell, his contact in the Nixon campaign, on October 12, one day after the North Vietnamese delegates asked U.S. negotiators if Johnson would stop the bombing in return for their agreeing to include Soviet Vietnam in the negotiations.[40] Kissinger's message this time, Nixon later wrote, was that "there was a strong possibility that the administration would move before October 23."[41]

No halt in the bombing occurred by that date, but a flurry of progress in the negotiations made such an action increasingly likely. For months, North Vietnam had insisted that the terms of its participation in the talks were an end to the bombing and the exclusion of South Vietnam from the negotiating table. On October 11, under severe pressure from Soviet officials who feared that Nixon was going to win the election, Hanoi had dropped the latter condition, and on October 27 it proposed that if the bombing was brought to an end within three days, it was prepared to resume negotiations as soon as November 2, three days before the election.[42] South Vietnam's president, Nguyen Van Thieu, was unhappy about this turn of events, but Johnson, assuming that Thieu would have to go along if the United States acted, scheduled a nationally televised address on Thursday, October 31. "I have now ordered that all air, naval, and artillery bombardment of North Vietnam cease as of 8 a.m., Washington time, Friday morning," Johnson said, in the course of reporting that negotiations with delegations from North Vietnam and the National Liberation Front would begin on November 6 and that South Vietnam was "free to participate."[43] Shortly before he went on the air, Johnson called the three candidates to tell them what was coming. Despite offering the president a "pledge of support," Nixon wrote, "I could feel my anger and frustration welling up."[44]

Johnson miscalculated Thieu's response. On November 2, backed by his parliament, the South Vietnamese president announced that his country would not participate in the talks because negotiations on these terms "would be just another trick toward a coalition government with the communists in South Vietnam." Johnson was furious. He had recently learned from FBI wiretaps that Anna Chan Chennault, the cochair of the Women for Nixon-Agnew National Advisory Committee and a leader of the pro-Taiwan China lobby in Washington, had been telling Bui Diem, South Vietnam's ambassador to the United States, that his government would get a better deal under Nixon. National Security Agency intercepts of messages between South Vietnam and its embassy revealed that Diem was passing on this advice to Thieu. Johnson was already aware that Mitchell had called Chennault right after his October 31 speech and, suspecting that the phone was tapped, guardedly told her "on behalf of Mr. Nixon it's very important that our Vietnamese friends understand our Republican position and I hope you have made that clear to them."[45] No such call was necessary. Thieu knew that anyway, as surely as he knew that to enter into four-party negotiations would put his country on the road to a coalition government and eventual defeat by the communists.[46] His problem was less with Johnson than with Humphrey. Thieu "felt that Humphrey would not be as staunch a supporter as President Johnson had been," according to Ambassador Ellsworth Bunker, "that he felt under greater pressure to get out more quickly."[47] In refusing to yield, Thieu arguably was exercising "the principle of self-determination" that the president had just told the country was "the very principle for which we are engaged in South Vietnam."[48]

Still, the idea that a candidate for president would have in his organization someone who was advising another country's government against her own was potentially explosive. On November 1, Humphrey was briefed by William Bundy, the assistant secretary of state for East Asian and Pacific Affairs, on the developments. After the election Humphrey wrote, "I wonder if I should have blown the whistle on Anna Chennault and Nixon. He must have known about her call to Thieu. I *wish* I could have been sure."[49] If he or Johnson had known about Nixon's October 22 instruction to campaign aide H. R. Haldeman to "keep Anna Chennault working on SVN [South Vietnam]," Humphrey surely would have.[50] But at the time, his decision to stay silent made sense. He could not be sure; also, it would be "difficult," Humphrey told aides, "to explain how we knew about what she had done."[51] Nixon would publicly deny any involvement, as he did in a November 3 phone call to Johnson, and the president was not about to confirm that his administration was wiretapping American citizens and the embassy of an allied government. To go public ran the risk of looking like a last-minute smear by a desperate candidate. Besides, Humphrey no longer felt desperate. The polls were moving his way: the final Harris Poll actually showed that he had taken a three-point lead over Nixon. Everyone knew that Harris tilted Democratic and discounted the results accordingly. But even Gallup showed that Humphrey had drawn within two points by November 2 and was gaining at a rate of about a half point per day.

In terms of political conduct, Secretary of Defense Clark Clifford rightly stated in his memoir that regardless of what Nixon personally knew, "the activities of the Nixon campaign constitute a gross, potentially illegal, interference in the security affairs of the nation."[52] James Rosen has argued that as president Nixon approved a break-in to the Washington headquarters of the Brookings Institution because he was concerned that documents demonstrating his campaign's efforts to undermine the Paris talks were in a safe on the premises.[53] In terms of immediate political consequence, however, the final-week flurry of activity concerning Vietnam was probably a wash. Johnson's announcement of a bombing halt and peace negotiations produced an immediate bubble of new support for Humphrey. Thieu's decision not to participate, which he did not need Anna Chennault to tell him was in his government's interest, burst it—all within a span of three or four days. According to Robert Dallek, Thieu had figured out for himself "that participation in the discussions would improve Humphrey's chances of winning. Thieu clearly preferred a more hardline Republican administration."[54]

FINAL DAYS

On the night before the election, with the race neck and neck, both major party candidates closed their campaigns with live four-hour telethons from Los Angeles, half telecast to the East and half to the West. Nixon's, on CBS, consisted almost entirely of his answering questions that were phoned in by viewers and then rewritten by Buchanan to evoke the themes he wanted to stress, nearly all of them centering on the nation's plight under Democratic rule and its need for new leadership. Nixon told Buchanan he wanted to include a Social Security question every hour so that he could highlight his plan to index benefits to inflation, an overt pitch to older voters.[55] Bud

Wilkinson, the former head football coach of the University of Oklahoma, read the questions to Nixon and listened devoutly to his answers.

Humphrey's telethon on the smaller ABC network (the only one he could afford) was more varied in format. In addition to his answering questions, it included a half-hour campaign film, a videotaped tribute by Senator Kennedy, a warm statement of support by McCarthy (at last), and frequent shots of Hollywood A-list celebrities such as Paul Newman, Kirk Douglas, and Burt Lancaster answering phone calls from viewers. Both candidates did fine, but Nixon was somber and Humphrey, fresh off an exhilarating motorcade through the city earlier that day, was animated. The most dramatic difference between the two programs was that Agnew was absent from Nixon's, dispatched to campaign in Virginia, a safe Republican state, while Muskie was not only present but featured on Humphrey's. One television critic noted that Humphrey's enthusiasm about his running mate was so great that he sometimes seemed to be hinting that, if elected, he would immediately resign.

Humphrey's rapid and formidable close in October and early November and Wallace's staying power in the Deep South evoked a host of nightmare scenarios, all of which began with an inconclusive election. The possibility that no candidate would secure a majority of electoral votes had loomed over the political process all year, but it had waned after the conventions when Nixon took a commanding lead. With the revival of Humphrey's candidacy it waxed once again.

Theoretically, if Wallace carried just one state in a close election, he could deny both Nixon and Humphrey the required 270 electoral votes. Realistically, the five states in which he was most competitive and the handful of others that he had a reasonable chance of winning made such an outcome plausible, especially because Wallace secured pledges from all of his candidates for elector "to go along with me in the matter"—that is, to cast their votes as he directed, even if the laws of their states, which were of doubtful constitutionality and carried no mechanism for enforcement, required them to vote for the candidate who received the most popular votes.[56] Such an outcome would create a bargaining situation in which Wallace could try to trade his votes for a host of concessions.

Ideally, from Wallace's standpoint, both Nixon and Humphrey would come to him, hat in hand, bidding to pay any price in exchange for his electors. Wallace did not know exactly what the price would be, but on February 19, 1968, he had told a Pittsburgh news conference that his conditions might include: "punish treason by putting some of these [antiwar] dissenters in jail"; eliminate federal antipoverty programs and foreign aid to nations not supporting the United States in Vietnam; "make a strong stand for law and order"; "abandon any type of civil rights legislation"; appoint people "differently oriented to the Supreme Court"; and "turn back to the states" decisions concerning racial integration and legislative apportionment.[57] In 1964 Wallace had mused aloud that his terms would include a pledge that civil rights activists "would never set foot in the White House," a commitment "to enforce the laws that would put communists in jail, where they belong," and a consulting role in the nomination of Supreme Court justices and the attorney general.[58] Wallace's hopes of gaining such concessions were almost certainly forlorn. Politically and otherwise, what major party candidate could afford to become president bearing the taint of such a bargain?

By law, electors were scheduled to meet in their various state capitals and cast their votes on December 16, the first Wednesday after the second Monday of the month. This meant that Wallace would have about six weeks after Election Day to entertain offers from his rivals or, if none were forthcoming, to either deny both of them his votes or support one of them anyway—"probably . . . Mr. Nixon," he later speculated, "because we were violently opposed to Mr. Humphrey's philosophy and ideology."[59] The candidates were not the only ones thinking about what to do if the eventuality arose. For example, James Michener, the best-selling novelist and a Pennsylvania elector pledged to Humphrey, decided that if Nixon won the national popular vote he would lead an effort to persuade other Humphrey electors to vote for the Republican.[60]

A handful of Democratic members of Congress explored another possibility. By law, Congress would meet in joint session on January 6, 1969, to count the electoral votes. The president of the Senate—Vice President Humphrey, as it happened—was slated to preside. If an objection to any state's tally was filed by at least one senator and one representative and both the House and the Senate, voting separately, upheld the objection, the state's votes would be thrown out. With Democratic majorities in both chambers, a series of upheld objections to the votes submitted by every state whose Wallace-pledged electors voted for Nixon was not inconceivable—especially if Humphrey won a plurality of either the national popular vote or the national electoral vote. The result, dictated by the Twelfth Amendment, would be that the president was elected by the House, with each state delegation casting a vote for one of the three leading electoral vote recipients. By House precedent dating back to the tied election between Thomas

Jefferson and Aaron Burr in 1801, evenly divided delegations would be recorded as casting no vote at all, which made getting a twenty-six-state majority more difficult than if, say, each candidate was awarded half a vote from every divided state. The vice president would be elected by the Senate in a much less complicated constitutional procedure: a simple majority vote of all senators—fifty-one out of a hundred—would choose one of the top two electoral vote recipients.[61]

Neither Humphrey nor Nixon could count on winning a House election because neither the Democrats nor the Republicans controlled a majority of the chamber's state delegations in the new 91st Congress. Controlled is the operative word: Democrats did constitute a majority of twenty-six delegations, compared with the Republicans' nineteen. But five of the Democratic delegations represented states carried by Wallace and could hardly be counted on to vote for Humphrey. In addition, three House Democrats from Virginia, the all-Democratic six-member House delegation from South Carolina, and the sole House member from Nevada, also a Democrat, had pledged during the campaign to support whichever presidential candidate carried their districts. The result would have been to swing these three states to Nixon in the House—not enough to win but enough to deny Humphrey a majority.

With the House stalemated, the majority Democratic Senate presumably would have much less trouble electing the highly regarded Senator Muskie as vice president over Governor Agnew. According to the Twentieth Amendment, if the stalemate in the presidential vote continued past January 20, Muskie would serve as acting president until such time as the House acted.[62] One remote possibility was that the House, despite the constitutional admonition to "choose immediately," would never be able to muster a majority of state delegations for any presidential candidate and Muskie would serve as acting president for the next four years. Less unlikely is that the House eventually would have chosen Nixon for president, with Muskie either continuing as vice president or resigning, in which case the Twenty-fifth Amendment, which had been added to the Constitution less than two years before, would allow Nixon to appoint, with the consent of both the House and Senate, a vice president of his own choosing.[63] Or, under massive pressure from House Democratic leaders, those Democrats who vowed to vote their district and support Nixon or Wallace may have considered that pledge fulfilled after a few ballots and then switched to Humphrey.

All of these scenarios in the event of an inconclusive result on November 5 were possible. None were probable. The pressure on all concerned—candidates, electors, and members of Congress—to improvise a solution during the six weeks between November 5 and December 16 would have been enormous. If either Nixon or Humphrey won a plurality of both the popular vote and the electoral vote, a solution probably would have been reached in a matter of days—perhaps the second-place candidate would tell his electors to vote for the plurality winner, or that candidate's electors would take matters into their own hands. But if one candidate led in the popular vote and the other in the electoral vote—plausibly Humphrey in the former and Nixon in the latter—the road to the White House during the "post-election election" would have been much less certain: poorly marked, riddled with deep potholes and fallen limbs, and beset by highwaymen.[64]

THE RESULTS

On election night, Nixon monitored the returns by himself, with the television off and the results coming in to him by phone. Humphrey watched the returns surrounded by family and friends, with televisions tuned to all three networks. Each chose the setting in which he was temperamentally most comfortable on this most stressful of nights.

The night proved suspenseful in some ways but not all. At no point did it seem possible that Humphrey would win a majority of electoral votes, although he did take a 600,000-vote lead in the national popular vote tally around midnight. The television networks, deploying their recently developed ability to call elections state by state based on returns from key precincts, made one thing clear soon after polls began closing along the East Coast and in certain midwestern states: Nixon's early victories in Kentucky, Florida, and North Carolina meant that Wallace's hopes of carrying the Outer South and border states were not going to be realized. But as the evening unfolded, and most of Nixon's targeted large states—specifically, Pennsylvania, Michigan, New York, and Texas—fell into Humphrey's column, it became apparent that even if Humphrey could not win, he might run strongly enough, in combination with Wallace's success in the Deep South, to throw the election into the House of Representatives.

That outcome remained possible until the next morning, when the networks declared that Illinois had gone for Nixon and its twenty-six electoral votes put him over the top. Certain that Mayor Richard J. Daley stole Illinois from Nixon in 1960 by waiting until all of the state's other returns were in before reporting the Chicago tally, Nixon campaign manager John Mitchell created Operation Eagle Eye to deploy precinct watchers throughout the city and to instruct election officials in Republican downstate counties not to release their results until Daley reported Chicago's.[65] In truth, Daley had written off Humphrey in September. Democratic billboards in Chicago, a Daley-supervised product, did not even mention him.

Nixon won a national victory. He carried at least a few states in every region of the country. In the eleven southern states Nixon outpolled Wallace by 58 to 45 electoral votes, with Humphrey carrying only Texas (25), where Lyndon Johnson finally had roused his supporters to a last-minute effort for fear of being embarrassed by a defeat for his vice president in the president's home state.[66] The Outer South went for Nixon by 49 to 25 (Humphrey) to 6 (Wallace). The Deep South, which as Matthew Lassiter points out had been on the losing side of all but one postwar election, favored Wallace over Nixon 39 to 8.[67] Nixon also carried the border states, shutting out Wallace and defeating Humphrey 29 to 17.

The Midwest went strongly for Nixon: he carried seven states with 98 electoral votes to Humphrey's two states and 31 electoral votes. So did the Mountain West, whose ten states and 41 electoral votes all went to Nixon. Of the Pacific states, Nixon carried three with 49 electoral votes and Humphrey two with 13 electoral votes. Humphrey ran strongly only in the Northeast, carrying seven states and 105 electoral votes. But even there Nixon won four states with 27 electoral votes. Nixon's total electoral vote was 301, thirty-one more than he needed but one fewer than he fairly won: a North Carolina elector pledged to him marked his ballot for Wallace instead. At 302, Nixon still would have had the lowest electoral vote total for a winning presidential candidate since Woodrow Wilson's reelection in 1916, a comparably close election from a half century before. Humphrey earned 191 electoral votes, more than half of them from the four large states he carried. Nixon, for his part, carried three of the seven large states he had targeted: California, Illinois, and Ohio. Wallace received only his 46 southern electoral votes, including the one intended for Nixon in North Carolina.

The electoral map was like a photographic negative of the maps from earlier periods, auguring the shift in the parties' geographical bases that later would be painted on television and computer screens in red and blue. In 1916 Wilson did best where Humphrey did worst, especially in the Mountain West and South. Wilson's opponent, Republican Charles Evans Hughes, did best where Nixon did worst: the Northeast and upper Midwest. Of Franklin D. Roosevelt's twenty best states in his four elections from 1932 to 1944, the height of the New Deal era, only three appeared on the list of Humphrey's twenty best states in 1968.[68] In fact, thirteen of the twenty states where Humphrey ran strongest, most of them northeastern, were on the GOP's top twenty list in the earlier period.[69] For the first time in history, a Republican was elected president without carrying New York, and, although he was competing in a three-candidate race, Humphrey surpassed John F. Kennedy's 1960 vote share in three New England states: Massachusetts, Maine, and Rhode Island. On the other hand, Humphrey lost ten southern states, the worst performance ever by a Democrat in the region that until recently had been the party's strongest—the fabled "Solid South."[70] Even in the Reconstruction contests of 1868 and 1872, when most southern whites and some entire states were disenfranchised, Democratic nominees managed to carry two southern states in each election.

The national popular vote was much closer than the electoral vote. Of the 73,211,875 ballots tallied in the election, Nixon won 31,785,480 (43.4 percent, the lowest percentage for a winning presidential candidate since Wilson was first elected in his own three-way contest in 1912). Humphrey received 31,275,166 votes (42.7 percent), and Wallace won 9,906,473 (13.5 percent). About 5.1 million of Wallace's votes came from the South, where he won 34.3 percent. He did considerably better in the Deep South, where he outpolled Nixon 50.6 percent to 23.8 percent, than in the Outer South, where Nixon bested him 39.6 percent to 26.7 percent. (Humphrey finished second in both subregions, earning 25.1 percent in the Deep South, mostly from recently enfranchised black voters, and 33.6 percent in the Outer South, largely on the strength of Texas.) The other 4.8 million Wallace votes came from the rest of the country, where he received 8.3 percent, with transplanted southern whites providing an especially strong source of support.[71]

As with most serious independent and third-party candidates, Wallace's support declined as the election drew closer, in his case by 7.5 percentage points—nearly 5.5 million votes—from his late September peak of 21 percent in the Gallup Poll. About one in five of his original southern supporters changed their minds, and 77 percent of them voted for Nixon. Outside the South, 57 percent of Wallace's original supporters defected, with 55 percent of them going for the Republican nominee and 45 percent for the Democrat. Humphrey did best among the roughly three-fifths of the previously pro-Wallace union members who abandoned him on Election Day, drawing 69 percent of their support. Thurmond's plea to southern conservatives not to "waste" their votes on Wallace clearly made a difference, as did Nixon's identical appeal to conservatives outside the South. Similarly, the efforts by Humphrey and union leaders to persuade their members that Wallace was antilabor had the desired effect on many of them. Overall, Nixon won

60 percent of the 5.5 million Wallace defectors and Humphrey 40 percent, amounting to a one-million-vote gain for the Republican—enough to give him his national popular vote plurality with about a half million votes to spare.[72]

Voter turnout in 1968 increased by 2.6 million from 1964, but that was an artifact of the country's growing population. The turnout rate—the share of voting-age citizens who turned out at the polls—declined a percentage point in 1968, down from 62 percent in 1964 to 61 percent. Spurred by the Voting Rights Act of 1965, the black turnout rate in the South rose from 44 percent to 51 percent and, in reaction, white turnout in the region rose by 2 percentage points. The decline in the national turnout rate was concentrated outside the South. Nonsouthern white turnout fell by 3 points. More significantly, turnout among African Americans living outside the South fell by 11 points. "We as a people, as a movement, misread the significance of a Humphrey victory," reflected civil rights leader Jesse Jackson years later. "If Humphrey had won, we'd have sustained all of the social justice programs, and no doubt ended the war as well."[73]

The surge in southern black voting did little for Humphrey in the region, where in every state except Texas he lost by margins ranging from 8.5 to 47.0 percentage points. In Illinois, California, and New Jersey, however, the decline in black voting may have cost Humphrey some or even all of these states' 83 electoral votes, which might have been enough to win him the election.[74] In a different race-based analysis, Omar Wasow argues that if Martin Luther King had not been assassinated and the fear-inducing post-assassination riots had not occurred, Humphrey would have won nearly one million more white votes, enabling him to carry enough additional states, including Illinois and New Jersey, to win the election.[75] Beyond that, some who had supported Robert F. Kennedy for the Democratic nomination chose not to vote, although those who did voted strongly for Humphrey. Supporters of Eugene McCarthy voted but backed Humphrey over Nixon only barely, and Wallace received 22 percent of their ballots.[76]

The election was not a landslide for Nixon, but it was a "negative landslide" against the Democrats.[77] Nixon won narrowly but Humphrey lost massively. Even though 1968 was a three-candidate race, Nixon added 4.9 percentage points to Goldwater's vote share in 1964. In contrast, Humphrey's share of the national popular vote fell 18.4 points from Johnson's, a falloff greater than was suffered by any major party candidate since Herbert Hoover in 1932. Even Humphrey's dramatic comeback in October only brought him from 29 percent to 43 percent. He carried thirteen states that

Johnson won but lost the other thirty-one, one of them (Arkansas) to Wallace and the remaining thirty to Nixon.

The Gallup Poll demonstrated the sources of the decline in Democratic support group by group in the electorate.[78] In the professional and business job category, Humphrey's share of the vote ran 20 percentage points behind Johnson's, dropping from 54 percent to 34 percent. He fell 21 points below Johnson's vote among manual workers, from 71 percent to 50 percent. Humphrey ran 20 points behind Johnson in the Protestant vote, falling from 55 percent to 35 percent, and 17 points behind him among Catholics, from 76 percent to 59 percent. There was no partisan gender gap in either 1964 or 1968: Humphrey ran 17 points below Johnson among both men and women, doing about equally well against Nixon in both categories. Wallace, in contrast, won 16 percent of men and just 12 percent of women, who were more likely—especially those living outside the South—to be turned off by the aura of violence around his stormy rhetoric and raucous rallies. Humphrey came close to holding on to his predecessor's 1964 majority only among black voters. He won 88 percent of their support, doing almost as well as Johnson, who won 94 percent. In the Deep South, newly enfranchised African Americans, many of them participating in their first presidential election, provided Humphrey with almost all the votes he received in some states.

Still, of the seven elements that made up the New Deal Democratic coalition, only the South abandoned Humphrey entirely. He carried Catholics by a 23-point margin over Nixon, with Wallace drawing 8 percent. Union members and their families supported Humphrey 56 percent to 29 percent (Nixon) and 15 percent (Wallace)—down but not dramatically from Johnson's 65 percent to 33 percent majority against Goldwater. Liberals and blacks (88 percent) also gave strong support to Humphrey, as did Jews, who backed him 86 percent to 14 percent. Although Humphrey did poorly among white voters in general, falling below 40 percent, whites in cities with populations of a million or more supported him over Nixon 50 percent to 44 percent, buttressing rather than diluting Humphrey's already strong big-city majority among minority voters.[79] Surprisingly, in view of the heckling from young protesters that plagued Humphrey during much of the campaign, he prevailed among voters under age thirty: Humphrey, 47 percent; Nixon, 38 percent; and Wallace, 15 percent. Muskie's ability to connect with college students seems to have been especially helpful to the ticket with younger voters.

Self-identified Democrats, including independents who leaned Democratic, outnumbered Republicans 55 percent to 37 percent in the University of Michigan's survey of voters in the 1968 election. But Republicans supported Nixon at a much higher rate than Democrats supported Humphrey. Nixon won 96 percent of the voters who called themselves strong Republicans. Humphrey did well but not as well among strong Democrats: 85 percent. Among weak Republicans and independent Republicans, Nixon received 83 percent and 82 percent, respectively. Humphrey's support among weak Democrats was only 58 percent; among independent Democrats it was 52 percent. The net effect was that the Democrats' 18-percentage-point advantage over the Republicans in party identification dwindled to a 5-point advantage in party loyalty–motivated voting for Humphrey over Nixon. Some of that advantage was erased by the 9 percent of voters who scored as pure independents, only 24 percent of whom voted for Humphrey.[80]

Nixon earned his popular vote plurality over Humphrey mostly from the voters' appraisals of the candidates themselves. Asked to rate them on a "feeling thermometer" that ran from "cold" to "warm" along a 100-degree scale, voters in the Michigan survey scored Nixon 67 and Humphrey 62.[81] Nixon's 5-point advantage in how people felt about the candidates translated into a lower but still substantial 3-point gain on Election Day from voters who based their decision mostly on those feelings.[82] Part of the falloff probably was traceable to the voters' assessments of the two major party vice presidential candidates. Muskie scored 61 and Agnew only 50.[83] Some Nixon campaign staffers argued after the election that Agnew's appeal to Wallace voters had made the difference for their candidate in Kentucky, North Carolina, Tennessee, and South Carolina, whose combined forty-two electoral votes raised Nixon above 270. No available data can prove or disprove this claim. What is clear is that nationally, the Agnew-Muskie comparison cost Nixon as much as 2 percent of the popular vote and that Muskie was able to swing his solidly Republican home state to Humphrey while Agnew failed to carry his generally Democratic home state for Nixon.

Wallace's support came neither from party loyalty nor voters' admiration for him as a candidate. Except in Alabama and perhaps Mississippi, where he was regarded by most white voters as the de facto Democratic nominee, Wallace's status as an independent earned him no votes at all from traditional partisans. Nor did most voters like or admire him: his thermometer score was 31, lower even than LeMay's 35. But more than either Humphrey or Nixon, Wallace won votes based on his stands on issues.

One ingredient of Wallace's issues-based success was that people believed they knew where he stood. On matters such as how to handle urban unrest and what to do in Vietnam, voters came nowhere near agreeing about where Nixon and Humphrey belonged on a seven-point scale from liberal to conservative. But they had little trouble agreeing that Wallace's positions fell squarely at the right end of the scale: "use all available force" to suppress urban violence and seek "complete military victory" in Vietnam. Among those who supported Wallace, about half mentioned his issue stands, nearly double the number that mentioned issues in explaining why they were for Nixon or Humphrey. Wallace's positions on Vietnam, civil rights, and law and order correlated strongly with how voters felt about him. This was considerably less true of Humphrey and, especially, Nixon.[84] To be sure, most voters disagreed with Wallace on the issues. But among the minority who cast their ballots for him, issues were the major motive.

Overall, Vietnam was the most important issue on voters' minds: 43 percent considered it one of the major problems facing the country, more than double the percentage that mentioned the next four problems combined: public disorder (8 percent), civil rights (5 percent), poverty (4 percent), and "Negro riots" (3 percent). But because voters saw little difference between Nixon, whom voters scored an average 4.4 (that is, slightly conservative) on the seven-point Vietnam scale, and Humphrey, who scored 4.1 (also slightly conservative), the war had little effect on how people decided between the two major party candidates.[85] Since 1964, the electorate itself had grown neither more hawkish nor more dovish on Vietnam and had, if anything, become a bit more liberal on civil rights. "What *had* changed," according to Philip Converse and colleagues, "was the public view of the success of Administration performance in these areas," which was of a "bungled war" and "racial confrontation."[86] This perception, more than any stand he took on the war, hurt Humphrey, whom voters associated with Johnson even more closely than they associated him with Muskie.[87] As the incumbent vice president, Humphrey also suffered from the public's steeply declining trust in government, from which Wallace benefited the most.[88]

Because of the looming possibility that the presidential election might be thrown into the House of Representatives, the length of the coattails, if any, of the winning presidential candidate was a focus of attention during the campaign. Although the election was decided without resort to the House, Nixon was nonetheless disappointed that his party gained only four seats in that chamber, leaving it in Democratic hands by a margin of 243 to 192. It was in these elections that the basic continuity of the Democrats' dominance in party identification was most manifest. Ever since 1952, when polling began, at least 50 percent of voters had identified themselves as Democrats of one variety or another. The party's 51 percent share of the national popular House vote in 1968 was about average for the period.[89]

One reason the Democrats did as well as they did is that 1968 turned out to be the best year yet for House incumbents, which worked to the advantage of the incumbent party. Aided by a 70 percent growth in taxpayer-funded personal staff during the past decade and a more than doubling, from five to twelve, in the number of members' free round trips home since 1966, all but twenty-six of the 435 incumbent representatives ran for reelection, and 396 of them, or 96.6 percent, won.[90] Neither party experienced significant gains or losses in any region of the country, but in New York City Democrat Shirley Chisholm became the first black woman ever elected to Congress. She took her seat alongside fellow freshmen Allard Lowenstein, who a year before had roused antiwar Democrats to challenge Johnson for the nomination, and future mayor Ed Koch. Chisholm's election, along with those of freshmen Louis Stokes in Cleveland and William Clay in St. Louis, raised the number of African Americans in the House to nine, exceeding the previous high of seven set in the Reconstruction Congress elected in 1872.

A second reason for the Democrats' success in the House contests was that the same southern voters who rejected the party's presidential nominee in every state but Texas elected Democratic House delegations in every state but Virginia, where the two parties each won five seats. Outside the South, 20.0 percent of congressional districts supported one party's candidate for president and another party's House candidate. In the South, the figure was 61.3 percent, and in fifty-nine cases out of sixty-five the district voted for the Democratic congressional candidate while rejecting Humphrey.[91] Going into the 1968 election, southern Democrats' long accumulation of seniority within the majority party meant that they held ten of twenty House standing committee chairmanships, including Ways and Means, Appropriations, Rules, and Armed Services. Not a single southern committee chair failed to gain reelection, and only one of several dozen subcommittee chairs, Basil Whitener of North Carolina, was defeated. Of the southerners who chaired nine of the Senate's sixteen standing committees—including Finance, Judiciary, Armed Services, and Foreign Relations—only two were on the ballot in 1968 and both of them, Foreign Relations Committee chair J. William Fulbright of Arkansas and Finance Committee chair Russell B. Long of Louisiana, were reelected handily. In an era when committee chairs still ran Congress and southerners chaired most committees, white voters in the South were not about to abandon their leading stronghold in Washington. In addition, Republicans in all but a few southern states had yet to build grassroots party organizations that were capable of winning the local and state legislative offices that create a farm system for congressional candidates.

Finally, the Supreme Court's reapportionment decisions in the 1960s—especially *Reynolds v. Sims* (1964), which established the "one man, one vote" principle of equal population in state legislative districts, and *Wesberry v. Sanders* (1964), which extended that principle to Congress's lower house—prompted some unusual mid-decade reapportionments of congressional districts. The nominal purpose of redistricting was to redraw district boundaries to ensure equal numbers of residents, but while Democratic state legislators were under the hood, some of them took the opportunity to help their party's candidates for Congress. Partly for that reason, in the forty-three states that conducted state legislative elections in 1968, Democrats lost only seventeen seats, or 0.2 percent of the total number of seats in all legislative houses.

Evidence that the unusual reapportionments that occurred before the 1968 election helped Democratic House candidates lay in the results of the statewide elections for senator and governor that also took place in 1968. After a string of good elections for Class 3 Democratic senators in 1950, 1956, and 1962, Democrats had to defend twenty-three seats in 1968 compared with eleven for the Republicans. Twenty-eight incumbents sought reelection, and eight, all but one of them Democrats, were defeated: Daniel B. Brewster of Maryland, who lost to Rep. Charles McC. Mathias; Joseph S. Clark of Pennsylvania, who lost to Rep. Richard S. Schweiker; A. S. Mike Monroney of Oklahoma, who lost to former governor Henry Bellmon; Wayne Morse of Oregon, who lost to state representative Robert W. Packwood; and primary losers Ernest Gruening of Alaska, who was defeated by real estate broker Mike Gravel; Frank J. Lausche of Ohio, who lost to Rep. John J. Gilligan (who was in turn defeated in November by Republican state attorney general William B. Saxbe); Edward V. Long of Missouri, who was defeated by Lt. Gov. Thomas F. Eagleton; and Thomas H. Kuchel of California, the only Republican primary loser, who was defeated by state education superintendent Max Rafferty (himself beaten in the general election by former state controller Alan Cranston). In elections with no incumbent seeking another term, Republicans carried previously Democratic seats in Florida, Ohio, and Arizona, where Goldwater won the seat that had been held since 1927 by retiring Senate president pro tempore Carl Hayden. Democrats won previously Republican open seats in California and Iowa. In all, the Republicans gained five seats in the Senate, increasing their ranks from thirty-seven to forty-two.

Gubernatorial elections, the other major statewide contests in 1968, also went well for the Republicans. In an era when eight states still elected their governors to two-year terms (compared with two such states in 2016) and thirteen states with four-year gubernatorial terms held their elections in conjunction with the presidential contest (compared with eleven in 2016), the governorships of twenty-one states were on the ballot in 1968.[92] The Democrats took the chief executive positions of two small states from the Republicans, Montana and Rhode Island, but they also surrendered seven to the GOP: three in the East, one in a border state, and three in the Midwest.[93] The Republicans' sweetest victory came in Illinois, where Cook County board president Richard B. Ogilvie's defeat of incumbent governor Samuel H. Shapiro left Republicans in charge of six of the seven largest states—every one but Texas. In all, the nation's thirty-one Republican governors, representing a net gain of five, led states comprising two-thirds of the nation's population.

In one sense the 1968 elections boded ill for Nixon's presidency. He was the first newly elected president since Zachary Taylor in 1848 to face a Congress controlled by the opposition party in both houses. But the GOP's gains in the Senate brought it within striking distance of a majority in 1970, when the Class 1 cohort of twenty-five Democrats and only eight Republicans, the product of dominating Democratic years in 1958 and 1964, would be on the ballot. As for the party's governors, they would be key figures in Nixon's effort to create a New Federalism that would delegate many federal grant programs to the states.

With Nixon eligible to seek a second term in 1972, Republicans spent little time examining their ranks of senators and governors with an eye toward the next presidential election. (Little could they have known that their 1996 nominee would be freshman senator Robert Dole of Kansas.) Democrats spent considerable time doing so. The pool of nineteen Democratic governors yielded no obvious presidential contenders, but that was no cause for concern: both parties had fallen into a pattern, soon to be broken, of choosing candidates for president from the ranks of current and former senators. A year before the election, Sen. George McGovern of South Dakota had informed Allard Lowenstein that he and most other critics of the Vietnam War were unavailable to challenge Johnson for the Democratic presidential nomination because they had to run for reelection in 1968. Morse, Clark, and Gruening were unsuccessful, but among the reelected were Fulbright, Gaylord Nelson of Wisconsin, Frank Church of Idaho, and McGovern himself. Along with senators Eugene McCarthy of Minnesota, Edward Kennedy of Massachusetts, and Edmund Muskie of Maine, the party's vice presidential nominee in 1968, McGovern emerged from the election as one of a small cohort of Democratic senators instantly identified as plausible contenders for the Democratic presidential nomination in 1972.

8

RESILIENT AMERICA

At 12:55 p.m. on January 6, 1969, Congress met in joint session to count the electoral votes submitted by the states. Hubert H. Humphrey was absent from the vice president's chair during such occasions on the dais of the House chamber, but his 1968 running mate, Sen. Edmund S. Muskie of Maine, was present. Attending the funeral of former United Nations secretary-general Trygve Lie in Oslo, where antiwar demonstrators threw rocks at the American embassy to mark his arrival and other Norwegians cheered him, Humphrey was spared the awkward assignment that Vice President Richard Nixon performed in 1961 and that Vice President Al Gore would perform again in 2001: announcing his own defeat in the presidential election.

The ritual nature of the occasion was interrupted when North Carolina's certificate of its electoral vote was opened by Sen. Richard B. Russell of Georgia, presiding as president pro tempore in Humphrey's absence. The certificate recorded twelve votes for Nixon and Spiro T. Agnew, who had carried the state, and one for George C. Wallace and Curtis LeMay. Lloyd W. Bailey, a physician and John Birch Society member who had run as a Nixon elector, was upset that during the postelection transition period Nixon announced the appointment of Harvard professor Henry Kissinger and other "members of the un-American and infamous Council on Foreign Relations" to positions in his administration, along with "the left-wing Democrat" Daniel Patrick Moynihan as urban policy adviser. Worst of all, Bailey charged, Nixon "asked Earl Warren to remain as Chief Justice of the United States Supreme Court until June. This is unthinkable!"[1]

Employing for the first time the procedure created by the 1887 Electoral Count Act, Senator Muskie, joined by six other senators, and Rep. James G. O'Hara of Michigan, joined by thirty-seven other representatives (including George Bush of Texas), formally challenged Bailey's vote as "not regularly given." Each house went off to deliberate separately on the matter. Some members argued that electors are constitutionally free to vote as they choose, and others who were sympathetic to the challenge opposed it because they feared it would "diminish pressures" for the thoroughgoing reform of the Electoral College that proponents of direct election of the president hoped to pass in the 91st Congress.[2] Both the House of Representatives, by 228 to 170, and the Senate, by 58 to 33, defeated the challenge, and the two houses reconvened at 4:45 p.m. EST to finish the vote count. When it was over, Senator Russell announced that Nixon had been elected president and Agnew vice president.

Bailey aside, Nixon's official election occurred exactly as elections nearly always have in the United States, proceeding from a constitutionally unofficial tally in November to the constitutionally mandated gathering of electors in their state capitals in December to the counting of the electoral votes by Congress in January.[3] Viewed in historical and comparative terms, the certainty of this process even in the wake of a turbulent year testified to the resilience of the American political system. After the results were in, no one plotted a revolution or coup to overturn Nixon's election. Neither the outgoing chief executive, the defeated vice president, nor anyone around them gave a second's thought to the possibility of refusing to turn over the reins of power to the newly elected president of the opposition party. No citizen woke up on the morning of January 20, 1969, wondering whether Nixon's inauguration would be allowed to proceed as scheduled at noon that day.

The practical consequence of this certain transfer of power was that Nixon was able to begin laying the foundation for his administration in the wee hours of November 6, the morning after the election. In his victory speech Nixon recalled a sign held up by a teenager at a campaign event in Deshler, Ohio. The sign read, "Bring Us Together," Nixon told the nation, "and that will be the great objective of this administration. . . . We want to bridge the generation gap. We want to bridge the gap between the races. We want to bring America together."[4] On January 20, Nixon struck a similarly unifying theme in his inaugural address. "In the orderly transfer of power, we celebrate the unity that keeps us free," he said, speaking from a platform on the East Front of the Capitol that included President Lyndon B.

After a politically acrimonious year, President Richard Nixon urged Americans in his inaugural address to "lower our voices." (Credit: Richard Nixon Presidential Library)

Johnson and Vice President Humphrey, who, along with Senator Muskie, had met with Nixon in a show of national unity right after the election. Calling on Americans to "lower our voices" because "we cannot learn from one another until we stop shouting at one another," the new president pledged: "Those who have been left out, we will try to bring in. Those left behind we will help to catch up."[5]

Nixon's words at the beginning of his presidency and those he uttered less than six years later, when he resigned the office in disgrace after perversely reuniting much of the nation in opposition to his leadership, constitute severely unmatched bookends. The war in Vietnam continued until the start of Nixon's second term, at enormous cost of life and treasure to the American and, especially, the Vietnamese people. Four years of additional fighting brought no progress in the U.S. negotiating position that Nixon inherited from President Johnson, and the peace agreement signed on January 27, 1973, merely postponed for another two years the fall of South Vietnam to the communists. In addition Nixon, leading members of his White House staff, prominent Justice Department officials, and a number of shady contract employees engaged in the ongoing series of criminal actions to subvert their political opponents that constituted the Watergate affair. Nearly forty administration officials and hired guns eventually went to jail for their crimes, including Nixon's chief of staff, H. R. Haldeman, domestic policy adviser John Ehrlichman, White House counsel John Dean, special counsel Charles Colson, and Attorney General John Mitchell. On August 8, 1974, Nixon announced his resignation as president in the face of certain and near-unanimous impeachment by the House and removal by the Senate. He escaped criminal indictment only because he was pardoned exactly one month later by his successor, President Gerald R. Ford.[6]

Nor was everything copacetic during the early days of Nixon's tenure, the eleven weeks between his election on November 5, 1968, and his first-term inauguration on January 20, 1969. On December 11, after the president-elect broke precedent by introducing all of his cabinet appointees at the same time on national television, much of the political community was unimpressed by the assemblage of uniformly middle-aged, white, male, Christian Republicans. "The cabinet was perhaps the least distinguished in the postwar era," sniffed Washington columnists Rowland Evans and Robert D. Novak.[7] The Democrats who controlled both houses of Congress— the first time in 120 years that a newly elected president had confronted this governing situation—were uninterested in seeing their longtime, strongly partisan Republican nemesis succeed. For the first time ever, violence marred a president's inaugural parade. Several thousand antiwar protesters, furious that the November ballot had offered them no way to express their strong desire that the United States withdraw from Vietnam, gathered near the end of the parade route chanting, "Ho, Ho, Ho Chi Minh / The NLF is gonna win." Some threw rocks, cans, bottles, and smoke bombs that struck cars in the presidential procession, including the limousine carrying Nixon and his family. A few days later Gallup reported that the new president's initial job approval rating was 59 percent, impressive compared with the 43 percent he won in the election but considerably below the initial ratings of his recent predecessors.[8]

Yet the start of the Nixon presidency affirmed the resilience of the American political system even while revealing the strains and stresses it still was under and to which he would contribute. Nothing guaranteed that the angry, often violent forces that divided American society in 1968 would be ameliorated by the institutions and processes of mainstream politics during the four years that followed the election. Nor was it clear that the system would be able to endure, albeit unhappily, what turned out to be the unprecedentedly long half century of divided party government that the 1968 elections began. But, for the most part, that is what happened.

CHANNELING DISSENT

Nineteen sixty-eight is rightly remembered for the discord and ire that marked it. But it is worth noting that most Americans were not entirely dissatisfied with how things were going in Washington, in no small measure because the economy had grown by 50 percent since 1960, the unemployment rate had fallen to 3.3 percent, and even though inflation was on the rise, wage increases were still surpassing it. The tens of millions of Republican voters were pleased, having elected the head of their united party just four years after the fractured GOP's 1964 nominee suffered a landslide defeat. Most Democratic voters of all stripes—southern, northern, and western; liberal and conservative; prowar and antiwar—felt well represented in Washington by their party's regionally and ideologically diverse majority in Congress, despite the loss of the presidency. Statistical measures of trust in the federal government had fallen from their peak in 1964, but on balance, the public remained more trustful than distrustful.[9]

Although discontent with politics and government was far from universal by January 1969, it was nonetheless widespread among large swathes of American society. The challenge facing the political system to reduce this discontent was formidable. Yet, broadly speaking, the challenge was met. This was partly because the various forms of violence and anger that pervaded the election year and contributed to the sense of America coming apart were substantially detached from each other. The antiwar protesters and the race rioters had little in common with each other, and even less with the politically alienated supporters of George Wallace. The assassinations of Martin Luther King and Robert F. Kennedy were disconnected from any organized insurgency (or counterinsurgency), as well as from the rise in other forms of violent crime that marked the year. Because the system-straining forces of discord were unaligned, they had no coherent political effect.

More important, from 1969 to 1972, the main cohorts of dissent that carried over from 1968 found ways of expressing their desire for substantial change through various channels of conventional politics and government.[10] This was true both of protesters on the left, motivated by the war and other causes, and of Wallace supporters on the right, provoked by many of the racial and cultural changes the country was experiencing.

THE LEFT

Of the major camps of dissidents, the greatest variety of conventional political channels opened up for the best organized, those on the left. To be sure, some operated outside the margins. In June 1969 a small group of violent opponents of the war commonly known as the Weatherman and later as the Weather Underground split off from Students for a Democratic Society and, starting in December, launched an erratic campaign of bombings that eventually encompassed banks, courthouses, police stations, and military facilities scattered across the country, including ROTC buildings on multiple campuses.[11] But the vast majority of antiwar protesters channeled their energies into a series of peaceful, legal protests, many of them under the aegis of a new umbrella organization, the Vietnam Moratorium Committee (VMC).

On October 15, 1969, more than a million people attended VMC-sponsored rallies in Washington, Boston, and cities and campuses across the country—the largest turnout of demonstrators, most of them college students, in American history.[12] (In London, Rhodes Scholar Bill Clinton helped organize a Moratorium event outside the U.S. embassy, even as he was scheming to avoid conscription and indefinitely postpone enrollment in the ROTC program at the University of Arkansas.)[13] Exactly one month later on November 15, about a quarter to a half million people assembled on the National Mall in Washington, again mostly students. "We're seeing one of the benefits of the McCarthy campaign," said the VMC's David Mixner. "You call four people in Iowa and you don't have to tell them what to do. They know how to organize, get up literature, deal with the press."[14] Nixon's chief of staff, H. R. Haldeman, grudgingly praised Moratorium leader and McCarthy campaign alumnus Sam Brown as "a genius for organization."[15]

Antiwar members of Congress, mostly Democrats but some Republicans, were featured speakers at the rallies organized by the VMC and allied groups. A number of legislators offered antiwar measures in Congress, evidence to many that the political process was at least partially responsive to pressure from below. For example, Republican senator John Sherman Cooper of Kentucky and Democratic senator Frank Church of Idaho sponsored legislation to end funding of the American military presence in Cambodia by July 1, 1970, and a version of the Cooper-Church amendment was enacted into law. Another bipartisan pair, Democratic senator George McGovern of South Dakota and Republican senator Mark Hatfield of Oregon, proposed an amendment to cut off funding for the war in Vietnam by the end of the year. The McGovern-Hatfield amendment failed on a 55–39 vote, but efforts to renew it in 1971 channeled the energies of many antiwar protesters into grassroots legislative politics.

Senator McCarthy, licking his wounds, played only a minor role in these endeavors and voluntarily yielded his seat on the Senate Foreign Relations

Committee to a hawkish colleague, Gale McGee of Wyoming. Asked to lead the battle in the Senate to cut off funding for the war, McCarthy said, peevishly, "Call me sometime when there's no one else to call on. Okay?"[16] He retired from the Senate at the end of his term in 1970 and began a loosely organized, almost offhand campaign for president in 1972. Humphrey, elected to fill McCarthy's seat, was sworn in by his vice presidential successor, Spiro Agnew, in January 1971. He launched his own campaign for the Democratic nomination in 1972, won a presidential primary for the first time in his career, and finished well ahead of Muskie, the early frontrunner, and second only to McGovern for the nomination.

Successful as the peaceful antiwar protests were, their decline with the passage of time was substantial. Participation in student-dominated demonstrations fell off following the November 1969 Moratorium event, with the exception of protests after Nixon's military incursion into Cambodia on May 1, 1970, and the killing of four antiwar Kent State University students by National Guardsmen on May 4 and of two Jackson State College students by police on May 15. By fall of 1970 the main form of campus protest against the war was called the Princeton Plan, since it originated at Princeton University: the scheduling of a two-week fall break at three dozen universities so that students could participate in the congressional elections. But even at Princeton, only 24 percent of students engaged in any form of campaign activity, and two years later the plan was abandoned.[17] An American incursion into Laos in late January 1971 was met "with protests of only slight and modest size," Tom Wells has observed.[18]

Much of the energy for the earlier protests was supplied by students who did not want to be drafted to fight in a war they did not support. Nixon moved to reduce that risk in three ways. First, in June 1969 he launched an incremental series of troop withdrawals that drew down the American presence in Vietnam from 540,000 when he took office to 16,000 by the end of his first term. American aerial bombing escalated steeply—Nixon was not pulling out of Vietnam in any meaningful sense—but the army's need for draftees fell accordingly. Second, in 1969 the president persuaded Congress to enact a draft lottery that, in a one-time drawing, would allow every young man to know, based on his date of birth, how likely he was to be drafted. With the need for troops declining, more than 60 percent of male college students and other males age nineteen to twenty-five received immediate assurance on December 1 that they were safe from the draft. This action alone removed "the most combustible element in the campus tinderbox," said Secretary of Defense Melvin Laird.[19] Third, in 1973, at Nixon's initiative, Congress enacted a law ending the draft entirely in favor of an all-volunteer force. Now every young man could be assured that he was immune to conscription.

Step by step, each of these moves drained energy from the antiwar movement. Young men's opinions about the war generally did not change, but the sense of personal jeopardy that had spurred many of them—and their girlfriends, sisters, and in some cases parents and grandparents—to active opposition did. Antiwar leader Doug Dowd, who had been "hoping like hell that the draft would continue," recalls thinking, "Shit, we're lost now."[20] Ironically, Beth Bailey has observed, "Although most of the protest Nixon hoped to quell came from the political left, it was conservatives and free-market economists who seized the momentum and shaped the path toward an all-volunteer military," motivated as Sen. Barry M. Goldwater had been in 1964 by their commitment to individual liberty.[21]

Besides opposition to the war, liberal political leaders promoted other causes that helped draw dissidents into the political process. In September 1969 Democratic senator Gaylord Nelson of Wisconsin planted the seed of what turned out to be the first Earth Day on April 22, 1970. Overnight, it seemed, environmentalism became a mass political crusade that was enormously appealing to young people. Feminists, out from the shadow of the antiwar and civil rights movements, whose leaders often had persuaded them to mute their own cause for the sake of draft-eligible white men and economically vulnerable black men, organized successfully to persuade Congress to propose the Equal Rights Amendment (ERA) to the states for ratification in 1972. Common Cause, founded in 1970 by former Health, Education and Welfare secretary John W. Gardner; Public Citizen, founded the following year by the ascetic activist attorney Ralph Nader; and other new public interest groups whose main purpose was to purge politics of corporate influence rallied in support of campaign finance reform, among other causes.

Nixon, preoccupied with foreign affairs, was generally dismissive of domestic policy as "building outhouses in Peoria."[22] To the extent that he paid attention to the home front, he did so either to mute protests and thereby strengthen his hand in negotiations with China and the Soviet Union or to help secure his reelection in 1972. Instead of vetoing the bills favored by young, liberal activists and passed by the Democratic Congress, Nixon signed and sometimes claimed credit for them. Clean air and clean water legislation became law with Nixon's blessing, to be enforced by the new Environmental Protection Agency, which he created using his executive reorganization authority. Nixon also endorsed the ERA and signed Title IX of the Education Amendments of 1972, opening up participation in school sports and other male-dominated educational programs to young women. He put up no resistance to congressional renewal of the Voting Rights Act in 1970 or enactment of the 1971 Federal Election Campaign Act and sometimes took the initiative on a host of other liberal measures: Keynesian-style deficit spending to spur the economy, wage and price controls to rein in inflation, a 20 percent boost in Social Security benefits indexed to increases in the cost of living, the labor-backed Occupational Safety and Health Act, and others. Stewart Alsop began calling Nixon "President Liberal" in his *Newsweek* column.[23]

As concerned as he was about quieting opposition from white antiwar protesters, the president was equally determined to forestall a renewed outbreak of violence in the nation's black ghettos. Nixon was uninterested in securing African American votes, and for the most part, he did not. Even as his share of white votes rose 20 percentage points, from 47 percent in 1968 to 67 percent in 1972, his share of black votes rose only 6 points, from 12 percent to 18 percent.[24] Providing enough benefits to African Americans to ward off riots, however, was a prime motive. Nixon championed the Family Assistance Plan, a kind of guaranteed income for poor people, and instituted the Philadelphia Plan, a quotas-based approach to increasing the number of blacks working on federally funded construction projects, initially in Philadelphia and later in nine other large cities. An added political bonus of the latter was that the quotas placed two Democratic constituencies—civil rights groups and overwhelmingly white construction unions—at odds with each other.[25]

The other branches of government were even more responsive to African American interests. Congressional Democrats pumped up spending on social welfare programs that were of particular benefit to minorities, and the still-liberal Supreme Court endorsed busing to effect school integration and other civil rights causes.[26] With blacks fully enfranchised in the South and constituting an increasing share of the population in big cities across the country, electoral politics became more open to African American candidates. The number of black elected officials rose from 1,469 in 1970 to 2,261 in 1973 and kept rising at a rate of several hundred per year for the next three decades.[27] First-ever black mayors in cities such as Gary, Cleveland, Newark, and Dayton were able to mute racial violence, and even white big-city mayors started appointing police forces that were more integrated and less hostile to black residents than in the past.[28]

Last on the list of conventional political channels that opened to absorb the left's residual anger from 1968 was the reformed presidential nominating process. Liberals' and activists' main grievance in that election was that neither party nominated a candidate who seemed in any way responsive to their opposition to the war, their support for the poverty-fighting recommendations of the Kerner Commission on urban violence, or other causes endorsed by Democratic candidates McCarthy and Kennedy and Republican contender Nelson A. Rockefeller. Acting on a resolution passed in the confusion of the Chicago convention, the Democratic Party created the Commission on Party Structure and Delegate Selection, initially chaired by Senator McGovern and then, when McGovern declared that he was running for president in January 1971, by Rep. Donald Fraser of Minnesota. The McGovern-Fraser Commission was guided by its members' concern that "if we are not an open party, if we do not represent the demands of change, then the danger is . . . that there will no longer be a way for people committed to orderly change to fulfill their needs and desires within our traditional political system"—in which case "they will turn to . . . the anti-politics of the street."[29]

The commission mandated eighteen detailed guidelines that state parties were obliged to follow in choosing delegates to the 1972 Democratic convention. Taken together, these changes transformed the nominating process. The commission required, for example, that racial minorities, women, and young voters be represented at the national convention in close proportion to their share of the population in each state. Most important, it demanded that all of a state's convention delegates be chosen through an open, participatory process, either a presidential primary or a caucus in which any Democrat could vote and be heard. No delegate could be appointed by party leaders or chosen before the start of the election year—both still common practices in 1968. Within a few years, the Republican Party adopted roughly similar reforms for choosing its own nominees.

Political scientists have tended to be strongly critical of the McGovern-Fraser Commission's effects on the parties, especially the Democrats.[30] Clearly the new rules seemed to hurt the Democratic Party badly in 1972, when the Republicans almost automatically renominated Nixon, who received 1,347 of 1,348 votes at the GOP convention, and the Democrats stumbled through a new and confusing process that only McGovern, the eventual nominee, really understood. McGovern brought a large number of new-style delegates to the convention—antiwar activists, feminists, reformist opponents of local party leaders, and others. Feeling their oats, they barred Chicago mayor Richard J. Daley from the convention in favor of civil rights leader Jesse Jackson; unsuccessfully but noisily pushed for a series of radical amendments to the party platform; and had so much fun with the vice presidential nomination on the convention's final evening that McGovern's acceptance speech was pushed to 2:45 a.m. EDT.

As a way of channeling dissent into mainstream politics, however, the McGovern-Fraser reforms were of tremendous value. In 1968 the Democratic Party had been deeply divided into three wings: the antiwar wing that supported McCarthy and Kennedy, won every primary, and felt cheated of victory; the Wallace wing, which defected from the party because in 1964 Wallace had not received a single convention delegate despite winning a substantial share of the vote in three Democratic primaries; and the Johnson-Humphrey wing, which carried off the prizes. The new rules created an incentive for all three wings to stay within the party in 1972 and fight to win the nomination and a favorable platform through open competition. For example, Wallace ran as a Democrat and, prior to being shot on May 15, 1972, by a twenty-one-year-old carpet cleaner who wanted to make "a statement of my manhood for the world to see," won a respectable number of delegates in the primaries, which at last counted for something.[31] McGovern lost the November election, but four years later the Democrats, having been through the new process once, nominated a supremely electable southern centrist, former governor Jimmy Carter of Georgia, and he defeated Republican president Ford in November.

Even McGovern's failure in 1972 was far from complete. His unabashedly liberal and antiwar campaign opened a doorway through which the disaffected left could reenter electoral politics with enthusiasm. From the standpoint of the political system, Bruce Miroff has written, "The openness of his campaign to young people, feminists, gays, and other activists for cultural change had lasting consequences . . . for these forces as they matured politically," election by election.[32] As for the Democratic Party, McGovern helped turn it into the political home of "suburban, issues-oriented, and college-educated activists," all of them growing sectors of the American electorate. Whether John B. Judis and Ruy Teixeira were correct in predicting the coming of *The Emerging Democratic Majority* in their 2002 book remains to be seen, but there is little doubt that they correctly identified the Democrats' renewed competitiveness in presidential elections as "George McGovern's revenge." The growing ranks of professionals, working women, and minorities—"groups that would become important components of today's Democratic party—made a clear statement during that [1972] election."[33]

Conventional political processes—peaceful demonstrations, congressional legislation, executive initiatives, Supreme Court decisions, party reforms, and presidential politics—were flexible enough to absorb most of the dissent that tore America so deeply from its left flank in 1968 and may otherwise have torn it apart. What remained was the challenge of reintegrating into mainstream politics the nearly ten million supporters of George Wallace, all of whom had made a conscious decision in 1968 to reject the moderately liberal and moderately conservative nominees of the Democratic and Republican parties, respectively.

This was a challenge that both major parties took on, as did the mainstream media. In 1969 and 1970 sympathetic stories about "forgotten" or "middle" America were published in the *New York Times* and *New York Times Magazine, Washington Post, Fortune, New Republic, Nation,* and other leading publications. *Time* made "The Middle Americans" its Man and Woman of the Year for 1969.[34] As for the parties, Democrats regarded Wallace's supporters as prodigals who had left their natural political home but would realize the rashness of their decision after a few years of Republican rule. North and South, Democrats believed, those who voted for Wallace were at heart children of the New Deal, economic populists whose real interests were served by the prolabor Democratic Party, not the probusiness GOP. Even Wallace acted as if his true home was among the Democrats. In 1970, two years after his independent campaign for president, he ran for and was elected governor of Alabama as a Democrat and then announced that he would enter the 1972 Democratic presidential primaries. "I'm tired of these kooks in this third party business," Wallace said, thinking of the John Birchers, Minutemen, and White Citizens' Council members who had populated his state campaign offices in 1968. Wallace promptly "hit the southern speakers' circuit with Richard Nixon as his primary target," Dan Carter has written, furious because Nixon had steered $400,000 to Wallace's gubernatorial primary opponent and urged the Internal Revenue Service to investigate several close associates, including his brother Gerald.[35]

All Democrats needed to do to create "a new majority," argued Jack Newfield and Jeff Greenfield, two erstwhile supporters of Robert Kennedy, was to issue "a populist manifesto" like the ones that in the 1890s had briefly united poor white and black farmers and workers across racial lines in the South.[36] "You are made to hate each other," Tom Watson of Georgia told the blacks and hardscrabble whites of his state in defending the People's Party platform of 1892, "because upon that hatred is rested the keystone of the arch of financial despotism which enslaves you both."[37] In the North, liberal Democrats urged, labor unions could build on the effort they made in 1968, with considerable success, to remind white workers that their real—that is, their economic—interests were best served by the Democratic Party. In their optimism, some Democrats even claimed that in the 1968 Democratic primaries "Kennedy, an earthy enemy of war, hunger, and crime, won the votes of both blacks and ethnic whites who had been tempted to follow George Wallace."[38] McGovern, the author of a doctoral dissertation sympathetic to the Ludlow miners who were massacred by corporate strike-breakers in 1914, was convinced that he could revive the cross-racial populist tradition in 1972.

Regarding the presidency, these Democratic hopes were largely delusional. In the South, the 1890s political alliances between blacks and poor whites had been scattered, fleeting, and easily overcome by appeals to white racial solidarity across class lines.[39] In the North, unions already were starting to decline in membership, in their ability to deliver the votes of their members, and in their loyalty to a national Democratic Party that they thought was intent on handing the reins of power to a congeries of antiwar protesters, feminists, blacks, and suburban reformers. "Contemptuous of the very idea that the Democratic party, within which they had long been powerful, needed reform," Miroff has written, "organized labor dropped off the [McGovern-Fraser] commission early on."[40] After the 1972 Democratic convention, at which union leaders were poorly represented, AFL-CIO president George Meany pressured his executive council to vote 27 to 3 not to endorse McGovern against Nixon in 1972.[41]

Republicans were equally consumed with drawing Wallace voters into the GOP. In their view, those who had voted for him in 1968 were cultural, not economic, populists, angry less at big business than at bureaucrats, intellectuals, journalists, and federal judges, whom they saw threatening their neighborhoods, schools, churches, values, and safety. Kevin P. Phillips, a young strategist in Nixon's 1968 campaign whom Attorney General Mitchell parked in the Justice Department, claimed to discover *The Emerging Republican Majority*, the title of a book he published in 1969, in simple arithmetic: 43 percent (the Nixon vote) plus 14 percent (the Wallace vote) equals 57 percent.[42] The Democrats' ardent embrace of civil rights in the mid-1960s and the new status of the monochromatically Democratic black electorate as a major electoral constituency were driving away southern whites from the party's presidential candidates. National Democrats' lukewarm concern about law and order and growing support or indifference regarding school busing, legalized abortion, prayer-free public schools, drug use, and pornography were similarly alienating many northern urban ethnic Catholics. All the Republicans needed to do to make a new home for these Wallace voters, Phillips argued, was appeal to their common cultural values.[43]

Nixon was happy to do so. He told the Departments of Justice and Health, Education and Welfare to support southern states' efforts to de-lay school integration and called on Congress to impose a moratorium on court-ordered busing in large metropolitan school districts, especially in the North. When Justice Abraham Fortas resigned from the Supreme Court in August 1969 in response to news reports of additional extrajudicial pay-ments from shady characters, Nixon nominated a widely respected South Carolina judge, Clement Haynsworth. After Haynsworth was rejected by the Democratic Senate, the president named a grotesquely incompetent Florida judge, G. Harrold Carswell—who was also rejected. The Senate had shown "regional discrimination" against these nominees based on "the fact that they were born in the South," Nixon charged, rubbing a raw nerve among white southerners.[44] Nixon also endorsed aid to parochial schools and, in a letter to Terence Cardinal Cooke, praised the Catholic Church's effort to repeal New York's liberal abortion law. He pursued anticrime mea-sures, declared a national drug abuse emergency, and unleashed Vice Pres-ident Agnew to attack student protesters, intellectuals, and the news media as, variously, "an effete corps of impudent snobs," "nattering nabobs of negativism," "pusillanimous pussyfoot[ers]," and a new-style "4-H Club: the hopeless, hysterical hypochondriacs of history."[45] Nixon himself went to the Pentagon after the Cambodia incursion to contrast the young men fighting the war—"the greatest"—with "these bums—you know, blowing up the campuses."[46]

Both parties knew what the other was doing to woo the Wallace vote and worked hard to counter it in the 1970 midterm elections. When two Democrats, Richard M. Scammon and Ben J. Wattenberg, published *The Real Majority* in May 1970, their fellow partisans took heed. Scammon and Wattenberg argued that the Democratic Party, longtime master of the "Economic Issue" in American politics, was losing control to the GOP of the new "Social Issue"—crime, drugs, patriotism, race, and other mostly cultural concerns. Democratic candidates for Congress in 1970 adapted ac-cordingly.[47] Nixon had especially hoped that with twenty-five Democratic and only ten Republican Senate seats on the November ballot, the GOP would make substantial gains in that chamber. But Democratic candidates began wearing American flag lapel pins, condemning illegal drug use, and airing television commercials that showed them riding shotgun in police cars. Race-based appeals to white voters were a landmine for Democrats, considering the prominence of black and liberal voters among their constituents. But the party held its own, losing only three Senate seats, gaining twelve in the House, and remaining firmly in control of both chambers. In response, Nixon began working hard to mute the Democrats' hold on the economic issue by promoting or at least accepting a long string of liberal welfare and regulatory programs. In 1972 he pumped up federal spending substantially to stimulate an election-year economic boom.[48]

In sum, both major parties addressed the concerns of Wallace voters in ways that drew them back into the system, just as those on the left were also being drawn. In 1972 support for Rep. John Schmitz, a California Republican and the presidential nominee of the Wallace-created American Independent Party, fell to 1.1 million, down from Wallace's 9.9 million in 1968. Nearly 90 percent of Wallace voters in 1968 cast their ballots for a major party nominee in 1972. Nixon outdid McGovern in this regard, virtually sweeping the Wallace vote en route to a 60.7 percent landslide. But the Democrats' efforts were not in vain. They gained back two of the three Senate seats they lost in 1970 and gave up only the twelve House seats they had gained in that election. The Democratic hold on Congress at the start of Nixon's first term was just as strong as Nixon's hold on the presidency: a 242 to 193 majority in the House and a 57 to 43 majority in the Senate.

DIVIDED GOVERNMENT

Resilience is more than the positive contribution of American political institutions and processes in opening doors to dissenters who feel locked out. Less happily, but no less significantly, resilience also involves endurance in the face of chronic stress. The political ailment ushered in by the 1968 elections remains unresolved: divided government, along with its corollary, a form of political conflict that Benjamin Ginsberg and Martin Shefter have called "politics by other means."[49]

The outcome in 1968—a Republican president and a Democratic Congress—seemed exceptional when it occurred. During the first two-thirds of the twentieth century, united party government, with the same political party controlling the presidency and both houses of Congress, prevailed 79 percent of the time, for all but eight years in the period 1901 to 1969. Not one newly elected president after Zachary Taylor ever faced an opposition-controlled Congress. But 1968 turned out to be less an exception than the inauguration of a new rule. From 1969 to 2017, when President Donald J. Trump and a Republican Congress took power, divided party government obtained 70 percent of the time, in all but fourteen of forty-eight years.

Divided government can take various forms. For all but the first two years of the Bill Clinton and Barack Obama administrations, it took the form of a Democratic president and a wholly or partially Republican Congress. But in the quarter century that began with Nixon's election in 1968, divided government always meant that the president was Republican and one or, typically, both houses of Congress were Democratic. From 1968 to 1988, the GOP won five of six presidential elections. Four were by landslides—Nixon in 1972, Ronald Reagan in 1980 and 1984, and George Bush in 1988. The Democrats' sole victory, Carter over Ford in 1976, was a squeaker.[50] In these six elections, Republican nominees won a total of 2,501 electoral votes to their Democratic rivals' 679.

In contrast, the House remained consistently Democrat-controlled from 1969 to 1993, with the Democratic majority never falling below fifty-one seats and sometimes reaching as high as 149. As many as 45 percent of congressional districts supported one party's presidential nominee, nearly always the Republican, and the other party's House candidate, nearly always a Democrat.[51] Except for the first six years of the Reagan presidency, the Senate also was Democratic during this period.

CAUSES OF DIVIDED GOVERNMENT

What accounts for the new pattern of governing that the 1968 elections inaugurated? Nixon bears part of the responsibility. As president, his interest in sustaining an emerging Republican majority was far outweighed by concern for his own agenda and reelection. In the 1970 midterm election Nixon pursued an ideological more than a partisan majority in Congress. For example, he tacitly supported James L. Buckley, the Senate nominee of New York's Conservative Party, over incumbent Republican Charles E. Goodell, who was more liberal. In Texas, as soon as conservative Lloyd Bentsen defeated liberal incumbent Ralph Yarborough for the Democratic nomination, Nixon pulled the plug on Republican nominee George Bush.[52] After the results were in, the president avowed satisfaction in the election of a conservative Senate majority even though the GOP remained the minority party.[53]

Two years later, Nixon's landslide reelection did little for his party's candidates for Congress, who made only small gains in the House and actually lost ground in the Senate. Nixon ran in 1972 less as the nominee of the Republican Party than of the organization he formed to manage his campaign, the Committee for the Re-Election of the President. As Robert Mason has observed, Nixon's strategy involved a de facto "acceptance of divided government."[54] Soon after the election, the public revulsion that drove Nixon from office in August 1974 in response to his crimes in the Watergate affair led to massive Republican losses in the November midterm as well as setting the stage for Carter's victory in 1976.

In the quarter century that began with Nixon's election in 1968, the electorate usually regarded Republican presidential candidates—more confident when asserting American global interests in the post-Vietnam Cold War era, more willing to express traditional cultural values from the nation's "bully pulpit," and less associated in the public mind with "special interest" groups—as their best guarantors of national well-being. But in voting for Congress, it was local, not national concerns that preoccupied voters, and their particular special interests in, for example, agricultural subsidies or airport construction, not special interests in general, that seemed at stake. The Democratic Party, with its more sympathetic view of government, came out ahead on both counts according to most voters' criteria for congressional elections.

The nature of the two parties also helps explain their contrasting success in presidential and congressional elections during the period ushered in by 1968. The Republicans were fairly homogeneous—white, Christian, prosperous, and at least moderately conservative at a time when the country was whiter and more Christian than in later decades. The Democrats, in contrast, were raucously heterogeneous—white and black; liberal and conservative; Christian and Jewish; uneducated and highly educated.

In fielding candidates for Congress, Democratic diversity was politically beneficial. Depending on the character of each state or district, the Democrats usually had little trouble finding a nominee who was ideologically and demographically suitable. In House and Senate elections, the Democrats could be virtually all things to all people: liberal in the North, conservative in the South; white in majority-white districts, black in majority-black districts; pro–gun control in the cities, anti–gun control in the countryside; and so on. Most erstwhile Wallace voters in the South, for example, had little trouble voting for ideologically compatible Democratic congressional candidates through the 1970s and 1980s. Candidates from the more homogeneous GOP, in contrast, tended everywhere to be cut from roughly the same cloth.

But heterogeneity hampered the Democrats in presidential elections.

Ideologically and otherwise, Republicans did not have to worry overmuch about defining their party's identity when writing a platform and choosing a candidate. They presented a united, confident front to the nation at their national conventions. In contrast, the Democrats, who thrived by being many parties in congressional elections, had to decide which one party they wanted to be when nominating a candidate for president. Typically, either the decision was contentious, as in 1968, producing angry losers and projecting to the voters an image of discord and incompetence, or, as in 1984 and 1988, the presidential nominee achieved temporary unity by making such sweeping concessions to the most vocal constituencies in the party as to alienate a substantial number of voters.[55]

The persistence of divided government after 1992, usually in the form of Democratic presidents and wholly or partially Republican Congresses, calls for an additional explanation, one less tied either to Nixon's lack of commitment to building a Republican majority or to any particular partisan balance of power. Such an explanation has been harder for scholars to come by. Perhaps divided government's persistence is due in part to the recent southernization of the Republican party, which, from the 1990s to the 2010s, grew to encompass more than 100 of the 136 southern House seats, all but three southern Senate seats, about three-fourths of the 11 southern governorships, and a majority of every southern state legislative house. The cost of this success has been to make the GOP seem more a regional than a national party, thereby undermining its appeal in presidential elections, of which it won only three of seven from 1992 to 2016, seldom by a margin of more than one state and only once with a plurality of the national popular vote.

In congressional elections, however, the "inefficient" concentration of contemporary core Democratic constituencies—minorities, singles, young adults, secular voters, and gays and lesbians—in a smaller number of urban districts that vote overwhelmingly Democratic has enabled Republicans to win about a 4 percent greater share of seats in the House than their share of the national popular vote.[56] In the thirty-two House elections that occurred from 1930 to 1994, Democrats won a higher proportion of seats than votes thirty-one times. The ratio of seats to votes has turned against them starting in 2012.[57] A similar Republican advantage inheres in the Senate, where the GOP tends to do better in small states such as Wyoming and Utah than in New York, California, and other large states. Fewer popular votes, more seats for Senate Republicans; more popular votes, fewer seats for Senate Democrats.

Finally, the obvious explanation for the modern prevalence of divided government—whether Republican presidents and Democratic Congresses from 1969 to 1993 or Democratic presidents and Republican Congresses since then—may be at least partly accurate: the voters elect a divided government because they do not wish to entrust the reins of power to either major party.[58] To be sure, only a minority of voters—sometimes less than 10 percent—split their ticket between a presidential candidate of one party and a congressional candidate of the other.[59] But that is a substantial number in close elections, especially when motivated, as some voters are, by an active desire to bring about divided control.[60] Not surprisingly, the persistence of the desire to not put complete control of the government in either party's hands correlates strongly with the decline of trust in the federal government that began in the 1960s and accelerated under Nixon.[61] It also is the case, as Gary C. Jacobson has argued, that voters continue to want the "low tax rates, low inflation, less intrusive government, greater economic efficiency, and strong national defense" that they associate with the Republican Party, as well as the "middle-class entitlements and other popular domestic programs" that they associate with the Democrats— however "self-contradictory" these preferences may be.[62]

CONSEQUENCES OF DIVIDED GOVERNMENT

The consequences of divided government have been mixed. Certainly the openness of the political system to the country's broad range of dissenting elements was greater in the immediate aftermath of the 1968 election because these elements could look to either a Republican president or a Democratic Congress for a response to their differing concerns. As for the performance of the federal government, after studying federal lawmaking from 1946 to 1990, David R. Mayhew concluded that divided government is as productive of "major statutes" as united party government.[63] Nixon's willingness to sign into law multiple bills that originated in the Democratic Congress provides strong evidence for Mayhew's argument. But, as Sarah A. Binder has shown, even in the period Mayhew studied, more issues on the national agenda were muzzled—that is, never came to a vote in Congress—under divided than united government. Further, as the parties have become more ideologically polarized since 1990, the final year of Mayhew's study, divided government has had a more stifling effect on policymaking than he found to be the case.[64] For example, divided government now "manifests in the form of more presidential vetoes, diverging budget projections by the two branches, less congressional delegation of authority to executive branch agencies, weakened presidential control over trade policy, and delayed confirmation of executive branch and judicial nominations."[65]

In at least two areas of fundamental importance to a constitutional system, the consequences of divided government have been dysfunctional bordering on corrosive. One is the effect on the third branch of government, the judiciary. Judicial appointments have become a political football in the partisan battle between presidents and senates of different parties. From 1900 to 1968, during the era of united government, only three of forty-five Supreme Court nominations (7 percent) were rejected by the Senate. Two of these rejections were of Fortas and Homer Thornberry in October 1968, a time of de facto divided government because the Republicans firmly expected to win control of the presidency but not the Senate in the election. Nearly two-thirds of Supreme Court nominations during the first two-thirds of the twentieth century (twenty-nine of forty-five) were approved *viva voce*, without controversy.

Since 1969, five of twenty-two Supreme Court nominations (23 percent) have been rejected, including five of thirteen (39 percent) when the president and Senate were of different parties. No nominee has been approved by voice vote, and even confirmed nominees in the twenty-first century have drawn an average of thirty-three dissenting votes. When Obama nominated Judge Merrick Garland in March 2016 to fill the vacancy on the court left by the death of Justice Antonin Scalia, Senate Republicans refused to hold committee hearings on the grounds that Obama was in his final year as president. Still worse, as John Anthony Maltese has shown, the "selling of Supreme Court nominees" has become indistinguishable from overtly partisan battles about public policy, a trend that began with Nixon's nominations to fill Justice Fortas's seat on the court.[66] Consequently, the legitimacy of the judicial system, dependent as it is on public trust in its nonpartisanship, has been placed in jeopardy.

An even greater consequence of divided government since the 1968 election has been the acceleration of "politics by other means." Because neither the Democratic nor Republican Party has been able to develop a stable majority in the electorate, Ginsberg and Shefter have argued, "contending forces are increasingly relying on such institutional weapons of political struggle as legislative investigations, media revelations, and judicial proceedings to weaken their political rivals and gain power for themselves."[67] The pursuit of Nixon's Watergate crimes by Congress, the courts, and the media was an exceptional event at the time. Since then, they note, "Character assassination has become a routine aspect of American politics."[68] The ranks of fallen or wounded political leaders include senators, party leaders in the House of Representatives, cabinet members, presidential aides, and presidents. In 2016 Republicans chanted "Lock her up!" at rallies, referring to Democratic nominee Hillary Clinton. "You'd be in jail [if I were elected]," Trump threatened her during their second presidential debate.

In terms of policymaking, filibusters to block Senate consideration of bills or nominations, which used to be relatively rare, now occur whenever almost any controversial measure or appointment is opposed by at least forty-one senators.[69] House Republican leaders have generally observed the "Hastert rule," introduced by former speaker Dennis Hastert to keep measures opposed by a majority of the GOP caucus from reaching the House floor even if a majority of all representatives support them. When divided government, as Binder has observed, began keeping national issues off the legislative agenda, liberal and then conservative groups began pursuing their policy agendas on matters such as abortion, race, the environment, gun rights, campaign finance, and land use in court cases rather than in election campaigns. The ideological polarization of the two parties, initially in Congress and among party activists and increasingly among voters, has left the center of the political spectrum, which many Republican and Democratic legislators once inhabited, barren ground.[70]

The late twentieth and early twenty-first centuries do not constitute the nation's first era of divided government: the periods 1848–1860 (the run-up to the Civil War) and 1874–1896 (the "Gilded Age") were, too. Few historians celebrate the government's performance during those eras. By most accounts, the contemporary era of divided government has been undistinguished as well. The morphing of consensus into polarized politics is in that way roughly similar to the transformation of warfare from World War I, which was fought between armies, to World War II, with its emphasis on civilian casualties.

CONCLUSION

Resilience, the theme of this book, is a term borrowed from metallurgy. It refers to the ability of a metal subjected to great stress to regain its former shape. As such, resilience is a variable. Different metals subjected to different stresses for different lengths of time will display resilience to varying degrees and in differing forms.

Not surprisingly, resilience has been applied by analogy to many areas of life. Type the word into the search box at amazon.com/books and thousands of titles come up, most of them pertaining to business, child-rearing, and various forms of self-help. Politics clearly belongs on that list. Not since the Civil War and Great Depression has the American political system been subjected to greater stress than in 1968. To a remarkable degree, the system survived. The parties adapted, partly by changing their rules and procedures and partly by developing new ways of appealing to alienated, even angry voters. Congress and the president also adapted, moving at least slightly leftward on foreign and economic policy and rightward on social policy.

But even a system that bounces back successfully is not unaffected by the stresses that bent it out of shape. The political system's response to the strains of 1968 included the inauguration of a period of divided government that has lasted longer than any previous period of its kind. In and of itself, divided government has not displeased most voters, who continue to perpetuate it with their votes and do not object to it in surveys taken on the subject. Nevertheless, some of divided government's tangible effects, notably the partisan politicization of the Supreme Court and the warlike resort to politics by other means, have contributed to declining trust in government and dissatisfaction with the Republican and Democratic Parties and with all three branches of government. The recent and growing ideological polarization of the parties has aggravated this dissatisfaction by combining partisan, interbranch, and ideological conflict in mutually reinforcing ways.

On balance, however, the resilience of the American political system since 1968 has been impressive and, in the aftermath of as angrily fought an election as 2016, reassuring. A half century has passed since the last assassination of a national political leader. National party conventions, now consisting of delegates openly chosen in primaries and caucuses, have gathered every four years without threat of disruption. Opposition to unpopular wars and to racial injustice has continued to spark organized mass protests, but they have been nonviolent. African Americans, Latinos, women, gays, and others who previously were excluded from Congress, the executive, and other public offices now are present in significant and growing numbers. And no one has woken up on the morning of a single presidential inauguration wondering even for an instant whether troops and tanks would be called out to overturn the verdict of the election.

1968 PRIMARIES*

	Republican			Democratic	
	Votes	%		Votes	%

March 12 New Hampshire

	Republican			Democratic	
Richard M. Nixon (N.Y.)	80,666	77.6	Lyndon B. Johnson (Texas)[1]	27,520	49.6
Nelson A. Rockefeller (N.Y.)[1]	11,241	10.8	Eugene J. McCarthy (Minn.)	23,263	41.9
Eugene J. McCarthy (Minn.)[1]	5,511	5.3	Richard M. Nixon (N.Y.)[1]	2,532	4.6
Lyndon B. Johnson (Texas)[1]	1,778	1.7	Others	2,149	3.9
George W. Romney (Mich.)	1,743	1.7			
Harold E. Stassen (Pa.)	429	0.4			
Others	2,570	2.5			

April 2 Wisconsin

	Republican			Democratic	
Nixon	390,368	79.7	McCarthy	412,160	56.2
Ronald Reagan (Calif.)	50,727	10.4	Johnson	253,696	34.6
Stassen	28,531	5.8	Robert F. Kennedy (N.Y.)[1]	46,507	6.3
Rockefeller[1]	7,995	1.6	Unpledged delegates	11,861	1.6
Unpledged delegates	6,763	1.4	George C. Wallace (Ala.)[1]	4,031	0.5
Romney[1]	2,087	0.4	Hubert H. Humphrey (Minn.)[1]	3,605	0.5
Others	3,382	0.7	Others	1,142	0.2

April 23 Pennsylvania

	Republican			Democratic	
Nixon[1]	171,815	59.7	McCarthy	428,259	71.7
Rockefeller[1]	52,915	18.4	Robert F. Kennedy[1]	65,430	11.0
McCarthy[1]	18,800	6.5	Humphrey[1]	51,998	8.7
George C. Wallace (Ala.)[1]	13,290	4.6	Wallace[1]	24,147	4.0
Robert F. Kennedy (N.Y.)[1]	10,431	3.6	Johnson[1]	21,265	3.6
Reagan[1]	7,934	2.8	Nixon[1]	3,434	0.6
Hubert H. Humphrey (Minn.)[1]	4,651	1.6	Others[1]	2,556	0.4
Johnson[1]	3,027	1.1			
Raymond P. Shafer (Pa.)[1]	1,223	0.4			
Others[1]	3,487	1.2			

April 30 Massachusetts

	Republican			Democratic	
Rockefeller[1]	31,964	30.0	McCarthy	122,697	49.3
John A. Volpe (Mass.)	31,465	29.5	Robert F. Kennedy[1]	68,604	27.6
Nixon[1]	27,447	25.8	Humphrey[1]	44,156	17.7
McCarthy[1]	9,758	9.2	Johnson[1]	6,890	2.8
Reagan[1]	1,770	1.7	Nelson A. Rockefeller (N.Y.)[1]	2,275	1.0
Kennedy[1]	1,184	1.1	Wallace[1]	1,688	0.7
Others[1]	2,933	2.8	Others[1]	2,593	1.0

	Republican				Democratic	
	Votes	%			Votes	%
May 7 District of Columbia						
Nixon-Rockefeller[2]	12,102	90.1	Robert F. Kennedy[3]		57,555	62.5
Unpledged delegates[2]	1,328	9.9	Humphrey[3]		32,309	35.1
			Humphrey[3]		2,250	2.4
May 7 Indiana						
Nixon	508,362	100.0	Robert F. Kennedy		328,118	42.3
			Roger D. Branigin (Ind.)		238,700	30.7
			McCarthy		209,695	27.0
May 7 Ohio						
James A. Rhodes (Ohio)	614,492	100.0	Stephen M. Young (Ohio)		549,140	100.0
May 14 Nebraska[4]						
Nixon	140,336	70.0	Robert F. Kennedy		84,102	51.7
Reagan	42,703	21.3	McCarthy		50,655	31.2
Rockefeller[1]	10,225	5.1	Humphrey[1]		12,087	7.4
Stassen	2,638	1.3	Johnson		9,187	5.6
McCarthy[1]	1,544	0.8	Nixon[1]		2,731	1.7
Others	3,030	1.5	Ronald Reagan (Calif.)[1]		1,905	1.2
			Wallace[1]		1,298	0.8
			Others		646	0.4
May 14 West Virginia						
Unpledged delegates at large	81,039	100.0	Unpledged delegates at large		149,282	100.0
May 28 Florida						
Unpledged delegates	51,509	100.0	George A. Smathers (Fla.)		236,242	46.1
			McCarthy		147,216	28.7
			Unpledged delegates		128,899	25.2
May 28 Oregon						
Nixon	203,037	65.0	McCarthy		163,990	44.0
Reagan	63,707	20.4	Robert F. Kennedy		141,631	38.0
Rockefeller[1]	36,305	11.6	Johnson		45,174	12.1
McCarthy[1]	7,387	2.4	Humphrey[1]		12,421	3.3
Kennedy[1]	1,723	0.6	Reagan[1]		3,082	0.8
			Nixon[1]		2,974	0.8
			Rockefeller[1]		2,841	0.8
			Wallace[1]		957	0.3
June 4 California						
Reagan	1,525,091	100.0	Robert F. Kennedy		1,472,166	46.3
			McCarthy		1,329,301	41.8
			Unpledged delegates		380,286	12.0
June 4 New Jersey						
Nixon[1]	71,809	81.1	McCarthy[1]		9,906	36.1
Rockefeller[1]	11,530	13.0	Robert F. Kennedy[1]		8,603	31.3

	Republican			Democratic	
	Votes	%		Votes	%
Reagan[1]	2,737	3.1	Humphrey[1]	5,578	20.3
McCarthy[1]	1,358	1.5	Wallace[1]	1,399	5.1
Others[1]	1,158	1.3	Nixon[1]	1,364	5.0
			Others[1]	596	2.2

June 4 South Dakota

Nixon	68,113	100.0	Robert F. Kennedy	31,826	49.5
			Johnson	19,316	30.0
			McCarthy	13,145	20.4

June 11 Illinois

Nixon[1]	17,490	78.1	McCarthy[1]	4,646	38.6
Rockefeller[1]	2,165	9.7	Edward M. Kennedy (Mass.)[1]	4,052	33.7
Reagan[1]	1,601	7.1	Humphrey[1]	2,059	17.1
Others[1]	1,147	5.1	Others[1]	1,281	10.6

TOTALS

Reagan	1,696,270	37.9	McCarthy	2,914,933	38.7
Nixon	1,679,443	37.5	Robert F. Kennedy	2,304,542	30.6
Rhodes	614,492	13.7	Unpledged delegates	670,328	8.9
Rockefeller	164,340	3.7	Young	549,140	7.3
Unpledged delegates	140,639	3.1	Johnson	383,048	5.1
McCarthy	44,358	1.0	Branigin	238,700	3.2
Stassen	31,598	0.7	Smathers	236,242	3.1
Volpe	31,465	0.7	Humphrey	166,463	2.2
Robert F. Kennedy	13,338	0.3	Wallace	33,520	0.4
Wallace	13,290	0.3	Nixon	13,035	0.2
Nixon-Rockefeller[2]	12,102	0.3	Rockefeller	5,116	0.1
Johnson	4,805	0.1	Reagan	4,987	0.1
Humphrey	4,651	0.1	Edward M. Kennedy	4,052	0.1
Romney	3,830	0.1	Others[6]	10,963	0.1
Shafer	1,223	–		7,535,069	
Others[5]	17,707	0.4			
	4,473,551				

Source: *Guide to U.S. Elections*, 5th ed. (Washington, D.C.: CQ Press, 2005), 363–365.

*Delegate selection primaries were held in Alabama and New York.

1. Write-in.

2. Prior to the primary, the District Republican organization agreed to divide the nine delegate votes, with six going to Nixon and three going to Rockefeller, according to the 1968 *Congressional Quarterly Almanac*, vol. 24.

3. Two slates favored Humphrey; a member of an "independent" Humphrey slate received 2,250 votes.

4. In the American Party presidential primary, Wallace received 493 of the 504 votes cast, or 97.8% of the vote, according to the office of the Nebraska secretary of state.

5. In addition to scattered votes, "others" includes Willis E. Stone who received 527 votes, Herbert F. Hoover who received 247 votes, David Watumull who received 161 votes, William W. Evans who received 151 votes, Elmer W. Coy who received 73 votes, and Don DuMont who received 39 votes in the New Hampshire primary; and Americus Liberator who received 1,302 votes in the Nebraska primary.

6. In addition to scattered votes, "others" includes John G. Crommelin who received 186 votes, Richard E. Lee who received 170 votes, and Jacob J. Gordon who received 77 votes in the New Hampshire primary.

1968 REPUBLICAN CONVENTION, BALLOTING FOR PRESIDENT

Delegation	Total Votes	First Pres. Ballot[1] (Before Shift)			First Pres. Ballot (After Shift)		
		Nixon	Rockefeller	Reagan	Nixon	Rockefeller	Reagan
Alabama	26	14	—	12	26	—	—
Alaska	12	11	1	—	12	—	—
Arizona	16	16	—	—	16	—	—
Arkansas	18	—	—	—	18	—	—
California	86	—	—	86	86	—	—
Colorado	18	14	3	1	18	—	—
Connecticut	16	4	12	—	16	—	—
Delaware	12	9	3	—	12	—	—
Florida	34	32	1	1	34	—	—
Georgia	30	21	2	7	30	—	—
Hawaii	14	—	—	—	14	—	—
Idaho	14	9	—	5	14	—	—
Illinois	58	50	5	3	58	—	—
Indiana	26	26	—	—	26	—	—
Iowa	24	13	8	3	24	—	—
Kansas	20	—	—	—	19	1	—
Kentucky	24	22	2	—	24	—	—
Louisiana	26	19	—	7	26	—	—
Maine	14	7	7	—	14	—	—
Maryland	26	18	8	—	26	—	—
Massachusetts	34	—	34	—	34	—	—
Michigan	48	4	—	—	48	—	—
Minnesota	26	9	15	—	26	—	—
Mississippi	20	20	—	—	20	—	—
Missouri	24	16	5	3	24	—	—
Montana	14	11	—	3	14	—	—
Nebraska	16	16	—	—	16	—	—
Nevada	12	9	3	—	12	—	—
New Hampshire	8	8	—	—	8	—	—
New Jersey	40	18	—	—	40	—	—
New Mexico	14	8	1	5	14	—	—

Delegation	Total Votes	First Pres. Ballot[1] (Before Shift)			First Pres. Ballot (After Shift)		
		Nixon	Rockefeller	Reagan	Nixon	Rockefeller	Reagan
New York	92	4	88	—	4	88	—
North Carolina	26	9	1	16	26	—	—
North Dakota	8	5	2	1	8	—	—
Ohio	58	2	—	—	58	—	—
Oklahoma	22	14	1	7	22	—	—
Oregon	18	18	—	—	18	—	—
Pennsylvania	64	22	41	1	64	—	—
Rhode Island	14	—	14	—	14	—	—
South Carolina	22	22	—	—	22	—	—
South Dakota	14	14	—	—	14	—	—
Tennessee	28	28	—	—	28	—	—
Texas	56	41	—	15	54	—	2
Utah	8	2	—	—	8	—	—
Vermont	12	9	3	—	12	—	—
Virginia	24	22	2	—	24	—	—
Washington	24	15	3	6	24	—	—
West Virginia	14	11	3	—	13	1	—
Wisconsin	30	30	—	—	30	—	—
Wyoming	12	12	—	—	12	—	—
District of Columbia	9	6	3	—	6	3	—
Puerto Rico	5	—	5	—	5	—	—
Virgin Islands	3	2	1	—	3	—	—
Total	1333	692	277	182	1238	93	2

Source: *Guide to U.S. Elections*, 5th ed. (Washington, D.C.: CQ Press, 2005), 650.

1. Other candidates: James A. Rhodes, 55 (Ohio); George Romney, 50 (44 in Michigan, 6 in Utah); Clifford P. Case, 22 (New Jersey); Frank Carlson, 20 (Kansas); Winthrop Rockefeller, 18 (Arkansas); Hiram L. Fong, 14 (Hawaii); Harold Stassen, 2 (1 in Minnesota, 1 in Ohio); John V. Lindsay, 1 (Minnesota).

1968 DEMOCRATIC CONVENTION, KEY BALLOTS

Delegation	Total Votes	Texas Credentials[1] Yea	Texas Credentials[1] Nay	Georgia Credentials[2] Yea	Georgia Credentials[2] Nay	Alabama Credentials[3] Yea	Alabama Credentials[3] Nay	End Unit Rule[4] Yea	End Unit Rule[4] Nay	Report on Vietnam[5] Yea	Report on Vietnam[5] Nay	First Presidential Ballot[6] Humphrey	First Presidential Ballot[6] McCarthy	First Presidential Ballot[6] McGovern	First Presidential Ballot[6] Philips
Ala.	32	32	—	10	22	—	—	5½	24½	1½	30½	23	—	—	—
Alaska	22	17	5	5	17	14	8	22	—	10	12	17	2	3	—
Ariz.	19	1¼	17	17	2	7½	11½	—	19	6½	12½	14½	2½	2	—
Ark.	33	33	—	3	29	8	23	—	32	7	25	30	2	—	—
Calif.	174	1	173	173	1	173	1	173	1	166	6	14	91	51	17
Colo.	35	—	35	30	5	34	1	35	—	21	14	16½	10	5½	3
Conn.	44	30	12	13	27	21	21	9	30	13	30	35	8	—	1
Del.	22	21	—	3	18	2	19	—	21	—	21	21	—	—	—
Fla.	63	58	4	9	54	6	57	11	52	7	56	58	5	—	—
Ga.	43	—	—	—	—	25	17½	39	4	19½	23½	19½	13½	1	3
Hawaii	26	26	—	4	22	—	26	3	23	—	26	26	—	—	—
Idaho	25	22½	2½	4½	20½	2	23	1	24	10	15	21	3½	½	—
Ill.	118	114	—	12	83	18	100	3	115	13	105	112	3	3	1
Ind.	63	34	10	25	38	13	41½	63	—	15	47½	49	11	2	—
Iowa	46	37½	8½	32	12	24½	21½	46	—	36	10	18½	19½	5	—
Kan.	38	38	—	3½	34½	5½	31½	6	20	4½	33½	34	1	3	—
Ky.	46	40½	5½	6	40	6½	39½	6½	39½	7	39	41	5	—	—
La.	36	32	4	7	29	—	36	—	36	2½	33½	35	—	—	—
Maine	27	25	1	5	22	—	26	27	—	4½	22½	23	4	—	—

Md.	49	46	3	3	46	2	47	49	—	12	37	45	2	2	—
Mass.	72	16	47	39	24	29	29	37	31	56	16	2	70	—	—
Mich.	96	70	23	35	58	26	67	43½	44½	52	44	72½	9½	7½	6½
Minn.	52	34½	14½	16	33	23½	28½	16	33½	16½	34½	38	11½	—	2½
Miss.	24	2	18½	18	2	12½	8½	21½	½	19½	2½	9½	6½	4	2
Mo.	60	48	12	12	48	8	52	60	—	10	50	56	3½	—	½
Mont.	26	20	4	2½	21½	3½	22½	12½	12	6	20	23½	2½	—	—
Neb.	30	12	16	11	18	13	15	26	2	19	11	15	6	9	—
Nev.	22	13	7	14	8	12½	9½	22	—	3½	18½	18½	2½	1	—
N.H.	26	6	20	23	2	25	—	23	3	23	3	6	20	—	—
N.J.	82	43	25	22	51	21	61	21	61	24	57	62	19	—	1
N.M.	26	13	13	11	15	11	15	11	15	11½	14½	15	11	—	—
N.Y.	190	—	190	190	—	80[e]	82[e]	190	—	148	42	96½	87	1½	2
N.C.	59	54½	4½	3½	55½	1	58	2	57	7	51	44½	2	½	—
N.D.	25	17	5	5	17	7	18	17	5	6	19	18	7	—	—
Ohio	115	37½	27	21	80	30½	65	23	92	48	67	94	18	2	—
Okla.	41	40	1	1	40	6½	34	6	35	4	37	37½	2½	½	½
Ore.	35	10	23	32	—	31	3	31	—	29	6	—	35	—	—
Pa.	130	80½	42½	31½	90½	22¼	100½	39¾	79½	35¼	92¼	103¾	21½	2½	1½
R.I.	27	24½	2½	12	11	2½	24½	3½	23½	5	22	23½	2½	—	—
S.C.	28	28	—	4	22	—	28	4½	23½	1	27	28	—	—	—
S.D.	26	1	25	26	—	24	2	26	—	26	—	2	—	24	—
Tenn.	51	48½	1	—	51	½	49½	2½	46½	2	49	49½	½	1	—
Texas	104	—	—	2.55	101.45	—	104	5	99	—	104	100½	2½	—	1
Utah	26	18	8	7	19	5	21	26	—	6	20	23	2	—	1
Vt.	22	5	13	17	4	14	7	22	—	17	5	8	6	7	—

Delegation	Total Votes	Texas Credentials[1] Yea	Texas Credentials[1] Nay	Georgia Credentials[2] Yea	Georgia Credentials[2] Nay	Alabama Credentials[3] Yea	Alabama Credentials[3] Nay	End Unit Rule[4] Yea	End Unit Rule[4] Nay	Report on Vietnam[5] Yea	Report on Vietnam[5] Nay	First Presidential Ballot[6] Humphrey	First Presidential Ballot[6] McCarthy	First Presidential Ballot[6] McGovern	First Presidential Ballot[6] Philips
Va.	54	21½	22½	8½	35½	1	53	9½	43½		46	42½	5½	—	2
Wash.	47	31½	15½	18	29	16	28	21½	25½	15½	31½	32½	8½	6	—
W.Va.	38	19	12	8	22	9	29	38	—	8	30	34	3	—	—
Wis.	59	5	54	52	7	54	4	58	1	52	7	8	49	1	1
Wyo.	22	18½	3½	2	20	6½	15½	3	19	3½	18½	18½	3½	—	—
Canal Z.	5	4	—	2	3	—	4	1	4	1½	3½	4	—	1	—
D. C.	23	—	22	22	—	23	—	23	—	21	2	2	—	—	21
Guam	5	4½	½	—	5	—	5	½	4½	½	4½	5	—	—	—
P.R.	8	8	—	7½	—	—	8	1	7	—	8	8	—	—	—
Vir. Is.	5	5	—	2½	—	—	5	5	—		5	—	—	—	—
Total	2622	1368¼[a]	956¾[b]	1043.55[c]	1415.45[d]	880¾[f]	1607[g]	1351¼[h]	1209[i]	1041¼	1567¾	1759¼[j]	601	146½	67½

Source: *Guide to U.S. Elections*, 5th ed. (Washington, D.C.: CQ Press, 2005), 651.

1. Not voting, 297.

2. Not voting, 163.

3. Not voting, 134.

4. Not voting, 61¾.

5. Not voting, 13.

6. Other candidates: Dan K. Moore, 17½ (12 in North Carolina, 3 in Virginia, 2 in Georgia, ½ in Alabama); Edward M. Kennedy, 12¾ (proceedings record, 12) (3½ in Alabama, 3 in Iowa, 3 in New York, 1 in Ohio, 1 in West Virginia, ¾ in Pennsylvania, 3 in Georgia); Bryant, 1½ (Alabama); George C. Wallace, ½ (Alabama); James H. Gray, ½ (Georgia); not voting, 15 (3 in Alabama, 3 in Georgia, 2 in Mississippi, 1 in Arkansas, 1 in California, 1 in Delaware, 1 in Louisiana, 1 in Rhode Island, 1 in Vermont, 1 in Virginia).

a. Sum of column; proceedings record, 1368.

b. Sum of column; proceedings record, 955.

c. Sum of column; proceedings record, 1041.

d. Sum of column; proceedings record, 1413.

e. New York vote announced after outcome of roll call.

f. Sum of column; proceedings record (without New York vote), 801.

g. Sum of column; proceedings record (without New York), 1525.

h. Sum of column; proceedings record, 1350.

i. Sum of column; proceedings record, 1206.

j. Sum of column; proceedings record, 1761¾.

1968 PRESIDENTIAL ELECTION RESULTS

State	Total Vote	Nixon (R) Votes	Nixon (%)	Humphrey (D) Votes	Humphrey (%)	Wallace (AI) Votes	Wallace (%)	Blomen (SL) Votes	Blomen (%)	Other Votes	Other (%)	Plurality	
Alabama	1,049,922	146,923	14.0	196,579	18.7	691,425	65.9	—	0.0	14,995	1.4	494,846	A
Alaska	83,035	37,600	45.3	35,411	42.6	10,024	12.1	—	0.0	—	0.0	2,189	R
Arizona	486,936	266,721	54.8	170,514	35.0	46,573	9.6	75	0.0	3,053	0.6	96,207	R
Arkansas	619,969	190,759	30.8	188,228	30.4	240,982	38.9	—	0.0	—	0.0	50,223	A
California	7,251,587	3,467,664	47.8	3,244,318	44.7	487,270	6.7	341	0.0	51,994	0.7	223,346	R
Colorado	811,199	409,345	50.5	335,174	41.3	60,813	7.5	3,016	0.4	2,851	0.4	74,171	R
Connecticut	1,256,232	556,721	44.3	621,561	49.5	76,650	6.1	—	0.0	1,300	0.1	64,840	D
Delaware	214,367	96,714	45.1	89,194	41.6	28,459	13.3	—	0.0	—	0.0	7,520	R
Florida	2,187,805	886,804	40.5	676,794	30.9	624,207	28.5	—	0.0	—	0.0	210,010	R
Georgia	1,250,266	380,111	30.4	334,440	26.7	535,550	42.8	—	0.0	165	0.0	155,439	A
Hawaii	236,218	91,425	38.7	141,324	59.8	3,469	1.5	—	0.0	—	0.0	49,899	D
Idaho	291,183	165,369	56.8	89,273	30.7	36,541	12.5	—	0.0	—	0.0	76,096	R
Illinois	4,619,749	2,174,774	47.1	2,039,814	44.2	390,958	8.5	13,878	0.3	325	0.0	134,960	R
Indiana	2,123,597	1,067,885	50.3	806,659	38.0	243,108	11.4	—	0.0	5,945	0.3	261,226	R
Iowa	1,167,931	619,106	53.0	476,699	40.8	66,422	5.7	241	0.0	5,463	0.5	142,407	R
Kansas	872,783	478,674	54.8	302,996	34.7	88,921	10.2	—	0.0	2,192	0.3	175,678	R
Kentucky	1,055,893	462,411	43.8	397,541	37.6	193,098	18.3	—	0.0	2,843	0.3	64,870	R
Louisiana	1,097,450	257,535	23.5	309,615	28.2	530,300	48.3	—	0.0	—	0.0	220,685	A
Maine	392,936	169,254	43.1	217,312	55.3	6,370	1.6	—	0.0	—	0.0	48,058	D
Maryland	1,235,039	517,995	41.9	538,310	43.6	178,734	14.5	—	0.0	—	0.0	20,315	D
Massachusetts	2,331,752	766,844	32.9	1,469,218	63.0	87,088	3.7	6,180	0.3	2,422	0.1	702,374	D
Michigan	3,306,250	1,370,665	41.5	1,593,082	48.2	331,968	10.0	1,762	0.1	8,773	0.3	222,417	D
Minnesota	1,588,506	658,643	41.5	857,738	54.0	68,931	4.3	285	0.0	2,909	0.2	199,095	D

													A
Mississippi	654,509	88,516	13.5	150,644	23.0	415,349	63.5	—	0.0	—	0.0	264,705	A
Missouri	1,809,502	811,932	44.9	791,444	43.7	206,126	11.4	—	0.0	—	0.0	20,488	R
Montana	274,404	138,835	50.6	114,117	41.6	20,015	7.3	—	0.0	1,437	0.5	24,718	R
Nebraska	536,851	321,163	59.8	170,784	31.8	44,904	8.4	—	0.0	—	0.0	150,379	R
Nevada	154,218	73,188	47.5	60,598	39.3	20,432	13.2	—	0.0	—	0.0	12,590	R
New Hampshire	297,298	154,903	52.1	130,589	43.9	11,173	3.8	6,784	2.3	633	0.2	24,314	R
New Jersey	2,875,395	1,325,467	46.1	1,264,206	44.0	262,187	9.1	—	0.0	16,751	0.6	61,261	R
New Mexico	327,350	169,692	51.8	130,081	39.7	25,737	7.9	—	0.0	1,840	0.6	39,611	R
New York	6,791,688	3,007,932	44.3	3,378,470	49.7	358,864	5.3	8,432	0.1	37,990	0.6	370,538	D
North Carolina	1,587,493	627,192	39.5	464,113	29.2	496,188	31.3	—	0.0	—	0.0	131,004	R
North Dakota	247,882	138,669	55.9	94,769	38.2	14,244	5.7	120	0.0	200	0.1	43,900	R
Ohio	3,959,698	1,791,014	45.2	1,700,586	42.9	467,495	11.8	—	0.0	483	0.0	90,428	R
Oklahoma	943,086	449,697	47.7	301,658	32.0	191,731	20.3	—	0.0	—	0.0	148,039	R
Oregon	819,622	408,433	49.8	358,866	43.8	49,683	6.1	4,977	0.6	2,640	0.3	49,567	R
Pennsylvania	4,747,928	2,090,017	44.0	2,259,405	47.6	378,582	8.0	—	0.0	14,947	0.3	169,388	D
Rhode Island	385,000	122,359	31.8	246,518	64.0	15,678	4.1	—	0.0	445	0.1	124,159	D
South Carolina	666,978	254,062	38.1	197,486	29.6	215,430	32.3	—	0.0	—	0.0	38,632	R
South Dakota	281,264	149,841	53.3	118,023	42.0	13,400	4.8	—	0.0	—	0.0	31,818	R
Tennessee	1,248,617	472,592	37.8	351,233	28.1	424,792	34.0	—	0.0	—	0.0	47,800	R
Texas	3,079,216	1,227,844	39.9	1,266,804	41.1	584,269	19.0	—	0.0	299	0.0	38,960	D
Utah	422,568	238,728	56.5	156,665	37.1	26,906	6.4	—	0.0	269	0.1	82,063	R
Vermont	161,404	85,142	52.8	70,255	43.5	5,104	3.2	—	0.0	903	0.6	14,887	R
Virginia	1,361,491	590,319	43.4	442,387	32.5	321,833	23.6	4,671	0.3	2,281	0.2	147,932	R
Washington	1,304,281	588,510	45.1	616,037	47.2	96,990	7.4	488	0.0	2,256	0.2	27,527	D
West Virginia	754,206	307,555	40.8	374,091	49.6	72,560	9.6	—	0.0	—	0.0	66,536	D
Wisconsin	1,691,538	809,997	47.9	748,804	44.3	127,835	7.6	1,338	0.1	3,564	0.2	61,193	R

State	Total Vote	Nixon (R) Votes	(%)	Humphrey (D) Votes	(%)	Wallace (AI) Votes	(%)	Blomen (SL) Votes	(%)	Other Votes	(%)	Plurality	
Wyoming	127,205	70,927	55.8	45,173	35.5	11,105	8.7	—	0.0	—	0.0	25,754	R
Dist. of Col.	170,578	31,012	18.2	139,566	81.8	—	0.0	—	0.0	—	0.0	108,554	D
Totals	73,211,875	31,785,480	43.4	31,275,166	42.7	9,906,473	13.5	52,588	0.1	192,168	0.3	510,314	R

Source: *Guide to U.S. Elections*, 5th ed. (Washington, D.C.: CQ Press, 2005), 710.

RICHARD M. NIXON'S INAUGURAL ADDRESS, JANUARY 20, 1969

Senator Dirksen, Mr. Chief Justice, Mr. Vice President, President Johnson, Vice President Humphrey, my fellow Americans—and my fellow citizens of the world community:

I ask you to share with me today the majesty of this moment. In the orderly transfer of power, we celebrate the unity that keeps us free.

Each moment in history is a fleeting time, precious and unique. But some stand out as moments of beginning, in which courses are set that shape decades or centuries. This can be such a moment.

Forces now are converging that make possible, for the first time, the hope that many of man's deepest aspirations can at last be realized. The spiraling pace of change allows us to contemplate, within our own lifetime, advances that once would have taken centuries.

In throwing wide the horizons of space, we have discovered new horizons on earth.

For the first time, because the people of the world want peace, and the leaders of the world are afraid of war, the times are on the side of peace.

Eight years from now America will celebrate its 200th anniversary as a nation. Within the lifetime of most people now living, mankind will celebrate that great new year which comes only once in a thousand years—the beginning of the third millennium.

What kind of a nation we will be, what kind of a world we will live in, whether we shape the future in the image of our hopes, is ours to determine by our actions and our choices.

The greatest honor history can bestow is the title of peacemaker. This honor now beckons America—the chance to help lead the world at last out of the valley of turmoil and onto that high ground of peace that man has dreamed of since the dawn of civilization.

If we succeed, generations to come will say of us now living that we mastered our moment, that we helped make the world safe for mankind.

This is our summons to greatness.

I believe the American people are ready to answer this call.

The second third of this century has been a time of proud achievement. We have made enormous strides in science and industry and agriculture. We have shared our wealth more broadly than ever. We have learned at last to manage a modern economy to assure its continued growth.

We have given freedom new reach. We have begun to make its promise real for black as well as for white.

We see the hope of tomorrow in the youth of today. I know America's youth. I believe in them. We can be proud that they are better educated, more committed, more passionately driven by conscience than any generation in our history.

No people has ever been so close to the achievement of a just and abundant society, or so possessed of the will to achieve it. And because our strengths are so great, we can afford to appraise our weaknesses with candor and to approach them with hope.

Standing in this same place a third of a century ago, Franklin Delano Roosevelt addressed a nation ravaged by depression and gripped in fear. He could say in surveying the Nation's troubles: "They concern, thank God, only material things." Our crisis today is in reverse.

We find ourselves rich in goods, but ragged in spirit; reaching with magnificent precision for the moon, but falling into raucous discord on earth.

We are caught in war, wanting peace. We are torn by division, wanting unity. We see around us empty lives, wanting fulfillment. We see tasks that need doing, waiting for hands to do them.

To a crisis of the spirit, we need an answer of the spirit.

And to find that answer, we need only look within ourselves.

When we listen to "the better angels of our nature," we find that they celebrate the simple things, the basic things—such as goodness, decency, love, kindness.

Greatness comes in simple trappings. The simple things are the ones most needed today if we are to surmount what divides us, and cement what unites us.

To lower our voices would be a simple thing.

In these difficult years, America has suffered from a fever of words; from inflated rhetoric that promises more than it can deliver; from angry rhetoric that fans discontents into hatreds; from bombastic rhetoric that postures instead of persuading.

We cannot learn from one another until we stop shouting at one another—until we speak quietly enough so that our words can be heard as well as our voices.

For its part, government will listen. We will strive to listen in new ways—to the voices of quiet anguish, the voices that speak without words, the voices of the heart—to the injured voices, the anxious voices, the voices that have despaired of being heard.

Those who have been left out, we will try to bring in.

Those left behind, we will help to catch up.

For all of our people, we will set as our goal the decent order that makes progress possible and our lives secure.

As we reach toward our hopes, our task is to build on what has gone before—not turning away from the old, but turning toward the new.

In this past third of a century, government has passed more laws, spent more money, initiated more programs than in all our previous history.

In pursuing our goals of full employment, better housing, excellence in education; in rebuilding our cities and improving our rural areas; in protecting our environment and enhancing the quality of life—in all these and more, we will and must press urgently forward.

We shall plan now for the day when our wealth can be transferred from the destruction of war abroad to the urgent needs of our people at home.

The American dream does not come to those who fall asleep.

But we are approaching the limits of what government alone can do.

Our greatest need now is to reach beyond government, to enlist the legions of the concerned and the committed.

What has to be done, has to be done by government and people together or it will not be done at all. The lesson of past agony is that without the people we can do nothing—with the people we can do everything.

To match the magnitude of our tasks, we need the energies of our people—enlisted not only in grand enterprises, but more importantly in those small, splendid efforts that make headlines in the neighborhood newspaper instead of the national journal.

With these, we can build a great cathedral of the spirit—each of us raising it one stone at a time, as he reaches out to his neighbor, helping, caring, doing.

I do not offer a life of uninspiring ease. I do not call for a life of grim sacrifice. I ask you to join in a high adventure—one as rich as humanity itself, and exciting as the times we live in.

The essence of freedom is that each of us shares in the shaping of his own destiny.

Until he has been part of a cause larger than himself, no man is truly whole.

The way to fulfillment is in the use of our talents. We achieve nobility in the spirit that inspires that use.

As we measure what can be done, we shall promise only what we know we can produce; but as we chart our goals, we shall be lifted by our dreams.

No man can be fully free while his neighbor is not. To go forward at all is to go forward together.

This means black and white together, as one nation, not two. The laws have caught up with our conscience. What remains is to give life to what is in the law: to insure at last that as all are born equal in dignity before God, all are born equal in dignity before man.

As we learn to go forward together at home, let us also seek to go forward together with all mankind.

Let us take as our goal: Where peace is unknown, make it welcome; where peace is fragile, make it strong; where peace is temporary, make it permanent.

After a period of confrontation, we are entering an era of negotiation.

Let all nations know that during this administration our lines of communication will be open.

We seek an open world—open to ideas, open to the exchange of goods and people—a world in which no people, great or small, will live in angry isolation.

We cannot expect to make everyone our friend, but we can try to make no one our enemy.

Those who would be our adversaries, we invite to a peaceful competition—not in conquering territory or extending dominion, but in enriching the life of man.

As we explore the reaches of space, let us go to the new worlds together—not as new worlds to be conquered, but as a new adventure to be shared.

With those who are willing to join, let us cooperate to reduce the burden of arms, to strengthen the structure of peace, to lift up the poor and the hungry.

But to all those who would be tempted by weakness, let us leave no doubt that we will be as strong as we need to be for as long as we need to be.

Over the past twenty years, since I first came to this Capital as a freshman Congressman, I have visited most of the nations of the world. I have come to know the leaders of the world and the great forces, the hatreds, the fears that divide the world.

I know that peace does not come through wishing for it—that there is no substitute for days and even years of patient and prolonged diplomacy.

I also know the people of the world.

I have seen the hunger of a homeless child, the pain of a man wounded in battle, the grief of a mother who has lost her son. I know these have no ideology, no race.

I know America. I know the heart of America is good.

I speak from my own heart, and the heart of my country, the deep concern we have for those who suffer and those who sorrow.

I have taken an oath today in the presence of God and my countrymen to uphold and defend the Constitution of the United States. To that oath I now add this sacred commitment: I shall consecrate my Office, my energies, and all the wisdom I can summon to the cause of peace among nations.

Let this message be heard by strong and weak alike:

The peace we seek to win is not victory over any other people, but the peace that comes "with healing in its wings"; with compassion for those who have suffered; with understanding for those who have opposed us; with the opportunity for all the peoples of this earth to choose their own destiny.

Only a few short weeks ago we shared the glory of man's first sight of the world as God sees it, as a single sphere reflecting light in the darkness.

As the Apollo astronauts flew over the moon's gray surface on Christmas Eve, they spoke to us of the beauty of earth—and in that voice so clear across the lunar distance, we heard them invoke God's blessing on its goodness.

In that moment, their view from the moon moved poet Archibald Mac-Leish to write:

"To see the earth as it truly is, small and blue and beautiful in that eternal silence where it floats, is to see ourselves as riders on the earth together, brothers on that bright loveliness in the eternal cold—brothers who know now they are truly brothers."

In that moment of surpassing technological triumph, men turned their thoughts toward home and humanity—seeing in that far perspective that man's destiny on earth is not divisible; telling us that however far we reach into the cosmos, our destiny lies not in the stars but on earth itself, in our own hands, in our own hearts.

We have endured a long night of the American spirit. But as our eyes catch the dimness of the first rays of dawn, let us not curse the remaining dark. Let us gather the light.

Our destiny offers not the cup of despair, but the chalice of opportunity. So let us seize it not in fear, but in gladness—and "riders on the earth together," let us go forward, firm in our faith, steadfast in our purpose, cautious of the dangers, but sustained by our confidence in the will of God and the promise of man.

Note: The President spoke at 12:16 p.m. from the inaugural platform erected at the East Front of the Capitol, immediately following administration of the oath of office by Chief Justice Earl Warren. The address was broadcast on radio and television.

Source: Richard Nixon, "Inaugural Address," January 20, 1969. Online by Gerhard Peters and John T. Woolley, *The American Presidency Project.* http://www.presidency.ucsb.edu/ws/?pid=1941.

NOTES

CHAPTER 1   THE VIEW FROM 1964

1   Gallup Poll, "U.S. Presidential Election Center," available at http://www.gallup
.com/poll/154559/US-Presidential-Election-Center.aspx.

2   The congressional vote, by chamber and party, is reported in Timothy N.
Thurber, *Republicans and Race: The GOP's Frayed Relationship with African
Americans, 1945–1976* (Lawrence: University Press of Kansas, 2013), chap. 6.
House Republicans supported the bill 138 to 34, and House Democrats 152 to
94. Senate Republicans supported it 27 to 6, and Senate Democrats 46 to 21.

3   "Barry M. Goldwater's Acceptance Speech to the Republican National Convention (1964)," in *Historical Documents on Presidential Elections, 1787–1988*, ed.
Michael Nelson (Washington, D.C.: Congressional Quarterly, 1991), 515–521.

4   Quoted in Gary Donaldson, *Liberalism's Last Hurrah: The Presidential Campaign
of 1964* (Armonk, N.Y.: M. E. Sharpe, 2003), 146–147. Goldwater's point in the
Kremlin comment was how accurate the military's targeting ability was, but
in the Cold War phase of the nuclear age any offhand reference to the use of
atomic weapons sounded alarming.

5   Tom Wicker, *JFK and LBJ: The Influence of Personality upon Politics* (Chicago:
Ivan R. Dee, 1968), 212.

6   Quoted in Rick Perlstein, *Before the Storm: Barry Goldwater and the Unmaking
of the American Consensus* (New York: Hill & Wang, 2001), 488.

7   Gallup Poll, "U.S. Presidential Election Center."

8   Kim Phillips-Fein, *Invisible Hands: The Making of the Conservative Movement
from the New Deal to Reagan* (New York: W. W. Norton, 2009), 141.

9   Theodore H. White, *The Making of the President 1964* (New York: Atheneum,
1965), 365.

10   David S. Broder, *The Party's Over: The Failure of Party Politics in America* (New
York: Harper & Row, 1972), 45.

11   Robert Dallek, *Flawed Giant: Lyndon Johnson and His Times, 1961–1973* (New
York: Oxford University Press, 1998), 184.

12   Quoted in Perlstein, *Before the Storm*, 513.

13   Robert J. Donovan, *The Future of the Republican Party* (New York: New American Library, 1964), 10.

14   Geoffrey Kabaservice, *Rule and Ruin: The Downfall of Moderation and the Destruction of the Republican Party from Eisenhower to the Tea Party* (New York:
Oxford University Press, 2012), 123.

15   James MacGregor Burns, *The Deadlock of Democracy: Four-Party Politics in
America*, rev. ed. (Englewood Cliffs, N.J.: Prentice-Hall, 1963), 252. See also the
1967 edition of the book, 3.

16 Gerald M. Pomper, "Classification of Presidential Elections," *Journal of Politics* 29 (August 1967): 535–566.

17 In two extensive 1964 surveys, pluralities of Americans regarded these characterizations of Goldwater as "true" rather than "untrue." Lloyd A. Free and Hadley Cantril, *The Political Beliefs of Americans: A Study of Public Opinion* (New York: Simon & Schuster, 1968), 159.

18 All but Gov. Adlai Stevenson of Illinois, the Democratic presidential nominee in 1952 and 1956, and Gov. Spiro Agnew of Maryland, the Republican vice presidential nominee in 1968. When Agnew ran for reelection in 1972 as the incumbent vice president, he had four years of experience in Washington.

19 Quoted in Merle Miller, *Lyndon: An Oral Biography* (New York: Ballantine Books, 1980), 292.

20 Quoted in Robert A. Caro, *The Passage of Power: The Years of Lyndon Johnson* (New York: Alfred A. Knopf, 2012), 33. See also John T. Shaw, *JFK in the Senate: Pathway to the Presidency* (New York: Palgrave Macmillan, 2013).

21 In the eight elections from 1928 to 1956, every Democratic vice presidential candidate was from a southern or border state except Henry A. Wallace in 1940—and Wallace was dropped from the ticket after one term in favor of border state senator Harry S. Truman.

22 Quoted in Jeff Shesol, *Mutual Contempt: Lyndon Johnson, Robert Kennedy, and the Feud That Defined a Decade* (New York: W. W. Norton, 1997), 45.

23 Quoted in Caro, *Passage of Power*, 125–126.

24 Michael Nelson, *A Heartbeat Away* (Washington, D.C.: Brookings Institution, 1988), 91–93.

25 Quoted in Randall B. Woods, *LBJ: Architect of American Ambition* (New York: Free Press, 2006), 361.

26 Quoted in Willie Morris, *North toward Home* (Dunwoody, Ga.: Norman S. Berg, 1977), 234.

27 Quoted in Shesol, *Mutual Contempt*, 47.

28 Quoted in Caro, *Passage of Power*, 205.

29 Evelyn Lincoln, *Kennedy and Johnson* (New York: Holt, Rinehart & Winston, 1968), 188, 161.

30 Bobby Baker, with Larry L. King, *Wheeling and Dealing: Confessions of a Capitol Hill Operator* (New York: W. W. Norton, 1978), 117.

31 Quoted in Shesol, *Mutual Contempt*, 86.

32 Harry McPherson, quoted in Miller, *Lyndon*, 373.

33 Quoted in Sidney M. Milkis and Michael Nelson, *The American Presidency: Origins and Development, 1776–2011* (Washington, D.C.: CQ Press, 2012), 486.

34 Caro, *Passage of Power*, 351.

35 Quoted in ibid., 410, 411.

36 Shesol, *Mutual Contempt*, 140.

37 David Greenberg, "Robert Caro's 'The Passage of Power: The Years of Lyndon Johnson' Book Review," *Washington Post*, May 1, 2012.

38 Quoted in Dallek, *Flawed Giant*, 63.

39 Quoted in Caro, *Passage of Power*, 562.

40 Clay Risen, *The Bill of the Century: The Epic Battle for the Civil Rights Act* (New York: Bloomsbury Press, 2014), 245–249.

41 Todd S. Purdum, *An Idea Whose Time Has Come: Two Presidents, Two Parties, and the Battle for the Civil Rights Act of 1964* (New York: Henry Holt, 2014), 313.

42 Lyndon B. Johnson, "Annual Message to Congress on the State of the Union, Jan. 8, 1964," available at http://www.presidency.ucsb.edu/ws/index.php?pid =26787.

43 Quoted in Dallek, *Flawed Giant*, 120.

44 Quoted in Nicholas Lemann, *The Promised Land: The Great Black Migration and How It Changed America* (New York: Alfred A. Knopf, 1991), 143.

45 "Lyndon B. Johnson's 'Great Society' Speech (1964)," in *The Evolving Presidency: Landmark Documents, 1787–2010*, ed. Michael Nelson (Washington, D.C.: CQ Press, 2012), 199–203.

46 Allen J. Matusow, *The Unraveling of America: A History of Liberalism in the 1960s* (New York: Harper & Row, 1984), 18.

47 "National Security Action Memorandum No. 52," Office of the Historian, U.S. Department of State, available at https://history.state.gov/historicaldocu ments/frus1961-63v01/d52.

48 Quoted in Perlstein, *Before the Storm*, 145.

49 Quoted in Eric Schlosser, *Command and Control: Nuclear Weapons, the Damascus Accident, and the Illusion of Safety* (New York: Penguin, 2013), 250.

50 Quoted in Fredrik Logevall, *Choosing War: The Lost Chance for Peace and the Escalation of the War in Vietnam* (Berkeley: University of California Press, 1999), 38.

51 Robert F. Kennedy, quoted in Miller, *Lyndon*, 463.

52 Quoted in Chris Matthews, *Jack Kennedy: Elusive Hero* (New York: Simon & Schuster, 2011), 396.

53 Quoted in Miller, *Lyndon*, 461.

54 Lyndon Baines Johnson, *The Vantage Point: Perspectives on the Presidency, 1963–1969* (New York: Holt, Rinehart & Winston, 1971), 42.

55 Quoted in Dallek, *Flawed Giant*, 254, 146.

56 Quoted in Doris Kearns, *Lyndon Johnson and the American Dream* (New York: Harper & Row, 1976), 253. Admirers of JFK who argue that after "keep[ing] Vietnam on the back burner until voting day" in November 1964, Kennedy would have negotiated a withdrawal seem unaware of how morally craven a president who allowed American soldiers to die for purely electoral reasons would be. See, for example, Fredrik Logevall, *Choosing War: The Lost Chance for Peace and the Escalation of War in Vietnam* (Berkeley: University of California Press, 1999), 395; and Larry J. Sabato, *The Kennedy Half-Century: The Presidency, Assassination, and Lasting Legacy of John F. Kennedy* (New York: Bloomsbury USA, 2013), 125–126. In truth, it seems at least as likely that Kennedy—who was committed to combatting "wars of national liberation," responsible for overthrowing South Vietnam's government, and politically vulnerable after agreeing to the neutralization of Laos in 1961 charges he had lost a Southeast Asian country to the communists—would have escalated the American involvement in Vietnam.

57   Marc J. Hetherington and Michael Nelson, "Anatomy of a Rally 'Round the Flag Effect," *PS: Political Science and Politics* 36 (Jan. 2003): 37–42. The resolution passed without dissent in the House of Representatives. In the Senate it was opposed by two members: Wayne Morse of Oregon and Ernest Gruening of Alaska.

58   Quoted in Joseph A. Califano, *The Triumph and Tragedy of Lyndon Johnson: The White House Years* (New York: Simon & Schuster, 1991), 172. He used the line elsewhere as well. See, for example, Matusow, *Unraveling of America*, 150.

59   John F. Kennedy's assassination in 1963 was preceded by the death in combat of the oldest Kennedy brother, Joseph P. Kennedy, Jr., in 1944.

60   William vanden Heuvel and Milton Gwirtzman, *On His Own: RFK, 1964–68* (New York: Doubleday, 1970), 22.

61   Arthur M. Schlesinger, Jr., *Robert Kennedy and His Times* (Boston: Houghton Mifflin, 1978), 133.

62   Quoted in Woods, *LBJ*, 357.

63   Quoted in Shesol, *Mutual Contempt*, 39, 35.

64   Quoted in Schlesinger, *Robert Kennedy and His Times*, 210.

65   Quoted in David Nasaw, *The Patriarch: The Remarkable Life and Turbulent Times of Joseph P. Kennedy* (New York: Penguin, 2012), 759.

66   Clark Clifford, with Richard Holbrooke, *Counsel to the President* (New York: Random House, 1991), 336.

67   According to Larry Tye, Robert Kennedy's account of the Cuban missile crisis, *Thirteen Days*, "is laced with fictions" that "cast him as the champion dove he would like to have been, rather than the unrelenting hawk he actually was through much of those two weeks." Tye, *Bobby Kennedy: The Making of a Liberal Icon* (New York: Random House, 2016), 239, 265–266.

68   "John F. Kennedy's Inaugural Address (1961)," in Nelson, *Evolving Presidency*, 187–191.

69   Michael Nelson, "Democratic Presidents, Protests, Elections, and the War in Vietnam: The Path to 1968 and Strategic Incoherence," in *War, Justice, and Peace in American Grand Strategy: From the Founding Era to the Twenty-first Century*, ed. Paul Carrese, Stephen F. Knott, and Bryan-Paul Frost (Baltimore: Johns Hopkins University Press, forthcoming).

70   Michael Cohen, *American Maelstrom: The 1968 Election and the Politics of Division* (New York: Oxford University Press, 2016), 36–37.

71   Quoted in Shesol, *Mutual Contempt*, 253.

72   Quoted in ibid., 172, 176.

73   Quoted in ibid., 178.

74   Quoted in Evan Thomas, *Robert Kennedy: His Life* (New York: Simon & Schuster, 2000), 292.

75   Quoted in Shesol, *Mutual Contempt*, 208, 209.

76   The quotation is from Act 3, Scene 2, of Shakespeare's *Romeo and Juliet*.

77   Joseph A. Califano, Jr., *Inside: A Public and Private Life* (New York: PublicAffairs, 2004), 145.

78 The Twenty-fifth Amendment, which was added to the Constitution in 1967, created a procedure for filling vice presidential vacancies.

79 Quoted in Carl Solberg, *Hubert Humphrey: A Biography* (New York: W. W. Norton, 1984), 77, 78.

80 Walter LaFeber, *The Deadly Bet: LBJ, Vietnam, and the 1968 Election* (Lanham, Md.: Rowman & Littlefield, 2005), 117.

81 "Hubert H. Humphrey's Civil Rights Speech to the Democratic National Convention (1948)," in Nelson, *Historic Documents on Presidential Elections*, 458–461.

82 "Education of a Senator," *Time*, January 17, 1949, 13–16.

83 Hubert H. Humphrey, *The Education of a Public Man: My Life and Politics* (New York: Doubleday, 1976), 165.

84 Harry McPherson, *A Political Education: A Washington Memoir* (Boston: Little, Brown, 1972).

85 LaFeber, *Deadly Bet*, 121.

86 Quoted in Solberg, *Hubert Humphrey*, 176.

87 Quoted in Schlesinger, *Robert Kennedy and His Times*, 200.

88 Quoted in ibid., 201.

89 Quoted in Solberg, *Hubert Humphrey*, 240.

90 Quoted in Dallek, *Flawed Giant*, 138.

91 Humphrey, *Education of a Public Man*, 301, 303.

92 Quoted in Albert Eisele, *Almost to the Presidency: A Biography of Two American Politicians* (Blue Earth, Minn.: Piper, 1972), 84; and Cohen, *American Maelstrom*, 72.

93 Quoted in Perlstein, *Before the Storm*, 401.

94 Mondale's role is described in Steven M. Gillon, *The Democrats' Dilemma: Walter F. Mondale and the Liberal Legacy* (New York: Columbia University Press, 1992), 70–75.

95 William H. Chafe, *Unfinished Journey: American since World War II*, 7th ed. (New York: Oxford University Press, 2011), 301.

96 Hubert H. Humphrey, "1964 Vice Presidential Acceptance Speech," available at http://www.speeches-usa.com/Transcripts/033_humphrey.html.

97 Quoted in Eisele, *Almost to the Presidency*, 84.

98 Quoted in Rick Perlstein, *Nixonland: The Rise of a President and the Fracturing of America* (New York: Scribner, 2008), 229.

99 Quoted in Dominic Sandbrook, *Eugene McCarthy: The Rise and Fall of Postwar American Liberalism* (New York: Alfred A. Knopf, 2004), 102.

100 Quoted in Lewis L. Gould, *1968: The Election That Changed America* (Chicago: Ivan R. Dee, 1993), 19.

101 Quoted in vanden Heuvel and Gwirtzman, *On His Own*, 286.

102 Quoted in Dan T. Carter, *The Politics of Rage: George Wallace, the Origins of Conservatism, and the Transformation of American Politics* (New York: Simon & Schuster, 1995), 54.

103 Stephen Lesher, *George Wallace: American Populist* (Reading, Mass.: Addison-Wesley, 1994), 61.

104 Quoted in ibid., 85.

105 Marshall Frady, *Wallace* (New York: Random House, 1996), 100, 101.

106 Quoted in ibid., 90.

107 Thomas Byrne Edsall and Mary D. Edsall, *Chain Reaction: The Impact of Race, Rights, and Taxes on American Politics* (New York: W. W. Norton, 1991), 41. See also Norman H. Nie, Sidney Verba, and John R. Petrocik, *The Changing American Voter* (Cambridge, Mass.: Harvard University Press, 1976), 243–269.

108 Quoted in Carter, *Politics of Rage*, 96.

109 Quoted in ibid., 103. See the full account in Jack Bass, *Taming the Storm: The Life and Times of Judge Frank M. Johnson, Jr., and the South's Fight over Civil Rights* (New York: Doubleday, 1993), chap. 14. The clash estranged Judge Johnson from Wallace, who thereafter attacked him frequently for his civil rights rulings.

110 Quoted in Carter, *Politics of Rage*, 106.

111 Quoted in ibid., 109.

112 Quoted in Lesher, *George Wallace*, 156.

113 Quoted in ibid., 174.

114 Quoted in ibid., 229.

115 Lewis Chester, Godfrey Hodgson, and Bruce Page, *An American Melodrama: The Presidential Campaign of 1968* (New York: Viking, 1969), 270.

116 See Robert J. Cook, *Troubled Commemoration: The American Civil War Centennial, 1961–1965* (Baton Rouge: Louisiana State University Press, 2007); and Maurice Isserman and Michael Kazin, *America Divided: The Civil War of the 1960s* (New York: Oxford University Press, 2000), 1.

117 Frady, *Wallace*, 180.

118 Quoted in Perlstein, *Before the Storm*, 326.

119 Lesher, *George Wallace*, 304; and Carter, *Politics of Rage*, 215.

120 Quoted in Perlstein, *Before the Storm*, 376.

121 Quoted in Kabaservice, *Rule and Ruin*, 118.

122 Facing no major party opposition, Nixon was reelected in 1948 with 87 percent.

123 Charles Peters, *Lyndon B. Johnson* (New York: Times Books, 2010), 41–42.

124 Evan Thomas, *Being Nixon: A Man Divided* (New York: Random House, 2015), 107.

125 Perlstein, *Before the Storm*, 74. Interestingly, John Kennedy offered himself to voters for the first time in 1946 as a "fighting conservative."

126 Donald T. Critchlow, *The Conservative Ascendancy: How the Republican Right Rose to Power in Modern America*, 2nd ed. (Lawrence: University Press of Kansas, 2011), 90.

127 Quoted in Jean Edward Smith, *Eisenhower in War and Peace* (New York: Random House, 2012), 522.

128 Quoted in Jeffrey Frank, *Ike and Dick: Portrait of a Strange Political Marriage* (New York: Simon & Schuster, 2012), 41.

129 "Richard Nixon's 'Checkers' Speech (1952)," in Nelson, *Historic Documents on Presidential Elections*, 474–482. See also Kevin Mattson, *Just Plain Dick: Richard*

Nixon's Checkers Speech and the "Rocking Socking" Election of 1952 (New York: Bloomsbury, 2012).

130 Quoted in Lee Huebner, "The Checkers Speech after 60 Years," *The Atlantic,* September 22, 2012, available at http://www.theatlantic.com/politics/archive /2012/09/the-checkers-speech-after-60-years/262172/.

131 Quoted in Thomas, *Being Nixon,* 81.

132 Quoted in Garry Wills, *Nixon Agonistes: The Crisis of the Self-Made Man* (Boston: Houghton Mifflin, 1969), 114.

133 This amount was equivalent to about $4.5 million in 2012. Smith, *Eisenhower in War and Peace,* 468.

134 Quoted in Conrad Black, *Richard M. Nixon: A Man in Full* (New York: PublicAffairs, 2007), 241.

135 Thomas, *Being Nixon,* 94; and Irwin F. Gellman, *The President and the Apprentice* (New Haven, Conn.: Yale University Press, 2015), 310–312.

136 Quoted in David A. Nichols, *Eisenhower 1956: The President's Year of Crisis—Suez and the Brink of War* (New York: Simon & Schuster, 2011), 237.

137 Quoted in Perlstein, *Nixonland,* 46.

138 Nelson, *Heartbeat Away,* chap. 5.

139 Quoted in Perlstein, *Before the Storm,* 84, 85.

140 Quoted in Perlstein, *Nixonland,* 52.

141 Quoted in Thomas, *Being Nixon,* 115.

142 William Rorabaugh, *The Real Making of the President: Kennedy, Nixon, and the 1960 Election* (Lawrence: University Press of Kansas, 2009), 201.

143 Jonathan Aitken, *Nixon: A Life* (Washington, D.C.: Regnery, 1993), 283.

144 Patrick J. Buchanan, *The Greatest Comeback: How Richard Nixon Rose from Defeat to Create the New Majority* (New York: Crown Forum, 2014), 13.

145 "Transcript of Nixon's News Conference on His Defeat by Brown in Race for Governor of California," *New York Times,* November 8, 1962.

146 William Safire, *Before the Fall: An Inside View of the Pre-Watergate White House* (Garden City, N.Y.: Doubleday, 1975), 21.

147 Quoted in Theodore H. White, *The Making of the President 1968* (New York: Atheneum, 1969), 49.

148 Perlstein, *Before the Storm,* 253.

149 "Nixon Gives Hint He Might Change Stand If Public Urges Him On," *Meriden (Conn.) Morning Record,* Jan. 10, 1964.

150 "Bryan Hears Cheers over the Phone" and "Son Born to Mrs. J. D. Rockefeller, Jr.," *New York Times,* July 10, 1908.

151 Quoted in Cary Reich, *The Life of Nelson A. Rockefeller: Worlds to Conquer, 1908–1958* (New York: Doubleday, 1996), xvii.

152 Richard Norton Smith, *On His Own Terms: A Life of Nelson Rockefeller* (New York: Random House, 2014), 319.

153 Ibid., 346.

154 Quoted in Perlstein, *Before the Storm,* 196.

155 David Frost, *The Presidential Debate, 1968* (New York: Stein & Day, 1968), 106.

156 "New York Governor Nelson Rockefeller Speaks on Extremism at the 1964 Republican National Convention, San Francisco, CA," available at http:// www.totalpolitics.com/speeches/america/republican-speeches/33388 /new-york-governor-nelson-rockefeller-speaks-on-extremism-at-the-1964-re publican-national-convention-san-francisco-ca.thtml.

157 Stephen Hess and David S. Broder, *The Republican Establishment: The Present and Future of the GOP* (New York: Harper & Row, 1967), 107.

158 Quoted in ibid., 95.

159 Quoted in ibid., 100.

160 Cohen, *American Maelstrom*, 186.

161 "Text of Romney's Letter to Goldwater after Defeat of Presidential Nominee in '64," *New York Times*, November 29, 1966. The letter was dated December 21, 1964.

162 Quoted in Lou Cannon, *Governor Reagan: His Rise to Power* (New York: Public Affairs, 2003), 58.

163 Hess and Broder, *Republican Establishment*, 249.

164 Matthew Dallek, *The Right Moment: Ronald Reagan's First Victory and the Decisive Turning Point in American Politics* (New York: Free Press, 2000), 32.

165 Quoted in Cannon, *Governor Reagan*, 99.

166 Thomas W. Evans, *The Education of Ronald Reagan: The General Electric Years and the Untold Story of His Conversion to Conservatism* (New York: Columbia University Press, 2006).

167 The text of the speech, known among Reagan admirers as "The Speech," is in ibid., 238–249.

168 Quoted in Rorabaugh, *Real Making of the President*, 93.

CHAPTER 2 PEAKS AND VALLEYS

1 Lawrence J. Grossback, Daniel A. M. Peterson, and James A. Stimson, *Mandate Politics* (New York: Cambridge University Press, 2006), 14, 16, 44.

2 Quoted in Harry McPherson, *A Political Education: A Washington Memoir* (Boston: Little, Brown, 1972), 268.

3 Lyndon B. Johnson, "Annual Message to Congress on the State of the Union, Jan. 12, 1966," available at http://www.presidency.ucsb.edu/ws/index.php?pid =28015.

4 Lyndon B. Johnson, "Remarks at the Lighting of the National Christmas Tree," December 18, 1964, available at http://www.presidency.ucsb.edu/ws/?pid=26766.

5 G. Calvin Mackenzie and Robert Weisbrot, *The Liberal Hour: Washington and the Politics of Change in the 1960s* (New York: Penguin, 2008), 113.

6 Lyndon B. Johnson, "Annual Message to Congress on the State of the Union, Jan. 4, 1965," available at http://www.presidency.ucsb.edu/ws/index.php?pid =26907.

7 James T. Patterson, *The Eve of Destruction: How 1965 Transformed America* (New York: Basic Books, 2012), 47.

8 Quoted in Joseph A. Califano, *The Triumph and Tragedy of Lyndon Johnson: The White House Years* (New York: Simon & Schuster, 1991), 113, 142. The task

forces are described in Michael Nelson, "Domestic Policy, Domestic Policy Advisers, and the American Presidency," in *Governing at Home: The White House and Domestic Policymaking*, ed. Michael Nelson and Russell L. Riley (Lawrence: University Press of Kansas, 2011), 1–23.

9   Randall B. Woods, *LBJ: Architect of American Ambition* (New York: Free Press, 2006), 561.

10 See the data in Edward G. Carmines and James A. Stimson, *Issue Evolution: Race and the Transformation of American Politics* (Princeton, N.J.: Princeton University Press, 1989), 45.

11 Gary May, *Bending toward Justice: The Voting Rights Act and the Transformation of American Democracy* (New York: Basic Books, 2013), 59.

12 The congressional vote, by chamber and party, is reported in Thomas Byrne Edsall and Mary D. Edsall, *Chain Reaction: The Impact of Race, Rights, and Taxes on American Politics* (New York: W. W. Norton, 1991), 61.

13 See the data in Michael K. Fauntroy, "Enforcing Section 5 of the Voting Rights Act," in *The Oxford Handbook of Southern Politics*, ed. Charles S. Bullock III and Mark J. Rozell (New York: Oxford University Press, 2012), 455.

14 Quoted in David T. Courtwright, *No Right Turn: Conservative Politics in a Liberal America* (Cambridge, Mass.: Harvard University Press, 2012), 62.

15 See, for example, James C. Davies, "The J-Curve of Rising and Declining Satisfactions as a Cause of Some Great Revolutions and a Contained Rebellion," in *Violence in America: Historical and Comparative Perspectives*, ed. Hugh Davis Graham and Ted Robert Gurr (New York: Bantam, 1969), 690–730.

16 Califano, *Triumph and Tragedy of Lyndon Johnson*, 338.

17 Mackenzie and Weisbrot, *Liberal Hour*, 328.

18 Lloyd A. Free and Hadley Cantril, *The Political Beliefs of Americans: A Study of Public Opinion* (New York: Simon & Schuster, 1968), 26–30.

19 Lyndon B. Johnson, "Commencement Address at Howard University: To Fulfill These Rights, June 4, 1965," available at http://www.lbjlib.utexas.edu/johnson/archives.hom/speeches.hom/650604.asp.

20 Michael W. Flamm, *Law and Order: Street Crime, Civil Unrest, and the Crisis of Liberalism* (New York: Columbia University Press, 2005).

21 Bevely Gage, "America Is Safer than It Used to Be. So Why Do We Still Have Calls for 'Law and Order,'" *New York Times Magazine*, August 30, 2016.

22 Omar Wasow, "Do Protest Tactics Matter? Evidence from the 1960s Black Insurgency" (working paper, 2016), available at http://www.omarwasow.com/Protests_on_Voting.pdf.

23 Quoted in Rick Perlstein, *Nixonland: The Rise of a President and the Fracturing of America* (New York: Scribner, 2008), 109.

24 Robert Dallek, *Flawed Giant: Lyndon Johnson and His Times, 1961–1973* (New York: Oxford University Press, 1998), 334.

25 Quoted in Doris Kearns, *Lyndon Johnson and the American Dream* (New York: Harper & Row, 1976), 251.

26 Quoted in Errol Morris, "Film: The Fog of War: Transcript," available at http://www.errolmorris.com/film/fow_transcript.html.

27 Quoted in ibid. See also Larry Berman, *Planning a Tragedy: The Americanization of the War in Vietnam* (New York: W. W. Norton, 1982).

28 Tom Wicker, *JFK and LBJ: The Influence of Personality upon Politics* (Chicago: Ivan R. Dee, 1968), 270.

29 Quoted in Tom Wicker, *One of Us: Richard Nixon and the American Dream* (New York: Random House, 1991), 281.

30 Eric Alterman and Kevin Mattson, *The Cause: The Fight for American Liberalism from Franklin Roosevelt to Barack Obama* (New York: Viking, 2012), 199.

31 Quoted in Courtwright, *No Right Turn*, 62.

32 Larry Tye, *Bobby Kennedy: The Making of a Liberal Icon* (New York: Random House, 2016), 233.

33 Lyndon B. Johnson, "Address at Johns Hopkins University: Peace without Conquest, April 7, 1965," available at http://www.lbjlib.utexas.edu/johnson/archives.hom/speeches.hom/650407.asp.

34 Dennis Wainstock, *The Turning Point: The 1968 United States Presidential Campaign* (Jefferson, N.C.: McFarland, 1988), 8.

35 Walter LaFeber, *The Deadly Bet: LBJ, Vietnam, and the 1968 Election* (Lanham, Md.: Rowman & Littlefield, 2005), 13.

36 Joseph A. Califano, Jr., *Inside: A Public and Private Life* (New York: PublicAffairs, 2004), 157.

37 Quoted in Carl Solberg, *Hubert Humphrey: A Biography* (New York: W. W. Norton, 1984), 289.

38 Quoted in Albert Eisele, *Almost to the Presidency: A Biography of Two American Politicians* (Blue Earth, Minn.: Piper, 1972), 247.

39 Quoted in Arthur M. Schlesinger, Jr., *Robert Kennedy and His Times* (Boston: Houghton Mifflin, 1978), 739.

40 Quoted in Eisele, *Almost to the Presidency*, 246.

41 Edgar Berman, *Hubert: The Triumph and Tragedy of the Humphrey I Knew* (New York: G. P. Putnam's Sons, 1979), 101.

42 Quoted in Adam Cohen and Elizabeth Taylor, *American Pharaoh: Mayor Richard J. Daley, His Battle for Chicago and the Nation* (Boston: Little, Brown, 2000), 444–445.

43 Quoted in Mackenzie and Weisbrot, *Liberal Hour*, 302.

44 Quoted in ibid., 308.

45 Quoted in Townshend Hoopes, *The Limits of Intervention: An Inside Account of How the Johnson Policy of Escalation in Vietnam Was Reversed* (New York: David McKay, 1969), 29.

46 Quoted in Charles Peters, *Lyndon B. Johnson* (New York: Times Books, 2010), 116–117.

47 Quoted in Merle Miller, *Lyndon: An Oral Biography* (New York: Ballantine Books, 1980), 521.

48 Sidney M. Milkis, *The President and the Parties: The Transformation of the American Party System since the New Deal* (New York: Oxford University Press, 1993).

49 Stephen Hess and David S. Broder, *The Republican Establishment: The Present and Future of the GOP* (New York: Harper & Row, 1967), 46.

50　The creation of the committee, and its contributions to the broadly consensual 1968 party platform, is discussed in David S. Broder, "Election of 1968," in *History of Presidential Elections, 1789–1968*, vol. 4, ed. Arthur M. Schlesinger, Jr., and Fred L. Israel (New York: Chelsea House, 1971), 3705–3752.

51　Carmines and Stimson, *Issue Evolution*, 190–191.

52　Timothy N. Thurber, *Republicans and Race: The GOP's Frayed Relationship with African Americans, 1945–1976* (Lawrence: University Press of Kansas, 2013), 192.

53　Quoted in Jon Margolis, *The Last Innocent Year: America in 1964, The Beginning of the "Sixties"* (New York: Perennial, 1999), 277, 334–335.

54　Carmines and Stimson, *Issue Evolution*, 188.

55　Wicker, *JFK and LBJ*, 214–215.

56　Daniel J. Galvin, *Presidential Party Building: Dwight D. Eisenhower to George W. Bush* (Princeton, N.J.: Princeton University Press, 2010), 5 and, more generally, chaps. 1 and 10.

57　Milkis, *President and the Parties*, 189 and, more generally, chap. 8.

58　The terms are not Johnson's but political scientist Frank J. Sorauf's in his classic *Political Parties in America* (Boston: Little, Brown, 1968), 10–11.

59　Clara Bingham, *Witness to the Revolution: Radicals, Resisters, Vets, Hippies, and the Year America Lost Its Mind and Found Its Soul* (New York: Random House, 2016), 10.

60　The most complete history of the antiwar movement is Tom Wells, *The War Within: America's Battle over Vietnam* (Berkeley: University of California Press, 1994).

61　"1966 Year in Review: Vietnam," available at http://www.upi.com/Audio/Year _in_Review/Events-of-1966/Vietnam%3A-1966/12301447861822-2/.

62　Quoted in Eisele, *Almost to the Presidency*, 265–266.

63　Dominic Sandbrook, *Eugene McCarthy: The Rise and Fall of Postwar American Liberalism* (New York: Alfred A. Knopf, 2004), 136.

64　Quoted in Jeff Shesol, *Mutual Contempt: Lyndon Johnson, Robert Kennedy, and the Feud That Defined a Decade* (New York: W. W. Norton, 1997), 316.

65　Quoted in Richard N. Goodwin, *Remembering America: A Voice from the Sixties* (Boston: Little, Brown, 1988), 405.

66　William vanden Heuvel and Milton Gwirtzman, *On His Own: RFK, 1964–68* (New York: Doubleday, 1970), 109.

67　Quoted in Evan Thomas, *Robert Kennedy: His Life* (New York: Simon & Schuster, 2000), 318.

68　Ronald Steel, *In Love with Night: The American Romance with Robert Kennedy* (New York: Simon & Schuster, 2000), 125–126.

69　Edwin O. Guthman and C. Richard Allen, *RFK: Collected Speeches* (New York: Viking, 1993), 271. Guthman, who was Kennedy's Senate press secretary, drafted the speech, along with former State Department Vietnam expert Roger Hilsman.

70　Quoted in Thomas, *Robert Kennedy*, 316.

71　Charles Schultze, budget director, quoted in Nicholas Lemann, *The Promised*

Land: The Great Black Migration and How It Changed America (New York: Alfred A. Knopf, 1991), 165.

72 Maurice Isserman and Michael Kazin, *America Divided: The Civil War of the 1960s* (New York: Oxford University Press, 2000), 193.

73 "Presidential Approval Ratings—Gallup Historical Statistics and Trends," available at http://www.gallup.com/poll/116677/presidential-approval-ratings -gallup-historical-statistics-trends.aspx#2.

74 Mary C. Brennan, *Turning Right in the Sixties: The Conservative Capture of the GOP* (Chapel Hill: University of North Carolina Press, 1995), 119.

75 Quoted in Geoffrey Kabaservice, *Rule and Ruin: The Downfall of Moderation and the Destruction of the Republican Party from Eisenhower to the Tea Party* (New York: Oxford University Press, 2012), 191.

76 Quoted in Hess and Broder, *Republican Establishment*, 263.

77 Quoted in ibid., 271.

78 Matthew Dallek, *The Right Moment: Ronald Reagan's First Victory and the Decisive Turning Point in American Politics* (New York: Free Press, 2000), 241.

79 Quoted in H. W. Brands, *Reagan: The Life* (New York: Doubleday, 2015), 146.

80 Robert H. Connery and Gerald Benjamin, *Rockefeller of New York: Executive Power in the Statehouse* (Ithaca, N.Y.: Cornell University Press, 1979), 41.

81 Quoted in Michael Kramer and Sam Roberts, *"I Never Wanted to Be Vice President of Anything": An Investigative Biography of Nelson Rockefeller* (New York: Basic Books, 1976), 310.

82 Quoted in Jules Witcover, *The Resurrection of Richard Nixon* (New York: G. P. Putnam's Sons, 1970), 183.

83 Connery and Benjamin, *Rockefeller of New York*, 50–51, 58.

84 Quoted in Dan T. Carter, *The Politics of Rage: George Wallace, the Origins of Conservatism, and the Transformation of American Politics* (New York: Simon & Schuster, 1995), 265.

85 Ibid., 264–265.

86 Quoted in Marshall Frady, *Wallace* (New York: Random House, 1996), 185.

87 Wallace later persuaded the legislature and voters to amend the state constitution and was elected to additional terms as governor in 1970, 1974, and 1982.

88 Quoted in Stephen Lesher, *George Wallace: American Populist* (Reading, Mass.: Addison-Wesley, 1994), 361.

89 DeGraffenreid had run a strong race against George Wallace in 1962, trailing by 7.2 percentage points in the primary and 11.8 points in the runoff.

90 Quoted in Carter, *Politics of Rage*, 290.

91 Quoted in Stephen E. Ambrose, *Nixon: The Triumph of a Politician, 1962–1972* (New York: Simon & Schuster, 1989), 71.

92 Richard Nixon, *RN* (New York: Grosset & Dunlap, 1978), 264.

93 Quoted in Terry Dietz, *Republicans and Vietnam, 1961–1968* (New York: Greenwood, 1986), 108.

94 Quoted in Perlstein, *Nixonland*, 159–160. In his memoirs, Nixon agreed: "I *was* a chronic campaigner, always out on the stump raising partisan hell." Nixon, *RN*, 278.

95 Quoted in Jules Witcover, *Very Strange Bedfellows: The Short and Unhappy Marriage of Richard Nixon and Spiro Agnew* (New York: PublicAffairs, 2007), 3.

96 Marc J. Hetherington, *Why Trust Matters: Declining Political Trust and the Demise of American Liberalism* (Princeton, N.J.: Princeton University Press, 2005), 19.

CHAPTER 3 JOHNSON, McCARTHY, KENNEDY, HUMPHREY

1 Quoted in Doris Kearns, *Lyndon Johnson and the American Dream* (New York: Harper & Row, 1976), 342.

2 Quoted in Townshend Hoopes, *The Limits of Intervention: An Inside Account of How the Johnson Policy of Escalation in Vietnam Was Reversed* (New York: David McKay, 1969), 29.

3 From March to November 1967, the share of the public favoring "total military victory" rose from 31 percent to 43 percent. Robert Dallek, *Flawed Giant: Lyndon Johnson and His Times, 1961–1973* (New York: Oxford University Press, 1998), 452.

4 Quoted in Tom Wells, *The War Within: America's Battle over Vietnam* (Berkeley: University of California Press, 1994), 154.

5 Quoted in Dallek, *Flawed Giant*, 277.

6 Quoted in Errol Morris, "Film: The Fog of War: Transcript" at http://www.errolmorris.com/film/fow_transcript.html.

7 Quoted in Dallek, *Flawed Giant*, 495.

8 For data on enrollment, see Table 143 of U.S. Bureau of the Census, *Statistical Abstract of the United States 1953* (Washington, D.C.: U.S. Government Printing Office, 1953) and Table 202 of the *Statistical Abstract of the United States 1973*.

9 James Fallows, "What Did You Do in the Class War, Daddy?" *Washington Monthly* (October 1975).

10 Quoted in Wells, *War Within*, 404.

11 George Q. Flynn, *The Draft, 1940–1973* (Lawrence: University Press of Kansas, 1993), 178.

12 John E. Mueller, *War, Presidents and Public Opinion* (New York: John Wiley, 1973), chaps. 2 and 6. Mueller points out that in contrast to Vietnam, much of the opposition to the Korean War came from the right.

13 Gail Collins, *When Everything Changed: The Amazing Journey of American Women from 1960 to the Present* (New York: Little, Brown, 2009), 183. See also Todd Gitlin, *The Sixties: Years of Hope, Days of Rage* (New York: Bantam Books, 1987), chap. 16.

14 David Maraniss, *They Marched into Sunlight: War and Peace, Vietnam and America, October 1967* (New York: Simon & Schuster, 2003), 400–401.

15 Quoted in Wells, *War Within*, 209.

16 Quoted in Nicholas Lemann, *The Promised Land: The Great Black Migration and How It Changed America* (New York: Alfred A. Knopf, 1991), 190; and Dallek, *Flawed Giant*, 367.

17 "Report of the National Advisory Commission on Civil Disorders—Summary of Report," at http://www.eisenhowerfoundation.org/docs/kerner.pdf.

18 "Johnson Unit Assails Whites in Negro Riots," *New York Times*, February 25, 1968.

19 Quoted in Randall B. Woods, *LBJ: Architect of American Ambition* (New York: Free Press, 2006), 695. As Mackenzie and Weisbrot have written, "Pouring federal money into neighborhoods that had been destroyed by the wanton violence of their own residents made no sense to many Americans, especially those who felt it was their money that was being poured." G. Calvin Mackenzie and Robert Weisbrot, *The Liberal Hour: Washington and the Politics of Change in the 1960s* (New York: Penguin, 2008), 361.

20 Aram Goudsouzian, *Down at the Crossroads: Civil Rights, Black Power, and the Meredith March against Fear* (New York: Farrar, Straus & Giroux, 2014), 252.

21 Quoted in Lewis L. Gould, *1968: The Election That Changed America* (Chicago: Ivan R. Dee, 1993), 63–64; and in Wells, *War Within*, 129.

22 Quoted in Jules Witcover, *Very Strange Bedfellows: The Short and Unhappy Marriage of Richard Nixon and Spiro Agnew* (New York: PublicAffairs, 2007), 11.

23 Patrick J. Buchanan, *The Greatest Comeback: How Richard Nixon Rose from Defeat to Create the New Majority* (New York: Crown Forum, 2014), 238.

24 Harry McPherson, *A Political Education: A Washington Memoir* (Boston: Little, Brown, 1972), 377–378, 382–383.

25 Quoted in Dallek, *Flawed Giant*, 396.

26 Maurice Isserman and Michael Kazin, *America Divided: The Civil War of the 1960s* (New York: Oxford University Press, 2000), 189.

27 Ibid., 398.

28 Donald F. Kettl, "The Economic Education of Lyndon Johnson: Guns, Butter, and Taxes," in *The Johnson Years, Volume 2: Vietnam, the Environment, and Science*, ed. Robert A. Divine (Lawrence: University Press of Kansas, 1987), 54–78.

29 Quoted in Goodwin, *Lyndon Johnson and the American Dream*, 251.

30 William vanden Heuvel and Milton Gwirtzman, *On His Own: RFK, 1964–68* (New York: Doubleday, 1970), 267.

31 Brian Dooley, *Robert Kennedy: The Final Years* (New York: St. Martin's, 1996), 99.

32 Quoted in Daniel J. Galvin, *Presidential Party Building: Dwight D. Eisenhower to George W. Bush* (Princeton, N.J.: Princeton University Press, 2010), 193–194.

33 Jan Jarboe Russell, *Lady Bird: A Biography of Mrs. Johnson* (New York: Scribner, 1999), 246, 282–284.

34 Johnson's fears were justified: he died of a massive heart attack five months after his sixty-fourth birthday.

35 Quoted in Lewis Chester, Godfrey Hodgson, and Bruce Page, *An American Melodrama: The Presidential Campaign of 1968* (New York: Viking, 1969), 183.

36 Glenn Fowler, "Lieut. Gen. James Gavin, 82, Dies; Champion and Critic of Military," *New York Times*, February 25, 1990.

37 Andrew Schlesinger and Stephen S. Schlesinger, *The Letters of Arthur Schlesinger, Jr.* (New York: Random House, 2013), 340.

38 Quoted in Jeff Shesol, *Mutual Contempt: Lyndon Johnson, Robert Kennedy, and the Feud That Defined a Decade* (New York: W. W. Norton, 1997), 378.

39   Quoted in ibid., 397.

40   Quoted in vanden Heuvel and Gwirtzman, *On His Own*, 268.

41   Their fears were justified. Both were defeated in November.

42   Quoted in Shesol, *Mutual Contempt*, 404.

43   Arthur M. Schlesinger, Jr., *Journals, 1952–2000* (New York: Penguin, 2007), 274.

44   Quoted in Rick Perlstein, *Nixonland: The Rise of a President and the Fracturing of America* (New York: Scribner, 2008), 222.

45   vanden Heuvel and Gwirtzman, *On His Own*, 280.

46   Peter S. Canellos, ed., *Last Lion: The Fall and Rise of Ted Kennedy* (New York: Simon & Schuster, 2009), 127–128.

47   William L. Chafe, *Unfinished Journey: America since World War II*, 7th ed. (New York: Oxford University Press, 2011), 340.

48   Quoted in Dominic Sandbrook, *Eugene McCarthy: The Rise and Fall of Postwar American Liberalism* (New York: Alfred A. Knopf, 2004), 162.

49   "Press Conference of Senator Eugene J. McCarthy, Senate Caucus Room, Washington D.C., November 30, 1968," http://www.4president.org/speeches /mccarthy1968announcement.htm.

50   William H. Chafe, *Never Stop Running: Allard Lowenstein and the Struggle to Save American Liberalism* (New York: Basic Books, 1993), 279.

51   Lawrence O'Brien, *No Final Victories: A Life in Politics from John F. Kennedy to Watergate* (Garden City, N.Y.: Doubleday, 1974), 215.

52   Quoted in Sandbrook, *Eugene McCarthy*, 175. The poll results are in George H. Gallup, *The Gallup Poll: Public Opinion, 1935–1971*, vol. 3 (New York: Random House, 1972), 2104.

53   Peter Braestrup, *Big Story: How the American Press and Television Reported and Interpreted the Crisis of Tet 1968 in Vietnam and Washington* (Boulder, Colo.: Westview, 1977).

54   Quoted in Clark Dougan and Stephen Weiss, *Nineteen Sixty-Eight: The Vietnam Experience* (Boston: Boston Publishing, 1983), 66.

55   Quoted in Gould, *1968*, 36.

56   Steven M. Gillon, *Politics and Vision: The ADA and American Liberalism, 1947– 1985* (New York: Oxford University Press, 1987), 207–212. The heads of the United Steelworkers of America, Communications Workers of America, and International Ladies Garment Workers resigned from the ADA board in protest of the McCarthy endorsement.

57   Quoted in George Rising, *Clean for Gene: Eugene McCarthy's 1968 Presidential Campaign* (Westport, Conn.: Praeger, 1997), 63.

58   Quoted in Douglas Brinkley, *Cronkite* (New York: Harper, 2012), 378.

59   The statement attributed to Johnson is debunked in W. Joseph Campbell, *Getting It Wrong: Ten of the Greatest Misreported Stories in American Journalism* (Berkeley: University of California Press, 2010), chap. 5.

60   Walter LaFeber, *The Deadly Bet: LBJ, Vietnam, and the 1968 Election* (Lanham, Md.: Rowman & Littlefield, 2005), 27–28.

61   Quoted in Jules Witcover, *The Year the Dream Died: Revisiting 1968 in America* (New York: Warner, 1997), 65.

62 Quoted in Shesol, *Mutual Contempt*, 414.

63 The Twenty-sixth Amendment, which became part of the Constitution in 1971, lowered the voting age to eighteen everywhere.

64 McCarthy staff member Steve Cohen's memo to volunteers is quoted in Richard T. Stout, *People: The Story of the Grassroots Movement That Found Eugene McCarthy and Is Transforming Our Politics Today* (New York: Harper & Row, 1970), 164.

65 Quoted in Clara Bingham, *Witness to the Revolution: Radicals, Resisters, Vets, Hippies, and the Year America Lost Its Mind and Found Its Soul* (New York: Random House, 2016), 166.

66 Richard N. Goodwin, *Remembering America: A Voice from the Sixties* (Boston: Little, Brown, 1988), 495.

67 Quoted in Kearns, *Lyndon Johnson and the American Dream*, 338.

68 Richard L. Strout, *TRB: Views and Perspectives on the Presidency* (New York: Macmillan, 1979), 319.

69 Quoted in Shesol, *Mutual Contempt*, 417.

70 Philip E. Converse, Warren E. Miller, Jerrold G. Rusk, and Arthur C. Wolfe, "Continuity and Change in American Politics: Parties and Issues in the 1968 Election," *American Political Science Review* 68 (December 1969): 1083–1105.

71 Herbert E. Alexander, *Financing the 1968 Election* (Lexington, Mass.: Lexington Books, 1971), 30.

72 Kennedy quoted in Thurston Clarke, *The Last Campaign: Robert F. Kennedy and 82 Days That Inspired America* (New York: Henry Holt, 2007), 33; and McGovern quoted in Merle Miller, *Lyndon: An Oral Biography* (New York: Ballantine Books, 1980), 616.

73 Quoted in Goodwin, *Remembering America*, 508–509.

74 Quoted in Gould, *1968*, 42.

75 Quoted in Theodore H. White, *The Making of the President 1968* (New York: Atheneum, 1969), 103.

76 Quoted in Larry Tye, *Bobby Kennedy: The Making of a Liberal Icon* (New York: Random House, 2016), 329; and Clarke, *Last Campaign*, 36.

77 Arthur M. Schlesinger, Jr., *Robert Kennedy and His Times* (Boston: Houghton Mifflin, 1978), 860.

78 Clark Clifford, with Richard Holbrooke, *Counsel to the President: A Memoir* (New York: Random House, 1991), 503–505.

79 Joseph A. Palermo, *In His Own Right: The Political Odyssey of Senator Robert F. Kennedy* (New York: Columbia University Press, 2001), 139.

80 Miller Center, University of Virginia, "Interview with Edward M. Kennedy (June 17, 2005)," Edward M. Kennedy Oral History, http://millercenter.org/oralhistory/interview/edward_m_kennedy_6-17-2005.

81 Arthur M. Schlesinger, Jr., *Journals,1952–2000* (New York: Penguin, 2007), 283.

82 Quoted in Sandbrook, *Eugene McCarthy*, 192.

83 Robert F. Kennedy, "Announcement of Candidacy for President, Washington, D.C., March 16, 1968" at http://www.4president.org/Speeches/rfk1968announcement.htm.

84   Quoted in Dennis Wainstock, *The Turning Point: The 1968 United States Presidential Campaign* (Jefferson, N.C.: McFarland, 1988), 30–31.

85   Miller Center, "Interview with Edward M. Kennedy."

86   Quoted in vanden Heuvel and Gwirtzman, *On His Own*, 318.

87   Bruce I. Miroff, *The Liberals' Moment: The McGovern Insurgency and the Identity Crisis of the Democratic Party* (Lawrence: University Press of Kansas, 2007), 18.

88   Quoted in Clarke, *Last Campaign*, 24–25.

89   Michael Cohen, *American Maelstrom: The 1968 Election and the Politics of Division* (New York: Oxford University Press, 2016), 148.

90   Quoted in Ray E. Boomheimer, *Robert F. Kennedy and the 1968 Indiana Primary* (Bloomington: Indiana University Press, 2008), 101.

91   Quoted in Shesol, *Mutual Contempt*, 425.

92   Gallup, *Gallup Poll*, vol. 3, 2112.

93   Quoted in Dallek, *Flawed Giant*, 528.

94   McPherson, *Political Education*, 264.

95   Maraniss, *They Marched into Sunlight*, 193.

96   Kearns, *Lyndon Johnson and the American Dream*, 313–317.

97   Quoted in Joseph A. Califano, *The Triumph and Tragedy of Lyndon Johnson: The White House Years* (New York: Simon & Schuster, 1991), 269. Busby's account of drafting the statement is in Horace Busby, *The Thirty-First of March: An Intimate Portrait of Lyndon Johnson's Final Days in Office* (New York: Farrar, Straus & Giroux, 2005), chap. 15.

98   Kearns, *Lyndon Johnson and the American Dream*, 343.

99   O'Brien, *No Final Victories*, 229.

100 Quoted in Gould, *1968*, 49.

101 Robert M. Collins, "The Economic Crisis of 1968 and the Waning of the 'American Century,'" *American Historical Review* 101 (April 1996): 396–422.

102 Quoted in Perlstein, *Nixonland*, 249; and Walter Isaacson and Evan Thomas, *The Wise Men: Six Friends and the World They Made* (New York: Simon & Schuster, 1986), 702. See also David M. Barrett, *Uncertain Warriors: Lyndon Johnson and His Vietnam Advisers* (Lawrence: University Press of Kansas, 1993), 144–152.

103 Collins, "Economic Crisis of 1968." See also Burton I. Kaufman, "Foreign Aid and the Balance-of-Payments Problem: Vietnam and Johnson's Foreign Economic Policy," in Divine, *Johnson Years*, 2:79–109. See also Kettl, "Economic Education of Lyndon Johnson."

104 Lyndon B. Johnson, "Televised Address, March 31, 1968," available at http://www.pbs.org/wgbh/americanexperience/features/primary-resources/lbjreelection/.

105 Hubert H. Humphrey, *The Education of a Public Man: My Life and Politics* (Garden City, N.Y.: Doubleday, 1976), 358.

106 Johnson, "Televised Address, March 31, 1968." See also Califano, *Triumph and Tragedy of Lyndon Johnson*, 270.

107 Quoted in Boomheimer, *Kennedy and the 1968 Indiana Primary*, 49–50.

108 Eugene McCarthy, *The Year of the People* (Garden City, N.Y.: Doubleday, 1969), 257.

109 Stout, *People*, 126–129.

110 Quoted in Wainstock, *Turning Point*, 67.

111 Chafe, *Unfinished Journey*, 351.

112 Quoted in Isserman and Kazin, *America Divided*, 227.

113 For an account of the riots, see Clay Risen, *A Nation on Fire: America in the Wake of the King Assassination* (New York: Wiley, 2009).

114 Quoted in Timothy N. Thurber, *Republicans and Race: The GOP's Frayed Relationship with African Americans, 1945–1976* (Lawrence: University Press of Kansas, 2013), 271.

115 Quoted in James R. Jones, "Behind LBJ's Decision Not to Run in '68," *New York Times*, April 18, 1988; and in Carl Solberg, *Hubert Humphrey: A Biography* (New York. W. W. Norton, 1984), 322, 323.

116 Quoted in Taylor E. Dark, *The Unions and the Democrats: An Enduring Alliance* (Ithaca, N.Y.: Cornell University Press, 1999), 82.

117 Humphrey, *Education of a Public Man*, 361.

118 "Interview II with George Ball (July 9, 1971)," Lyndon B. Johnson Oral History Collection, available at http://www.lbjlibrary.net/assets/documents/archives /oral_histories/ball_g/BALL-G2.PDF.

119 Steven M. Gillon, *The Democrats' Dilemma: Walter F. Mondale and the Liberal Legacy* (New York: Columbia University Press, 1992), 112.

120 Michael Nelson, *A Heartbeat Away* (Washington, D.C.: Brookings Institution, 1988), chap. 5. See also Joel K. Goldstein, *The White House Vice Presidency: The Path to Significance, Mondale to Biden* (Lawrence: University Press of Kansas, 2016).

121 Quoted in Califano, *Triumph and Tragedy of Lyndon Johnson*, 292.

122 Solberg, *Hubert Humphrey*, 332.

123 Strout, *TRB*, 337.

124 With 40 percent, Humphrey led among Democratic voters over Kennedy (31 percent) and McCarthy (19 percent). The order was different among self-identified independents: McCarthy (36 percent), Humphrey (27 percent), Kennedy (23 percent). Gallup, *Gallup Poll*, vol. 3, 2127.

125 O'Brien, *No Final Victories*, 236.

126 Quoted in Witcover, *Year the Dream Died*, 176.

127 Quoted in Boomheimer, *Kennedy and the 1968 Indiana Primary*, 56.

128 David Frost, *The Presidential Debate, 1968* (New York: Stein & Day, 1968), 26.

129 Quoted in Witcover, *Year the Dream Died*, 201.

130 Ben Stavis, *We Were the Campaign: New Hampshire to Chicago for McCarthy* (Boston: Beacon Press, 1969), 51, 53.

131 Jeremy Larner, *Nobody Knows: Reflections on the McCarthy Campaign of 1968* (New York: Macmillan, 1969), 81.

132 Quoted in Boomheimer, *Kennedy and the 1968 Indiana Primary*, 6.

133 Quoted in Jeff Greenfield, *Then Everything Changed: Stunning Alternate Histories of American Politics: JFK, RFK, Carter, Ford, Reagan* (New York: G. P. Putnam's Sons, 2011), 124.

134 Quoted in Witcover, *Year the Dream Died*, 154–155.

135 Quoted in ibid., 177.

136 Quoted in Schlesinger, *Robert Kennedy and His Times*, 882.

137 Quoted in Clarke, *Last Campaign*, 179.

138 Quoted in Perlstein, *Nixonland*, 267.

139 Quoted in Chester, Hodgson, and Page, *American Melodrama*, 164.

140 Frost, *Presidential Debate, 1968*, 121.

141 Quoted in Clarke, *Last Campaign*, 219.

142 Jules Witcover, *85 Days: The Last Campaign of Robert Kennedy* (New York: G. P. Putnam's Sons, 1969), 186.

143 Tom Wicker, "The Impact of Indiana," *New York Times*, May 8, 1968.

144 Quoted in Boomheimer, *Robert F. Kennedy and the 1968 Indiana Primary*, 120.

145 Quoted in White, *Making of the President 1968*, 204.

146 McCarthy, *Year of the People*, 150.

147 Quoted in Witcover, *Year the Dream Died*, 217.

148 Quoted in Wainstock, *Turning Point*, 75.

149 Quoted in ibid., 223.

150 Quoted in Chester, Hodgson, and Page, *American Melodrama*, 302.

151 Quoted in ibid., 331.

152 Quoted in Witcover, *Year the Dream Died*, 234.

153 Quoted in ibid., 344.

154 Quoted in vanden Heuvel and Gwirtzman, *On His Own*, 87.

155 Quoted in Gould, *1968*, 83.

156 vanden Heuvel and Gwirtzman, *On His Own*, 123.

157 "Interview XXII with Lawrence F. O'Brien (June 19, 1987)," Lyndon B. Johnson Oral History Collection, available at http://www.lbjlibrary.net/assets/docu ments/archives/oral_histories/obrien_l/OBRIEN22.PDF.

158 Quoted in Schlesinger, *Robert Kennedy and His Times*, 913.

159 Goodwin, *Remembering America*, 537. Ronald Steel argues that after seeing how disrespectfully both John and Robert Kennedy had treated Secretary of State Dean Rusk, McCarthy would surely have turned down the job under any circumstances. Steel, *In Love with Night: The American Romance with Robert Kennedy* (New York: Simon & Schuster, 2000), 187.

160 Converse et al., "Continuity and Change in American Politics," 1090.

161 See the appendix to Richard M. Scammon and Ben J. Wattenberg, *The Real Majority: An Extraordinary Examination of the American Electorate* (New York: Coward, McCann & Geoghegan, 1970), 339.

162 The document is reprinted as the appendix to vanden Heuvel and Gwirtzman, *On His Own*.

CHAPTER 4   REAGAN, ROMNEY, NIXON, ROCKEFELLER

1   Richard Nixon, *RN: The Memoirs of Richard Nixon* (New York: Grosset & Dunlap, 1978), 297.

2   Ellsworth made his statement as part of CBS News's live coverage of the Republican National Convention on August 8, 1968, as found in the recording of the broadcast available at the Vanderbilt Television News Archive, Vanderbilt University, Nashville, Tenn.

3   William Safire, *Before the Fall: An Inside View of the Pre-Watergate White House* (New York: Doubleday, 1975), 43.

4   Quoted in ibid., 289.

5   Robert J. Donovan, *The Future of the Republican Party* (New York: New American Library, 1964), 73.

6   Quoted in Rick Perlstein, *Nixonland: The Rise of a President and the Fracturing of America* (New York: Scribner, 2008), 184.

7   Quoted in Lou Cannon, *Governor Reagan: The Rise to Power* (New York: Public Affairs, 2003), 260.

8   Ibid., chap. 18.

9   For a detailed account if these events, see Thomas C. Reed, *The Reagan Enigma, 1964–1980* (Los Angeles: Figueroa Press, 2015), chap. 11 and Appendix B.

10 Quoted in Jules Witcover, *The Year the Dream Died: Revisiting 1968 in America* (New York: Warner, 1997), 14.

11 Michael Nelson, "Who Vies for President?" in *Presidential Selection,* ed. Alexander Heard and Michael Nelson (Durham, N.C.: Duke University Press, 1987), 120–154.

12 Herbert E. Alexander, *Financing the 1968 Election* (Lexington, Mass.: Lexington Books, 1971), 10.

13 Quoted in Clark Raymond Mollenhoff, *George Romney: Mormon in Politics* (New York: Meredith, 1968), 337. See also the account of the "brainwashing" episode in Theodore H. White, *The Making of the President 1968* (New York: Atheneum, 1969), 66–69.

14 Quoted in Geoffrey Kabaservice, *Rule and Ruin: The Downfall of Moderation and the Destruction of the Republican Party from Eisenhower to the Tea Party* (New York: Oxford University Press, 2012), 220.

15 "George Romney Brainwash Interview on WKBD-TV 50," available at http://www.youtube.com/watch?v=fSdSiBehQpI.

16 Jonathan Alter, *The Center Holds: Obama and His Enemies* (New York: Simon & Schuster, 2013), 209.

17 Paul Taylor, *See How They Run: Electing the President in a Mediaocracy* (New York: Alfred A. Knopf, 1990), 86–89.

18 Quoted in Witcover, *Year the Dream Died,* 15.

19 Quoted in Perlstein, *Nixonland,* 204–205.

20 Quoted in Witcover, *Year the Dream Died,* 15.

21 Richard J. Whalen, *Catch the Falling Flag: A Republican's Challenge to His Party* (Boston: Houghton Mifflin, 1972), 24.

22 Quoted in Jules Witcover, *The Resurrection of Richard Nixon* (New York: G. P. Putnam's Sons, 1970), 219. The *Time* cover story was called "Anchors Away."

23 Richard Norton Smith, *On His Own Terms: A Life of Nelson Rockefeller* (New York: Random House, 2014), 497.

24 Quoted in Witcover, *Resurrection of Richard Nixon,* 171.

25 Patrick J. Buchanan, *The Greatest Comeback: How Richard Nixon Rose from Defeat to Create the New Majority* (New York: Crown Forum, 2014), 93.

26 David Halberstam, *The Powers That Be* (New York: Alfred A. Knopf, 1979), 589–590.

27 Robert B. Semple, Jr., "The Nixon Phenomenon," *New York Times Magazine*, January 21, 1968, 24–25, 77–83. Nixon remained grateful for the article: in May 1970 he told Haldeman, "*No one* from the White House staff under any circumstances [is] to answer any call or see anybody from the *New York Times* except for Semple." Quoted in Tom Wells, *The War Within: America's Battle over Vietnam* (Berkeley: University of California Press, 1994), 449.

28 Quoted in Wells, *War Within*, 303.

29 Joe McGinniss, *The Selling of the President 1968* (New York: Simon & Schuster, 1969). See also Leonard Garment, *Crazy Rhythm: My Journey from Brooklyn, Jazz, and Wall Street to Nixon's White House, Watergate, and Beyond* (New York: Times Books, 1997), 129–134.

30 Donald T. Critchlow, *Phyllis Schlafly and Grassroots Conservatism: A Woman's Crusade* (Princeton, N.J.: Princeton University Press, 2005), 186.

31 Quoted in Harry S. Dent, *The Prodigal South Returns to Power* (New York: John Wiley & Sons, 1978), 77.

32 Evan Thomas, *Being Nixon: A Man Divided* (New York: Random House, 2015), 156.

33 Quoted in Perlstein, *Nixonland*, 277. Ironically, Nixon picked up "silent center" from Paul Douglas, the liberal Democratic former senator from Illinois.

34 Richard M. Nixon, "Asia after Viet Nam," *Foreign Affairs* 46 (October 1967), 111–125.

35 Richard M. Nixon, "What Has Happened to America?" *Reader's Digest* (October 1967), 49–54.

36 Quoted in Semple, "Nixon Phenomenon."

37 Whalen, *Catch the Falling Flag*, 12.

38 Quoted in Safire, *Before the Fall*, 101.

39 Quoted in Stephen Lesher, *George Wallace: American Populist* (Reading, Mass.: Addison-Wesley, 1994), 403.

40 Quoted in Dennis Wainstock, *The Turning Point: The 1968 United States Presidential Campaign* (Jefferson, N.C.: McFarland, 1988), 39.

41 Quoted in White, *Making of the President 1968*, 7.

42 Quoted in Wainstock, *Turning Point*, 38; Witcover, *Resurrection of Richard Nixon*, 240.

43 Quoted in Wainstock, *Turning Point*, 40.

44 Richard Melvin Eyre, "George Romney in 1968, From Front-runner to Dropout, An Analysis of Cause," M.A. thesis, Department of Political Science, Brigham Young University, Provo, Utah, 1969.

45 Quoted in Witcover, *Resurrection of Richard Nixon*, 183.

46 Quoted in Michael Kramer and Sam Roberts, *"I Never Wanted to Be Vice President of Anything": An Investigative Biography of Nelson Rockefeller* (New York: Basic Books, 1976), 287.

47 Quoted in ibid., 7.

48 Witcover, *Year the Dream Died*, 88.

49   Quoted in Jules Witcover, *Very Strange Bedfellows: The Short and Unhappy Marriage of Richard Nixon and Spiro Agnew* (New York: PublicAffairs, 2007), 9.

50   Quoted in ibid., 30.

51   A draft of the speech constitutes the appendix to Whalen, *Catch the Falling Flag*, 283–294.

52   Quoted in Edward W. Knappman, ed., *Presidential Election 1968* (New York: Facts on File, 1970), 67.

53   Stephen E. Ambrose, *Nixon: The Triumph of a Politician, 1962–1972* (New York: Simon & Schuster, 1989), 144.

54   Mark Kurlansky, *1968: The Year That Rocked the World* (New York: Ballantine, 2004), 207.

55   James Rosen, *The Strong Man: John Mitchell and the Secrets of Watergate* (New York: Doubleday, 2008), 39.

56   Buchanan, *Greatest Comeback*, 200.

57   Geoffrey Kabaservice, *Rule and Ruin: The Downfall of Moderation and the Destruction of the Republican Party from Eisenhower to the Tea Party* (New York: Oxford University Press, 2012), 53.

58   Tom Wicker, *One of Us: Richard Nixon and the American Dream* (New York: Random House, 1991), 330.The thirteen states included all the nation's largest states—New York, California, Texas, Ohio, Pennsylvania, Illinois, New Jersey, and Massachusetts—plus states where Rockefeller thought his candidacy would be popular: Oregon, Maryland, Washington, and (mostly because the St. Louis and Kansas City media markets reached into other states) Missouri.

59   Smith, *On His Own Terms*, 500.

60   Quoted in Witcover, *Year the Dream Died*, 196.

61   Alexander, *Financing the 1968 Election*, 10; Herbert E. Alexander, *Money in Politics* (Washington, D.C.: PublicAffairs Press, 1972), 61.

62   Quoted in Cannon, *Governor Reagan*, 261.

63   Quoted in Witcover, *Year the Dream Died*, 211.

64   Buchanan, *Greatest Comeback*, 261.

65   Alexander, *Financing the 1968 Election*, 10.

66   Reed, *Reagan Enigma*, 147.

67   Quoted in Gene Kopelson, *Reagan's 1968 Dress Rehearsal: Ike, RFK, and Reagan's Emergence as a World Statesman* (Los Angeles: Figueroa Press, 2016), 603.

68   Allen J. Matusow, *The Unraveling of America: A History of Liberalism in the 1960s* (New York: Harper & Row, 1984), 401.

69   Nixon himself acknowledged that southern Republican leaders "in their hearts would have preferred Reagan, but they had been burned by Goldwater and had learned a lesson of political pragmatism." Nixon, *RN*, 287.

70   Quoted in Perlstein, *Nixonland*, 283.

71   *Green v. County School Board of New Kent County*, 391 U.S. 430 (1968). See Joseph Crespino, *Strom Thurmond's America* (New York: Hill & Wang, 2012), 213–214.

72   Condemned by Republican leaders such as Nixon and conservative leaders such as *National Review* editor William F. Buckley, Jr., some ultraconservative

John Birch Society members did shift their allegiance from Goldwater to Wallace.

73 Quoted in Witcover, *Resurrection of Richard Nixon*, 198.

74 Jody Carlson, *George C. Wallace and the Politics of Powerlessness: The Wallace Campaigns for the Presidency, 1964–1976* (New Brunswick, N.J.: Transaction Books, 1981), 74.

75 *Williams v. Rhodes*, 393 U.S. 23 (1968). The court decided that Ohio's election law gave the Republicans and Democrats such an advantage over independent candidates and third parties as to deny voters the constitutionally guaranteed "equal protection of the laws."

76 Petition signing often represents more a response to a personal request than a statement of belief. In a study of Wallace petition signers in one western city in October 1968, only 27.3 percent said they intended to vote for Wallace, less than the 34.0 percent who planned to vote for Nixon. Allen R. Wilcox and Leonard B. Weinberg, "Petition-Signing in the 1968 Election," *Western Political Quarterly* 24 (December 1971): 731–739.

77 Brewer ended up losing this election to George Wallace.

78 Quoted in Marshall Frady, *Wallace* (New York: Random House, 1996), 246.

79 Quoted in Lesher, *George Wallace*, 367.

80 Quoted in Lewis Chester, Godfrey Hodgson, and Bruce Page, *An American Melodrama: The Presidential Campaign of 1968* (New York: Viking, 1969), 282, 283. A bit taken aback by the passion he was rousing, Wallace later slightly tempered the threatened violence of this line from "lays down in front of" to "feels like laying down in front of."

81 Quoted in John Judis, *The Populist Explosion: How the Great American Recession Transformed American and European Politics* (New York: Columbia Global Reports, 2016), 35.

82 "The Omaha Platform," available at http://historymatters.gmu.edu/d/5361/.

83 "New York Campaign Speech by George C. Wallace (1968)," in *Historic Documents on Presidential Elections 1787–1988*, ed. Michael Nelson (Washington, D.C.: Congressional Quarterly, 1992), 566–573; see also Thomas Byrne Edsall and Mary D. Edsall, *Chain Reaction: The Impact of Race, Rights, and Taxes on American Politics* (New York: W. W. Norton, 1991), 77.

84 Quoted in Lewis L. Gould, *1968: The Election That Changed America* (Chicago: Ivan R. Dee, 1993), 66.

85 Donald I. Warren, *The Radical Center: Middle Americans and the Politics of Alienation* (Notre Dame, Ind.: University of Notre Dame Press, 1976).

86 Quoted in Frady, *Wallace*, 143.

87 Quoted in ibid., 9.

88 Quoted in John Dickerson, *Whistlestop: My Favorite Stories from Presidential Campaign History* (New York: Twelve, 2016), 373.

CHAPTER 5 THE CONVENTIONS

1 Quoted in Stephen E. Ambrose, *Nixon: The Triumph of a Politician, 1962–1972* (New York: Simon & Schuster, 1989), 157.

2   Theodore H. White, *The Making of the President 1968* (New York: Atheneum, 1969), 167, 387–388.
3   Norman Mailer, *Miami and the Siege of Chicago* (New York: New York Review of Books, 1968), 44.
4   Archibald M. Crossley and Helen M. Crossley, "Polling in 1968," *Public Opinion Quarterly* 33 (Spring 1969): 1–16.
5   Lou Cannon, *Governor Reagan: The Rise to Power* (New York: PublicAffairs, 2003), 270.
6   Quoted in Dennis Wainstock, *The Turning Point: The 1968 United States Presidential Campaign* (Jefferson, N.C.: McFarland, 1988), 92.
7   Harry S. Dent, *The Prodigal South Returns to Power* (New York: John Wiley & Sons, 1978), 80.
8   William Rusher, "The Blunder of 1968," *American Spectator*, April 2006, 16–19; Cannon, *Governor Reagan*, 265.
9   Quoted in Lewis Chester, Godfrey Hodgson, and Bruce Page, *An American Melodrama: The Presidential Campaign of 1968* (New York: Viking, 1969), 447–448.
10   Quoted in Cannon, *Governor Reagan*, 266.
11   Quoted in Chester et al., *American Melodrama*, 465.
12   Quoted in Lewis L. Gould, *1968: The Election That Changed America* (Chicago: Ivan R. Dee, 1993), 102.
13   Quoted in Chester et al., *American Melodrama*, 437.
14   Quoted in ibid., 440.
15   Quoted in Wainstock, *Turning Point*, 106.
16   Quoted in Chester et al., *American Melodrama*, 462.
17   Quoted in Gould, *1968*, 104.
18   Quoted in Rick Perlstein, *Nixonland: The Rise of a President and the Fracturing of America* (New York: Scribner, 2008), 298.
19   Miller Center, University of Virginia, "Interview with Stuart Spencer," November 15–16, 2001, http://millercenter.org/oralhistory/interview/stuart-spencer.
20   Unless otherwise noted, all quotations from the Republican and Democratic conventions were transcribed by the author from the video recordings of CBS News's live coverage of the proceedings made by the Vanderbilt University Television News Archive.
21   In this book, the South is defined as the eleven states of the Confederacy: Alabama, Arkansas, Florida, Georgia, Louisiana, Mississippi, North Carolina, South Carolina, Tennessee, Texas, and Virginia. The border states are Kentucky, Maryland, Missouri, Oklahoma, and West Virginia. The Pacific states are Alaska, California, Hawaii, Oregon, and Washington. The Mountain West states are Arizona, Colorado, Idaho, Montana, Nevada, New Mexico, North Dakota, South Dakota, Utah, and Wyoming. The Midwest consists of Illinois, Indiana, Iowa, Kansas, Michigan, Minnesota, Nebraska, Ohio, and Wisconsin. Connecticut, Delaware, the District of Columbia, Maine, Massachusetts, New Hampshire, New Jersey, New York, Pennsylvania, Rhode Island, and Vermont comprise the Northeast.
22   "The Making of the President 1968," CBS television documentary, September

8, 1969, available at http://www.amazon.com/The-Making-President-1968/dp/B00779UACK.

23 Quoted in Jules Witcover, *The Year the Dream Died: Revisiting 1968 in America* (New York: Warner, 1997), 303.

24 William Rorabaugh, *The Real Making of the President: Kennedy, Nixon, and the 1960 Election* (Lawrence: University Press of Kansas, 2009), 166. Kennedy is quoted in Timothy N. Thurber, *Republicans and Race: The GOP's Frayed Relationship with African Americans, 1945–1976* (Lawrence: University Press of Kansas, 2013), 128.

25 Quoted in Jules Witcover, *Very Strange Bedfellows: The Short and Unhappy Marriage of Richard Nixon and Spiro Agnew* (New York: PublicAffairs, 2007), 26.

26 Quoted in ibid.

27 Quoted in Joseph Crespino, *Strom Thurmond's America* (New York: Hill & Wang, 2012), 220.

28 Michael Nelson, "George Bush: Texan, Conservative," in *41: Inside the George H. W. Bush Presidency*, ed. Michael Nelson and Barbara A. Perry (Ithaca, N.Y.: Cornell University Press, 2014), 27–47.

29 William Safire, *Before the Fall: An Inside View of the Pre-Watergate White House* (New York: Doubleday, 1975), 56.

30 Richard Nixon, *RN: The Memoirs of Richard Nixon* (New York: Grosset & Dunlap, 1978), 312.

31 As part of a plea bargain that enabled him to avoid prison, Agnew resigned as vice president on October 12, 1973.

32 Stephen Hess and David S. Broder, *The Republican Establishment: The Present and Future of the GOP* (New York: Harper & Row, 1967), 6–9.

33 Kevin M. Kruse, *White Flight: Atlanta and the Making of Modern Conservatism* (Princeton, N.J.: Princeton University Press, 2005), 253.

34 "Richard Nixon's Acceptance Speech to the Republican National Convention," in *Historic Documents on Presidential Elections, 1787–1988*, ed. Michael Nelson (Washington, D.C.: Congressional Quarterly, 1991), 557–565.

35 Safire, *Before the Fall*, 55.

36 Geoffrey Kabaservice, *Rule and Ruin: The Downfall of Moderation and the Destruction of the Republican Party from Eisenhower to the Tea Party* (New York: Oxford University Press, 2012), 246.

37 Quoted in Richard T. Stout, *People: The Story of the Grassroots Movement That Found Eugene McCarthy and Is Transforming Our Politics Today* (New York: Harper & Row, 1970), 320.

38 Jeremy Larner, *Nobody Knows: Reflections on the McCarthy Campaign of 1968* (New York: Macmillan, 1969), 132–133. With support from a broad coalition that included the National Rifle Association, the Gun Control Act of 1968 was passed into law, a modest piece of legislation that banned the sale of most firearms through the mail.

39 Quoted in Stout, *People*, 248.

40 Quoted in Dominic Sandbrook, *Eugene McCarthy: The Rise and Fall of Postwar American Liberalism* (New York: Alfred A. Knopf, 2004), 206.

41 George McGovern, *Grassroots: The Autobiography of George McGovern* (New York: Random House, 1977), 118.

42 Joshua M. Glasser, *The Eighteen-Day Running Mate: McGovern, Eagleton, and a Campaign in Crisis* (New Haven, Conn.: Yale University Press, 2012), 11.

43 Quoted in White, *Making of the President 1968*, 311.

44 Hubert H. Humphrey, *The Education of a Public Man: My Life and Politics* (Garden City, N.Y.: Doubleday, 1976), 375.

45 Ken Hughes, *Chasing Shadows: The Nixon Tapes, the Chennault Affair, and the Origins of Watergate* (Charlottesville: University of Virginia Press, 2014), 11.

46 Quoted in Wells, *War Within*, 252.

47 Doris Kearns, *Lyndon Johnson and the American Dream* (New York: Harper & Row, 1976), 351.

48 Norman Mailer calculated that of the 834 delegates seated near the podium, Humphrey ended up with 730. Of the 720 seated farthest away, he only received 297. Mailer, *Miami and the Siege of Chicago*, 113–114.

49 Quoted in Chester et al., *American Melodrama*, 404–405.

50 Quoted in Witcover, *Year the Dream Died*, 275.

51 Quoted in Carl Solberg, *Hubert Humphrey: A Biography* (New York: W. W. Norton, 1984), 342.

52 Quoted in ibid., 348.

53 Secretary of Defense Clark Clifford quoting Johnson in Witcover, *Year the Dream Died*, 312.

54 Ted Van Dyk, *Heroes, Hacks, and Fools: Memoirs from the Political Inside* (Seattle: University of Washington Press, 2007), 74.

55 Quoted in ibid.

56 Humphrey, *Education of a Public Man*, 6.

57 Quoted in Albert Eisele, *Almost to the Presidency: A Biography of Two American Politicians* (Blue Earth, Minn.: Piper, 1972), 337.

58 Quoted in Witcover, *Year the Dream Died*, 309.

59 Adam Cohen and Elizabeth Taylor, *American Pharaoh: Mayor Richard J. Daley, His Battle for Chicago and the Nation* (Boston: Little, Brown, 2000), 446–447.

60 Humphrey, *Education of a Public Man*, 384–385.

61 Quoted in Cohen and Taylor, *American Pharaoh*, 455.

62 Quoted in White, *Making of the President 1968*, 101.

63 Mark Kurlansky, *1968: The Year That Rocked the World* (New York: Ballantine, 2004), 276.

64 Quoted in Stout, *People*, 326.

65 "The McGovern-Fraser Commission Report," in Nelson, *Historic Documents on Presidential Elections*, 574–584.

66 The only convention to meet later was the 1864 Democratic convention, which met August 29–31.

67 John W. Soule and James W. Clarke, "Issue Conflict and Consensus: A Comparative Study of Democratic and Republican Delegates to the 1968 National Conventions," *Journal of Politics* 33 (February 1971): 72–91.

68 See the account in Justin A. Nelson, "Drafting Lyndon Johnson: The Presi-

dent's Secret Role in the 1968 Democratic Convention," *Presidential Studies Quarterly* 30 (December 2000): 688–714.

69 John Connally with Mickey Hershkowitz, *In History's Shadow: An American Odyssey* (New York: Hyperion, 1993), 203.

70 Quoted in Randall B. Woods, *LBJ: Architect of American Ambition* (New York: Free Press, 2006), 863.

71 Joseph A. Califano, *The Triumph and Tragedy of Lyndon Johnson: The White House Years* (New York: Simon & Schuster, 1991), 321.

72 Quoted in James Reston, Jr., *The Lone Star: The Life of John Connally* (New York: Harper & Row, 1989), 359, 362.

73 "Interview IV with Carl Albert (August 13, 1969)," Lyndon B. Johnson Oral History Collection, available at http://www.lbjlibrary.net/assets/documents/archives/oral_histories/albert/ALBER-C4.PDF.

74 Quoted in Richard N. Goodwin, *Remembering America: A Voice from the Sixties* (Boston: Little, Brown, 1988), 6.

75 Califano, *Triumph and Tragedy of Lyndon Johnson*, 322.

76 Miller Center, University of Virginia, "Interview with David Burke (April 2008)," Edward M. Kennedy Oral History, http://millercenter.org/oralhistory/interview/david-burke-2008.

77 Arthur M. Schlesinger, Jr., *Journals,1952–2000* (New York: Penguin, 2007), 298.

78 Miller Center, University of Virginia, "Interview with Milton Gwirtzman (August 2009)," Edward M. Kennedy Oral History, http://millercenter.org/oralhistory/interview/milton_gwirtzman_08-2009.

79 Quoted in White, *Making of the President 1968*, 333.

80 Edward M. Kennedy, *True Compass: A Memoir* (New York: Twelve, 2009), 273.

81 Miller Center, University of Virginia, "Interview with Edward M. Kennedy (June 17, 2005)," Edward M. Kennedy Oral History, http://millercenter.org/oralhistory/interview/edward_m_kennedy_6-17-2005.

82 Quoted in Adam Clymer, *Edward M. Kennedy: A Biography* (New York: William Morrow, 1999), 125–126.

83 Quoted in Solberg, *Hubert Humphrey*, 359.

84 See the account in Byron E. Shafer, *Quiet Revolution: The Struggle for the Democratic Party and the Shaping of Post-Reform Politics* (New York: Russell Sage, 1983).

85 Quoted in ibid., 34.

86 Timothy N. Thurber, *The Politics of Equality: Hubert H. Humphrey and the African American Freedom Struggle* (New York: Columbia University Press, 1999), 209.

87 Quoted in ibid., 353.

88 Humphrey, *Education of a Public Man*, 388.

89 Ibid., 389.

90 Ibid., 390.

91 Quoted in Kurlansky, *1968*, 284.

92 Quoted in Stout, *People*, 363.

93 Quoted in White, *Making of the President 1968*, 353.

94 Mailer, *Miami and the Siege of Chicago*, 180.

95 Quoted in Witcover, *Year the Dream Died*, 336–337.

96 Quoted in ibid., 326.

97 Ibid.

98 Tom Wicker, *One of Us: Richard Nixon and the American Dream* (New York: Random House, 1991), 354.

99 See the account in Scott Stossel, *Sarge: The Life and Times of Sargent Shriver* (New York: Smithsonian Books, 2004).

100 Quoted in Solberg, *Hubert Humphrey*, 366.

101 Quoted in Witcover, *Year the Dream Died*, 338.

102 Humphrey, *Education of a Public Man*, 391.

103 Quoted in Theo Lippman, Jr., and Donald C. Hansen, *Muskie* (New York: W. W. Norton, 1971), 23. See also Max M. Kampelman, "Hubert Humphrey: Political Scientist," *PS: Political Science and Politics* 11 (Spring 1978): 228–236.

104 Hubert H. Humphrey, "Address Accepting the Presidential Nomination at the Democratic National Convention in Chicago," available at http://www.presidency.ucsb.edu/ws/index.php?pid=25964.

105 Humphrey, *Education of a Public Man*, 396.

106 Quoted in Sandbrook, *Eugene McCarthy*, 212.

107 Quoted in Wainstock, *Turning Point*, 146; and White, *Making of the President 1968*, 390.

CHAPTER 6 THE GENERAL ELECTION: SEPTEMBER

1 Quoted in Rick Perlstein, *Nixonland: The Rise of a President and the Fracturing of America* (New York: Scribner, 2008), 52.

2 All Gallup Poll results reported in this chapter may be found in George H. Gallup, *The Gallup Poll: Public Opinion, 1935–1971*, vol. 3 (1959–1971) (New York: Random House, 1972).

3 Quoted in Jules Witcover, *The Resurrection of Richard Nixon* (New York: G. P. Putnam's Sons, 1970), 367.

4 Members of the Business Council, who had divided almost evenly in their financial support for Republicans and Democrats in 1964, broke three to one for Nixon in 1968. Herbert E. Alexander and Harold B. Meyers, "A Financial Landslide for the GOP," *Fortune* (March 1970).

5 Herbert E. Alexander, *Financing the 1968 Election* (Lexington, Mass.: Lexington Books, 1971), 87; and Dan T. Carter, *The Politics of Rage: George Wallace, the Origins of Conservatism, and the Transformation of American Politics* (New York: Simon & Schuster, 1995), 336–337.

6 Michael Kazin, *The Populist Persuasion: An American History* (New York: Basic Books, 1995), 236.

7 Carl Solberg, *Hubert Humphrey: A Biography* (New York. W. W. Norton, 1984), 373, 391; and Dennis Wainstock, *The Turning Point: The 1968 United States Presidential Campaign* (Jefferson, N.C.: McFarland, 1988), 163.

8 Lawrence O'Brien, *No Final Victories: A Life in Politics from John F. Kennedy to Watergate* (Garden City, N.Y.: Doubleday, 1974), 258.

9 Ibid., 265.

10 Lewis Chester, Godfrey Hodgson, and Bruce Page, *An American Melodrama: The Presidential Campaign of 1968* (New York: Viking, 1969), 632.

11 David S. Broder, "Election of 1968," in *History of Presidential Elections, 1789–1968*, vol. 4, ed. Arthur M. Schlesinger, Jr., and Fred L. Israel (New York: Chelsea House, 1971), 3743.

12 Chester et al., *American Melodrama*, 612.

13 Tom Wells, *The War Within: America's Battle over Vietnam* (Berkeley: University of California Press, 1994), 325.

14 William Safire, *Before the Fall: An Inside View of the Pre-Watergate White House* (New York: Doubleday, 1975), 57.

15 Gabriel Sherman, *The Loudest Voice in the Room: How the Brilliant, Bombastic Roger Ailes Built Fox News—and Divided a Country* (New York: Random House, 2014), 50.

16 Theodore H. White, *The Making of the President 1968* (New York: Atheneum, 1969), 371; and Joe McGinniss, *The Selling of the President 1968* (New York: Simon & Schuster, 1969). In the view of Kathleen Hall Jamieson, McGinniss's book "does not make the case it claims"—namely, that Nixon's advisers promulgated a false version of the candidate. See Jamieson, *Packaging the Presidency: A History and Criticism of Presidential Campaign Advertising* (New York: Oxford University Press, 1984), 258–269.

17 McGinniss, *Selling of the President*, 89–90; and "Vietnam," available at http://www.livingroomcandidate.org/commercials/1968. Some Republicans objected to the final image on the screen, which was a soldier with "Love" written on his helmet. The Nixon campaign removed the image, only to find out that Love was his name.

18 Alexander, *Financing the 1968 Election*, 92; Jamieson, *Packaging the Presidency*, 234.

19 John G. Geer, *In Defense of Negativity: Attack Ads in Presidential Campaigns* (Chicago: University of Chicago Press, 2006), 91.

20 Quoted in Lewis L. Gould, *1968: The Election That Changed America* (Chicago: Ivan R. Dee, 1993), 112.

21 Quoted in Chester et al., *American Melodrama*, 682.

22 William F. Gavin, *Speechwright: An Insider's Take on Political Rhetoric* (East Lansing: Michigan State University Press, 2011), 54.

23 Quoted in McGinniss, *Selling of the President*, 15; Jules Witcover, *The Year the Dream Died: Revisiting 1968 in America* (New York: Warner, 1997); and *ABC Evening News*, September 19, 1968. All quotations from network news programs are from original recordings of the broadcasts available at the Vanderbilt Television News Archive, Vanderbilt University, Nashville, Tenn.

24 Quoted in Safire, *Before the Fall*, 64.

25 Stephen E. Ambrose, *Nixon: The Triumph of a Politician, 1962–1972* (New York: Simon & Schuster, 1989), 186.

26 Quoted in Chester et al., *American Melodrama*, 625.

27 Quoted in White, *Making of the President 1968*, 379–380.

28 Norman Mailer, *Miami and the Siege of Chicago* (New York: New York Review of Books, 1968), 172.

29 Quoted in Solberg, *Hubert Humphrey*, 372.

30 Quoted in Wainstock, *Turning Point*, 156–157.

31 *CBS Evening News*, September 10, 1968.

32 Hubert H. Humphrey, *The Education of a Public Man: My Life and Politics* (Garden City, N.Y.: Doubleday, 1976), 8.

33 Quoted in Nancy Gibbs and Michael Duffy, *The Preacher and the Presidents: Billy Graham in the White House* (New York: Center Street, 2007), 168.

34 Eugene McCarthy, *The Year of the People* (Garden City, N.Y.: Doubleday, 1969), 236.

35 Quoted in Chester et al., *American Melodrama*, 740.

36 *CBS Evening News*, September 19, 1968.

37 *CBS Evening News*, September 24, 1968.

38 Edgar Berman, *Hubert: The Triumph and Tragedy of the Humphrey I Knew* (New York: G. P. Putnam's Sons, 1979), 197.

39 "Bureau of Labor Statistics, "Union Members in the United States, 1935–1980," available at ftp://ftp.bls.gov/pub/special.requests/collbarg/unmem.txt.

40 A survey of five UAW locals in New Jersey found support for Wallace ranging from 52 percent to 92 percent. Kevin Boyle, *The UAW and the Heyday of American Liberalism, 1945–1968* (Ithaca, N.Y.: Cornell University Press, 1995), 253.

41 *CBS Evening News*, September 9, 1968.

42 *CBS Evening News*, September 11, 1968.

43 Michael W. Flamm, *Law and Order: Street Crime, Civil Unrest, and the Crisis of Liberalism* (New York: Columbia University Press, 2005), 167–168.

44 Jeremy D. Mayer, "Nixon Rides the Backlash to Victory: Racial Politics in the 1968 Presidential Campaign," *The Historian* 64 (Winter 2002): 351–366.

45 Herbert Asher, *Presidential Elections and American Politics: Voters, Candidates, and Campaigns since 1952*, rev. ed. (Homewood, Ill.: Dorsey Press, 1980), 91. Strong Democrats outnumbered strong Republicans 22 percent to 11 percent. Weak Democrats outnumbered weak Republicans 24 percent to 16 percent. Independent-leaning Republicans outnumbered independent-leaning Democrats 10 percent to 9 percent.

46 *Huntley-Brinkley Report* (NBC), September 24, 1968.

47 Boyle, *UAW and the Heyday of American Liberalism*, 250; *Huntley-Brinkley Report* (NBC), September 19, 1968.

48 *CBS Evening News*, September 13, 1968.

49 *CBS Evening News*, September 20, 1968.

50 Richard Nixon, *RN: The Memoirs of Richard Nixon* (New York: Grosset & Dunlap, 1978), 319.

51 *CBS Evening News*, September 27, 1968.

52 "Ball of Confusion: The 1968 Presidential Election," an American Public Tele-

vision documentary produced by the University of Virginia Center for Politics (2016).

53 The Agnew quotations in this paragraph are from Wainstock, *Turning Point*, 150; and Witcover, *Year the Dream Died*, 363, 368, 394–395.

54 Quoted in Theo Lippman, Jr., and Donald C. Hansen, *Muskie* (New York: W. W. Norton, 1971), 13.

55 Joel K. Goldstein, "Campaigning for America: Edmund S. Muskie's 1968 Vice Presidential Campaign," *New England Journal of Political Science* 4 (Fall 2009): 153–174.

56 Ibid., 40.

57 "Laughter," available at http://www.livingroomcandidate.org/commercials/1968.

58 Witcover, *Year the Dream Died*, 428. Humphrey spent more than $6 million on advertising—a larger percentage of total expenditures than Nixon did, but a smaller amount. Wallace's advertising campaign cost more than $2 million. Alexander, *Financing the 1968 Election*, 84, 89.

59 *ABC Evening News*, September 23, 1968.

60 "Interview XXII with Lawrence F. O'Brien (June 19, 1987)," Lyndon B. Johnson Oral History Collection, available at http://www.lbjlibrary.net/assets/docu ments/archives/oral_histories/obrien_l/OBRIEN22.PDF.

61 Quoted in Solberg, *Hubert Humphrey*, 377.

62 Quoted in Gould, *1968*, 145.

63 Ibid., 146.

64 *CBS Evening News*, October 15, 1968.

65 Quoted in Richard T. Stout, *People: The Story of the Grassroots Movement That Found Eugene McCarthy and Is Transforming Our Politics Today* (New York: Harper & Row, 1970), 375.

66 *CBS Evening News*, October 9, 1968; *Huntley-Brinkley Report* (NBC), October 1, 1968.

67 Humphrey, *Education of a Public Man*, 403.

68 Alexander, *Financing the 1968 Election*, 84; Chester et al., *American Melodrama*, 715; "Interview IX with Lawrence F. O'Brien (April 9, 1986)," Lyndon B. Johnson Oral History Collection, available at http://www.lbjlibrary.net/assets/docu ments/archives/oral_histories/obrien_l/OBRIEN09.PDF.

69 Quoted in White, *Making of the President 1968*, 415.

70 "New York Campaign Speech by George C. Wallace (1968)," in Michael Nelson, ed., *Historic Documents on Presidential Elections 1787–1988* (Washington, D.C.: Congressional Quarterly, 1992), 566–573.

71 *Huntley-Brinkley Report* (NBC), September 13, 1968.

72 Joseph Crespino, *In Search of Another Country: Mississippi and the Conservative Counterrevolution* (Princeton, N.J.: Princeton University Press, 2007), 221. In general, Phillips's advice about where to show ads, based on his detailed knowledge of local voting patterns, was sound. Leonard Garment, *Crazy Rhythm: My Journey from Brooklyn, Jazz, and Wall Street to Nixon's White House, Watergate, and Beyond* (New York: Times Books, 1997), 134.

73 Quoted in Chester et al., *American Melodrama*, 708.

74 Quoted in Solberg, *Hubert Humphrey*, 389.

75 Ben A. Franklin, "As a 'Spoiler,' Wallace Could Produce a National Crisis," *New York Times*, February 11, 1968.

76 Bernard Schwartz, *Super Chief: Earl Warren and the Supreme Court: A Judicial Biography* (New York: New York University Press, 1983), 680–682.

77 Warren political aide M. F. "Pop" Small, quoted in Roger Morris, *Richard Milhous Nixon: The Rise of an American Politician* (New York: Henry Holt, 1990), 324.

78 Quoted in James Worthen, *The Young Nixon and His Rivals: Four California Republicans Eye the White House, 1946–1958* (Jefferson, N.C.: McFarland, 2010), 73.

79 Quoted in Morris, *Richard Milhous Nixon*, 741. See also Jim Newton, *Justice for All: Earl Warren and the Nation He Made* (New York: Riverhead, 2006), 248.

80 Quoted in Lyndon Baines Johnson, *The Vantage Point: Perspectives on the Presidency, 1963–1969* (New York: Holt, Rinehart & Winston, 1971), 546.

81 In order to keep the Subversive Activities Control Board from expiring on June 30, Dirksen also wanted the attorney general to refer some cases to it. Johnson agreed. See Mark Silverstein, *Judicial Choices: The Politics of Supreme Court Appointments*, 2nd ed. (New York: W. W. Norton, 2007), 19–20.

82 Quoted in Bruce Allen Murphy, *Fortas: The Rise and Ruin of a Supreme Court Justice* (New York: William Morrow, 1988), 302.

83 Ibid.

84 Ibid., 315.

85 David Alistair Yalof, *Pursuit of Justices: Presidential Politics and the Selection of Supreme Court Nominees* (Chicago: University of Chicago Press, 1999), 92.

86 Quoted in ibid., 350. For a full account of the Lawrence nomination, see Robert Mann, *The Walls of Jericho: Lyndon Johnson, Hubert Humphrey, and the Struggle for Civil Rights* (New York: Harcourt and Brace, 1996), 494–498.

87 Robert Dallek, *Flawed Giant: Lyndon Johnson and His Times, 1961–1973* (New York: Oxford University Press, 1998),559.

88 Fortas's White House activities while on the court are thoroughly assayed in Laura Kalman, *Abe Fortas: A Biography* (New Haven, Conn.: Yale University Press, 1990), chap. 14. See also Henry J. Abraham, *Justices and Presidents: A Political History of Appointments to the Supreme Court*, 3rd ed. (New York: Oxford University Press, 1992), 288–291.

89 A prominent example of the rampant press speculation about Fortas's role in the Johnson administration was Fred P. Graham, "The Many-Sided Justice Fortas," *New York Times Magazine*, June 24, 1967. A pull quote from the article read: "Fortas still does chores for L.B.J."

90 Joseph A. Califano, Jr., *The Triumph and Tragedy of Lyndon Johnson: The White House Years* (New York: Simon & Schuster, 1991), 313.

91 Randall B. Woods, *LBJ: Architect of American Ambition* (New York: Free Press, 2006), 852.

92 Quoted in Murphy, *Fortas*, 448.

93   Ibid.; Kalman, *Abe Fortas*, 358.

94   John Ehrlichman, *Witness to Power: The Nixon Years* (New York: Simon & Schuster, 1982), 113.

95   Patrick J. Buchanan, *The Greatest Comeback: How Richard Nixon Rose from Defeat to Create the New Majority* (New York: Crown Forum, 2014), 276.

96   Max Frankel, "Humphrey Scores 'The Same Nixon,'" *New York Times*, September 14, 1968.

97   Witcover, *Year the Dream Died*, 459.

98   Marjorie Hunter, "Fortas Refuses to Appear Again in Senate Inquiry," *New York Times*, September 14, 1968.

99   For a fuller account of these associations, see Kalman, *Abe Fortas*, chap. 15.

100 Quoted in Murphy, *Fortas*, 521.

101 Quoted in ibid., 316–317.

CHAPTER 7   THE GENERAL ELECTION: OCTOBER AND NOVEMBER

1   "Will HHH Come in Third?" *Newsweek*, September 23, 1968, 25–26.

2   "Wallace Presidential Campaign Organization," *Congressional Quarterly Weekly Report*, September 27, 1968, 2556. The quoted words are from Marshall Frady, *Wallace* (New York: Random House, 1996), 14.

3   Joseph E. Lowndes, *From the New Deal to the New Right: Race and the Southern Origins of Modern Conservatism* (New Haven, Conn.: Yale University Press, 2008), 98.

4   Just a few years earlier LeMay had been lionized in the popular film *Strategic Air Command*, in which he was fictionalized as General Ennis C. Hawkes. See Eric Schlosser, *Command and Control: Nuclear Weapons, the Damascus Accident, and the Illusion of Safety* (New York: Penguin, 2013), 147–149.

5   *CBS Evening News*, October 3, 1968. All quotations from network news programs are from original recordings of the broadcasts available at the Vanderbilt Television News Archive, Vanderbilt University, Nashville, Tenn.

6   Ibid.

7   Robert D. Novak, *The Prince of Darkness: Fifty Years of Reporting in Washington* (New York: Crown Forum, 2007), 174.

8   Dan T. Carter, *The Politics of Rage: George Wallace, the Origins of Conservatism, and the Transformation of American Politics* (New York: Simon & Schuster, 1995), 361.

9   Roy Reed, "Wallace Issues Platform Urging Tougher Policies," *New York Times*, October 14, 1968. The complete platform may be accessed at http://www.presidency.ucsb.edu/ws/index.php?pid=29570.

10   Lowndes, *From the New Deal to the New Right*, 100.

11   Richard M. Scammon and Ben J. Wattenberg, *The Real Majority: An Extraordinary Examination of the American Electorate* (New York: Coward, McCann & Geoghegan, 1970), 171.

12   See Paul Felix Lazarsfeld, Bernard Berelson, and Hazel Gaudet, *The People Decide: How the Voter Makes Up His Mind in a Presidential Campaign* (New York: Columbia University Press, 1944).

13   Warren Weaver, Jr., "Study Finds Nixon Winning 34 States to 7 for Wallace," *New York Times,* October 6, 1968.

14   Quoted in Theodore H. White, *The Making of the President 1968* (New York: Atheneum, 1969), 418.

15   Ibid., 424.

16   Hubert H. Humphrey, *The Education of a Public Man: My Life and Politics* (Garden City, N.Y.: Doubleday, 1976), 8.

17   Daniel C. Hallin, "Sound Bite News: Television Coverage of Elections, 1968–1988," *Journal of Communication* 42 (1992): 5–24; Erik P. Bucy and Maria Elizabeth Grabe, "Taking Television Seriously: A Sound and Image Bite Analysis of Presidential Campaign Coverage, 1992–2004," *Journal of Communication* 57 (2007): 652–675.

18   *CBS Evening News,* October 10, 1968.

19   Quoted in James Reston, Jr., *The Lone Star: The Life of John Connally* (New York: Harper & Row, 1989), 374.

20   *CBS Evening News,* October 29, 1968.

21   *Huntley-Brinkley Report* (NBC), October 31, 1968.

22   Kathleen Hall Jamieson, *Packaging the Presidency: A History and Criticism of Presidential Campaign Advertising* (New York: Oxford University Press, 1984), 232, 243; Connie Bruck, *When Hollywood Had a King: The Reign of Lew Wasserman, Who Leveraged Talent into Power and Influence* (New York: Random House, 2003), 362.

23   Jamieson, *Packaging the Presidency,* 233.

24   White, *Making of the President 1968,* 365.

25   Herbert E. Alexander, *Financing the 1968 Election* (Lexington, Mass.: Lexington Books, 1971), 122–123.

26   Jack Nelson, *Scoop: The Evolution of a Southern Reporter* (Jackson: University Press of Mississippi, 2013), 130.

27   *Huntley-Brinkley Report* (NBC), October 18, 1968.

28   *CBS Evening News,* October 24, 1968; *Huntley-Brinkley Report* (NBC), October 22, 1968; and *Huntley-Brinkley Report* (NBC), October 18, 1968.

29   Quoted in William Safire, *Before the Fall: An Inside View of the Pre-Watergate White House* (New York: Doubleday, 1975), 76. Brief excerpts from these speeches may be found in Edward K. Knappman, *Presidential Election 1968* (New York: Facts on File, 1970), 206–207.

30   Beth Bailey, *America's Army: Instituting the All-Volunteer Force* (Cambridge, Mass.: Harvard University Press, 2009), chap. 1.

31   *CBS Evening News,* October 28, 1968.

32   Quoted in Safire, *Before the Fall,* 75.

33   Stephen E. Ambrose, *Nixon: The Triumph of a Politician, 1962–1972* (New York: Simon & Schuster, 1989), 191.

34   Patrick J. Buchanan, *The Greatest Comeback: How Richard Nixon Rose from Defeat to Create the New Majority* (New York: Crown Forum, 2014), 340.

35   Quoted in Jules Witcover, *The Resurrection of Richard Nixon* (New York: G. P. Putnam's Sons, 1970), 423.

36 *Newsweek* concluded in mid-October that even a 400-electoral-vote Nixon land-slide would not be enough to secure a Republican majority in the House of Representatives. "The GOP's House Hopes," *Newsweek*, October 14, 1969, 32–33.

37 Quoted in Safire, *Before the Fall*, 79.

38 *CBS Evening News*, October 1, 1968.

39 Quoted in Walter Isaacson, *Kissinger: A Biography* (New York: Simon & Schuster, 1992), 131.

40 Ken Hughes, *Chasing Shadows: The Nixon Tapes, the Chennault Affair, and the Origins of Watergate* (Charlottesville: University of Virginia Press, 2014), 26–27. In his memoir Humphrey indicated that he would have brought Kissinger into the White House if he had won the election. Humphrey, *Education of a Public Man*, 9. Nixon did bring him in as his national security adviser.

41 Richard Nixon, *RN: The Memoirs of Richard Nixon* (New York: Grosset & Dunlap, 1978), 324.

42 Soviet ambassador Anatoly Dobrynin later wrote: "Moscow believed that as far as its relations with Washington were concerned, Humphrey would make the best president." Quoted in Larry Berman, *No Peace, No Honor: Nixon, Kissinger, and the Betrayal in Vietnam* (New York: Free Press, 2001), 28.

43 "President Lyndon B. Johnson's Address to the Nation upon Announcing His Decision to Halt the Bombing of North Vietnam," available at http://www.lbjlib.utexas.edu/johnson/archives.hom/speeches.hom/681031.asp.

44 Nixon, *RN*, 322.

45 Quoted in James Rosen, *The Strong Man: John Mitchell and the Secrets of Watergate* (New York: Doubleday, 2008), 54.

46 See, for example, Melvin Small, "The Election of 1968," *Diplomatic History* 18 (September 2004): 513–528.

47 "Interview III with Ellsworth Bunker (October 12, 1983)," Lyndon B. Johnson Oral History Collection, available at http://www.lbjlibrary.net/assets/documents/archives/oral_histories/bunker_e/bunker3.pdf.

48 "President Lyndon B. Johnson's Address to the Nation."

49 Humphrey, *Education of a Public Man*, 8.

50 John A. Farrell, *Richard Nixon: The Life* (New York: Doubleday, 2017), 343.

51 Quoted in Robert Dallek, *Flawed Giant: Lyndon Johnson and His Times, 1961–1973* (New York: Oxford University Press, 1998), 591.

52 Clark Clifford, with Richard Holbrooke, *Counsel to the President: A Memoir* (New York: Random House, 1991), 583.

53 Rosen, *Strong Man*, 62.

54 Robert Dallek, *Nixon and Kissinger: Partners in Power* (New York: Harper, 2007), 77.

55 Buchanan, *Greatest Comeback*, 361.

56 Quoted in Neal R. Peirce and Lawrence D. Longley, *The People's President: The Electoral College in American History and the Direct Vote Alternative*, rev. ed. (New Haven, Conn.: Yale University Press, 1981), 75. As it happens, none of the five states Wallace actually carried had such laws.

57 "The Public Record of George C. Wallace," *Congressional Quarterly Weekly Report*, September 27, 1968, 2553–2567.

58 Ben A. Franklin, "As a 'Spoiler,' Wallace Could Produce a National Crisis," *New York Times*, February 11, 1968. See also Stephen Lesher, *George Wallace: American Populist* (Reading, Mass.: Addison-Wesley, 1994), 401.

59 Quoted in Peirce and Longley, *People's President*, 75.

60 James A. Michener, *Presidential Lottery: The Reckless Gamble in Our Electoral System* (New York: Random House, 1969), 16.

61 According to the Twelfth Amendment, enacted in 1804, "if no person have a majority [of electoral votes], then from the two highest numbers on the list the Senate shall choose the Vice President."

62 The Twentieth Amendment, enacted in 1933, provides: "If a President shall not have been chosen by the time fixed for the beginning of his term, . . . then the Vice President elect shall act as President until a President shall have qualified."

63 The Twenty-fifth Amendment, enacted in 1967, provides: "Whenever there is a vacancy in the office of the Vice President, the President shall nominate a Vice President who shall take office upon confirmation by a majority vote of both Houses of Congress."

64 The term "post-election election" is from Michael Nelson,"The Post-election Election: Politics by Other Means," in *The Elections of 2000*, ed. Michael Nelson (Washington, D.C.: CQ Press, 2001), 211–224.

65 Rosen, *Strong Man*, 55. For a firsthand account of Operation Eagle Eye in action, see Novak, *Prince of Darkness*, 177–179.

66 For a list of which states are included in each region in this book, see chapter 5, note 21.

67 Matthew D. Lassiter, *The Silent Majority: Suburban Politics in the Sunbelt South* (Princeton, N.J.: Princeton University Press, 2006), 239.

68 "Best" is measured by the average percentage of the popular vote received by FDR in those four presidential elections. The three states Humphrey carried from that list were Texas, Washington, and Maryland. A map showing the Democrats' best twenty states in the earlier period is in Michael Nelson, "Partisan Bias in the Electoral College," *Journal of Politics* 36 (November 1974): 1033–1048.

69 Maine, New Hampshire, Vermont, Massachusetts, Connecticut, Rhode Island, New York, New Jersey, Pennsylvania, West Virginia, Ohio, Michigan, and Illinois. For the Republicans' best twenty states in the earlier period, see the map in ibid.

70 The classic account of southern politics in this era is V. O. Key, *Southern Politics in State and Nation* (New York: Alfred A. Knopf, 1949). See also Dewey W. Grantham, *The Life and Death of the Solid South: A Political History* (Lexington: University Press of Kentucky, 1988).

71 Philip E. Converse, Warren E. Miller, Jerrold G. Rusk, and Arthur C. Wolfe, "Continuity and Change in American Politics: Parties and Issues in the 1968 Election," *American Political Science Review* 63 (December 1969): 1083–1105.

72 Drawn from data presented in Seymour Martin Lipset and Earl Raab, *The Politics of Unreason: Right-Wing Extremism in America, 1790–1977*, 2nd ed. (Chicago: University of Chicago Press, 1978), 395–397. A mid-October NBC-Quayle national survey that prodded voters supporting Wallace at the time to choose between the two major party candidates found 58 percent for Nixon and 22 percent for Humphrey, with most of the rest saying they would not vote under those circumstances. Daniel A. Mazmanian, *Third Parties in Presidential Elections* (Washington, D.C.: Brookings Institution, 1974), 71.

73 "Ball of Confusion: The 1968 Presidential Election," an American Public Television documentary produced by the University of Virginia Center for Politics (2016).

74 Ronald W. Walters, *Black Presidential Politics in America: A Strategic Approach* (Albany: State University of New York Press, 1988), 32.

75 Omar Wasow, "Do Protest Tactics Matter? Evidence from the 1960s Black Insurgency" (working paper, 2016), available at http://www.omarwasow.com /Protests_on_Voting.pdf.

76 Priscilla L. Southwell, "The Politics of Disgruntlement: Nonvoting and Defection among Supporters of Nomination Losers, 1968–1984," *Political Behavior* 8 (1986): 81–95. According to the University of Michigan's Survey Research Center poll of New Hampshire voters, a plurality of those who supported Eugene McCarthy in the 1968 Democratic primary said they would vote for George Wallace in November. See Converse et al., "Continuity and Change in American Politics."

77 White, *Making of the President 1968*, 462.

78 "Election Polls—Vote by Groups, 1968," available at http://www.gallup.com /poll/9457/Election-Polls-Vote-Groups-19681972.aspx; and "Election Polls— Vote by Groups, 1960–1964," available at http://www.gallup.com/poll/9457 /Election-Polls-Vote-Groups-19601964.aspx.

79 The data on Jewish and big-city voting come from the American Institute for Public Opinion poll, reported in Lipset and Raab, *Politics of Unreason*, 380–382.

80 Herbert B. Asher, *Presidential Elections and American Politics: Voters, Candidates, and Campaigns since 1952*, rev. ed. (Homewood, Ill.: Dorsey Press, 1980), 91–94.

81 Herbert F. Weisberg and Jerrold G. Rusk, "Dimensions of Candidate Evaluation," *American Political Science Review* 64 (December 1970): 1167–1178.

82 Asher, *Presidential Elections and American Politics*, 135–136.

83 A Harris Poll conducted about a month before the election that showed Nixon with a strong lead also found that voters preferred Muskie to Agnew by a 17-percentage-point margin. Asher, *Presidential Elections and American Politics*, 183.

84 Converse et al., "Continuity and Change in American Politics."

85 Richard A. Brody and Benjamin I. Page, "Policy Voting and the Electoral Process: The Vietnam War Issue," *American Political Science Review* 66 (September 1972): 979–995.

86 Converse et al., "Continuity and Change in American Politics."

87 Weisberg and Rusk, "Dimensions of Candidate Evaluation."

88 Richard W. Boyd, "Popular Control of Public Policy: A Normal Vote Analysis of the 1968 Election," *American Political Science Review* 66 (June 1972): 429–449; Paul Abramson, *Political Attitudes in America: Formation and Change* (San Francisco: Freeman, 1983), 199–200; and Marc J. Hetherington, "The Effect of Political Trust on the Presidential Vote, 1968–1996," *American Political Science Review* 93 (June 1999): 311–326.

89 Asher, *Presidential Elections and American Politics*, 91. Democrats in all category of self-identification—strong, weak, or independent—were considerably more likely to vote Democratic for Congress in 1968 than for president. See Abramson, *Political Attitudes in America*, 79.

90 The relevant data is in Gary C. Jacobson, *The Politics of Congressional Elections*, 3rd ed. (New York: HarperCollins, 1992), 27, 39. The record for incumbency reelection was broken in 1986, when 98 percent of reelection-seeking incumbents were successful.

91 Calculated from data, with assistance from Alex McGriff, in *Congressional Quarterly Almanac 1969* (Washington, D.C.: Congressional Quarterly, 1969), 1202–1238.

92 In 1940 most states elected their governors to two-year terms, and as recently as 1964, fifteen states still did. In the three years prior to the 1968 election, seven states changed to four-year terms, and another five did so in the seven years after 1968. In making this change, the great majority of states set the gubernatorial election midway through the president's term so that it would not be overshadowed by the national contest. Larry Sabato, *Goodbye to Good-Time Charlie: The American Governorship Transformed*, 2nd ed. (Washington, D.C.: CQ Press, 1983), 99.

93 In Montana the Democratic state attorney general, Forrest H. Anderson, defeated incumbent Republican Tim M. Babcock, and in Rhode Island Democrat and former state judge Frank Licht unseated Republican governor John H. Chafee. The seven states where Republicans replaced Democrats as governor were Illinois, where Ogilvie unseated Shapiro; Delaware, where DuPont executive Russell W. Peterson defeated Gov. Charles L. Terry, Jr.; Indiana, where Secretary of State Edgar D. Whitcomb defeated Lt. Gov. Robert L. Rock; Iowa, where former state GOP chair Robert Ray defeated Paul Franzenburg; New Hampshire, where state house speaker Walter R. Peterson defeated Emile R. Bussiere; Vermont, where attorney Deane C. Davis defeated Lt. Gov. John J. Daley; and West Virginia, where Rep. Arch A. Moore defeated attorney James M. Sprouse.

CHAPTER 8   RESILIENT AMERICA

1 Quoted from a statement by Lloyd W. Bailey on December 16, 1968, *Congressional Record—Senate* (January 6, 1969), 205.

2 Lawrence D. Longley and Neal R. Peirce, *The Electoral College Primer* (New Haven, Conn.: Yale University Press, 1996), 116–118. See also Walter Berns, ed., *After the People Vote: Steps in Choosing the President* (Washington, D.C.: Amer-

ican Enterprise Institute for Public Policy Research, 1983), chap. 4; and Jack Maskell and Elizabeth Rybicki, "Counting Electoral Votes: An Overview of Procedures at the Joint Session, Including Objections by Members of Congress," Congressional Research Service, November 30, 2012. A direct election amendment to the Constitution passed the House in 1969 by a vote of 338 to 70 but failed to overcome a Senate filibuster in 1970. Subsequent efforts to pass such an amendment have been defeated in Congress by a coalition of small states, which are especially well represented in the Senate and fear losing what little advantage they have in the Electoral College, and liberal interest groups, which argue that minority, union, and urban voters, who are concentrated in the large states, would lose their strategic advantage if these states were no longer as central to the fortunes of presidential candidates as they are in the Electoral College. Michael Nelson, "Constitutional Change and the Modern Presidency: The Twentieth, Twenty-second, and Twenty-fifth Amendments to the Constitution," in Pierre Lagayette, ed., *L'empire de l'executif (1933–2006): la présidence des Etats Unis de Franklin Roosevelt à George W. Bush [Executive Supremacy: The American Presidency from Franklin D. Roosevelt to George W. Bush]* (Paris: Presses de l'Université Paris—Sorbonne, 2007), 63–85.

3   The four exceptions, out of fifty-eight elections through 2016, were 1800 and 1824, when the election went to the House; 1876, when it was resolved by a specially appointed commission; and 2000, when it was resolved by the state of Florida and the U.S. Supreme Court.

4   Quoted in Jonathan Aitken, *Nixon: A Life* (Washington, D.C.: Regnery, 1993), 368.

5   "First Inaugural Address of Richard Milhous Nixon," available at http://avalon .law.yale.edu/20th_century/nixon1.asp.

6   Under the recently enacted Twenty-fifth Amendment, Ford was appointed vice president after Agnew resigned. He succeeded to the presidency when Nixon resigned.

7   Rowland Evans, Jr., and Robert D. Novak, *Nixon in the White House: The Frustration of Power* (New York: Random House, 1971), 51. Nixon did offer several cabinet positions to Democrats, including secretary of defense (first to Sen. Henry Jackson of Washington, then to Gov. John Connally of Texas) and ambassador to the United Nations (Sargent Shriver and Hubert Humphrey). All declined. Melvin Small, *The Presidency of Richard Nixon* (Lawrence: University Press of Kansas, 1999), 36.

8   "Presidential Job Approval Center," The Gallup Poll, available at http://www .gallup.com/poll/124922/presidential-approval-center.aspx.

9   Marc J. Hetherington, *Why Trust Matters: Declining Political Trust and the Demise of American Liberalism* (Princeton, N.J.: Princeton University Press, 2005), 18.

10   The main cohorts of dissent, but not all of them, were able to express themselves. See Bryan Burroughs, *Days of Rage: America's Radical Underground, the FBI, and the Forgotten Age of Revolutionary Violence* (New York: Penguin Press, 2015).

11 Maurice Isserman and Michael Kazin, *America Divided: The Civil War of the 1960s* (New York: Oxford University Press, 2000), 266–267.

12 Clara Bingham, *Witness to the Revolution: Radicals, Resisters, Vets, Hippies, and the Year America Lost Its Mind and Found Its Soul* (New York: Random House, 2016), chap. 10.

13 David Maraniss, *First in His Class: A Biography of Bill Clinton* (New York: Simon & Schuster, 1995), chaps. 9–10.

14 Quoted in Tom Wells, *The War Within: America's Battle over Vietnam* (Berkeley: University of California Press, 1994), 365.

15 Quoted in ibid., 376.

16 Quoted in Dominic Sandbrook, *Eugene McCarthy: The Rise and Fall of Postwar American Liberalism* (New York: Alfred A. Knopf, 2004), 232.

17 Anastasia Erbe, "Born of Unrest, Fall Break Legacy Lives On," *Daily Princetonian*, October 24, 2008.

18 Wells, *War Within*, 477.

19 Quoted in ibid., 324.

20 Quoted in ibid., 403.

21 Beth Bailey, *America's Army: Making the All-Volunteer Force* (Cambridge, Mass.: Harvard University Press, 2009), 33. On Nixon and the draft, see also George Q. Flynn, *The Draft, 1940–1973* (Lawrence: University Press of Kansas, 1993), chap. 9.

22 Quoted in Richard Reeves, *President Nixon: Alone in the White House* (New York: Touchstone, 2001), 33.

23 Quoted in ibid., 295. In interviews conducted in 2004, radical linguist Noam Chomsky and former Harvard president Derek Bok concurred in this assessment. According to Chomsky, "the last liberal president in the United States was Nixon." Berbard von Bothmer, *Framing the Sixties: The Use and Abuse of a Decade from Ronald Reagan to George W. Bush* (Amherst: University of Massachusetts Press, 2010), 17.

24 "National Exit Polls Table," *New York Times*, November 5, 2008, available at http://elections.nytimes.com/2008/results/president/national-exit-polls .html; and "Election Polls by Groups, 1968–1972," Gallup Poll, available at http://www.gallup.com/poll/9457/election-polls-vote-groups-19681972.aspx.

25 In 1970 Nixon thwarted an effort by congressional Democrats to repeal the Philadelphia Plan, telling Republican leaders that the plan would weaken labor unions and divide them from civil rights groups. Timothy N. Thurber, *Republicans and Race: The GOP's Frayed Relationship with African Americans, 1945–1976* (Lawrence: University Press of Kansas, 2013), 335. But in preparation for the 1972 election, in which he hoped to sweep the Wallace vote, Nixon abandoned both the Family Assistance Plan and the Philadelphia Plan.

26 See, for example, *Green v. County School Board of New Kent County*, 391 U.S. 430 (1968) and *Swann v. Charlotte-Mecklenburg Board of Education*, 402 U.S. 1 (1970), which endorsed the use of busing as a remedy for racial imbalance in public school systems. For a different perspective on the Burger court, see

Michael J. Graetz and Linda Greenhouse, *The Burger Court and the Rise of the Judicial Right* (New York: Simon & Schuster, 2016).

27 "Types of Office Held by All Black Elected Officials," Russell Sage Foundation, available at https://www.russellsage.org/sites/all/files/Conyers_Tables%20 Figures.pdf.

28 The demand for greater police protection often came from African American neighborhood leaders. See Michael Javen Fortner, *Black Silent Majority: The Rockefeller Drug Laws and the Politics of Punishment* (Cambridge, Mass.: Harvard University Press, 2015).

29 "The McGovern-Fraser Commission Report," in *The Evolving Presidency: Landmark Documents, 1787–2011*, ed. Michael Nelson (Washington, D.C.: CQ Press, 2011), 210–216.

30 The leading account and critique of the reforms is Byron E. Shafer, *Quiet Revolution: The Struggle for the Democratic Party and the Shaping of Post-Reform Politics* (New York: Russell Sage, 1983). See also Nelson W. Polsby, *Consequences of Party Reform* (Institute of Governmental Studies Press, 1983); and James W. Ceaser, *Reforming the Reforms: Critical Analysis of the Presidential Selection Process* (New York: Harper & Row, 1983).

31 "Portrait of an Assassin: Arthur Bremer," *American Experience*, available at http://www.pbs.org/wgbh/amex/wallace/sfeature/assasin.html.

32 Bruce Miroff, *The Liberals' Moment: The McGovern Insurgency and the Identity Crisis of the Democratic Party* (Lawrence: University Press of Kansas, 2007), 139.

33 John B. Judis and Ruy Teixeira, *The Emerging Democratic Majority* (New York: Scribner, 2002), 37–38.

34 Donald I. Warren, *The Radical Center: Middle Americans and the Politics of Alienation* (Notre Dame, Ind.: University of Notre Dame Press, 1976), xix–xx. The *Time* cover appeared on the January 5, 1970, issue.

35 Dan T. Carter, *The Politics of Rage: George Wallace, the Origins of Conservatism, and the Transformation of American Politics* (New York: Simon & Schuster, 1995), 410.

36 Jack Newfield and Jeff Greenfield, *A Populist Manifesto: The Making of a New Majority* (New York: Praeger, 1972).

37 Quoted in Robert C. McMath, Jr., *American Populism: A Social History, 1877–1898* (New York: Hill & Wang, 1993), 11.

38 Newfield and Greenfield, *Populist Manifesto*, 11.

39 C. Vann Woodward, *Origins of the New South, 1877–1913* (Baton Rouge: Louisiana State University Press, 1951). Even Watson's transracial politics only lasted a few years until he became virulently antiblack. Woodward, *Tom Watson: Agrarian Rebel* (New York: Oxford University Press, 1938).

40 Miroff, *Liberals' Moment*, 20.

41 Taylor E. Dark, *The Unions and the Democrats: An Enduring Alliance* (Ithaca, N.Y.: Cornell University Press, 1999), 87–88.

42 Kevin P. Phillips, *The Emerging Republican Majority* (New Rochelle, N.Y.: Arlington House, 1969).

43 Phillips acknowledged that the pursuit of Wallace voters would cost the GOP

support in the Northeast. Such losses in a demographically declining region would be more than offset, he argued, by gains in the booming "Sunbelt," a term he coined to describe the rapidly growing metropolitan areas of the South, Southwest, and southern California, which would be attracted by Republican economic policies.

44 Quoted in Stephen E. Ambrose, *Nixon: The Triumph of a Politician, 1962–1972* (New York: Simon & Schuster, 1989), 338.

45 The quotations and others like them are sprinkled throughout Jules Witcover, *Very Strange Bedfellows: The Short and Unhappy Marriage of Richard Nixon and Spiro Agnew* (New York: PublicAffairs, 2007).

46 Quoted in Ambrose, *Nixon: The Triumph of a Politician*, 348.

47 Richard M. Scammon and Ben J. Wattenberg, *The Real Majority: An Extraordinary Examination of the American Electorate* (NewYork: Coward, McCann & Geoghegan, 1970).

48 Edward R. Tufte, *Political Control of the Economy* (Princeton, N.J.: Princeton University Press, 1980).

49 Benjamin Ginsberg and Martin Shefter, *Politics by Other Means: The Declining Importance of Elections in America* (New York: Basic Books, 1990).

50 The election took place under unusually adverse conditions for the Republican Party. Ford lost as the first president never to be elected to either the presidency or vice presidency, in the aftermath of the Watergate crisis, after a divisive Republican primary battle, and in a time of economic distress.

51 Harold W. Stanley and Richard G. Niemi, *Vital Statistics on American Politics, 2011–2012* (Washington, D.C.: CQ Press, 2011).

52 Michael Nelson, "George Bush: Texan, Conservative," in *41: Inside the George H. W. Bush Presidency,* ed. Michael Nelson and Barbara A. Perry (Ithaca, N.Y.: Cornell University Press, 2014), 27–47.

53 Evans and Novak, *Nixon in the White House,* chap. 11; and Robert Mason, *Richard Nixon and the Quest for a New Majority* (Chapel Hill: University of North Carolina Press, 2004), 111.

54 Mason, *Richard Nixon and the Quest for a New Majority*, 164.

55 For example, in 1984 Democratic presidential nominee Walter F. Mondale, facing intense demands from feminists within the party to select a woman as his vice presidential running mate, chose the underqualified Rep. Geraldine Ferraro of New York. In 1988 presidential nominee Michael S. Dukakis, under similar pressure from African American delegates, ceded a major place on the convention program to civil rights activist Jesse Jackson.

56 Gary C. Jacobson, "The Electoral Connection, Then and Now," paper originally prepared for "Representation and Governance: A Conference in Honor of David Mayhew," Center for the Study of American Politics, Yale University, May 29–30, 2013.

57 "56 Interesting Facts About the 2016 Election," Cookpolitical.com, December 16, 2016. Cookpolitical/story/10201.

58 For evidence to support this argument, see Morris P. Fiorina, *Divided Government* (Boston: Allyn & Bacon, 1996), chap. 5. For a strongly differing perspec-

tive, see Barry C. Burden and David C. Kimball, *Why Americans Split Their Tickets: Campaigns, Competition, and Divided Government* (Ann Arbor: University of Michigan Press, 2004). Samuel Kernell and his colleagues argue against Fiorina's view but do cite surveys showing that more than twice as many people prefer divided government as prefer united party government. Samuel Kernell, Gary C. Jacobson, and Thad Kousser, *The Logic of American Politics*, 6th ed. (Washington, D.C.: CQ Press, 2014), 561.

59 Jacobson, "The Electoral Connection, Then and Now."

60 Fiorina, *Divided Government*, 72–91.

61 Hetherington, *Why Trust Matters.*

62 Gary C. Jacobson, *The Politics of Congressional Elections*, 5th ed. (New York: Longman, 2001), 259.

63 David R. Mayhew, *Divided We Govern: Party Control, Lawmaking, and Investigations, 1946–1990* (New Haven, Conn.: Yale University Press, 1991).

64 Sarah A. Binder, *Stalemate: Causes and Consequences of Legislative Gridlock* (Washington, D.C.: Brookings Institution Press, 2003).

65 Burden and Kimball, *Why Americans Split Their Tickets.*

66 John Anthony Maltese, *The Selling of Supreme Court Nominees* (Baltimore: Johns Hopkins University Press, 1995).

67 Ginsberg and Shefter, *Politics by Other Means*, x.

68 Benjamin Ginsberg, Walter R. Mebane, Jr., and Martin Shefter, "The President and the 'Interests': Why the White House Cannot Govern," in *The Presidency and the Political System*, 6th ed., ed. Michael Nelson (Washington, D.C.: CQ Press, 2000), 371.

69 Despite Senate rules changes easing confirmation of most appointments in November 2013, most controversial measures can only be brought to a vote in the Senate if three-fifths, or sixty senators, vote to impose cloture on the debate. In some instances a single senator's "hold" can significantly delay, even prevent Senate action.

70 In an extreme case of politics by other means, George W. Bush won the 2000 presidential election against Al Gore by successfully pressing all of the advantages that he enjoyed in the institutional combat that constitutes politics by other means. Because the cochair of his Florida presidential campaign was Florida's secretary of state, deadlines for conducting manual recounts that might otherwise have been extended at Gore's request were strictly enforced. Because Bush's brother was the governor of Florida, Bush could expect that, in the absence of clear evidence that Gore had carried the state, the slate of electors that received the governor's official signature would be his. Bush also knew that any disputes about the election that reached Washington would be resolved by a Republican-dominated Supreme Court or, if that strategy failed, by a Republican House of Representatives. About three weeks before the House was scheduled to meet, the Supreme Court settled the election in Bush's favor in the case of *Bush v. Gore*. See Michael Nelson, "The Post-election Election: Politics by Other Means," in *The Elections of 2000*, ed. Michael Nelson (Washington, D.C.: CQ Press, 2001), 211–224.

BIBLIOGRAPHIC ESSAY

Although none make the argument this book makes about the 1968 election and its aftermath, many fine general accounts of the election have been written by journalists and historians. As in most sections of this essay, these works are listed in the order they were published: Lewis Chester, Godfrey Hodgson, and Bruce Page, *An American Melodrama: The Presidential Campaign of 1968* (New York: Viking, 1969); Theodore H. White, *The Making of the President 1968* (New York: Atheneum, 1969), along with the CBS News documentary "The Making of the President 1968," which aired on September 8, 1969; David S. Broder, "Election of 1968," in *History of Presidential Elections, 1789–1968*, vol. 4, ed. Arthur M. Schlesinger, Jr., and Fred L. Israel (New York: Chelsea House, 1971), 3705–3752; Dennis Wainstock, *The Turning Point: The 1968 United States Presidential Campaign* (Jefferson, N.C.: McFarland, 1988); Lewis L. Gould, *1968: The Election That Changed America* (Chicago: Ivan R. Dee, 1993); Jules Witcover, *The Year the Dream Died: Revisiting 1968 in America* (New York: Warner, 1997); Melvin Small, "The Election of 1968," *Diplomatic History* 18 (September 2004): 513–528; Walter LaFeber, *The Deadly Bet: LBJ, Vietnam, and the 1968 Election* (Lanham, Md.: Rowman & Littlefield, 2005); Rick Perlstein, *Nixonland: The Rise of a President and the Fracturing of America* (New York: Scribner, 2008); and Michael A. Cohen, *American Maelstrom: The 1968 Election and the Politics of Division* (New York: Oxford University Press, 2016). See also Edward W. Knappman, ed., *Presidential Election 1968* (New York: Facts on File, 1970), a daily account of election-related news events in 1968; David Frost, *The Presidential Debate, 1968* (New York: Stein & Day, 1968), a series of interviews with the candidates; Herbert E. Alexander, *Financing the 1968 Election* (Lexington, Mass.: Lexington Books, 1971); and "Ball of Confusion: The 1968 Presidential Election," an American Public Television documentary produced by the University of Virginia Center for Politics (2016).

In terms of political influence at the time, the two most important interpretations of the election were Kevin P. Phillips, *The Emerging Republican Majority* (New Rochelle, N.Y.: Arlington House, 1969); and Richard M. Scammon and Ben J. Wattenberg, *The Real Majority: An Extraordinary Examination of the American Electorate* (New York: Coward, McCann & Geoghegan, 1970)—the former offered as a Republican's advice to his party and the latter as two Democrats' advice to theirs.

The 1968 election cannot be understood apart from those of 1960 and 1964. The best accounts of the 1960 election are W. J. Rorabaugh, *The Real Making of the President: Kennedy, Nixon, and the 1960 Election* (Lawrence: University Press of Kansas, 2009); and Theodore C. White, *The Making of the President 1960* (Atheneum, 1961). White also wrote *The Making of the President 1964* (New York: Atheneum, 1965), which is one of several useful books on that election, including Robert D. Novak, *The Agony of the GOP 1964* (New York: Macmillan, 1965); Jon Margolis, *The Last Innocent Year: America in 1964, The Beginning of the "Sixties"* (New York: Perennial, 1999); Rick Perlstein, *Before the Storm: Barry Goldwater and the Unmaking of the American Consensus* (New York: Hill & Wang, 2001); and Gary Donaldson, *Liberalism's Last Hurrah: The Presidential Campaign of 1964* (Armonk, N.Y.: M. E. Sharpe, 2003).

Valuable accounts of the 1960s in general or of 1968 in particular include Allen J. Matusow, *The Unraveling of America: A History of Liberalism in the 1960s* (New York: Harper & Row, 1984); Todd Gitlin, *The Sixties: Years of Hope, Days of Rage* (New York: Bantam, 1987); Maurice Isserman and Michael Kazin, *America Divided: The Civil War of the 1960s* (New York: Oxford University Press, 2000); G. Calvin Mackenzie and Robert Weisbrot, *The Liberal Hour: Washington and the Politics of Change in the 1960s* (New York: Penguin, 2008); James T. Patterson, *The Eve of Destruction: How 1965 Transformed America* (New York: Basic Books, 2012); and the relevant chapters in several books about the postwar United States: Michael Barone, *Our Country: The Shaping of America from Roosevelt to Reagan* (Free Press, 1990); William H. Chafe, *Unfinished Journey: America since World War II*, 7th ed. (New York: Oxford University Press, 2011); and Eric Alterman and Kevin Mattson, *The Cause: The Fight for American Liberalism from Franklin Roosevelt to Barack Obama* (New York: Viking, 2012).

Several nonelectoral developments pervaded the politics of 1968, none more important than the war in Vietnam. Among the many useful books on American politics and policy concerning the Vietnam War are Townshend Hoopes, *The Limits of Intervention: An Inside Account of How the Johnson Policy of Escalation in Vietnam Was Reversed* (New York: David McKay, 1969); John E. Mueller, *War, Presidents, and Public Opinion* (New York: John Wiley, 1973); Peter Braestrup, *Big Story: How the American Press and Television Reported and Interpreted the Crisis of Tet 1968 in Vietnam and Washington* (Boulder, Colo.: Westview, 1977); Larry Berman, *Planning a Tragedy: The Americanization of the War in Vietnam* (New York: W. W. Norton, 1982), and *No Peace, No Honor: Nixon, Kissinger, and the Betrayal in Vietnam* (New York: Free Press, 2001); Clark Clifford, with Richard Holbrooke, *Counsel to the President* (New York: Random House, 1991); and Fredrik Logevall, *Choosing War: The Lost Chance for Peace and the Escalation of War in Vietnam* (Berkeley: University of California Press, 1999).

Three important books on the antiwar movement are William H. Chafe, *Never Stop Running: Allard Lowenstein and the Struggle to Save American Liberalism* (New York: Basic Books, 1993); Tom Wells, *The War Within: America's Battle over Vietnam* (Berkeley: University of California Press, 1994); and David Maraniss, *They Marched into Sunlight: War and Peace, Vietnam and America, October 1967* (New York: Simon & Schuster, 2003). More recent works on the movement after 1968 are Bryan Burroughs, *Days of Rage: America's Radical Underground, the FBI, and the Forgotten Age of Revolutionary Violence* (New York: Penguin Press, 2015); and Clara Bingham, *Witness to the Revolution: Radicals, Resisters, Vets, Hippies, and the Year America Lost Its Mind and Found Its Soul* (New York: Random House, 2016).

On the draft see George Q. Flynn, *The Draft, 1940–1973* (Lawrence: University Press of Kansas, 1993); and Beth Bailey, *America's Army: Instituting the All-Volunteer Force* (Cambridge, Mass.: Harvard University Press, 2009).

A congeries of issues relating to race, civil rights, and law and order also animated the politics of 1968. Those sources worth consulting include Ronald W. Walters, *Black Presidential Politics in America: A Strategic Approach* (Albany: State University of New York Press, 1988); Edward G. Carmines and James A. Stimson, *Issue Evolution: Race and the Transformation of American Politics* (Princeton, N.J.: Princeton University Press, 1989); Thomas Byrne Edsall and Mary D. Edsall, *Chain Reaction: The Impact of Race, Rights, and Taxes on American Politics* (New York: W. W. Norton, 1991); Robert Mann, *The Walls of Jericho: Lyndon Johnson, Hubert Humphrey, and the Struggle for Civil Rights* (New York: Harcourt & Brace, 1996); Kevin M. Kruse, *White Flight: Atlanta and the Making of Modern Conservatism* (Princeton, N.J.: Princeton University Press, 2005); Michael W. Flamm, *Law and Order: Street Crime, Civil Unrest, and the Crisis of Liberalism* (New York: Columbia University Press, 2005); Matthew D. Lassiter, *The Silent Majority: Suburban Politics in the Sunbelt South* (Princeton, N.J.: Princeton University Press, 2006); Clay Risen, *A Nation on Fire: America in the Wake of the King Assassination* (New York: Wiley, 2009); Gary May, *Bending toward Justice: The Voting Rights Act and the Transformation of American Democracy* (New York: Basic Books, 2013); Aram Goudsouzian, *Down at the Crossroads: Civil Rights, Black Power, and the Meredith March against Fear* (New York: Farrar, Straus & Giroux, 2014); and Michael Javen Fortner, *Black Silent Majority: The Rockefeller Drug Laws and the Politics of Punishment* (Cambridge, Mass.: Harvard University Press, 2015).

Two additional influences on the political climate in 1968 were the era's rising conservatism and the changing politics of the South. On conservatism, see Mary C. Brennan, *Turning Right in the Sixties: The Conservative Capture of the GOP* (Chapel Hill: University of North Carolina Press, 1995); Joseph E. Lowndes, *From the New Deal to the New Right: Race and the Southern Origins of Modern Conservatism* (New Haven, Conn.: Yale University Press, 2008); Kim Phillips-Fein, *Invisible Hands: The Making of the Conservative Movement from the New Deal to Reagan* (New York: W. W. Norton, 2009); and especially Donald T. Critchlow, *The Conservative Ascendancy: How the Republican Right Rose to Power in Modern America*, 2nd ed. (Lawrence: University Press of Kansas, 2011).

The classic account of southern politics prior to the 1960s is V. O. Key, *Southern Politics in State and Nation* (New York: Alfred A. Knopf, 1949). For later developments, see Harry S. Dent, *The Prodigal South Returns to Power* (New York: John Wiley & Sons, 1978); Dewey W. Grantham, *The Life and Death of the Solid South: A Political History* (Lexington: University Press of Kentucky, 1988); Alexander P. Lamis, *The Two-Party South*, expanded ed. (New York: Oxford University Press, 1988); Earl Black and Merle Black, *The Vital South: How Presidents Are Elected* (Cambridge, Mass.: Harvard University Press, 1992), and *The Rise of Southern Republicans* (Cambridge, Mass.: Harvard University Press, 2002); Jason Sokol, *There Goes My Everything: White Southerners in the Age of Civil Rights, 1945–1975* (New York: Alfred A. Knopf, 2006); and Joseph Crespino, *In Search of Another Country: Mississippi and the Conservative Counterrevolution* (Princeton, N.J.: Princeton University Press, 2007).

Some illuminating books on political parties in this era are: on the GOP, Robert J. Donovan, *The Future of the Republican Party* (New York: New American Library, 1964); Stephen Hess and David S. Broder, *The Republican Establishment: The Present and Future of the GOP* (New York: Harper & Row, 1967); Terry Dietz, *Republicans and Vietnam, 1961–1968* (New York: Greenwood, 1986); Geoffrey Kabaservice, *Rule and Ruin: The Downfall of Moderation and the Destruction of the Republican Party from Eisenhower to the Tea Party* (New York: Oxford University Press, 2012); and Timothy N. Thurber, *Republicans and Race: The GOP's Frayed Relationship with African Americans, 1945–1976* (Lawrence: University Press of Kansas, 2013). On the Democrats: Byron E. Shafer, *Quiet Revolution: The Struggle for the Democratic Party and the Shaping of Post-Reform Politics* (New York: Russell Sage, 1983); Steven M. Gillon, *Politics and Vision: The ADA and American Liberalism, 1947–1985* (New York: Oxford University Press, 1987); Kevin Boyle, *The UAW and the Heyday of American Liberalism, 1945–1968* (Ithaca, N.Y.: Cornell University Press, 1995); and Taylor E. Dark, *The Unions and the Democrats: An Enduring Alliance* (Ithaca, N.Y.: Cornell University Press, 1999).

On third parties, see Daniel A. Mazmanian, *Third Parties in Presidential Elections* (Washington, D.C.: Brookings Institution, 1974); and Steven J. Rosenstone, Roy L. Behr, and Edward H. Lazarus, *Third Parties in America: Citizen Response to Major Party Failure,* 2nd ed. (Princeton, N.J.: Princeton University Press, 1996). On the parties in general in this period: James MacGregor Burns, *The Deadlock of Democracy: Four-Party Politics in America,* rev. ed. (Englewood Cliffs, N.J.: Prentice-Hall, 1963); and David S. Broder, *The Party's Over: The Failure of Party Politics in America* (New York: Harper & Row, 1972). On parties and the presidency: Sidney M. Milkis, *The President and the Parties: The Transformation of the American Party System since the New Deal* (New York: Oxford University Press, 1993); and Daniel J. Galvin, *Presidential Party Building: Dwight D. Eisenhower to George W. Bush* (Princeton, N.J.: Princeton University Press, 2010).

Many excellent books have been written on the candidates and their campaigns in 1968. Democrats are listed first, Republicans second, then Wallace.

On Lyndon B. Johnson: Johnson, *The Vantage Point: Perspectives on the Presidency, 1963–1969* (New York: Holt, Rinehart & Winston, 1971); Harry McPherson, *A Political Education: A Washington Memoir* (Boston: Little, Brown, 1972); Doris Kearns, *Lyndon Johnson and the American Dream* (New York: Harper & Row, 1976); Merle Miller, *Lyndon: An Oral Biography* (New York: Ballantine Books, 1980); Joseph A. Califano, *The Triumph and Tragedy of Lyndon Johnson: The White House Years* (New York: Simon & Schuster, 1991), and *Inside: A Public and Private Life* (New York: Public Affairs, 2004); Robert Dallek, *Flawed Giant: Lyndon Johnson and His Times, 1961–1973* (New York: Oxford University Press, 1998); Randall B. Woods, *LBJ: Architect of American Ambition* (New York: Free Press, 2006); Charles Peters, *Lyndon B. Johnson* (New York: Times Books, 2010); and Robert A. Caro, *The Passage of Power: The Years of Lyndon Johnson* (New York: Alfred A. Knopf, 2012). Books chronicling Johnson's troubled relationship with the Kennedy brothers are Tom Wicker, *JFK and LBJ: The Influence of Personality upon Politics* (Chicago: Ivan R. Dee, 1968); Evelyn Lincoln, *Kennedy and Johnson* (New York: Holt, Rinehart & Winston, 1968); and especially Jeff Shesol, *Mutual Contempt: Lyndon Johnson, Robert Kennedy, and the Feud That Defined a Decade* (New York: W. W. Norton, 1997).

On Robert F. Kennedy: William vanden Heuvel and Milton Gwirtzman, *On His*

Own: RFK, 1964–68 (New York: Doubleday, 1970); Arthur M. Schlesinger, Jr., *Robert Kennedy and His Times* (Boston: Houghton Mifflin, 1978); Edwin O. Guthman and C. Richard Allen, *RFK: Collected Speeches* (New York: Viking, 1993); Ronald Steel, *In Love with Night: The American Romance with Robert Kennedy* (New York: Simon & Schuster, 2000); Evan Thomas, *Robert Kennedy: His Life* (New York: Simon & Schuster, 2000); Joseph A. Palermo, *In His Own Right: The Political Odyssey of Senator Robert F. Kennedy* (New York: Columbia University Press, 2001); and Larry Tye, *Bobby Kennedy: The Making of a Liberal Icon* (New York: Random House, 2016). On RFK's campaign for president: Jules Witcover, *85 Days: The Last Campaign of Robert Kennedy* (New York: G. P. Putnam's Sons, 1969); Richard N. Goodwin, *Remembering America: A Voice from the Sixties* (Boston: Little, Brown, 1988); Thurston Clarke, *The Last Campaign: Robert F. Kennedy and 82 Days That Inspired America* (New York: Henry Holt, 2007); and Ray E. Boomheimer, *Robert F. Kennedy and the 1968 Indiana Primary* (Bloomington: Indiana University Press, 2008).

On Eugene McCarthy: Albert Eisele, *Almost to the Presidency: A Biography of Two American Politicians* (Blue Earth, Minn.: Piper, 1972), which also treats Humphrey at equal length; and Dominic Sandbrook, *Eugene McCarthy: The Rise and Fall of Postwar American Liberalism* (New York: Alfred A. Knopf, 2004). On the McCarthy campaign: Ben Stavis, *We Were the Campaign: New Hampshire to Chicago for McCarthy* (Boston: Beacon Press, 1969); Jeremy Larner, *Nobody Knows: Reflections on the McCarthy Campaign of 1968* (New York: Macmillan, 1969); Eugene McCarthy, *The Year of the People* (Garden City, N.Y.: Doubleday, 1969); Richard T. Stout, *People: The Story of the Grassroots Movement That Found Eugene McCarthy and Is Transforming Our Politics Today* (New York: Harper & Row, 1970); and George Rising, *Clean for Gene: Eugene McCarthy's 1968 Presidential Campaign* (Westport, Conn.: Praeger, 1997).

On Hubert H. Humphrey: Eisele, *Almost to the Presidency;* Humphrey, *The Education of a Public Man: My Life and Politics* (New York: Doubleday, 1976); Edgar Berman, *Hubert: The Triumph and Tragedy of the Humphrey I Knew* (New York: G. P. Putnam's Sons, 1979); Carl Solberg, *Hubert Humphrey: A Biography* (New York: W. W. Norton, 1984); Timothy N. Thurber, *The Politics of Equality: Hubert H. Humphrey and the African American Freedom Struggle* (New York: Columbia University Press, 1999). On the Humphrey campaign: Lawrence O'Brien, *No Final Victories: A Life in Politics from John F. Kennedy to Watergate* (Garden City, N.Y.: Doubleday, 1974); and Ted Van Dyk, *Heroes, Hacks, and Fools: Memoirs from the Political Inside* (Seattle: University of Washington Press, 2007).

On George S. McGovern: McGovern, *Grassroots: The Autobiography of George McGovern* (New York: Random House, 1977); and Bruce I. Miroff, *The Liberals' Moment: The McGovern Insurgency and the Identity Crisis of the Democratic Party* (Lawrence: University Press of Kansas, 2007).

On Edward M. Kennedy: Adam Clymer, *Edward M. Kennedy: A Biography* (New York: William Morrow, 1999); Edward M. Kennedy, *True Compass: A Memoir* (New York: Twelve, 2009); and Peter S. Canellos, ed., *Last Lion: The Fall and Rise of Ted Kennedy* (New York: Simon & Schuster, 2009). See also Kennedy's oral history at the University of Virginia's Miller Center, available at http://millercenter.org/oral history/edward-kennedy.

On Edmund S. Muskie: Theo Lippman, Jr., and Donald C. Hansen, *Muskie* (New York: W. W. Norton, 1971); and Joel K. Goldstein, "Campaigning for America: Edmund S. Muskie's 1968 Vice Presidential Campaign," *New England Journal of Political Science* 4 (Fall 2009): 153–174.

On Richard Nixon: Garry Wills, *Nixon Agonistes: The Crisis of the Self-Made Man* (Boston: Houghton Mifflin, 1969); Jules Witcover, *The Resurrection of Richard Nixon* (New York: G. P. Putnam's Sons, 1970); Rowland Evans, Jr., and Robert D. Novak, *Nixon in the White House: The Frustration of Power* (New York: Random House, 1971); William Safire, *Before the Fall: An Inside View of the Pre-Watergate White House* (Garden City, N.Y.: Doubleday, 1975); Nixon, *RN* (New York: Grosset & Dunlap, 1978); John Ehrlichman, *Witness to Power: The Nixon Years* (New York: Simon & Schuster, 1982); Stephen E. Ambrose, *Nixon: The Triumph of a Politician, 1962–1972* (New York: Simon & Schuster, 1989); Roger Morris, *Richard Milhous Nixon: The Rise of an American Politician* (New York: Henry Holt, 1990); Tom Wicker, *One of Us: Richard Nixon and the American Dream* (New York: Random House, 1991); Jonathan Aitken, *Nixon: A Life* (Washington, D.C.: Regnery, 1993); Melvin Small, *The Presidency of Richard Nixon* (Lawrence: University Press of Kansas, 1999); Richard Reeves, *President Nixon: Alone in the White House* (New York: Touchstone, 2001); Conrad Black, *Richard M. Nixon: A Man in Full* (New York: PublicAffairs, 2007); James Worthen, *The Young Nixon and His Rivals: Four California Republicans Eye the White House, 1946–1958* (Jefferson, N.C.: McFarland, 2010); Jeffrey Frank, *Ike and Dick: Portrait of a Strange Political Marriage* (New York: Simon & Schuster, 2012); Kevin Mattson, *Just Plain Dick: Richard Nixon's Checkers Speech and the "Rocking Socking" Election of 1952* (New York: Bloomsbury, 2012); Irwin F. Gellman, *The President and the Apprentice* (New Haven, Conn.: Yale University Press, 2015); Evan Thomas, *Being Nixon: A Man Divided* (New York: Random House, 2015); and John A. Farrell, *Richard Nixon: The Life* (New York: Doubleday, 2017).

On the Nixon campaign: Joe McGinniss, *The Selling of the President 1968* (New York: Simon & Schuster, 1969)—but see also Kathleen Hall Jamieson, *Packaging the Presidency: A History and Criticism of Presidential Campaign Advertising* (New York: Oxford University Press, 1984) for a critique of McGinniss; Richard J. Whalen, *Catch the Falling Flag: A Republican's Challenge to His Party* (Boston: Houghton Mifflin, 1972); Leonard Garment, *Crazy Rhythm: My Journey from Brooklyn, Jazz, and Wall Street to Nixon's White House, Watergate, and Beyond* (New York: Times Books, 1997); William F. Gavin, *Speechwright: An Insider's Take on Political Rhetoric* (East Lansing: Michigan State University Press, 2011); and Patrick J. Buchanan, *The Greatest Comeback: How Richard Nixon Rose from Defeat to Create the New Majority* (New York: Crown Forum, 2014).

On George Romney: Clark Raymond Mollenhoff, *George Romney: Mormon in Politics* (New York: Meredith Press, 1968).

On Ronald Reagan: Matthew Dallek, *The Right Moment: Ronald Reagan's First Victory and the Decisive Turning Point in American Politics* (New York: Free Press, 2000); Lou Cannon, *Governor Reagan: His Rise to Power* (New York: PublicAffairs, 2003); Thomas W. Evans, *The Education of Ronald Reagan: The General Electric Years and the Untold Story of His Conversion to Conservatism* (New York: Columbia University Press, 2006); H. W. Brands, *Reagan: The Life* (New York: Doubleday, 2015); and Thomas C. Reed, *The Reagan Enigma, 1964–1980* (Los Angeles: Figueroa Press, 2015).

On Nelson A. Rockefeller: Michael Kramer and Sam Roberts, *"I Never Wanted to Be Vice President of Anything": An Investigative Biography of Nelson Rockefeller* (New York: Basic Books, 1976); Robert H. Connery and Gerald Benjamin, *Rockefeller of New York: Executive Power in the Statehouse* (Ithaca, N.Y.: Cornell University Press, 1979); Cary Reich, *The Life of Nelson A. Rockefeller: Worlds to Conquer, 1908–1958* (New York: Doubleday, 1996); and Richard Norton Smith, *On His Own Terms: A Life of Nelson Rockefeller* (New York: Random House, 2014).

On Spiro T. Agnew: Theo Lippman, *Spiro Agnew's America: The Vice President and the Politics of Suburbia* (New York: W. W. Norton, 1972); and Jules Witcover, *Very Strange Bedfellows: The Short and Unhappy Marriage of Richard Nixon and Spiro Agnew* (New York: PublicAffairs, 2007).

On George C. Wallace: Stephen Lesher, *George Wallace: American Populist* (Reading, Mass.: Addison-Wesley, 1994); Dan T. Carter, *The Politics of Rage: George Wallace, the Origins of Conservatism, and the Transformation of American Politics* (New York: Simon & Schuster, 1995); and Marshall Frady, *Wallace* (New York: Random House, 1996). On the Wallace campaign: Seymour Martin Lipset and Earl Raab, *The Politics of Unreason: Right-Wing Extremism in America, 1790–1977*, 2nd ed. (Chicago: University of Chicago Press, 1978); and Jody Carlson, *George C. Wallace and the Politics of Powerlessness: The Wallace Campaigns for the Presidency, 1964–1976* (New Brunswick, N.J.: Transaction Books, 1981).

Worthy books by or about other major political or media figures of the era include Richard L. Strout, *TRB: Views and Perspectives on the Presidency* (New York: Macmillan, 1979); James Reston, Jr., *The Lone Star: The Life of John Connally* (New York: Harper & Row, 1989); John Connally with Mickey Hershkowitz, *In History's Shadow: An American Odyssey* (New York: Hyperion, 1993); Robert Alan Goldberg, *Barry Goldwater* (New Haven, Conn.: Yale University Press, 1995); Adam Cohen and Elizabeth Taylor, *American Pharaoh: Mayor Richard J. Daley, His Battle for Chicago and the Nation* (Boston: Little, Brown, 2000); Scott Stossel, *Sarge: The Life and Times of Sargent Shriver* (New York: Smithsonian Books, 2004); Donald T. Critchlow, *Phyllis Schlafly and Grassroots Conservatism: A Woman's Crusade* (Princeton, N.J.: Princeton University Press, 2005); Arthur M. Schlesinger, Jr., *Journals,1952–2000* (New York: Penguin, 2007); Robert D. Novak, *The Prince of Darkness: Fifty Years of Reporting in Washington* (New York: Crown Forum, 2007); James Rosen, *The Strong Man: John Mitchell and the Secrets of Watergate* (New York: Doubleday, 2008); Jean Edward Smith, *Eisenhower in War and Peace* (New York: Random House, 2012); Joseph Crespino, *Strom Thurmond's America* (New York: Hill & Wang, 2012); Jack Nelson, *Scoop: The Evolution of a Southern Reporter* (Jackson: University Press of Mississippi, 2013); Gabriel Sherman, *The Loudest Voice in the Room: How the Brilliant, Bombastic Roger Ailes Built Fox News—and Divided a Country* (New York: Random House, 2014); and Michael Nelson and Barbara A. Perry, eds., *41: Inside the Presidency of George H. W. Bush* (Ithaca, N.Y.: Cornell University Press, 2014).

On the 1968 conventions, see Norman Mailer, *Miami and the Siege of Chicago*

(New York: New York Review of Books, 1968); John W. Soule and James W. Clarke, "Issue Conflict and Consensus: A Comparative Study of Democratic and Republican Delegates to the 1968 National Conventions," *Journal of Politics* 33 (February 1971): 72–91; and Justin A. Nelson, "Drafting Lyndon Johnson: The President's Secret Role in the 1968 Democratic Convention," *Presidential Studies Quarterly* 30 (December 2000): 688–714.

On the Fortas nomination: Bernard Schwartz, *Super Chief: Earl Warren and the Supreme Court: A Judicial Biography* (New York: New York University Press, 1983); Bruce Allen Murphy, *Fortas: The Rise and Ruin of a Supreme Court Justice* (New York: William Morrow, 1988); and Laura Kalman, *Abe Fortas: A Biography* (New Haven, Conn.: Yale University Press, 1990).

On the strong possibility of an electoral college deadlock in 1968: Neal R. Peirce and Lawrence D. Longley, *The People's President: The Electoral College in American History and the Direct Vote Alternative*, rev. ed. (New Haven, Conn.: Yale University Press, 1981), and *The Electoral College Primer* (New Haven, Conn.: Yale University Press, 1996); and Walter Berns, ed., *After the People Vote: Steps in Choosing the President* (Washington, D.C.: American Enterprise Institute for Public Policy Research, 1983).

Helpful analyses of voting and other forms of political behavior especially relevant to 1968 are Gerald R. Pomper, "Classification of Presidential Elections," *Journal of Politics* 29 (August 1967): 535–566; Lloyd A. Free and Hadley Cantril, *The Political Beliefs of Americans: A Study of Public Opinion* (New York: Simon & Schuster, 1968); Archibald M. Crossley and Helen M. Crossley, "Polling in 1968," *Public Opinion Quarterly* 33 (Spring 1969): 1–16; Philip E. Converse, Warren E. Miller, Jerrold G. Rusk, and Arthur C. Wolfe, "Continuity and Change in American Politics: Parties and Issues in the 1968 Election," *American Political Science Review* 68 (December 1969): 1083–1105; Herbert F. Weisberg and Jerrold G. Rusk, "Dimensions of Candidate Evaluation," *American Political Science Review* 64 (December 1970): 1167–1178; Richard W. Boyd, "Popular Control of Public Policy: A Normal Vote Analysis of the 1968 Election," *American Political Science Review* 66 (June 1972): 429–449; Richard A. Brody and Benjamin I. Page, "Policy Voting and the Electoral Process: The Vietnam War Issue," *American Political Science Review* 66 (September 1972): 979–995; Herbert Asher, *Presidential Elections and American Politics: Voters, Candidates, and Campaigns since 1952*, rev. ed. (Homewood, Ill.: Dorsey Press, 1980); Paul Abramson, *Political Attitudes in America: Formation and Change* (San Francisco: Freeman, 1983); Priscilla L. Southwell, "The Politics of Disgruntlement: Nonvoting and Defection among Supporters of Nomination Losers, 1968–1984," *Political Behavior* 8 (1986): 81–95; and Marc J. Hetherington, "The Effect of Political Trust on the Presidential Vote, 1968–1996," *American Political Science Review* 93 (June 1999): 311–326, and *Why Trust Matters: Declining Political Trust and the Demise of American Liberalism* (Princeton, N.J.: Princeton University Press, 2005).

On divided government, see Benjamin Ginsberg and Martin Shefter, *Politics by Other Means: The Declining Importance of Elections in America* (New York: Basic Books, 1990); David R. Mayhew, *Divided We Govern: Party Control, Lawmaking, and Investigations, 1946–1990* (New Haven, Conn.: Yale University Press, 1991);

Morris P. Fiorina, *Divided Government* (Boston: Allyn & Bacon, 1996); Sarah A. Binder, *Stalemate: Causes and Consequences of Legislative Gridlock* (Washington, D.C.: Brookings Institution Press, 2003); and Barry C. Burden and David C. Kimball, *Why Americans Split Their Tickets: Campaigns, Competition, and Divided Government* (Ann Arbor: University of Michigan Press, 2004). On judicial nominations in the post-1968 era of divided government: John Anthony Maltese, *The Selling of Supreme Court Nominees* (Baltimore: Johns Hopkins University Press, 1995); David Alistair Yalof, *Pursuit of Justices: Presidential Politics and the Selection of Supreme Court Nominees* (Chicago: University of Chicago Press, 1999); and Mark Silverstein, *Judicial Choices: The Politics of Supreme Court Appointments*, 2nd ed. (New York: W. W. Norton, 2007).

For election data for president, Congress, and governor, see *Guide to U.S. Elections*, 6th ed. (Washington, D.C.: CQ Press, 2009). For poll data, see George H. Gallup, *The Gallup Poll: Public Opinion, 1935–1971* (New York: Random House, 1972); also search the Gallup Poll website (http://www.gallup.com) for data on issues, trial heats, exit polls, presidential approval ratings, and other relevant survey results. For a broad range of data on American government and politics, see the biennial editions of Harold W. Stanley and Richard G. Niemi, *Vital Statistics on American Politics* (Washington, D.C.: CQ Press, published in odd-numbered years). Television commercials are archived at the Museum of the Moving Image's "The Living Room Candidate" website (http://www.livingroomcandidate.org). The indispensable Vanderbilt Television News Archive has been recording and making available both regular and special news broadcasts since August 5, 1968.

INDEX

Abel, I. W., 96
Acheson, Dean, 14, 92
Adams, Sherman, 32
AFL-CIO, 89, 96, 174, 181, 200, 247.
    See also Committee on Political
    Education (COPE)
African Americans
    affirmative action and, 50, 243, 318n25
    "black power," 24, 74, 124, 132
    civil rights legislation, 2, 10–11, 46, 48,
        57, 62, 189, 243, 279n2
    elected officials, 243
    Kerner Commission and, 75–76, 123,
        244
    1956 election, 2, 187–188
    1960 election, 2, 152–153, 187–188
    1964 election, 2, 187
    1968 election, 95–96, 104, 108, 124, 131,
        177, 187–188, 191–192, 197, 226–228,
        231
    1972 election, 243
    voter registration, 59, 62, 226
Agnew, Spiro T.
    bribe-taking as governor and vice
        president, 154
    electoral college deadlock possibility, 223
    favorite-son candidacy, 146
    King assassination and, 127–128, 154
    1966 election as governor, 63, 121
    Nixon and, 126–127, 147, 150–151, 221
    Rockefeller and, 126, 142, 147
    vice presidency of, 248, 303n31
    vice presidential candidate, 193, 194,
        196, 221, 235–236, 280n18, 315n83
    vice presidential nomination, 153–154,
        155, 178
Ailes, Roger, 119, 120, 186
Albert, Carl, 162, 168, 172
Allen, Richard, 186
Alsop, Joseph, 35
Alsop, Stewart, 243
Alter, Jonathan, 116
Alterman, Eric, 52

Ambrose, Stephen, 216
American Conservative Union, 63
Americans for Democratic Action, 20
    endorses Humphrey for president, 214
    endorses McCarthy for Democratic
        nomination, 77, 81, 293n56
    Humphrey helps found, 20
American Friends Service Committee, 60
American Independent Party, 135, 209, 211,
    249
American Legion, 67, 90, 189
American Party (Know Nothings), 134
Anderson, Forrest H., 316n93
Andreas, Dwayne, 199
antinepotism law, 76
antiwar movement, 59–60, 71–73, 161,
        238–241, 244, 245
    decline of, 241–242
    Democratic Convention, 165–166,
        175–176
    women and, 72
    *See also individual antiwar organizations
    and leaders*
Appalachian Regional Development Act, 46
Arvey, Jake, 20
"Ask Nixon," 186
Austin, Paul, 206
Automobile Manufacturers Association, 39

Babcock, Tim M., 316n93
Bailey, Beth, 242
Bailey, John M., 58, 77
Bailey, Lloyd W., 235, 236
Baker, Howard
    election to Senate in 1966, 63
    1968 election, 153
Ball, George
    Humphrey campaign and, 97, 198
    Vietnam War and, 55
Ball, Joseph, 20
Barkan, Al, 200
Barkley, Alben, 20
Barr, Joseph, 94

Wallace, George C., 1968 election, *continued*
    campaign organization, 134–135, 209
    campaign rhetoric and themes, 136–137,
        199, 301n80
    electoral vote count, 235
    hecklers, 199, 215
    independent candidate strategy, 112,
        133–134, 183–184, 208–209, 216–217,
        221–223
    law and order issue, 137, 191, 215
    platform, 210–211
    race issue, 136, 137, 140
    support from union members, 191, 192,
        200, 211, 213, 227, 308n40
    vice presidential selection, 193–194, 196,
        209–210, 211
    Vietnam War and, 209, 221
    voting patterns, 225–230
    "Wallace Girls," 199
Wallace, Gerald, 246
Wallace, Henry A., 20, 158, 280n21
Wallace, Lurleen
    Alabama gubernatorial career, 133, 135
    1966 election as governor, 65–66
War on Poverty, 11, 46, 49, 50, 61
    controversies about community action
        programs, 11–12, 50, 62
    declared by Johnson, 11–12
Warren, Earl, 148, 201, 203, 204, 206, 236
Washington Post, 131, 246
Wasow, Omar, 50, 227
Wasserman, Lew, 214
Watergate crisis, 237–238, 251, 254, 320n50
Watson, Marvin, 58, 161
Watson, Tom, 246–247, 319n39
Wattenberg, Ben, 248
Weatherman (Weather Underground), 165,
    239–240

Webb, James, .
Weisbrot, Robert, 46–47, 49
Wells, Tom, 241
Welsh, Matthew, 29, 99
Wesberry v. Sanders, 232
West, politics of, 57, 141
    defined, 302n21
    Mountain West, 113, 146, 151, 182, 183,
        225
    Pacific West, 151, 177, 225
Westmoreland, William C., Vietnam War
    and, 53, 69, 81–82, 91
Wheeler, Earle, Vietnam War and, 53, 82,
    91
Whig Party, 43–44
Whitcomb, Edgar D., 316n93
White, F. Clifton, 132, 145, 147–148, 150
White, Theodore H., 37, 43, 141, 186
White Citizens' Council, 10, 209, 246
Whitener, Basil, 231
Wicker, Tom, 3, 51, 104, 177
Wilkinson, Bud, 221
Williams, John, 63
Williams v. Rhodes, 135, 301n75
Willkie, Wendell, 111
Wilson, Woodrow, 90, 225, 226
Wise Men, 92–93
Witcover, Jules, 103
Wolfson, Louis, 207
    Wolfson Family Foundation, 207
Women Strike for Peace, 59–60
Wyman, Jane, 42

Yarborough, Ralph, 9, 250
Young, Stephen, 60, 94
Youth International Party (Yippies),
    Democratic National Convention
    and, 165–166